Le Jazz

Jazz and
French Cultural
Identity

Le Jazz

Matthew F. Jordan

UNIVERSITY OF ILLINOIS PRESS
Urbana, Chicago, and Springfield

© 2010 by the Board of Trustees
of the University of Illinois
All rights reserved
Manufactured in the United States of America
1 2 3 4 5 C P 5 4 3 2 1
∞ This book is printed on acid-free paper.

Library of Congress Cataloging-in-Publication Data
Jordan, Matthew F.
Le jazz : jazz and French cultural identity / Matthew F. Jordan.
p.   cm.
Includes bibliographical references and index.
ISBN 978-0-252-03516-6 (cloth : alk. paper)
ISBN 978-0-252-07706-7 (pbk. : alk. paper)
1. Jazz—France—History and criticism. I. Title.
ML3509.F7J67   2010
781.660944—dc22   2009048716

For Claire and Ellis

Contents

Acknowledgments

I want to acknowledge the many people who supported, guided, and pushed me through the many stages of this project. The generous support of the Claremont Graduate University, pedagogical and material, allowed me to spend a year in Paris doing archival work. In Paris, the hospitality of Marianne Bastid-Brugière, Ian and Valeria Kent, and countless others helped keep me going. When I was a graduate student in European studies at Claremont, Elazar Barkan and Robert Dawidoff helped me make sense of a very protean research project, and Michael Roth has continued to teach me in ways I can only begin to acknowledge. I am much beholden. I am grateful to the Humanities Institute and the Division of the Humanities at the University of Louisville, especially for the help of Tom Byers and Elaine Wise. At Penn State University, I am grateful for the material support provided by the College of Communication and the Department of Film/Video and Media Studies, especially Deans Doug Anderson and John Nichols. Colleagues and friends like John Christman, Matt McAllister, Mary Beth Oliver, Jeremy Packer, and Michael Elavsky have enriched my work and life. Thanks also to the State College jazzmen who have played with me over the last several years, especially Barry Kernfeld and Brian Tuttle, for keeping me in touch with the music.

I benefited greatly from collegial conversations, jam sessions, and lasting social bonds that emerged from a conference in Seysses, France, organized by Colin Nettelbeck and Jackie Dutton, on the importance of jazz in French culture and of French culture to jazz. As this book took its present form, I have continued to learn from many of the participants, including David

Looseley, Ludovic Tournès, Nick Hewitt, and Terri Gordon, by reading their work and collaborating with them on other projects. Laurie Matheson and Angela Burton do the University of Illinois Press proud as editors, and I am grateful for their help as the book came to press. The anonymous reviewers who read and engaged with the manuscript were extremely helpful to the editing process.

None of this would have been possible without the support of my family. My parents, Don and Mary Kay Jordan, saw me through my days as a vagabond graduate student. Along with the many things she does to help me every day, my wife, Meredith Doran, helped me in every way on this project: negotiating the peculiarities of French culture during a year in Paris, translating the nuances of the French language, and listening to me talk about my material and work through my ideas.

Le Jazz

The Meaning and Function of French Debates about Jazz

Our values are interpreted into things.
Is there then any meaning in the in-itself?!
—Friedrich Nietzsche

An event, consequently, is not a decision, a treaty,
a reign, or a battle, but the reversal of a relationship
of forces, the usurpation of power, the appropriation of a
vocabulary turned against those who had once used it.
—Michel Foucault

If this book has a tonic root or dominant mode to its harmonic structure, it is the notion that cultures are constantly defining and constituting themselves by debating which forms of cultural production and enjoyment are appropriate and which are not. The endless conversation about what kinds of music, art, dance, and expression should be embraced or repressed is what allows cultures to delineate the boundaries of cultural identity and maintain a meaningful relationship to the world.[1] Examining what is contested in public debate, what is characterized as foreign, dangerous, or other, and what is accepted or uncontested and assimilated allows one to understand subtle changes in how a culture sees and defines itself. This self-examination is ongoing; there is no timeless essence to culture or cultural identity, only the constant drive to define the self in relation to historical circumstance.

Beginning with Raymond Williams, cultural studies has focused on the way in which popular culture, and the ongoing discourse on popular culture, provides a quotidian site for the generation of community meaning and identity formations: "Human community grows by the discovery of common meanings and common means of communication . . . Since our way of seeing things is literally our way of living, the process of communication is in fact the process of community: the sharing of common meanings, and thence common activities and purposes; the offering, reception and comparison of new meanings, leading to the tensions and achievements of growth and change."[2] Following from this notion that communication is an ongoing process through which community meaning is generated, this book will argue that there is no "true" French culture or "truly" French identity that transcends time. Rather, throughout the twentieth century, one sees a constant struggle to define the meaning of true French culture, often of the "invented" kind as Hobsbawm and Ranger define it,[3] in relation to important changes in popular culture. The by-products resulting from this ongoing activity, public debate and media discourse, allow the observer to see changes in how France saw itself over time. In the twentieth century, a new foreign import, jazz, became an important spur for such cultural work as France sought to make sense of a rapidly changing modernity.

Jazz is one of the great cultural innovations of the twentieth century, and no music had greater impact on cultures around the world or met with as much resistance. France is a nation proud of its rich tradition of public debate, and the story of how the French came to terms with this foreign music during a period that saw the rise of mass media as a cultural force is particularly interesting. Unlike the many cultural imports that are resisted for being un-French, there are also things that people seem to have achieved a kind of general consensus about and are accepted as part of French culture. From today's perspective, jazz is one of those imports that has been integrated into French culture and French cultural identity.

Today, there is a widespread belief that "the French love jazz." But as in all stories of passion, love, and betrayal, this love has been a rocky affair. After jazz was first experienced as a foreign threat to traditional French culture, the initial hostility of listeners and critics waned and, as the French modernized their sense of self, jazz became an accepted and important form of expression that was compatible with most notions of Frenchness and visions of true French culture. Through their active encounter with difference as part of popular culture in everyday life, the French came to live with, and eventually interpolate, the difference that jazz represented.[4]

A host of institutions, infrastructures, and media bear witness to the French embrace of jazz: there are clubs, concerts, *festivals du jazz,* piano bars, radio stations, magazines, recording studios, and record stores dedicated to promoting it. In 1986, the French Ministry of Culture created the Orchestre National de Jazz,[5] the first of its kind in the world. Scores of black American jazz musicians have lived (or live) in France as heroes,[6] and many American jazz musicians have been officially recognized by the French Ministry of Culture as treasured parts of the national cultural heritage. Louis Armstrong was honored with the *vase de Sèvres* in 1949; Josephine Baker, once seen as a sexualized savage, became a *citoyenne,* was welcomed into the *Légion d'honneur,* and bought a castle in the French countryside; a monument of Sidney Bechet sits as a bronzed *lieu de mémoire* to the Jazz Age in the southern town of Juan-les-Pins. While these and many other examples bear witness to the French love of jazz, what one does *not* find in contemporary media discourse are critics who label jazz a threat to their notion of French culture. I read this discursive absence, one that did not appear until after the German occupation, as a sign that jazz is now an assimilated or naturalized part of French culture. Though obviously some like jazz more than others, the cultural debate surrounding it today in France is no longer marked by contestation about its basic legitimacy. For it to be accepted in this way, not only did the French perspective on the music and what it meant for French culture have to change, but the meaning of true Frenchness and true French culture had to undergo a metamorphosis, as well. In roughly forty years, French cultural identity renewed and remodeled itself through an encounter with and assimilation of a host of cultural differences that jazz symbolized. This book will show how the characteristics or qualities initially heard and seen in jazz as markers of otherness against which Frenchness gained coherence went through a historical process of transvaluation, so that those traits once seen and heard as un-French came to be recognized as internal markers, or normal, commonsense conceptions of an emerging modern sense of Frenchness.

Jazz's acceptance as a legitimate part of French culture is all the more remarkable because France has welcomed it in a way that most American media and cultural forms have not: In fact, the relationship between the French and other American cultural imports—like action movies, game shows, Coca-Cola, fast food, and more recently, American business practices—is, if anything, fiercely ambivalent.[7] This separation of jazz from such American imports was not immediate, and the process through which jazz was integrated into French cultural identity via the communicative action that surrounded it tells us much about how the process of cultural assimilation takes place. To be sure, it took jazz a long time to shed the "hate" side of the love/hate relationship that the French have with much of American culture.[8] Indeed, heated debate about the appropriateness of jazz for French culture existed until after the Occupation, when publicly denouncing jazz in the media as a degenerate form or saying that it was un-French to love jazz became like saying one was a collaborator. This reversal, this tacit acceptance of jazz by a culture whose sense of self had changed enough to embrace a form once seen as culturally other, marks an "event" in the sense evoked in the Foucault epigraph that opens this chapter. Yet despite the change in what counted as truly French, the strength of this contemporary consensus on jazz conceals the contested ground on which it was built, a terrain that tells us much about crucial cultural values before the liberation.

While jazz is not the only foreign form that has been assimilated into modern French culture, as a powerful new mass-media music it is a certainly one of the most revealing. Since Plato, music has been accorded a special epistemological status in culture because of its ability to move people. Music, perhaps more than other forms of cultural production, is able to cross borders, define places, and change socially understood forms of taste. Because jazz did move into French culture, define new cultural spaces, and shift popular taste in music, the discourse surrounding it provides a perfect screen for the projection of important ideologies and beliefs about cultural identity that were in tension within French culture.[9] As such, it dramatizes Simon Frith's thesis that "the essence of popular cultural practice is making judgments and assessing differences."[10] Looking to the first half of the twentieth century, writing on jazz in France—on what it was and whether it should be accepted or rejected—allows us to get attuned to important beliefs about what it meant to be French and to live in an authentically French culture. Though, of course, these beliefs about the "true," "authentic," or "real" France were always contingent and imaginary, the debates about jazz provide us with an important opening to hear how ideas about "true" French culture changed over time. In what follows, it should be understood that these terms were always contested and that I am not trying to argue the contrary.

Many of the seminal thinkers in cultural studies have focused on the way that debates about popular culture often serve a function similar to recounting myths. In *Mythologies*, Roland Barthes showed how all forms of semiotic production in contemporary culture are subject to having their meanings changed in a functional process that works a lot like myth. The changes in meaning, he offered, would speak to the underlying ideologies of the societies that produced them. Similarly, Claude Lévi-Strauss noted long ago that our statements about music, like our telling of myths, often reveal concealed ideological beliefs about the meaning of culture even if they are nominally about something else. Debating what kind of music is good or bad, or culturally appropriate, allows writers and critics to generate important stories about what a culture is like and what forms of enjoyment and behaviors are good for it.[11] Jane Fulcher has shown how music was in important site for ideological work in twentieth-century France.[12] Indeed, discourse on music seems to be an important site for constructing ideology. Simon Frith, borrowing Pierre Bourdieu's ideas about distinction, has argued that all cultural judgments expressed in discourse about music are functional. Not only does ritualized debate about the significance of popular music allow dominant classes to display their *distinction* or social superiority, it also enables all communities to generate their sense of taste, values, and shared purpose. "If social relations are constituted in cultural practice, then our sense of identity and difference is established in the processes of discrimination . . . These relationships between aesthetic judgment and the formation of social groups are obviously crucial to popular cultural practice, to genres and cults and subcultures."[13] In a nutshell, Frith argues that music provides us with an intense "subjective sense of being social" that is something like "the immediate experience of collective identity."[14] David Hesmondhalgh, in discussing why evaluating musical aesthetics matters, states it succinctly: "Music makes clear that people's pleasures, tastes and values are connected to their emotional lives . . . Although music can be deeply personal, it is also tied in important ways to our relationships with others, and to the various forms of collective identity which help to make us who we are."[15] I see the debates surrounding jazz in France as just such a ritualized cultural practice, one that mattered in that it enabled people to negotiate their cultural identity. Through coming to terms with this music, the debate about aesthetics allowed for important cultural work that slowly shifted the unconscious ideological frames that Gramsci would call the "national-popular" by emphasizing certain constructions about what it meant to be French.

Though Lévi-Strauss often found universals in myths where modern cultural studies would find historically contingent ideological constructions, he was on to something when he described the recurrence of certain component parts of the mythologies that are used and exchanged with one another depending on the contingent needs of the storyteller. I assert that a similar dynamic operates within French debates on jazz, in which certain terms, themes, tropes, and clichés—what we could call "discursive riffs"—are used, exchanged, and updated so as to define jazz or Frenchness again and again. Depending on circumstances, these clusters of signifiers are encoded and decoded[16] as commensurate with or oppositional to dominant or resistant ideas about normative Frenchness. In relation to jazz, these riffs are played out as writers ask questions and posit answers about its ontology (What is jazz?), ponder its origin (Where does jazz come from?), speculate about its symbolic importance for French culture (What does it mean for us?), and make claims and counterclaims about its true *ethos* (What are the emotional effects of jazz on French men and women, and what does the fact that people like it imply for society and for the future of "true" French culture?).[17] Each of these inquiries and the constellations of possible questions and answers around them are heard again and again as leitmotifs in the discourse surrounding jazz, and they always contain certain assumptions about "normal" or everyday Frenchness. In short, media debates about jazz gave French critics a forum through which to make sense of their changing lives and times. The stories they told about jazz and the way they used the debate about jazz allowed them to cluster discursive riffs together and construct normative notions of Frenchness. To use jazz music as an analogy, riffing on what was or was not French about jazz allowed critics to perform variations, sometimes dramatically different-sounding ones, about what true French culture meant to them.

There are important reasons for using jazz music as an analogy to understand how debates on cultural identity function. In jazz music, individual players improvise on the themes and over the chord changes of standard songs that are well known to musicians and jazz fans. The sequences of notes they play resonate as consonant or dissonant depending on what those chord changes allow. I assert that there is an analogous relationship between the ritualized utterances about French popular culture and the underlying ideologies of that culture. In debates about jazz, what a speaker says about jazz or Frenchness is guided or determined by what he or she believes about culture, by the ideologies that serve as the cultural harmonics or architectonics. These beliefs about culture operate on an unconscious level, which is to say following a Gramscian or post-Althusserian notion of ideology, that ideologies structure the social fantasy of the individual though they remain hidden; though they are often not aware of it, people act in accordance with the ideologies that function as the chord changes over which the individual writer can sound off on the meaning of jazz or "true" French culture. To follow the analogy further, when playing the chord changes of well-known songs like "I've Got Rhythm"—which jazz musicians just refer to as "rhythm changes"—a host of motifs or riffs fit and will work harmonically. So, too, for an individual entering into debates on jazz and its relation to French culture, certain discursive riffs make sense in relation to the ideological harmonics of their identity and thus ring true to them. Their choices as to what things are in harmony with Frenchness, which discursive features are encoded as normal, and what things seem dissonant or abnormal to them are immensely revealing. To be sure, improvisation plays an important role in both jazz music and in the negotiation of cultural identity through debates on popular culture. By studying how the subtle rules governing discourse on French culture determined what could be said within historically situated conversations, one can chart how the kinds of things said about true French culture and Frenchness changed over time.

Simon Frith has posited that music is heard through three overlapping and sometimes contradictory grids of meaning related to three types of discourse. This cognitive mapping is helpful for contextualizing French debates on jazz as they fit into a wider context of public discourse on music, which David Looseley rightly contends often plays a bigger role in French musical life than music itself.[18] There is art discourse—discourse on jazz relating to some particular notion of great music—that tells us about the values and tastes of dominant bourgeois culture; there is folk discourse, whereby the value of jazz is generated by imagining a folk world in which music is tied to its social function and then comparing this construct to jazz; finally, there is pop discourse, whereby the value of the music is determined by thinking about its relation to the commercial musical world and about the values created by the culture industry. French discourse on jazz can be mapped along these lines so as to understand the particularities of these debates as they relate to larger issues about culture.

Three standard themes also are repeatedly heard in French discourse on jazz. Writers perform variations on these themes depending on their needs. First, there are endless attempts to elaborate on the nature of "true" or "authentic" Frenchness as it relates to some notion of great art or folk art. Second, one hears variations on the mentality or spirit of the primitive "*nègre*" performed to define the life-world of the writer by way of differentiation. Sometimes the primitive is described in relation to great art, sometimes in relation to some imaginary folk ethnos, sometimes expressing nostalgia, sometimes revealing disgust. Finally, one repeatedly hears standard descriptions of America and of what would count as the Americanization of culture, often used to think through the implications of French culture in the age of mechanized cultural production and mass media. A writer can use one or all of these themes when constructing her sense of community values or the meaning of Frenchness or of "true" French culture that jazz is either clashing against or in harmony with. As such, this intersection of discourses and themes come to constitute what Lawrence Grossberg has defined as "mattering maps."[19]

In relation to the first standard theme, the meaning of Frenchness might be composed by riffing on the idea of *egalité, liberté, fraternité* as a foundational cultural ideal; or one might hear passages on the true legacy of the French Revolution;[20] variations on authentic French characteristics or psychological traits—such as Cartesianism or the notion that the French have a propensity for clarity and an innate sense of logic—might recur as leitmotifs; or some might utilize republican riffs on cultural missions or duties for France, such as the *mission civilisatrice* (the need to spread sophisticated civilization to the world[21]) to make their vision of the true France sound more persuasive. These standard myths of self-description are repeatedly used in one form or another in mass-media discourse on the meaning of jazz for French culture. Once particular ideological formations gain standing, meaning that they work on the level of a stereotype or "common sense," they begin to ring true for people and are thus available for use and abuse. According to the critic's concerns about where French culture is headed, standard cultural riffs like those just described are often drawn on as the basis for judgment about the meaning of jazz and its relation to what might be seen as an imaginary notion of the true France.

The second group of themes heard in debates about jazz, variations on the characteristics of the primitive *nègre*, are usually used by French media critics for purposes of negation to construct an un-French other. Throughout the book, I retain the French category *nègre* and other French racial terms rather than translating them, in order to highlight not only the difference between *nègre* and the English term *Negro*, but because French writers contested these categories and substituted different ones when they thought it necessary to underline the sense of what they heard in jazz. The word *nègre* was used in many different ways, sometimes as a noun and sometimes as an adjective, but always used as a signifier of difference from being French. As such, I try to show what the word signifies in the context of its usage rather than searching for an English equivalent. For instance, writers used this construct to underline the extent to which jazz was not true French music because it expressed the ethos of another people or race. Statements about the un-French *nègre* are based on certain tropes or clichés about racial tendencies, like the old riff about blacks being naturally rhythmic. These stereotypic notions of racial sensibilities are examples of what postcolonial theorists like Homi Bhabha have described as markers of "fixity."[22] This process of constructing an Other by using riffs about fixed or innate racial characteristics is constantly repeated in the ongoing construction of French cultural identity. The binary works like this: if the French are civilized, some argued, then *les nègres* are savage; where the true Frenchman could be (and often was) characterized as reasonable or intellectual, the *nègre* was thought to be ruled by the passions and the body. Such cultural stereotypes about race have a long standing, and their use in Orientalist literature, pseudoscience, and voyagers' tales has been well analyzed.[23] As we shall see, one of the changes in the sense of Frenchness that made jazz acceptable for "true" French people to enjoy was that, over time, many of the characteristics of *nègre* otherness came to be internalized and recoded; the markers of otherness described at the beginning of our story were, by the liberation period, often seen as tensions within the French sense of self. This metamorphosis is extremely important for understanding the sense of Frenchness that emerged after the German occupation. The history of the debates on jazz show that it was not merely that French writers asserted their Frenchness by repressing foreign cultural influences; rather, one can see that, over time, notions of jazz and of various conceptions of Frenchness evolved, allowing one to enjoy jazz, even the kind of jazz once hailed for its exotic otherness, and still be very French.

The third variety of leitmotifs heard in debates about jazz are statements characterizing American culture and the meaning of Americanization. Many critics read the existence of jazz in France as a symptom of the loss of traditional French culture and of the modern Americanization of that culture. Constructing an imaginary notion of America[24] allowed writers to constitute important features of the French imagined community, such as "Frenchness," and the "true" French culture placed at risk by American culture.[25] Indeed, much recent writing in cultural studies has concentrated on the process through which cultures come to recognize themselves through their relation to an Other. If French writing on *le nègre* often reveals preconceptions about the relation between French civilization and a primitive state of nature, then discourse on America has often been used to differentiate American cultural modernity from "*la vraie culture française*" (real French culture).[26] Jean-Philippe Mathy, for instance, has analyzed different narrative constructions about America that French writers repeatedly used to talk about possible French futures. He has emphasized how commentaries on the meaning of American culture for France can be read as statements that reflect the antagonisms contained within French culture in its description of itself.[27] Using America as an external example allows French writers to construe notions of cultural difference fundamental to French cultural identity, such as fear about the modern mechanization of traditional culture. Indeed, Baudelaire is said to have coined the verb *americaniser*—"to Americanize"—as part of his criticism of modern French life when he wrote that "mechanization will Americanize us."[28] What such cultural change meant for French culture—whether high artisan culture would become subordinate to popular mass culture, whether commercialism would triumph over traditional taste, whether jazz would triumph over *la chanson française* as the most important *musique populaire*—depended on the writer's imaginary America. Though the three themes established here (writing on "true" Frenchness, writing on the primitive *nègre,* writing on America) are the standards that dominate the debates on jazz, they are by no means the only ones. By examining what form variations of these leitmotifs took in relation to historical circumstances and changing notions of normative Frenchness, one can begin to understand the changing stakes in French debates over jazz and the shifts in the "national-popular" or cultural unconscious—the chord changes—over which these statements rang true.

Lévi-Strauss once theorized that there was no one true historical fact behind any myth. The substance of the myth—its meaning—he believed, was to be uncovered by examining the way in which *mythemes* are used according to the needs of the teller.[29] Though I substitute the search for competing ideologies for the search for deep structures, I begin with the idea that there is no one "truth" about jazz—or about what "true" French culture might be—that French writers either did or did not get right. Rather, I focus on the ways in which writers used debates about jazz to locate themselves within the changing landscape of modern French culture. In each case, the importance of what a writer said about jazz is not determined by whether or not the writer "got jazz right," but what he or she chose to emphasize and how particular standard ideas were clustered together to make sense of jazz and its relationship to what the writer imagined France to be. The issue, to quote Foucauldian phrasing, is not merely whether critics said yes or no to jazz, whether they formulated prohibitions or permissions, whether they asserted its importance for the health of French culture or denied its effects, but to understand the positions and viewpoints from which they spoke, and the issues, affiliations, and ideologies that dictated the kinds of things that they said. My main concern is to understand how debates on jazz were used to fine-tune notions of what it meant to be French. As we will see, jazz became an important locus for the elaboration of aesthetics-as-politics[30] in the interwar era, a way of determining what forms of cultural enjoyment were appropriate for modern France. As a result, the public debates over jazz became a site of contestation in the power struggle to define Frenchness and true French culture, functioning as what rhetoricians would call epideictic discourse that promotes values that are shared in a community by ascribing praise or blame.

Since contestation over the nuances of jazz and its relation to different notions of Frenchness changed over time and make sense only within a particular temporal framework or cultural context, each chapter is based upon historically situated conversations in the media. Accordingly, the chapters are organized chronologically around shifts in the debates on jazz. To emphasize the dialogic nature of the discourse, I try to play the anti-jazz protesters off the pro-jazz proponents in each chapter—except in the last, where the former are absent—as a kind of counterpoint, not only because the conceptual changes follow a kind of dialectical progression, but because more than its referentiality to the music, French writing on jazz depended upon these oppositions for its consistency. Just as in music, there can be no resolution to consonance in cultural discourse without dissonance and tension. Moreover, certain identity formations—conservative, modernist, cosmopolitan, fascist, royalist, communist, and so on—came to be associated with particular statements about jazz. This association between the kind of person one was and what one said about jazz is especially important for my conclusion, since by the liberation period, the performance of anti-jazz discourse became almost as impossible as performing the protofascist identity that had so violently denounced jazz during the occupation: both faded away as features of debate on French culture.

There are, of course, epistemological conflicts herein resulting from my choice to highlight intertextuality and changes in language and concepts over the biographies of the writers when looking at what was said about jazz. In any historical analysis, there is always a tension between the study of collective discursive formations that emerge from the dynamics of a social field and the individual expression of these collective ways of making sense of the world, used in specific texts by specific authors. Ideas are neither directly determined by social and economic processes, nor free-floating entities without agency determined only through discursive conventions fixed by invisible systems of power. There is always a bit of both, of course, and they need to be blended judiciously. For the sake of lending a certain amount of relative autonomy to the field of French media discourse on jazz, I emphasize the life of the discourse more than the lives of the writers and the minutiae of political or economic history. Though biography is often the primary device used to mediate between ideas and the culture in which they are produced, such an approach often deemphasizes the changes in categories or terminology through excessive personalization. Of course, just as in the history of jazz musicians, some writers are innovative, and many are derivative. Accordingly, I highlight the innovative critics who found their own voices and made the language their own—like jazz players whose signature ways of playing and phrasing changed the ways the music was played—and who changed the sound and nature of the debates on jazz. Each chapter focuses on one or more of these important players. However, I am wary about overemphasizing these dominant critics' later retrospective writings, as autobiographical accounts written from a hindsight perspective often manifest a retroactive causality that injects issues into historically specific conversations that could not have been present at the time.

I situate my account of the French debates over jazz with other similar histories but diverge from them in different ways. Colin Nettelbeck has looked both at the way in which the initial explosion of jazz in 1918 worked as a foundational story[31] and about how the post-occupation consensus of jazz was linked to contemporary ideas about freedom.[32] American literary scholar Michael Haggerty and jazz critic A. David Franklin both began preliminary studies of the acceptance of jazz by French critics but did not deal with the cultural and ideological stakes in the debates.[33] Tyler Stovall, Michel Fabre, William Shack, T. Denean Sharpley-Whiting, and Brent Hayes Edwards have written about the Jazz Age in France as it relates to the African Americans who visited or lived there, but they are primarily interested in the African American experience in France as opposed to the French perceptions of the music and how descriptions of jazz were used to constitute Frenchness.[34] What it was like for Josephine Baker, Duke Ellington, Langston Hughes, and many other African Americans to live in France, where they were often more accepted than in America, is certainly an interesting story that has many implications for our understanding of contemporary identity and cultural practices; it is just not one I am trying to tell. Jody Blake has examined the spiritual and intellectual relation between what modern French visual artists were trying to do and the jazz they loved in the 1920s.[35] Charles Rearick's work on French popular culture in the interwar period is helpful for understanding the importance of jazz as part of a rapidly changing popular culture and French way of life, but jazz is only one part of a much larger story.[36] Most often, analysis of French debates on jazz has taken the form of tangential remarks by authors whose subjects are jazz musicians working in France. Take, for instance, the brief remarks of jazz biographer James Lincoln Collier in his biography of Duke Ellington: "Moreover, the European musical establishment did not share Lambert's enthusiasm for Ellington's music and jazz in general: by and large, it looked down on it. The French intellectuals were generally scornful of it."[37] Similarly, in his book on the reception of jazz in

America, he turns briefly to European audiences and France but lapses into hagiographic accounts that deal only with major critics like Hugues Panassié. Such comments, obviously, conceal a rich cultural debate, a debate that I try to reconstruct.

Ludovic Tournès and Jeffrey Jackson have done the most to suggest the importance of jazz for negotiating and defining French culture in the interwar years.[38] Tournès's *New Orleans sur Seine: histoire du jazz en France* is a sweeping study of the people and places in France that slowly embraced jazz, from its initial moment to the present. Jackson's *Making Jazz French* tackles the growing impact of jazz in French culture during the interwar period and makes the case for its assimilation in the mid-1930s by virtue of jazz being present in musicals, movies, and popular music. It is a good book, but the historiographic fiction of the interwar period presents a liability for following and understanding the genealogy of the media discourse surrounding jazz from its roots to its resolution. As such, we differ on when jazz was assimilated and what count as the signs of that assimilation. Like many retrospective observers, Jackson assumes that because a number of liberal humanists, French cosmopolitans, or professional jazz critics embraced jazz by the mid-1930s, the same can be said for French culture at large. His analysis stops at the end of the interwar period, before the battle over jazz in French cultural discourse was truly over. I see the debate in the media, and jazz's utility as a powerful metonymic symbol for culture critics, persisting until after World War II.

In many ways, the foreshortening of the duration of the debate on jazz is a problem of faulty retrospective causality shared by many contemporary critics. It is a form of "genesis-amnesia"[39] akin to Russo's "Vichy Syndrome" that I have come to think of as the *Casablanca complex:* as time goes by, writers continue to round up the usual suspects, the jazz critics and liberal humanists who marked the beginning of the beautiful friendship that the French have with jazz. For instance, the famous American critic Whitney Balliett wrote about Hugues Panassié's 1934 book *Le jazz hot:* "Aside from the erratic *Aux frontières du jazz,* brought out two years before by the Belgian Robert Goffin, it was the first book of jazz criticism, and it put jazz on the map in Europe and in its own country."[40] Similarly, James Lincoln Collier declared that "the case for the priority of European appreciation of jazz rests to a substantial extent on Panassié's shoulders."[41] Not only do such statements conceal the existence of the highly nuanced discourse that Panassié and other dominant critics' work emerged from and depended on, they also silence the voices of those who tried to keep jazz off the map, those anti-jazz writers whose contestation is essential for understanding the dialogic nature of the debates.

Contemporary French jazz critics like André Hodeir, Lucien Malson, Frank Ténot, and Jacques Hess often dramatize the Casablanca complex in their work, mentioning only those critics whose work set the stage for their own. Since they are more interested in the music and musicians than the changes in the language used to make sense of both, they exclude those who, from their post-occupation perspective, got jazz wrong. To avoid the Casablanca complex and to try to reconstruct the debates more fully, I focus on the genealogical changes in the tropes, descriptive procedures, and standard discursive riffs used to make sense of jazz, as well as on their relation to the changing notions of Frenchness and true French culture. Moreover, since I see the absence of anti-jazz writing in the post–World War II period as the key marker or sign of jazz's assimilation into French cultural identity, my narrative follows the debates over jazz beyond the occupation.

In a book that traces linguistic and semiotic changes in the debates over jazz, the starting point for this conversation is difficult to pin down. The discourse on jazz did not just emerge out of the still-reverberating post–World War I air along with the music; the debate over the meaning of jazz in France arrived, to borrow a Heideggerian metaphor, as an echo within a space that had long been cleared by conversations about art, music, popular song, French culture, and the French way of life. As such, the thematic riffs that came to dominate the debates on jazz—variations on ideas about the primitive, the civilized, Americanization, modernization, authentic Frenchness and French tradition—were, in fact, already standards in epideictic debates on the nature of true French culture.

In each chapter, statements about jazz that represent the dominant positions of the time are analyzed in relation to the ideological and material conditions that served as the cultural harmonics or architectonics. Chapter 1 serves as a preliminary vamp on how such cultural discourse functioned in relation to the cakewalk dance craze of 1903. Chapter 2 stresses how the debates on jazz were used as a way to diagnose the state of French cultural health after the trauma of World War I. The third chapter deals with how the debates on jazz were used to make sense of the difference between high culture, traditional culture, and modern popular culture in relation to emerging media technologies like the phonograph, radio, and cinema that were spreading jazz to a new kind of French public. Chapter 4 examines the attempts to rethink the racial and cultural hybridity of jazz and modern French culture in the wake of Josephine Baker and *La revue nègre*'s arrival in France. Chapter 5 examines the emergence of the specialized professional jazz critic that seized hold of the discourse in France. It shows the rhetorical and logical similarities between the discourse of the "Hot Club" movement and its critics and that of the culture movements on the right, whereby both developed strict orthodoxies and constructed cults of personality around their "great leaders" who embodied "true" cultural values they were trying to spread. Chapter 6 focuses on the sometimes bloody battles over the symbolic importance of jazz during the occupation as they played out between Vichy collaborators and the swing subculture, culminating in the "hunt for the Zazous." The concluding chapter examines key differences in the debates on jazz after the liberation, when anti-jazz voices fell silent after the music had been accepted in France as a naturalized form.

This book lays no claims to the truth about jazz or about French culture. I do argue that examining historically situated conversations about the relationship between the two can show how aesthetic judgment about the nature of popular culture is often an important component of generating cultural values. As such, debate on popular music plays an important role in the construction of cultural identity. I would hope that my analysis of the how the French assimilated jazz into its cultural identity would demonstrate why a cultural-studies approach is valuable for coming to terms with the function of popular culture in our own lifeworld.

1

Vamp on the Meaning of Jazz
The Cakewalk Comes to Town

As established in the introduction, jazz discourse was used by French observers to construct competing notions of Frenchness as part of an ongoing process of generating cultural identity. In jazz music, many songs begin with a *vamp,* in which the band plays the chord changes and establishes the rhythm, key, and feel of the piece for a number of bars before the head theme is played, to get the listener into the groove. This chapter serves as a similar function, as I use the pre-jazz transatlantic phenomenon of the ragtime cakewalk, which took Paris by storm in 1903, as a vamp to show how fin-de-siècle writers used these themes in relation to the new American music to define what Frenchness and "true" French culture meant to them. Examining how writers made sense of this jazz ancestor at a moment when a new democratic mass media culture was changing the way French people enjoyed themselves can help prepare us to hear how debate on jazz was later used to construct competing notions of true French culture and to negotiate cultural identity.

Les Joyeux Nègres and the French Public

At the end of the nineteenth century, Parisian popular culture was undergoing a dramatic change in its look and sound. With bicycles, telephones, and automobiles, people had a new relationship to time and space, one that they heard externalized in the new popular dances and songs that reigned in the emerging popular culture venues like the café-concert and the music hall.[1] Along with being new, many of these cultural forms came from outside the traditional boundaries of the imaginary French nation. As a result of this change, in the final decade of the *belle époque,* debates about what counted as properly French forms of enjoyment or leisure activity were increasingly important in the ongoing negotiation of cultural identity.[2] Indeed, only during the last part of the nineteenth century did statements about something like a consistent notion of Frenchness—as opposed to more localized identity constructions[3]—emerge in the French media. At the very moment that French identity was gaining consistency, the new thriving popular culture was shaking its imaginary foundations by constantly introducing new and exotic forms of enjoyment.

Critics in the new century saw the changes in culture and leisure activity as profound. Many argued that the new popular entertainment, as opposed to high-culture art, reflected a shift in sensibility related to a rapidly changing modern world and way of life. Some embraced this change; others rejected it as a sign of cultural loss. Though as Eugen Weber has shown, French culture was still largely local and heterogeneous,[4] performers came from everywhere to Paris and transformed their own acts to reflect the emerging national popular culture. In 1902, Gaby Deslys and Maurice Chevalier were the rising stars of the Parisian music hall, singing songs about modern life and drawing in audiences like never before. Like the new autobuses that seated the poor next to the very rich, this new modern *culture populaire* was leveling class distinctions and pushing the limits of what it meant to be French.

Economic conditions in fin-de-siècle France were as protean as popular culture. Though the end of the *belle époque* saw rapid economic growth, allowing for the surplus wealth and leisure necessary for the boom in popular entertainment,[5] a serious recession was stinging France when the cakewalk first came to town. Yet in October 1902, while American dancer Loie Fuller was being paid handsomely to perform at the luxurious Casino de Paris, more than 120,000 miners in the countryside were waging a sometimes bloody strike to protest their oppressive working conditions. When the general strike reached Paris, it spread to meat cutters, bakers, and almost every sector of the economy. By November, even the market for high culture was affected, and more than two thousand symphony orchestra musicians joined the marching *grévistes* (strikers) and called for better pay and overtime. Disturbed by this trend, tradition-minded French musical *maîtres* (masters) like Camille Saint-Saëns, Vincent d'Indy, and Gabriel Fauré—all suspicious of the new popular culture—thought that true artists ought to separate themselves from such mundane economic considerations. "I find this strike ridiculous," quipped Saint-Saëns. "Musicians should make art and not business."[6] For them, true

French culture was high culture and had no business responding to the vicis-situdes of contemporary life. Yet despite the support of these very visible and powerful champions, established high-culture venues had trouble competing at the box office. Popular cultural ventures for music and dancing, on the other hand, seemed to thrive.[7] Many critics began to argue that true French culture, which they saw as *haute culture,* needed protection. The aesthetic and political question of the day became: should the French state continue to support what some described as *"la vraie musique française"* (true French music) and protect it against the democratic distractions offered by *la culture populaire?* Critics were divided on this point and debated whether it made sense to uphold traditional standards of value, whatever they might be, in the face of an increasingly commercialized public that seemed to follow the whims of fashion. Many writers drew on Tocqueville's ideas about the tyranny of the majority among the American masses to characterize the behavior of the modern democratic *grand public* (general public) in France; the masses and markets in both countries, they argued, were driven by modern adver-tisement, which led hedonistic individuals to think more of pleasure than of cultural propriety.[8] Using American culture as a counterexample, both con-servative and modern vanguard critics often admonished the French public for being too fickle, though for different reasons. For instance, conservatives diagnosed the public's openness to the new *culture populaire* as a symptom of a true French culture in decay. Fashion, they argued, had replaced tradi-tion as the basis for judgment. Modernist promoters of popular culture, on the other hand, read the French embrace of the new as a sign of a healthy cosmopolitan sensibility that stayed up-to-date with progress. For them, the true France was one that had the ability to change with the times.

While popular acts came and went, the institutions that staged them— and the media forms in which their significance was debated—grew and grew. By 1900, Paris, the pleasure capital for France's new millennium, had 27,000 cafés,[9] more than it had before or since. Two hundred and sixty-four of these were *café-concerts*—cafés with a small stage for music and dance that charged only for food and drink—that attracted a working-class cli-entele. Dance halls were the cheapest places to dance and hear music, with tickets costing 25 centimes. Music halls were the most luxurious option, and tickets ranged in cost from 2 to 6 francs.[10] Yet with the very cheapest seats at the state-subsidized Opéra costing 4 francs, and the pit at the Comédie-Française charging 2.5 francs for a seat, even the expensive music hall was a relatively feasible entertainment venue for most of the French populace. For members of all social classes, there were places to hear and see the new music and dance, and these spaces far outnumbered—and were far more accessible than—the public spaces promoting elite culture.

Amid this economic, social, and cultural instability, the new ragtime dance from America called the cakewalk was unleashed on the French public. It is unclear exactly where it first appeared in France, but anxious critics quickly seized on it to make sense of the turbulent times. As they tried to show how it differed from traditional French dances, writers had to explain why this foreign rhythmic phenomenon seemed to appeal to even the highest French brows. In a sense, the cakewalk was not entirely new to the French cultural imaginary, as both African exhibitions and American minstrel shows had been regular features of the Parisian spectacle scene since the mid-1870s. After the Exposition Universelle in 1878, the Zulus danced at the Folies Bergère. Subsequent *expositions* in 1889 and 1900 featured similar groups from Dahomey (today's Benin), the Congo, and Senegal. In 1893 the Casino de Paris featured a show with 100 Dahomeyans that was attended by 2.7 million spectators. By the 1890s, minstrel shows were so normal that Footit and Chocolat, two black American clowns featured in the art of Toulouse-Lautrec,[11] were mainstays at the Nouveau-Cirque, one of the most fashionable and expensive venues in Paris.[12] Audiences had long developed a taste for their burlesque humor, dances, and songs.[13] Yet when *Les joyeux nègres* (The Happy Negroes) opened at the Nouveau-Cirque on October 20, 1902, their act created an immediate stir that unleashed a wave of cultural anxiety in the press. One can hear the excitement resonating in a review of the show in the newspaper *Le Gaulois:* "The show is composed of a series of fully loaded sketches about the life of *nègres* in the U.S. It forms a spectacle of giddy craziness."[14] Like this reviewer, most critics used standard racial riffs, stressing the uncontrolled and unmediated expression of *les nègres,* in order to show how the American *nègre* sense of musical expression and enjoyment was different from what they believed true Frenchness to be.

To open a window on the past, *Les Joyeux Nègres* was a typical slapstick Vaudeville review. The show began with a billiard match between Footit and Chocolat. Their burlesque gags included a mule who refused to budge, a pickpocketing dog, and a boxing match, all of which were, according to one reviewer, "interlaced with songs, dances and disheveled jigs."[15] While the *Le Gaulois* critic passed over most of the performance as normal minstrel-show fare, the new cakewalk captured his imagination. "We see a clearing where a contest of *nègre* dancers doing the cakewalk is going to be performed . . . What is the cakewalk, you say? The cakewalk is a dance, baptized as such because the couple who brings the most fantasy and grace to their execution

of it receives a cake as a prize. It was born in the U.S., where it quickly became very fashionable. This year, it was introduced to England, where it set
off the same craze . . . Imported to Paris by Houke, the cakewalk will entice
Parisians and cause a furor in the salons . . . Nothing could be more original,
more lively, or more agreeable to the eye than these new cakewalk dances,
which have the advantage of being unlike anything we have previously seen
in this genre."[16] Several themes used here help prepare us for the dynamics
of reception that would later dominate French jazz criticism. For instance,
one hears the hyperbolic description of a new, rhythmic, and exotic popular
American phenomenon, followed by a prediction about its dramatic impact
on French popular culture. Both are typical gestures by a culture critic whose
job is to reveal the latest trend. One should also note how this critic, as others would later do, drew upon stereotypic riffs about *nègre* racial sensibility
to characterize the music and dance.

As many critics predicted, this "strange and captivating"[17] foreign dance
quickly caught on in the most fashionable salons and inspired French theater owners to put it on their stages. "Today, in all the reviews of the end of
the year, in the music halls and in Montmartre theaters—that means everywhere—we dance the cakewalk with *frénésie*."[18] Note the critic's use of the
word *frénésie* (frenzy), a standard signifier in descriptions of *nègre* expression
through song and dance. Here, as it would be later with jazz, *frénésie* was
used to characterize not only the instability of the music, but the mimetic
reaction of the French public, conveying the idea that the new dance was
disturbing the French ethos and that French people were becoming more like
les nègres because of it. In the magazine *Le Rire* one critic warned, "While
there is still time, before the cakewalk obsession has taken over all classes of
society, let it be known that this Negro dance is all the rage . . . Attend the
big protest meeting against [the new dance]."[19] Neither reviewer was wholly
exaggerating, at least about the dance being everywhere. A partial list of venues integrating versions of this new transatlantic "*danse nègre*" reveals that
it had indeed reached all levels of popular culture. The cakewalk was seen
in the revue *C'est d'un raid!* (It's a raid), at the Scala, a music hall; the song
and dance troupes *Seven Floridas* and *The Elks* could be seen dancing it at
the Casino de Paris; *Elle est rien bath!* presented the dance to a working-class
audience at the Bataclan, a café-concert; *Le nègre continue* stayed on at the
Boîte à Fursy; *Cakewalk,* a socialite comedy by Louis Varney, took the stage
at the Théâtre des Nouveautés; the *Olympia-révue* at the Olympia music hall
included a lighthearted number in which chorus girls danced the cakewalk
with the devil; the *opérette* called *La petite duchesse du casino* had a cakewalk

scene, and performance of the cakewalk served as the warm-up act for the *opérette Cabriole* at the ritzy music hall Le Parisiana.[20] At the Ambassadeurs, the entertainer Strit performed "La cakewalkomanie" and Odette Auber sang "Professeur de cakewalk."[21] Le Gai Tivoli, a dance hall that advertised itself as "the only Parisian ball open every night," boasted that all of Paris came there to "amuse itself nightly" with the new dance. From the café-concert and the music hall, to the circus and the *cabaret-artistique,* it seemed that everywhere, everyone was doing the cakewalk. As is often the case in compliance with fashion, the performance and enjoyment of this dance became a way of marking oneself as modern.

Yet critics who had a more traditional and highbrow vision of true French culture began wondering aloud in the media if being up-to-date meant being Americanized. What, they asked, did the popularity of the exotic cakewalk mean about the strength of traditional French cultural identity? What, they demanded, was the appropriate collective response to this foreign threat? Such questions about the direction of culture and about proper ways of being French in the new century were raised by Abel Hermant (1862–1950) in *Les transatlantiques,* one of the most popular books—and dramas—of the decade. It is a story about the interactions of an emerging transatlantic elite in a rapidly changing culture, and Hermant used its characters to answer the questions he raised about how France should negotiate these changes. Blanche de Tiercé, the youngest daughter of a "pure-blooded" but bankrupt French aristocratic family looking to alleviate its troubles by marrying into American industrial wealth, is described as "wanting to modernize herself a bit." Her father, the count, prefers "the old America of Fenimore Cooper and de Chateaubriand"[22] to the new, modern America represented by industrialist Jerry Shaw, the patriarch "King of Gold," who brags that Americans "have mechanics for everything."[23] Like many French writers after Chateaubriand, Hermant seemed to be arguing that the "natural" America, characterized by vast forests and noble savages, had been supplanted by a modern America dominated by great cities and machines. The de Tiercés are looking to find a way out of debt, and the Shaws are looking to marry into a European royal family befitting its wealth. Blanche befriends Biddy, the youngest daughter of the Shaw family, on the transatlantic voyage back to France. It is through this younger generation, learning to engage the challenges of American cultural influence, that the appropriate way of being French is dramatized. When Biddy, dressed in a Loie Fuller–like costume, tries to teach Blanche modern American dances, Blanche declines. In this test of cultural propriety, Blanche, even at the tender age of fourteen, politely says no.

She befriends Americans even as she remains ambivalent about the trappings of modern American popular culture, retaining her difference and distinct sense of French taste. Thus one can see that the proper way to be modern and French, for Hermant, was to accept certain aspects of modernity (like American economic hegemony) while distancing oneself from un-French forms of culture by not taking part in them.

Most Parisians, despite the popularity of Hermant's book, seemed to lack Blanche's protective reserve and rushed to take their first awkward cakewalk step. The cakewalk quickly became the most modern of dances, de rigueur even in high-class salon society. To meet the demand, music-hall impresarios hired "authentic" black American dancers, such as the seven-member Creole group *The Floridas,* to give the public the kind of exotic *nègre frénésie* it wanted to see. As the cakewalk craze continued into 1903, many observers expressed concern about the implications of this trend in France and defended what they believed to be true Frenchness. Whereas its proponents valued its *frénésie* as authentic, its opponents read such demeanor as a mark of bad taste, acceptable for *nègres* who lived in oppressive conditions in the southern states of America[24] but completely unbecoming in civilized French salon society, which valued corseted grace and self-control. The poem "Pavane et Cakewalk," by Jacques Redelsberger, put it succinctly: "Alas, today French brains are topsy-turvy and the prancing of monkeys has turned the universe upside-down . . . The epileptic cakewalk makes us look like broken toys who spin like madmen . . . O little society women, keep the waltz and the Boston, and let this dance be sweated out by the inmates of Charenton."[25] Redelsberger was not alone in associating the dance with mental instability and asylums. Newspapers, magazines, and other print media of the era were filled with cartoon images of the cakewalk that give a sense of the stakes as aesthetics became political in French debates on culture. Artists caricatured salon *danseurs* in tails and starched collars, absentmindedly dancing the salon version of the cakewalk with corseted *danseuses* in heels, hair wound tightly in a bun. Several cartoons by *L'Illustration* artist Henriot, published amid the ads on the weekly's last page, showed disfavored politicians, who followed public opinion too much, doing the dance; maids questioned whether their cakewalking masters had lost their sense of reason. One cartoon wondered if good manners and politeness rituals would be displaced in France by the cakewalk craze. For these artists, the dance carried the stigma of being disruptive for the cultural ethos and being distinctly un-French, so they satirized those who seemed unable to resist its thrill. These media critics were not against the cakewalk per se—they just found it ridiculous when French men and women tried to do it.

One of the most representative examples of this nuanced position on the "latest Parisian craze" can be found in a 1903 article in *L'Illustration,* an expensive glossy journal with a large and solidly bourgeois readership. The story was illustrated by two paintings of the dance in its different cultural contexts. In each setting, the cakewalk took an appropriate form. *Les nègres* performed it one way, and French men and women another. One was disheveled and ragged; the other starched and reserved. Along with the paintings and text, readers were given sheet music and dance-step instructions. So while it educated its readers about the cakewalk, it also warned them about

An artist's depiction of French dancers doing the cake-walk.
"Dance of Today." *L'Illustration,* no. 3128 (February 7, 1903).
Reproduced with permission from the Bibliothèque Nationale
de France.

L'ambassadeur, pour montrer la cordialité de, ses relations répondra en dansant le cake-walk : — J'ai un pied qui remue...

Three examples of the artist Henriot's humorous take on the cultural implications of the cake-walk (see also pp. 26, 27). "The ambassador, to show the warmth of relations between countries, responds by dancing the cake-walk. 'I have a foot that moves . . .'" *L'Illustration,* no. 3132 (March 7, 1903). Reproduced with permission from the Bibliothèque Nationale de France.

the larger forces of Americanization it represented. "We know that the Yankees are in the process of conquering, by seduction or by force, all of our old world. They started with the investment of money in Paris. In 1900 they gave us the Souza band, the 'orchestra of Souza,' with its American fanfare, epileptic marches, and frenetic gallops. Now the winter of 1902–3 reveals the cakewalk to us, that 'danse du gâteau' of the North American *nègre.*"[26] Again, several important themes play off one another in this passage. First and foremost, there is the evocation of cultural conquest, a conjuring of the specter of Americanization where the traditions of the Old World are threatened both by economic power and by rhythmic seduction. The seductive Souza marches are described as *epileptic* or *frenetic,* adjectives associated with sickness, abnormality, or *les nègres* but not used at the time to convey a sense of true Frenchness.

"Oh, my God! . . . Monsieur is crazy! . . . Imbecile . . . I am learning to dance the cake-walk!" *L'Illustration,* no. 3126 (January 24, 1903). Reproduced with permission from the Bibliothèque Nationale de France.

It is important to note that the article links culturally appropriate rhythm to individual and cultural health. As would be the standard procedure in later debates about jazz in France, the difference between healthy and unhealthy is paralleled to the distinction between syncopated and nonsyncopated rhythm. This imaginary construct, like many received ideas, has old and deep cultural roots. For centuries, writers have argued that "true" French music is grounded in the rhythm of the healthy body, a rhythm rooted in the mythic French past. An example of such an origin myth, and the sense of Frenchness generated

En résumé, la politesse, qui était l'aïeule des belles manières, sera supprimée définitivement en France, et le coup de chapeau antique sera remplacé par un simple pas de cake-walk.

"In short, politeness, the ancestor of good manners, will be replaced permanently in France, and the old tip of the hat will be replaced by an easy step of the cake-walk." *L'Illustration,* no. 3142 (May 16, 1903). Reproduced with permission from the Bibliothèque Nationale de France.

by it, can be found in the work of Michelet, the famously romantic nationalist historian who wanted to restore France to its roots in the rhythms of *le peuple.* "The mystic weavers of the Middle Ages were famous under the name of Lollards because while they worked they actually lulled—that is, sang and hummed in low tones some nursery rhyme. The rhythm of the shuttle, pushed forth and pulled back at equal intervals, patterned itself to the rhythm of the heart, and by evening it often happened that in addition to the cloth, a hymn or a ballad had been woven."[27] For Michelet and many other French critics who had similar traditional ideas about true Frenchness linked to an ethnic folk culture, good rhythm was linked to repetitious work and was a calm, rational expression of a healthy body and mind. True French rhythm, such critics argued, should have a salutary effect on the cultural ethos. Syncopated music, on the other hand, is often described as "frenetic" or "epileptic" and, even before the cakewalk, had a wholly different and altogether unhealthy connotation. In academic musicological discourse, the beat in syncopated music is characterized as irregular. Indeed, according to the *Litrée* dictionary, the word *syncope* was first used as a medical term to describe the irregular heartbeat associated with "sickness of the heart." As opposed to the strong regular pulse of the industrious peasants evoked by Michelet, a *coeur* (heart) *syncope* is a sign of sickness. Thus, by virtue of the linguistic connotations, it was standard practice when describing "French rhythm" to convey the idea that a healthy French body would naturally express itself in regular meter, while the *nègre* or the unhealthy Frenchman would exude (and be attracted to) syncopated rhythms. Variations of this standard imaginary opposition were repeatedly used to characterize the ragtime cakewalk and would later return in media debates about jazz.

Like other observers, the *Illustration* critic described the cakewalk craze as a cultural contagion. Yet though it had been "introduced into Franco-American salons by transatlantic girls," the catalyst for the dance craze was the improvisational element that the *nègre* dancers brought to it. The dance "was improvised by the *nègre* troops who, in front of an enthusiastic public, carry themselves away each night with the most disheveled frolics of the cakewalk."[28] Thus the missing ingredient that the *nègres* added, the element of ragged exotic otherness that attracted the French public and set off the "contagion," was the spirit of unrestrained rhythmic improvisation. The critic believed French people should not mimic the kind of enjoyment associated with the primitive *nègre*. Rather, the French should take part only in the sophisticated or regulated ballroom dances taught in classes by dance masters according to rules. One can see how this critic used the black American dance to draw an imaginary line of racial difference: whereas grace, poise, and precision were, for him, valued as markers of a civilized and rule-bound Frenchness, the *nègre* cakewalk dancers improvised "acrobatic variations on an original rhythm." Yet their "disheveled originality" was precisely what appealed to a "high society, happy to encounter a little of the new."[29] Though the modern French public seemed to have a taste for the new, he did not believe the cakewalk would stay exotic for long, as French tastes started to assert themselves. "The dance masters have undertaken to regulate the movements and figures in order to transform them into a dance of society."[30] In other words, he hoped that a dialectic of cultural appropriation would tame the dance and that the strength of French republican civilization would triumph over *nègre* improvisation. The proof of this, to him, was that all over Paris, the cakewalk was being "civilized" and made to conform to a sophisticated French sensibility so that it would be acceptably French.

Moreover, the *Illustration* critic argued that the cakewalk that most French people knew was "nothing but a caricature on the stages of the café-concert and, in the salons, nothing but a very pale imitation. The cakewalk really lacks all the picturesque and passionate charm that it has in its original milieu, that of the *nègres* of the southern states of the American Union."[31] Parisians had been seduced by a caricature, a regulated pale imitation that they learned by method and continued to misrecognize as the real. The "real" cakewalk, on the other hand, as depicted in the picturesque painting, was truly exotic and corresponded to the differences between the races: it could be seen in the facial expressions (one animated, the other reserved), the differences in posture (one loose, the other stiff), and the clothes (one kind ragged, the other elegant). The authenticity of the dance in its "natural setting," that of the American *nègres,* was conveyed by the critic's use of standard riffs on racial fixity. "There, it is really the cakewalk . . . This crazy party usually takes place outside, as long as the bad weather of the season doesn't force the band of 'darkies,' dressed in rags of lively colors and indescribable throwaways, to take refuge in some broken-down shack or some straw hut with a dirt floor."[32] The authenticity of the *nègre* cakewalk is conveyed by stressing its naiveté and its naturalness, markers of wildness related to fixed racial stereotypes. Opposite the standard depiction of white, civilized, and reasoned French dancers is a "crazy party" of "darkies." In contrast to the exquisite salon, the *nègres* dance outside or in a "broken-down shack." In contrast to the stiff and pale imitation, which the French learned by method, everything with *les nègres* is natural, unmediated, and authentic. "The gestures, the steps, the attitude, the physiognomy, and the accessories of the dancers, the audience, the musicians, the judges, the director of the scene, and the rhythm of the music, everything here forms a harmonious blend of local colors. The grotesqueness of the details disappears in the picturesqueness of the ensemble and the contagiousness of the general joy that illuminates their faces. We admire the incomparable suppleness of the dancers, the precise ease of all their movements."[33] The sense of community and communal enjoyment—the contagious joy—was possible for the dance only in its "natural" (read *nègre*) context. This authentic cakewalk, he seemed to be saying, could be truly enjoyed only by those who were not conscious of the rules of civilized French culture. Therefore, French imitators could never achieve the same kind of rhythmic enjoyment and suppleness that the *nègres* did, as they were determined by a wholly different racial physiognomy and constitution. For him, this was a good thing, a sign of the permanence of something truly French.

Indeed, the imaginary notion that different races had specific varieties of enjoyment related to their ontology was, and is, a persistent idea in France. This idea could explain why so many culture critics disapproved of the cakewalk in its Parisian setting, where it clashed with the demeanor and ethos appropriate for civilized French society. Here, as would later be the case with jazz, the primitive was out of tune with the civilized. For instance, many critics argued that the posture and carriage required for the cakewalk, arching the back and raising the arms in front of the dancer (a position described by one observer as that of "a dog begging for food"), lacked grace and were unnatural, not to mention being very difficult for women dressed in the whalebone corsets worn in polite society at the time. They thought the French body was incapable of the *nègre* suppleness the dance required.

"The cake-walk in a Parisian Salon." *L'Illustration,* no. 3124 (January 10, 1903). Reproduced with permission from the Bibliothèque Nationale de France.

"The cake-walk in its country of origin: the kangaroo step at a nègre dance in the United States." *L'Illustration,* no. 3124 (January 10, 1903). Reproduced with permission from the Bibliothèque Nationale de France.

On a cultural level, the cakewalk required something lacking in a Parisian social world ordered by rules of decorum, protocol, and tradition: improvisation. As the *Illustration* critic worried: "How can we define the particular character of the dance? No rules really exist. It is the triumph of personal improvisation."[34] The nature of improvisation and its relation to both individual and cultural identity is a theme that is still playing itself out in relation to jazz. Many of the ideas about improvisation used in debates on jazz date back at least to the eighteenth century in France, when Rameau and Rousseau battled over whether harmony or melody was the basis of music. While Rameau insisted that music was based on physical and cosmological laws,[35] Rousseau felt that music originated in melodic expression of heartfelt sentiment. Whereas Rameau followed the traditional Pythagorean notion that music was better when it was a product of the rational, detached intellect, Rousseau believed good music was possible only when one unleashed the passions. Rameau argued that musicians should study and obey physical laws and social conventions, but Rousseau felt the best musicians were natural, unschooled, and free to express themselves in their own way. Rameau argued that *musique doit adoucir les moeurs*—music should soothe the soul and the social ethos; Rousseau wanted music to set them free. Variations on these two positions on the appropriate expression of music and its effect on the cultural ethos—the spiritual, emotional, or psychological state of society—were rehearsed in relation to the cakewalk and are still heard today in French debates about music.

Critic Henri de Rive, for instance, condemned the "Yankee dance" in 1903 for its unhealthy effect on French culture. The "uncoordinated and burlesque" dance, he argued, was characterized by an "unstable equilibrium."[36] Repeatedly evoking the abnormal or unhealthy, his description dramatizes how notions of French tradition or the "true France" are often invented in opposition to a perceived cultural threat. In his mind, the dance clashed with the grace and restraint that he believed characterized traditional French culture. Therefore, the enjoyment it engendered was unnatural for the French race. Performing a variation on the standard cultural riff about France's civilizing duty linked to normative ideals of French femininity, he demanded a call to action to protect tradition. "Are you not there, Ladies, to close the door on it? If some exceptional fantasy keeps you from doing so, it will be too late, assuredly, to make a return to the gracious minuets of your grandmothers. And so, abandoning the past, you want to be of your time, to sacrifice yourselves to the fashion of the day, to rejuvenate the national traditions with a bit of exoticism. To the eccentric choreography and epileptic extravagances of a *danse sauvage,* you should prefer the reasonably regulated steps and rhythmic cadences of a music more captivating and . . . civilized."[37] One can hear how he linked racial difference to the ethos of their natural music and dance by contrasting *nègre* "primitiveness" or "wildness" with French civility and reason. While his true French dances were "gracious" and "reasonably regulated," he described the "*danse sauvage*" as eccentric and epileptic. In fact, de Rive's normative plea dramatizes how important having culturally appropriate desire is for constituting cultural identity.[38] Should one enjoy things that are part of one's own time, such as the exotic cakewalk (or its spin-off, the kangaroo hop), or was it the duty of self-respecting French men and women to desire more traditional or "civilized" forms of enjoyment, such as the quadrille or the minuet?[39]

The reflexive gesture toward true French tradition or traditional French values exemplified by de Rive, whereby tradition is posited through conscious reflection, is a constant leitmotif in media debates on jazz. The logic behind this move can be understood in this way: when a speaker performs a variation on this theme and calls for a return to tradition, he or she imagines a culture in which such tradition is accepted unconditionally. From this nostalgic position, traditional cultures possessed values that were accepted without reflection, which is why critics always find them so worthy of imitation. The logical twist, however, is that the return to tradition evoked by culture critics is a choice based entirely on conscious reflection. One could say that cultures never know what values or traditions they have, only those that they believe to have lost. This is what cultural theorist Slavoj Žižek means when he says that the moment we start to talk about "values," we have "*a priori* posited values as something relative, contingent, whose preserve is not unquestionable, as something which it is necessary to discuss—that is to say, precisely to value."[40] When French writers invoke "French tradition"—whether it be musical tradition, traditional forms of enjoyment, or traditional values—as a way to ground their tastes, judgments, and pleasures, they often follow this same constitutive logic. Within de Rive's variation, his notion of "true" Frenchness was distinctly Cartesian. Thus it followed that true French ladies and gentlemen *should* value reason over fantasy, gracious control over epileptic extravagances, and French over *sauvage*. But the dilemma for fin-de-siècle culture critics like de Rive was that, in spite of knowing better, French people really enjoyed getting carried away by an un-French dance like the cakewalk. What did this mean about the state of tradition in modern France?

How widespread was the impact of the cakewalk on the new century's *culture populaire*? Ample evidence points to its influence on some of the biggest stars of French popular music. For instance, Maurice Chevalier, today an icon of Frenchness around the world, later declared that his own style of dancing and singing came from the cakewalk, whose foreign rhythms had given him the sensation of "a completely new physical enjoyment."[41] That so many French people, like Chevalier, seemed to be taking pleasure in this foreign *jouissance* (enjoyment) was a cause for anxiety among cultural purists in 1903. What did the collective desire to dance the cakewalk mean about the potency of traditional forms of enjoyment and the health of traditional French culture? To frame the paradox another way, if conservative critics were convinced it was necessary to return to the gracious dances of the past, had an unreflexive enjoyment of traditional French dance steps already been lost? Was the cakewalk, as many critics argued, a symptom of a dramatic and potentially dangerous cultural change?

Ragtime Projections

Several short films about the cakewalk from 1903 dramatize the deep-seated anxieties provoked by the imagined loss of true French culture. Though less than a decade old, the cinema had already gained standing as an immensely popular and democratic cultural media form.[42] Film was a powerful way to display, frame, and lend meaning to all kinds of cultural phenomena. Several early filmmakers noticed how well film conveyed rhythm, and they turned to dance, and the new rhythms of the cakewalk, as subject matter for their short films.[43] The first films on the cakewalk were *actualité* films—early documentary films that set up cameras in front of spectacles or scenes to give viewers an "actual" perspective—such as *Le cakewalk, danse par les Elks du Casino de Paris,* by Siegmund Lubin, that merely recorded live performances. Soon, filmmakers such as the famous Georges Méliès (1861–1938) were using it in narrative films, projecting cultural anxieties about the cakewalk for mass audiences and lending the dance a moral resonance through the normative views they constructed on screen.

Méliès's *Le cake-walk infernal* (1903), for instance, was a thinly veiled condemnation of the dance craze. Set in hell, the short scenario has the Devil conjuring up out of thin air—in an early use of double exposure—a dancing couple who do the cakewalk. As if warning about the danger of cultural mimesis, first a demon and then two dancers in blackface do the cakewalk in front of hell's inhabitants, who all begin to follow blithely along. The desires stirred by the dance stimulate a dispute over a girl, and two men begin to fight over her. The Devil, watching the effect of the cakewalk on all the figures, laughs and consumes the quarreling dancers in flames. Finally, for his pièce de résistance, Méliès used a double-exposure technique he had first employed in *Dislocations mystérieuses* (1901) to show the arms and the legs of the remaining dancers coming off of their bodies and dancing by themselves before all the dancers are consumed in flames.[44]

In many ways, the lesson of this morality tale has to do with social disintegration through rhythmic enjoyment and desire: dancing the cakewalk, introduced by blackfaced devils, will lead to damnation. The short is thus contributing to the debate about the ethos of the cakewalk, which degrades social order and degenerates the French body. Poor souls are manipulated by un-French rhythms into losing control of themselves. As the rhythms take over their bodies, the limbs literally begin dancing by themselves, and this unnatural *jouissance* gives rise to desires that turn men against one another.

Pathé Frères[45] also made several short films about the new American dance: *La célèbre danse du cake-walk* (1903), *Le cake-walk* (1904), and *Le cake-walk chez les nains* (1903), another allegory about cultural loss. A different mythic external agent threatens Frenchness in *Le cake-walk chez les nains:* a barely blackfaced American minstrel figure who looks uncannily like Uncle Sam with his beard, coattails, and top hat. His status as a symbolic agent in the drama is made explicit by his monumental size in comparison to the other figures in the film, who are "dwarfs" (*nains*) by comparison. He sweeps his magic hat across a chair, and two miniature French peasants appear out of the hat and begin to dance a traditional peasant jig on the chair. The American magician then waves a handkerchief over the peasants and transforms them into a modern bourgeois city couple. He then conjures up on the cushion a miniature mirror image of himself, and it shows the city couple how to do the cakewalk. While the big Uncle Sam watches approvingly, smiling and tapping his cane to the rhythm, the modern French dancers follow the little Yankee, reproducing his motions and rhythm. Now with the figures all in step, literally and symbolically, the film ends with them saluting the viewer in harmony with their hats.[46] On an allegorical level, the film is a variation on the theme of the Americanization of French culture. The symbolic American behind the scenes transforms peasants, with their traditional jigs, into bourgeois Frenchmen who readily imitate Yankee dances and enjoy American rhythms. Americanization takes place through rhythmic conquest, which causes traditional forms of dress and customs to literally disappear.

Such anxiety about a perceived metamorphosis in Frenchness and French popular culture due to the influence of foreign rhythm and dance is common in French discourse on culture. Following the standard discursive riffs, the unhealthy syncopated foreign rhythms are usually contrasted with healthy Frenchness linked to regular meter and rationality. This binary, at work in the distinctions between primitive and civilized, frenzied and calm, or *nègre* and French, continued to manifest itself in all types of cultural criticism of the cakewalk for the rest of the decade as more and more French men and women came to enjoy the dance. Despite the critical protest, the cakewalk (along with other American dances, such as the kangaroo hop and the Boston) not only thrived in popular culture, but found a place in high-society salons alongside the traditional polkas, mazurkas, quadrilles, and minuets.

Though the cakewalk had taken a regular place in many levels of culture, many critics continued to call for resistance to the so-called *nègre* elements of the dance. For instance, the description of the cakewalk in a best-selling dance manual by Lussan-Borel, published in 1909, shows the anxiety the cakewalk still provoked some six years after its first appearance. "We will confess that, for a long time, we weighed the question of whether that *nègre* dance imported from North America would figure or not in our treatment of salon dances . . . Like all laws, fashion has its requirements; *la mode* has decided, and the cakewalk, having made a furor in the most elegant salons in Paris, contrary to sane notions of grace and good taste [is no different]. Thus we have resigned ourselves to regulate and publish a theory of the cakewalk—at least so that the fashion of this dance, little recommendable in our opinion, not come from just anywhere and might vanish like it came."[47] Along with the standard discursive opposition between sane notions of grace, good taste, and elegance—things Lussan-Borel associated with "true" Frenchness—and the riffs on the unhealthy ethos of the *nègre* dance, one can again hear anxiety about the tyranny of public opinion transforming popular culture as it relentlessly searched for the new. The un-French forces represented by the cakewalk threaten the imaginary true French culture, which he equated with the traditional high-society salon. The great threat was the desire to be modern, which, he feared, trumped "sane notions of grace and good taste."

Yet despite his resignation about the power of public opinion causing French people to forsake normative Frenchness for the sake of fashion, Lussan-Borel offered a remedy. Regulate this "syncopated polka, with its posture which is both difficult and has very little grace, and make it more elegant and tasteful."[48] Even while denouncing it, dance teachers could change it and make it more French. Yet even in a more Frenchified form, learned by method and performed without improvisation, he still believed cultured French men and women should avoid this "fantasy of the crowd": "In our opinion, the attitude demanded by the cakewalk will never lend itself to the varieties of gracious and restrained combinations of the regular salon dances, which permit a natural body position. The cakewalk, all in all, appears to us a fantasy of the café-concert and the music hall but does not seem to have a place in the salon."[49] Since Lussan-Borel argued that the body position and mentality demanded by the cakewalk were unnatural for French men and women, the dance was incompatible with true Frenchness. As the salon dances could be dictated by the host rather than the law of fashion, Lussan-Borel hoped that by denouncing the cakewalk for being "epileptic," "frenetic," "unnatural," "primitive," and "*sauvage*," he could convince high-culture hosts of the impropriety of the dance and help restore traditional salon dancing.

Many critics framed the cakewalk as un-French in this way, but the public continued to follow its ragtime rhythm. Nor did the elite anti-cakewalk critics stop these rhythms from entering into music normally deemed the highest of culture. For instance, Claude Debussy, who had become the star of French symphonic music in the new century, showed his interest in the syncopated American music by writing *Golliwogg's Cakewalk* in 1908 and following it with a composition titled *Minstrels* two years later. That such an influential and iconic high-culture French figure would write a piece like *Golliwogg's*

Cakewalk still provoked the ire of conservative critic Louis Laloy some six years after its composition in 1914. "The cakewalk of Debussy will corrupt children, who, bit by bit, will clumsily imitate the well-known postures of that *nègre* dance."[50] It bothered Laloy that Debussy, who as the leading French composer should have been promoting "true" French music, chose foreign themes and rhythms. He worried that the bodies and constitutions of French children, who were naturally mimetic, could be permanently marked by the adaptation of *nègre* posture and enjoyment. Yet beyond Laloy arguing that Debussy was not sufficiently French, there is an exemplary paradox here that would surface again and again in relation to jazz: "true Frenchness" is often based upon the idea that there is a core essence of Frenchness that is immutable. As such, French enjoyment, rather than being learned, is believed to be ontologically natural, as natural as the frenetic and epileptic *nègre* enjoyment critics constantly described. But if Frenchness was natural to Frenchmen, then what was the cause for alarm? One could posit that on some level, critics knew that cultural identity *was* mutable and *could* change, despite their rhetorical assertions to the contrary.

Within months of Laloy's critique of the cakewalk, a strange new twentieth-century *danse macabre* had begun that would change the face of French culture forever. The threat was no longer imaginary or symbolic, but took the form of the German military, armed with tanks, barbed wire, and mustard gas. As a result, when dancers Irene and Vernon Castle, backed by the music of James Reese Europe, launched the new ragtime dance the Castle-Walk in 1914[51] with the hope of inspiring a new international craze, newspapers had little space—or concern—for debates about its appropriateness for French culture. Though the dance was immensely popular in America and England, the horrors of war captured the public's attention in France, and the Castle-Walk stumbled there. Vernon himself gave up promoting the dance and joined the Royal Air Force.

America entered World War I in April of 1917: "We make love to ragtime and we die to it,"[52] wrote the American writer Walter Lippmann. In France, pro-American sentiment continued to rise with the presence of U.S. soldiers, and as it did, so did a shared love of their music. There are innumerable stories of American popular songs being sung in the trenches and being taught to French soldiers by "Les Sammies," as the American soldiers were called.[53] Popular culture was exchanged. Away from the front, ragtime songs and other examples of the latest recorded sounds of American culture had also entered the French salon and home through a new cultural force: the phonograph.[54]

Some time in 1917, amid the noise and chaos of trench warfare, jazz entered

French culture; over the cries of anguish and grief, no one paid much attention to it. That last year of the war, Erik Satie is reported by Darius Milhaud to have made the prophetic statement, "Jazz tells us about its sadness—& we don't give a damn [*on s'en fou*] . . . That is why it is beautiful, real."[55] Jazz had arrived.

This chapter introduced important discursive procedures, tropes, themes, and riffs used by fin-de-siècle culture critics to describe the significance of the ragtime cakewalk for French culture. Variations on the same ideas, and ways of using them to define "true" Frenchness and "true" French culture, would return in the cultural debates about jazz. The next chapter deals with the explosion of jazz into French culture during the chaotic period after World War I. It examines the process by which the French public came to give a damn about jazz as it became an important part of the postwar celebration and mourning process for a traumatized culture trying to heal its wounds.

2

The First Wave

Jazz and Cultural Recovery

Man is visibly made for thinking; all his dignity
and skill go into it, and it is his duty to think like one
must. Now the order of thought is to begin
with itself, its author and his ends.

So what does everyone think about?
Never of all that, but of dancing.
—Pascal, *Pensées*

When America entered into World War I, a certain optimism seemed
to accompany the American soldiers into France. On the Fourth of July, 1917,
American troops marched through Paris to the cheers of welcoming crowds.
L'Intransigeant reported that the troops whistled and sang tunes "already
very popular in Paris, and the happy crowd has taken them to heart."[1] Henri
Bergson wrote that "we have had, until now, a moral certitude of victory. The
American intervention brings us mathematical certainty."[2] Indeed, more than
three million American soldiers would arrive between this time and the end
of the war, anxiously enjoying Parisian life before shipping out to the front.[3]
This chapter traces the public reaction to the music the soldiers brought
with them, a music so new that it defied traditional cultural categories and
resonated in almost every sector of French society as a marker of change.
Jazz and jazz dancing became contested signs of the times, symptoms of
cultural health in the postwar period that writers and culture critics rushed
to diagnose. For some, they signified sickness; for others, they meant that
French culture was getting over the wounds of war.

The summer of 1917 was hardly a cakewalk, as bread was being made from
potato flour and there were rations on milk, sugar, and fruit, but the presence of American troops brought hope that the war might finally be end-

ing. The French public seemed to have a fascination with American things. General Pershing's populist man-of-the-people attitude, so different from the aristocratic airs of Maréchal Foch and Maréchal Pétain, captivated the crowds. The songs that the "Sammies" taught French men and women were not traditional American patriotic songs, but rather the popular songs of America's Tin Pan Alley. "In order to please our allies from the other side of the Atlantic," wrote columnist Le Wattman in *L'Intransigeant*, "no . . . no . . . don't sing Yankee Doodle. Though it is certainly well known, the old balanced rhythms of the cakewalk are now held more dearly than anything else."[4] The syncopated songs from the American culture industry celebrated modern men, women, and life, and they fascinated the French public.[5] With the new optimism, the cakewalk, once opposed as an epileptic dance of an inferior race, was now heard as a sign of cultural balance and equilibrium.

Jean Cocteau (1889–1963), who had been to America in 1915,[6] tapped into this pro-American sentiment and, along with Erik Satie, Pablo Picasso, and the Ballets Russes, staged the ballet *Parade* in the fall of 1917. They combined cubism and modern composition to "parade" a variety of dance scenes depicting modern life in America and France. Picasso's costumes were unlike anything seen before. Satie's theme for "le Manager New-Yorkais," a dancer costumed in a cubist vision of skyscrapers, stoplights, and loudspeakers, was the *Ragtime du Paquebot*. Arguably the first instance of "jazz" influence on European composition, it was inspired by Scott Joplin's "Mysterious Rag," which Satie had heard on phonograph. Poet Guillaume Apollinaire wrote in *L'Excelsior* that *Parade* marked a "point of departure for a new spirit,"[7] which he called "*sur-réalisme.*" Satie's embrace of the new American music made him an idol for the young group of modernist composers known as the Six.[8] These composers, Darius Milhaud, Francis Poulenc, George Auric, Albert Roussel, Arthur Honegger, and Germaine Tailleferre, all began to texture their music with the new syncopated idiom. So, too, did Russian émigré Igor Stravinsky, who drew on it for his ragtime-tinted *Histoire du Soldat,* a ballet on wartime suffering. Everywhere, American music seemed to be capturing the French imagination.

A Kind of Domesticated Catastrophe

On December 12, 1917, just after the German Gothas bombed Paris, a new musical revue directed by George Arnold and Jacques Charles inaugurated the newly refurbished Casino de Paris. *Laissez-les tomber* (Let Them Drop / Don't Worry About It) starred the French Gaby Deslys and the American

Harry Pilcer and featured the music of brother Murray Pilcer's "Ragtime" band. The defiant show, comprising two acts, fifty backdrops, over three hundred artists—including fifty clowns and forty-eight "Beautiful Girls" wearing plumed hats over four feet tall—and eight hundred costumes, was designed to dazzle with its over-the-top extravagance. The publicity and reviews for the show brought the new American music dramatically into conversations about the future of French popular culture.

For Cocteau, *Laissez-les tomber* marked a defining moment, which he announced in his book *Le coq et l'arlequin: notes autour de la musique* (The Cock and the Harlequin: Notes on Music). Cocteau crowed over the arrival of a new revolutionary musical aesthetic, that of a "generation that no longer blinked."[9] He argued that this shocking foreign music was to be "felt," not judged according to traditional standards and academic rules. "*Bad* music, scorned by beautiful spirits, is very agreeable. What is disagreeable is their *good* music."[10] According to this logic, the new good music was the inverse of traditional good music. Based on simplicity, it was a perfect antidote to the overly intellectual music and music criticism of high culture. "It is not necessary to make simplicity a synonym for poverty, nor for retreat . . . The simplicity that comes in reaction to sophistication relieves itself of that sophistication; it releases and digests the acquired richness."[11] As opposed to French academic music based on "numbers and geometry," this heartfelt American popular music was perfect "for the fatigue of our ears."[12]

Cocteau thought there were two French musical "prejudices" that needed to be overcome: Wagner and impressionism. He blamed the former on the influence of Baudelaire, as the famous poet and critic was one of the most ardent proponents of Wagnerian romanticism, and the latter on the artistic tastes of the *haute bourgeoisie*. Cocteau rallied the anti-Wagnerian Friedrich Nietzsche to his cause: "Reread *The Case of Wagner* by Nietzsche. Never has something more light and more profound been said. When Nietzsche praised *Carmen*, he praised the frankness that our generation looks for at the music hall . . . That which brushes aside the impressionist music is a certain American dance which I saw at the Casino de Paris."[13] By analogy, Cocteau and *Laissez-les tomber* were to "impressionist music"—read Debussy—what Nietzsche and *Carmen* were to Wagner. Cocteau was convinced by Nietzsche's admonitions that true music should "serve recreation," exhilarate, or "give pleasure," rather than serve an ideal, "lie," and "redeem" as Wagner's music had. In the new American music, Cocteau heard this same explosive power and argued that it might be the homeopathic cure that France needed to get over the noisy chaos of war. "Here is what that dance was like. The

American band accompanied it on banjos and fat nickel pipes. To the right of the little troop in black clothes, there was a *barman de bruit* [noise] under a gold pergola, responsible for bells, triangles, boards, and motorcycle horns. He mixed cocktails with them, each time topping them off with a slice of cymbal, raising himself, waddling around, and smiling like an angel . . . Mr. Pilcer was in coattails, thin, and made up in red, and Miss Gaby Deslys, the great ventriloquist doll with a porcelain face, had cornsilk hair and a dress with ostrich feathers. They danced together on that whirlwind of rhythms and drums a sort of domesticated catastrophe that left them completely drunk and nearsighted under a shower of six air-raid lights."[14] Hearing the music was like drinking one of the newly introduced American cocktails that, in Cocteau's experience, left one drunk and happy. His characterization of the American music as a "domesticated catastrophe" never mentioned the word *jazz,* but he would claim for years to have discovered it.[15] Though the music was new, his description of it repeated the same standard discursive riffs on modern America used in *Parade:* America was a land of machines, cocktails, motorcycles, and, above all, noise.

Cocteau did not champion this new music over all French music. Rather, he advocated its use as a power tool to scrape off the hardened layers of convention muting "true" musical expression. This "music of American machines," he argued, could serve "as an antidote against a useless beauty that encourages superfluousness."[16] It had an avant-garde "spirit of shock" for a new generation. In other words, Cocteau believed that this musical "catastrophe" could be used to redeem a corrupted civilization. Paradoxically, though he claimed to uphold an art based only on feeling and that smashed any sense of duty to traditional or academic beauty, he transformed resistance to duty into a duty to resist. This avant-garde ethic, a variation of a theme common to modernist writers that Hayden White has characterized as a desire to lighten the "burden of History,"[17] would be one shared by many other culture critics who embraced the new American music as an antidote to a stifling French tradition.

The shock-treatment aesthetic, however, did not sit well with many French traditionalists, who were concerned about the cultural impact of this new American music. An unsigned review in *Le Courrier Musical,* an established high-culture music journal, gives a sense of this growing anxiety. It diagnosed the popularity of the café-concert, the music hall, and the new American music as a symptom of cultural illness. "The war and our allies have had the unforeseen result of developing our taste for the music hall. Now is not the time to deplore this looseness in morals, and to do so would require a rather long and developed study. We will simply note today the vogue of the Casino de Paris, of the Folies Bergère, of the Olympia, the Eldorado, the Cigalle, etc. . . . It's a sickness."[18] In other words, the popularity of these venues and the taste for the American music that they played, the reviewer believed, was a sign that "true" French high culture and musical sensibility were under siege. Indeed, as David Looseley points out, the music hall was taking over. The café-concert, which had been the dominant space for popular song before the war, largely vanished after the war, giving way to the more spectacular English-style music halls.[19]

By March 1918, the time of the last major German offensive, the original cast of *Laissez-les tomber* had performed the show more than one hundred times and was replaced by a new group of musicians and dancers. Its second version, directed by Léon Volterra and starring Mistenguett and Maurice Chevalier, still got good reviews for its rendering of the "drunken American dance."[20] However, even with the success of the show there was still no mention of the word *jazz*, merely of the "American orchestra." One could speculate that the word *jazz* remained with the 150,000 black American troops who were still largely segregated in special regiments.[21] As the tide turned in the war and the Allies drove back the Germans, the French public would begin to hear an authentic jazz that evoked something more.

One reason that the word *jazz* became known at this time was that "Negro regiment" bands had begun to play it all over France. The 369th Infantry band, known as the "Hellfighters" and directed by the first "king of jazz," James Reese Europe,[22] was the most famous. Europe, music director for the Clef Club in New York, became the first black entertainer to record with a major record label when he recorded the "Castle-Walk" with Vernon and Irene Castle in 1914. He enlisted in Harlem's regiment in 1917 as a machine gun operator, but Colonel William Haywood decided not to waste Europe's musical talent and gave him ten thousand dollars to recruit a band of the best black musicians available to entertain Allied troops.[23] Europe signed up around seventy musicians from all over, including eighteen clarinet players from Puerto Rico, cornetist Jaçon Frank Debraithe from Chicago, and the arranger Noble Sissle. He even hired dancer Bill "Bojangles" Robinson to be the drum major for this musical arm of the American Expeditionary Force. The Hellfighters were so extraordinary that General Pershing kept them with him as his personal band for months. As soon as the French public heard their sound, they wanted more. Europe later recalled the enthusiasm of French audiences for his band, which opened in Paris at the Théâtre des Champs-Elysées. "Before we had played two numbers, the audience went wild. We had conquered Paris . . . Everywhere we gave a concert it was a riot, but the supreme moment came in the Tuileries Gardens when we gave a concert in conjunction with the greatest bands in the world—the British Grenadier's Band, the band of the *Garde Républicaine,* and the royal Italian band. My band, of course, could not compare with any of these, yet the crowd, and it was such a crowd as I never saw anywhere in the world, deserted them for us. We played to fifty thousand people at least, and had we wished it, we might be playing yet."[24]

Indeed, the reaction was so strong that, at the request of the French government, General Pershing ordered the band on a six-week tour of France. Between February 12 and March 29, 1918, the Hellfighters, who could break down into several small ensembles when necessary, traveled more than two thousand miles and played in twenty-five French cities. Their music seemed to herald the celebration to come and did much to raise the spirits of the troops and the citizens. Lieutenant Arthur W. Little later described the typical scene following one of their concerts: "The crowd cheered without ceasing; women and children wept. When at last, the call *en voiture* passed down the line, the cheeks of the few remaining unkissed babies of that town were presented to me for attention."[25] Europe wrote to Fred Moore, editor of the *New York Age,* of his amazing reception into French society, so different from the treatment that blacks endured in America: "The French simply cannot be taught to comprehend that despicable thing called prejudice . . . *Vive la France* should be the song of every black American over here and over there."[26] Indeed, *jazz nègre,* as it was now called by culture critics, had captured the French imagination, and the public embraced the black American musicians. In a letter to Jean Cocteau on September 2, 1918, about a reception Count Étienne de Beaumont held on rue Duroc that featured such a jazz band (probably some of the Hellfighters), composer Francis Poulenc wrote of the "gold and silver trombones of these *nègres* at Duroc. I'm beginning to be rather black in order to be a part of the orchestra."[27] He found himself identifying with these black Americans after listening to their music.

Other Negro regiments also formed their own bands. The 350th Field Artillery Band, headed by Tim Brymn—who had been a Clef Club rival of Europe's back in New York—and known as the Seventy Black Devils, caused a sensation at the Paris peace conference when they played for French and American dignitaries. The competition between Europe and Brymn, already strong in New York, continued on French soil with Brymn describing his band as "a military symphony engaged in a battle of jazz."[28]

James Reese Europe and the Hellfighters stayed on in France after the fighting stopped, touring and spreading their music until February 1919.

When they finally returned to New York, the Hellfighters marched down Fifth Avenue. Europe brought with him the good news of the success in France and a validation of "Negro music." "I have come back from France more firmly convinced than ever that Negroes should write Negro music. We have our own racial feeling and if we try to copy whites, we will make bad copies."[29] He also went back to Harlem a very rich man and inspired a number of bands, and promoters, to return and pick up where he left off in France. As one of the refrains recorded by the Hellfighters on the Pathé phonograph label testified: "How ya goin' keep 'em down on the farm . . . after they've seen Paris?"[30]

Jazz Bands Everywhere

Even after the Hellfighters returned to America, the popularity of jazz music continued to grow in France. The overwhelming desire to dance to "*nègre* rhythms" raised the eyebrows of culture critics who valued traditional French music that inspired intellectual restraint. Critic Emmanuel Bourcier explained the significance of jazz dancing for French culture in this way: "The couples know the path and the rally cry. One-step, two-step, foxtrot—oh, yes—squeezing and releasing themselves weakly to the rhythms of the jazz band. There is a kind of audacity in dancing like that . . . And everyone will dance, soon, very soon; there is a general permission. Itchy legs . . . It's the peace."[31] The rally cry for celebration, the names of the dances whose rhythms carried the couples away, and the new cultural spaces where they performed them—*les dancings*—were not in French, but in English. How long, he seemed to say, would this permissiveness toward such foreign cultural influence and such unbecoming behavior last?

The conservative columnist Le Semainier, in the glossy haute-bourgeois magazine *L'Illustration*, thought it was time to stop the madness. Like Cocteau, he thought the dominant feature of jazz was the loud rhythmic drumming. Yet where Cocteau concluded that the shocking rhythms of jazz might be a cultural cure, Le Semainier believed the noise was a symptom of sickness. He argued that the music and the instruments left behind by the American troops had a significance for France that should not be ignored:

> That infernal machine is there, silent and innocent, at the disposal of the dilettantes. One rarely has a chance to see these terrible mechanisms of diabolic ingeniousness at work. When they are in full action, who would dare to approach these explosive engines? Look at them with attention. See how everything is

calculated to obtain the maximum racket with the minimum labor using an all-powerful pedal. One simple press of the foot and the heavy mallet beats onto a huge drum making the noise of a cannon, while a triangle comes down with the *danse de Saint-Guy*, and two cymbals collide frenetically, and a third is irritated by a shivering stick. Basque drums shudder and explode one after another, and a gong sounds gloomily, and an automobile horn sounds, then a bell rings, and a Chinese hat succumbs to an epileptic fit.[32]

Just as the cakewalk had brought on fears about cultural equilibrium, concern about the effect of jazz on French cultural health brought these same tropes of criticism into the public. Importantly, raising the specter of the *danse de Saint-Guy*, often used as a synonym for hysteria, linked the cultural impact of jazz to the growing concern about cultural health in the postwar era. Le Semainier believed that France needed traditional music that helped calm the cultural ethos, not music that would exacerbate the disequilibrium. Hence, jazz had no place in a postwar France already suffering from a lack of order.

Indeed, Le Semainier's characterization of the presence of jazz in French culture resembled the description of a contagious disease: "Dark vision: The Americans are not going to take these formidable ragtime grinders back home with them. After having gravely wounded the little French muse of the operetta, the review and the song, are they going to leave it like a knife in the wound? Our music hall is dying from that contagious madness of racket. Instead of having pity for eardrums so cruelly afflicted by the noisiest of wars, we try to weaken them again by organizing these orchestras of gunfire and these assaults of heavy artillery! Light, spiritual and gracious music has disappeared. And so our Yanks, after having inoculated us with this *nègre houravari* fever, pull out while forgetting to take back with them their instruments of torture."[33] In sum, the eardrums of the French muse, already weakened by war, had been further damaged by the American music. The "ragtime apparatus" facilitating this racially tainted Yankee contagion was the trap set. After the troops left, jazz continued to spread the "*nègre*" fever throughout French culture. In his mind, it was a case of modern American technology being used in the service of primitive rhythmic music against "true" Frenchness. Like other critics, he blended standard stereotypes about modern America with those about the primitive *nègre* when he described jazz as a "heavy artillery" music, "enraged like a savage," which shocked people into a "tribe of Parisians"[34] dancing an epileptic *danse de Saint-Guy*. In other words, he thought jazz inoculated people with a primitive desire to dance that was neither healthy nor French. For Le Semainier, the editorial voice of *L'Illustration*, the jazz band, with all its symbols and cymbals, was a noisy negation of almost every civilized and French sensibility. Good French people, he believed, needed to return to traditional cultural values and musical tastes.

One can only begin to imagine the symbolic importance of jazz to a French public that had just endured such a terrible war and suffered such incredible losses. To scratch the surface of the wound, between 1915 and 1919, over 1.3 million French men and women were killed and more than 3 million were crippled. The psychic damage was even more pervasive. At the time, the French medical community was only beginning to understand *maladies de la guerre* (shell shock). Doctors like Paul Sollier, Jean Vinchon, and Georges Dumas led this field of medicine, which grew with the numbers of victims. National and local governments also did their part, erecting more than 38,000 war monuments to honor the fallen *poilus* (infantrymen).[35]

The government could do little to keep down inflation, which soared over 400 percent between 1914 and 1919. Even if they had money, French families faced shortages in almost every category of consumable, from tobacco, milk, bread, and meat to chocolate and beer. The nation's war debt, mostly owed to America, was 175 billion francs, five times what it had been in 1913. Thus it was not surprising that the increased consumption of American music, not to mention the amount of money that jazz bands were making, produced a certain anxiety for those who kept tabs on French culture in the media.

In this context, shifts in popular culture were linked directly to cultural instability. Jacques Florange expressed his concerns in *Paris-Midi* about the ramifications of the French public's changing musical tastes. "The first 'jazz band' that brought Paris a sample of American tunes made lots of money. It was as new, fantastic, and unforeseen as the rhythm, and as disheveled as the orchestration. The funny faces and brio with which these musicians played attracted lots of sympathy. Their way of playing was as funny as the music itself . . . and *la mode* adopted them. Soon, each establishment wanted to have its own 'jazz band' and everyone wanted to dance to the sound of banjos accompanied by huge box drum-horn-bell-train-whistles and kitchen pots, so these 'jazz bands' made a sensation. Like before the war, when our musicians became tango gypsies, they have now become 'American' . . . Several musicians of the *Garde* [army] have themselves entered into these orchestras . . . Which foreign orchestra will succeed the jazz band?"[36] The worry was that French performers were changing their style according to the dictates of fashion rather than following their innate French taste. Though French musicians became proficient with the tools of "jazz" mimicry—the drum sets, the automobile horns, the train whistles, and the pots and pans—Florange did not believe they could reproduce the "grimaces" and carefree spirit of the black musicians who fascinated the public.

Yet it was precisely this carefree spirit, so different from traditional French reserve, that attracted most modernist critics to jazz. In Cocteau's words, jazz bands were changing public tastes by "familiarizing our public with stronger spices."[37] But was the music itself causing the change in French taste? Editorialist Lazarille in *La Semaine Littéraire* blamed the popularity of jazz on the media, which continued to focus the public's attention on the music; even those who wrote *against* jazz, he believed, unwittingly aided its promotion. He declared that the only way to make the affront to "true" French sensibility go away was to stop talking about it. "By this means . . . we will impose silence on the jasz-band [*sic*]. We hope that the jasz-band will not enfranchise our frontier. But will you dare to hope?"[38] But though Lazarille and *La Semaine Littéraire* remained silent about jazz, few others did.

One question that troubled critics was what the public's taste for jazz meant for the future of high-culture French music. According to classical music critic Jean Chantovoine, French musicians were indeed giving up traditional forms in response to the public's demands for more jazz. Such a market-driven change in taste and enjoyment was, he believed, an expression of "cultural anarchy": "If several worried spirits had feared that the war had not exposed French music to a crisis of anemia, they should be convinced now . . . We see this music [jazz] multiply from day to day in cinemas, restaurants and '*dancings,*' where it is the obligatory accompaniment to the 'filmed' novel and lobster *à l'américaine.*"[39] Chantovoine believed that left to the democratic rules of the market, French music was losing its traditional consistency and becoming sick. A market-driven culture, he seemed to say, was an unhealthy culture, and he argued that outbreaks of this jazz influence on the cultural body—and it is important to note the constant use of the body as a metaphor for cultural health—could be seen and heard everywhere. The best way to cure the "blood" of French music, he believed, was a dose of better state organization from above. "The state should first of all be able to impose musical education . . . In short, for some time all the artistic politics of the state have been a primer for mediocrity. It should be the contrary. Without imposing anything, we should recruit and maintain a musical elite—strongly menaced at the moment in our country—so that the level of arts and taste will not decline toward zero."[40] By arguing that the state should reorder musical culture by recruiting an elite class of musicians who would judge and disseminate good French taste, Chantovoine identified himself with those who believed that only a society with a traditional hierarchy had values. *Culture populaire,* according to such an aristocratic vantage point, was "valueless," as it turned away from authentic French cultural ideals and swayed along with the contingent tyranny of the democratic masses.

Yet the smashing of old hierarchies and the reordering of cultural values was exactly what many modernist critics and musicians—who saw fixed hierarchies and values as the real problem of civilization—valued in jazz. Maurice Ravel, for instance, wrote to Colette de Jouvenal, who had written a libretto for an operetta and commissioned him to do the music, about his desire to unsettle elitist cultural conservatives by using ragtime. "What would you think of the cup and teapot, in old Wedgwood—black—singing a ragtime? I confess that the idea of having a ragtime sung by two *nègres* at our National Academy of Music fills me with great joy."[41] French culture, such thinkers believed, needed to find its way in a new world, not by looking to the past, but by embracing the future. For them, jazz represented that future.

La Musique Nègre N'est Pas Matière, Elle Est Esprit

Many writers sought to describe the musical form and the particular spirit of jazz. The best example came in the summer of 1919 from Ernest Ansermet (1883–1969), conductor of the famous *Ballets Russes* orchestra. During a tour in London, he heard one of the first waves of American jazz bands to travel to Europe. Having moved from Switzerland to France in 1903 to study at the Sorbonne, Ansermet stayed in Paris and became part of the flourishing postwar international music scene. He had heard a lot of music all over the world claiming to be jazz, some of it good, some of it bad. His article "Sur un orchestre nègre," on the Southern Syncopated Orchestra (SSO), stands as one of the most serious attempts to pin down the formal aspects of jazz during this initial moment.

For Ansermet, jazz was the latest manifestation of "rag," the musical creation of Africans from the southern states of America. The most important element of rag music, he argued, was neither harmony nor melody, the two conceptual poles of European music, but rather rhythm, "in particular, syncopated rhythm."[42] Ragtime was so popular and its influence so pervasive in America that "one could say that ragtime has become the true American national music."[43] During the war, American troops sang the ragtime songs of Tin Pan Alley to remember life back home, "like the Swiss, in foreign lands, who start singing a yodel to remember their country." This was how native

Europeans first heard jazz, and it soon caught on all over Europe. Yet most of the music heard in French music halls and dance halls was inauthentic, a "new art of insipid and sentimental taste, catering to the mediocre and crude sensuality of their clientele." In its authentic form, however, jazz was something totally fresh. "Here, under the name of the Southern Syncopated Orchestra, an ensemble of authentic musicians of the *nègre* race . . . presented us, *pêle-mêle,* all kinds of demonstrations of their art, old and new, the best and the worst. Theirs is a mysterious world that we know only by its repercussions, more or less far away, and that has finally appeared to us in its living reality."[44] He believed that anyone who heard the authentic jazz of Will Marion Cook's Southern Syncopated Orchestra, this echo of a "mysterious world," would be forever changed. It gave him great hope.

Despite what many high-culture critics said, this was serious music. Indeed, jazz was only one of the varieties of music they played, along with arrangements of classical favorites and ragtime standards. Ansermet used his vast musical and critical skills to treat the jazz they did play with the seriousness it deserved. Knowing that many conservative music critics, "our police of musical morals," placed European music on an intellectual and spiritual pedestal, he emphasized how jazz equaled European music in its sincerity, nobility, and courage without being dominated by the "idea" of music. As such, jazz did not strictly follow musical logic and its harmony was not grounded in mathematics, as was the music of students taught at the dominant schools of French composition, like the nationalistic Schola Cantorum or the Paris conservatory. Whereas classical training taught students to be disciplined, sound alike, and rigorously follow the score and the conductor, these "authentic musicians of the *nègre* race" never used scores and never played a song the same way twice. The SSO's authentic jazz, he argued, was serious without being overly rational. Whereas classical music conveyed the idea of musicians performing an intellectual duty toward a guiding ideal by obeying a maestro and his rational rules, jazz expressed the obvious enjoyment of musicians playing in the moment for the audience and themselves. "I see clearly that they have a very precise sense of the music that they love, and a pleasure that communicates itself to the listener with an irresistible force, a pleasure that pushes them to ceaselessly outbid one another, to enrich and refine their means constantly. I imagine that, knowing the voice that is attributed to them within the harmonic ensemble, and being conscious of the role that their instrument should play, they are able to let themselves go, in a certain sense and within limits, according to their hearts."[45] One can hear strains of a Rousseauian riff on natural man in

Ansermet's description of a group of individuals who expressed what they felt and who outbid one another to be heard: a collective manifestation of natural improvisers following the sentiment of their hearts. Unlike trained European musicians, who followed strict rules of written composition and even stricter conductors, these "authentic" musicians were "possessed" by the music they improvised.

Their musical "material," he noted, came from everywhere. There were themes drawn from religious songs, popular American tunes, blues, and syncopated renditions of classical favorites. Though most of the music they played was "foreign," it sounded perfectly "natural" when they played it. "How is such a thing possible? It is because *la musique nègre* is not matter, it is spirit."[46] Their appropriative "spirit," he believed, was an extension of an original "African" musical taste that manifested itself as a kind of nostalgic force in the musicians of the SSO and guided their interpretation of the music. He argued that "in losing their homeland, the *nègres* lost their songs" but not their spirit or their African musical taste. "In their new villages, close to the cotton fields, the first music they found were the hymns taught to them by missionaries. And very quickly, they recast them in their own manner."[47]

According to Ansermet, this *nègre* manner of recasting music had several essential characteristics. The first was syncopation, a tendency that he linked to the slaves' expressive need to transform their masters' ballads and religious music and make it their own. *Nègre* music, he argued, seemed to express a "desire to give to certain syllables a particular suddenness, or a prolonged resonance. In other words, there is a preoccupation of an expressive order that seems to give *nègre* songs their anticipation of or hesitation to the subtleties of rhythm."[48] The plantation slaves had "appropriated" the Anglo-Saxon songs in this way and turned them into rags. This interpretive spirit could not be learned, and this was why inauthentic European imitators lacked it. Instead, Ansermet believed the talent for syncopation was linked to race. "We have seen that syncopation itself is nothing but the effect of an expressive need, the rhythmic manifestation of a particular taste, and, to say it all, the genius of race. This genius marks itself in all the elements of the music, and it will transfigure all the music it appropriates."[49] Thus the innate syncopation heard in "authentic jazz" was a racial trait.

The distinctive use of tones was another characteristic of jazz that Ansermet linked to race. *Nègre* musicians had a way of playing instruments, be they trombones, clarinets, violins, or banjos, that transformed their sounds into something new. Ansermet believed this tonal tendency came from the musicians' ability to imitate the sound of the "*nègre* voice" with their horns.

Yet Ansermet heard more than just a deformation of proper European musical tones in the SSO's jazz; he heard an African melodic and harmonic order that spoke through the music as they played. "In the melodic order, even though his habituation to our scales has erased the memory of African modes, an old instinct pushes the *nègre* to search for his pleasure outside these orthodox intervals."[50] Though American slavery had uprooted slaves and effaced conscious memory of African modalities, Ansermet believed that a deeper memory remained at an instinctual level, a memory of freedom, which pushed the *nègre* toward liberation outside the master's laws. Ansermet did not place this racial instinct on equal footing with the longstanding Western philosophical idea of spirit striving toward freedom. The memory was not located in the mind, but was retained in the body as a physiological necessity. "There is nothing in the harmonic order that the *nègre* has not realized in his own physiognomy."[51]

Jazz was thus the latest form of *la musique nègre,* based upon an African harmonic and rhythmic order. For his readers, Ansermet tried to translate this "African" sound into the language of Western music theory, but he found that it did not quite fit. "It utilizes thirds that are neither major nor minor . . . and often instinctually falls into these natural harmonics after one given note. This, along with the idea of its play, is something that no written music could represent."[52] Though *nègre* musicians were unaware of it, these African harmonies were expressed in the music that the SSO musicians played. Yet since they were not consciously playing these harmonies, Ansermet believed that jazz was an unconscious musical symptom of a culture that had lost its home but was evolving elsewhere.

Indeed, though some of the SSO's jazz showed that it had moved across the evolutionary line from the oral tradition to the written tradition, "or if we want, from popular art to learned art," this was where Ansermet believed they were weakest. Their real strength was in more primitive forms, like the blues: "It is in the blues that the genius of the race manifests itself with the most force."[53] But what were the blues? "The blues, that's what happens when the *nègre* has ennui, when he is far from his *home,* or from his *mammy,* or from his *sweetheart.* So he thinks of a tune or a rhythm for his predilection, and he takes his trombone, or his violin, or his banjo, or his clarinet, or his drum, or better he sings, or simply, he dances. And playing that tune he decides upon, he exhausts his fantasy. That allows his *ennui* to pass. That's the blues."[54] The blues were the expressive form—equal, he believed, to the verse of the greatest European poets—through which the genius of the race bemoaned its predilection and found relief from suffering: it was a kind of talking cure through music.

Ansermet believed that the SSO's Sidney Bechet exemplified such racially grounded artistic genius. This virtuoso of the blues had a style of his own through which to express his nostalgia and relieve his suffering. "I would like to say the name of that artist of genius, as for my part I will never forget him: it is Sidney Bechet. We have so often looked to the past to rediscover one of these figures who herald the coming of our art—those men of the seventeenth and eighteenth century, for example, whose dance songs and expressive works opened the path on which Haydn and Mozart were not the point of departure, but the first result. What a moving thing to encounter this fat black man there, with his white teeth and scrunched-up forehead, who is happy that one likes what he does but has nothing to say of his art except that he follows his 'own way,' *sa propre voie,* and when we think of this 'own way,' that's perhaps the great route through which the world will be pulled into [*s'engouffrera*] tomorrow."[55]

Thus Bechet's position in the evolution of *la musique nègre* was similar to the one occupied by the trailblazers of European music. In both cases, Ansermet found natural musicians who *felt* their own individual relationship to music rather than followed established rules. However, Ansermet seemed to acknowledge an important difference between the early European musicians and these black musicians despite their similarity; it was uncanny when one went looking to rediscover the origins of European art and found Sidney Bechet waiting at the end of the road. Yet this was, he believed, a problem only for the critic. Bechet, Ansermet argued, was not conscious of the status of his music as an art, he did not reflect upon his relationship to musical tradition, and thus he did not feel its weight. He was just happy that you liked what he played when he followed his "own way." Ansermet thought that this individualism, this *nègre* manner of expressing the suffering of existence in its own sweet way, free from the burden of history, offered the world a way to get over its blues.[56]

Dansomania

Certainly, there was a basis for French people identifying with the suffering of black Americans and hearing the expression of that suffering in their music. Many French men and women, to follow Ansermet, had also lost their sweethearts and loved ones. They, too, had the blues and were looking for a way to get over them. Whether or not singing the blues or losing oneself in the rhythm of dance to get over the blues was an appropriately French response to loss, however, was a heated point of contestation in the media between traditionalists and modernists struggling to define the future of French culture. One conservative institution, the Catholic Church, believed that jazz music was destroying France's moral foundations. Church leaders argued in public and in print that jazz dancing caused more psychological and constitutional damage to the individual than any war trauma ever could. The secular temptations of the body associated with jazz dancing, the church argued, were contrary to the heady cultivation of spiritual life associated with Christianity. The archbishop of Paris, Cardinal Amette (1850–1920), condemned jazz dancing as a modern perversion. "It is said that it is useless to warn Christians, who hardly frequent the kind of salons where they dare this [dancing]. This is not my opinion. Even the best supports of social order are deplorably permeable to this perverting snobbism."[57] He believed that the cure for France's troubled soul was to be found in confession and chapel, not in *dancings* or bars. Soon after, the Catholic Church forbade jazz dancing for practicing Catholics.

Yet for the avant-garde and those who saw the church as another of the burdens of history, such a reaction was proof of the repressive problems of civilization. Jean Cocteau, for one, continued to promote jazz as a form of resistance to restrictive social order. He wrote the musical drama *Le bœuf sur le toit* in response to the news that an oppressive reactionary spirit had taken over in America: Prohibition. As such, the drama was set in a speakeasy, where jazz, in this case jazz-inflected music by Darius Milhaud, was played underground and enjoyed by surrealists who danced and recited poetry. Living his artistic ethic of enraging the bourgeoisie, Cocteau opened a real bar in Paris by the same name, where pianist Jean Wiéner played "rags," the "negro Vance" played saxophone, and Cocteau played the *barman des bruits,* banging on pots, pans, and drums. Surrealist Louis Aragon described the ensemble there as a kind of "*poète-orchestre*"[58] for avant-garde artists who identified with the liberating cause of jazz against the prohibitive powers of the past. This "jazz Parisien," as Georges Auric would later describe it,[59] represented a new way of life. They were not the only ones to embrace it. Jazz bars popped up all over Paris in 1919 as a jazz dance craze swept through France.

From the traditionalist's perspective, represented again by *L'Illustration*'s editorial voice, Le Semainier, the public's ravenous appetite for jazz was a tragic effect of war trauma. It was a symptom of the disease, not the cure. "Humanity has sick nerves . . . the war has dislocated our planet. The great temple of civilization is cracked. We dance, the vanquished and the victor, an exasperated and nervous dance, an aggressive dance without courtesy."[60] There was only one way for the citizens of a "penitent and sadistic France" to repair a crumbling civilization: just say no to dancing. True Frenchmen, he believed, would show "a bit more resolve [sang-froid] and restraint and never imitate these hypocritical people who seem to have taken as a maxim: never say no."[61]

The media debate over jazz dancing and cultural health was not limited to critics and editorialists. The French medical establishment also had something to say about healing traumatic war wounds, and those comments can help us make sense of the debate over jazz. Neurologist Paul Sollier, for instance, concluded that there were many causes for the weakened nerves and reflexes—nervous tics and acting out—that one saw in those who suffered from "maladies de la guerre." He identified two general types of sicknesses. The first, hysterotraumatic problems, were disorders caused by "a shock or a commotion, direct or indirect,"[62] which led to functional alterations in the nervous system. Many doctors argued that these physiological changes caused chemical modifications in the body and made patients act out in some way. The second variety of sickness was a form of hysteria with purely psychological causes. In this theory, closer to the thinking of Charcot's influential characterization of hypnosis, physiological damage to the body or nerves was not the cause. Rather, hysteria was a constitutional tendency to "cling to attitudes that he [the patient] has learned under diverse influences and remain in these induced states."[63] Most hysterical states resulted from suggestion, when an individual psyche came under the influence of an outside power and was unable to return to its "normal state." If a patient had too much plasticity in response to external suggestion, or a lack of plasticity in response to environmental change, he or she would develop hysterical symptoms. When confronted with patients who suffered from symptoms of "war sickness," doctors tried to determine if the cause was physiological—if the noise and shock had caused changes in the nervous system—or psychological. Observers of the dance craze in the media framed the cultural debate in a similar way: did the jazz and dancing result from battle-weary nerves, or was the desire to dance symptomatic of psychological or spiritual attraction, a hysteric "dansomania" brought on by the external suggestion of jazz?

The idea that dansomania was a symptom of war trauma began to manifest itself in Parisian culture. It was dramatized, for instance, in the musical Ça vaut le voyage (It's worth the trip), performed at the Bataclan music hall in the spring of 1920. Madame Daussane, a traditional culture critic and actress at the state-supported high-brow *Comédie-Française,* reviewed the show and commended its diagnosis of jazz dancing as a kind of cultural hysteria: "A brave doctor, inspector of lunatic asylums, enters by chance into a strange house where all the inhabitants have fallen prey to a sort of bacchanalian frenzy. He believes himself in a nut house. No! He is simply in a *dancing!*"[64] After seeing the show and wanting to experience the collective dansomania firsthand, Madame Daussane descended to a *dancing* to report on the epidemic. As someone who associated true Frenchness with civilized reserve and sophistication, she found cause for alarm. "I found it rather curious and altogether melancholic. I know very well that like all the actors of the *Comédie-Française,* I am rather burdened by the gravity of my nature, but really, one must drink lots of champagne in order to keep up the appearance of enjoyment. Again and again, I heard the sliding of feet, of all the feet together, serving as an underhanded and monotonous accompaniment to the melodies of the musical orchestra . . . When the jazz band unleashed itself, it was even more sad. Amid this racket, the people continued to undulate with mournful and continuous movements. For me, that irresistibly evoked a troop of cowards crossing through the woods at night on tiptoe, who force themselves to sing as loudly as they can to prove that they are not afraid."[65] In her opinion, the cowardly French public was moved to dance so as to conceal their fears from themselves. Rather than confront the ghosts of the past, they tried desperately to ignore them. In the end, she believed that jazz dancing was unnatural for French men and women and was an embarrassment to the Republic. If people wanted distraction, Madame Daussane recommended the circus; if they wanted to enjoy truly French things, she believed they should try more "gracious" French dances.

Music critic and composer Charles Tenroc also touted the importance of upholding traditional sophistication and reserve. He could not understand why the public was giving up its true Frenchness in exchange for jazz revelry. He understood that France was going through a "troubled period," but he had difficulty believing that "Parisian music lovers can taste the curiosity of the jazz band and its *nègre* uproar for more than five minutes."[66] People had already had over fifteen months "to calm nerves agitated for too long." Dancing, he argued, was not the cure French people needed for battle fatigue: "It is in contact with healthy music that they will rediscover quietude and health."[67] Like Madame Daussane, he went to a *dancing* to witness the pathological behavior. "The owner of the house of the dead [*nécrocome*] where I choked or absorbed these opiates swore to me that 'this will not last.' No matter. The shame will last. The contagion enters the salons daily. The infectious virus spreads itself in respectable houses. We must stop this disaster . . . The police should have no other mission than to watch over [*surveiller*] the closing of these sad, tolerated houses and to board up their fronts."[68] In Tenroc's mind, *les dancings,* those houses of the dead, were marks of shame, outbreaks of a cultural disease that should be cured by the state. He thought that true French music, tempered by what he described as "innate" French reserve, should "adoucit les moeurs"—soften social conventions. If it did not, Tenroc argued, then those who promoted such disruptive music ought to pay a heavy tax that, in turn, would support those who performed proper music. He was not alone in his desire to tax jazz in popular culture to help raise funds to repair true French culture. In June of 1920, the French senate created a system of taxes on "spectacles" designed to raise money for the "arts." Cinemas were taxed 10 percent if their monthly receipts were 25,000 francs, 15 percent if receipts were 50,000, and 20–25 percent for amounts above. "Les dancings," which could never claim to be promoting art, were taxed right away at 25 percent.[69] Phonograph players and records, expensive technological innovations that let listeners dance at home, were also taxed at 25 percent.[70]

When they denounced the presence of jazz in France, cultural traditionalists often echoed standard discursive riffs about the dangers of Americanization. In *Le Courrier Musical,* a music journal that promoted conservative politics and high-culture aesthetics, Louis-Charles Bataille used the powerful anti-American symbol of phylloxera—aphid-like, root-destroying insects—to describe jazz as a disease that threatened the roots of true French culture. Just as phylloxera had destroyed many of the old noble grape varieties, jazz, in his mind, was weakening the strength of "pure" French music. "Never has music been more threatened. Its enemies are legion, and it is more necessary than ever that a sacred union of its friends be formed so that French music will not succumb."[71] He argued that the symptoms of this American disease and the "enemies of French music" could be found at all levels of society. "Children, adults, men, women, young and old, all of them dance those bizarre steps designated by names as various as they are assorted . . . The contagion spreads, and the numbers of those who, having to choose between a beautiful musical recital and dancing, opt for the latter are becoming more considerable day by day."[72] The names of the dances were indeed numerous, ranging from the foxtrot and the Boston to the "furious madness of the shimmy, that new epileptic dance in vogue."[73] However, though the vine—the public—was sick, Bataille did not think it was too late to save the root, which he associated with traditional culture and a Frenchness once again grounded in sophistication and reserve. "These diverse phylloxera have not completely ruined the plant;

the roots remain good and the soil is still excellent. To keep the contagion from reaching the roots, we must vigorously combat the plague by first creating a sacred union, and then by starting and pursuing a serious campaign to achieve success. Certain public powers should understand that the appearance of this music is not their fault, but they should still try to wipe it out for fear that it will return . . . We must combat the *dancings* by all possible means, be it by suppressing them or by regulating the place which they merit and keeping them contained . . . And when we have attained these diverse results, the defenders of the Muse will be able to say that they truly deserve her."[74] Bataille's metaphor does not work, of course, as phylloxera ravages the vine from the roots up. Nevertheless, the fear that an American disease was threatening the patrimony and true French culture was transmitted to the reading public. Not only was this another variation on the argument for an elite control of culture, but by linking the roots of French culture to the French muse, he located the basis for cultural identity in an imaginary idea. Thus, for Bataille, the problem with French culture was one of mind or will, not one related to the body. To return to the medical community's categories, one could say that he was diagnosing a cultural hysteria caused by external suggestion rather than a physiological problem caused by trauma to the body. To cure French culture, he argued, the external influence working its power of suggestion on the weary nerves of the French public, jazz music and dancing, needed to be eliminated.

The Return of the Repressed

One cannot reduce the ideological split between French critics over the significance of jazz during this time to those who promoted it as a healthy cure for French culture and those who thought it was a threat to true Frenchness. By 1920, many critics questioned whether the music that so many seemed to crave was really as un-French as the public was being led to believe. Indeed, some questioned the consistency of the true French music and musical enjoyment that opponents of jazz held up as a static ideal. Perhaps Frenchness had not always been so reserved? Critic and ethnomusicologist Gabrielle Choubley, for instance, brought her own expertise to bear on the question of French musical taste. She challenged both the idea that rhythmic sensibility was an exclusively *nègre* characteristic and the notion that French cultural sensibility was exclusively white. Choubley argued that it was necessary to understand the true origin of jazz rhythms—and French ethnicity—if one wanted to understand the public's need for syncopated music after the war. "Following a very human process, a scandal was caused by these unique harmonies that troubled the quietude of our grandmothers and fatigued the eardrums of certain critics; it became a curiosity, then an attraction . . . Now it has become a form of fashion! We imitate them. In sum, we go to lots of trouble in order to 'make it *nègre*' . . . So we will relearn, painfully, that which we already knew long ago—or at least which some of our ancestors did."[75] Choubley believed that the desire to transform music, to "make it *nègre*," was not caused by foreign influence, but rather it was the expression of an original French characteristic that civilization had concealed over time. Choubley argued that modern archeological studies had established a genealogical link between a distant group of French ancestors and the black rhythms of jazz. Exploding cherished myths about the original racial purity of France, she explained how "black peoples" had once inhabited southern France. Contrary to the standard claims about the Latin or Gallic ancestry of the true France, she cited studies proving that the Etruscans had actually been colored and that, if one examined the Etruscan instruments found by archeologists, it was obvious that these forbears had had a developed "rhythmic sense." In actuality, innate rhythmic sensibility was not foreign to France at all, but had been repressed, she claimed, by the invasions of Aryans from the north who drove the indigenous black people elsewhere. "Little by little, repressed by the invasions of the self-described Aryans, who were in reality very mixed, [the indigenous blacks] ended up settling in Algeria and Tunisia at the time of the Punic wars . . . Descending little by little toward the south, due to various causes that would take too long to enumerate, these tribes dug themselves in near central Africa . . . Their musical technique was already strongly superior to those of the people who surrounded them."[76] Accordingly, the Aryans, who were actually a mixed rather than pure race, drove the rhythmic peoples out of France, and these lost ancestors relocated in Africa, where they spread their superior musical techniques and forms. Before the arrival of these groups, she postulated, the indigenous African peoples had only had "music of invocation, with a magical tendency—to bring about hypnotic sleep."[77]

Choubley argued that by the time that Africans were brought to America as slaves, their music combined indigenous hypnotic rhythms and harmonies rooted in pre-Aryan Mediterranean culture. Now, she claimed, this music had been returned to France. Thus, to close the circle, the French public's taste for the "black rhythms" of jazz was not the result of suggestion from an external influence, but rather the return of a repressed "colored" rhythmic sentiment in French culture that had finally made its way back home through this unlikely prodigal son.

Conservative philosopher Albert Leclère took a similar tack by describing the taste for jazz as a sign of a primal return. Yet unlike Choubley, he made this return pathological rather than natural. The enjoyment of "primitive" rhythms, he argued, was a symptom of "psychic regression" in the civilized Frenchman. In his view, every human existence and culture, "normal and sane or not," was marked by moments when the past "reappeared, more or less as a semblance of what it was."[78] Such a return was at work, he claimed, when individuals of one race identified with the habits of another, as French men and women were doing with les nègres when they danced to jazz. Some races were "lower than others" on the ladder of progress toward civilization, and thus their racial characteristics were related to earlier times in the distant past. As such, if one mimicked the activities of a "lower" race by enjoying their rhythms, one was experiencing a regression into a deeper past. Jazz dancing, he believed, caused such a regressive identification.

Leclère used the analogy of "irregularities" in individual sexual development to explain how jazz dancing made people regress. In normal development, he argued, autoerotism ended after infancy, but when psychic degeneration occurred, there were frequent returns of "primitive taste" and infantile behavior. Moreover, a number of "primitive vices" were associated with the return of such a state. Regressed cultures—read uncivilized cultures—typically displayed an analogous lack of control. Of these, "fetishistic nègre" cultures, as he described them, displayed an exclusive preference for the pleasures of the body, "This fetishism is the sign of infantilism . . . One sees there the phenomenon of arrested development."[79] By contrast, normal adult states, and the state of civilization that Leclère believed true Frenchmen and -women should identify with, was marked by an absence of autoerotic behavior and a dominance of "clear and distinct" Cartesian self-control.

In civilized adults, he argued, the most common form of regression was a desire to play instead of work, a state that he associated with infantile vanity and exhibitionism. This was precisely the kind of primitive and regressive behavior that he saw at les dancings:

> What is there to say if we speak of dance? It's there like the door to self-decoration that appears in the highest form of adult vanity . . . It accentuates the body and all its advantages. It materializes, for the eyes of the public, all of its intellectual value and social morality. Dance perfects the movements

through which the infant pleases itself. The uncoordinated, ineptly combined movements of infancy are subjected to an aesthetic rhythm that multiplies by a hundred times the pleasures they give. But it is also, and principally, in certain conditions and at certain times, a means of sexual enjoyment [*jouissance*] that is more or less hypocritical. These dances of today are quite simply a softened and more elegant mode of *coitus interruptus,* a manifestation of *satyriasis.* Thus one sees juvenile behavior along with infantilism in adults as a result of dancing. More logically, savages make their dances, which resemble these new dances, a direct preparation to the work of the flesh.[80]

In the end, Leclère's argument against jazz dancing echoed standard republican riffs on civilized duty, as he warned French people about the danger of identifying with such regressed racial habits and falling into a state of "arrested development." They should, he admonished, show more self-control and do away with the noisy "sensual tickling" that caused the degeneration into childish behavior. True Frenchness, to Leclère, was about self-control, not losing control through jazz and dance.

Despite such calls to combat cultural regression—or maybe *because of* enticing descriptions of the forbidden enjoyment to be found in such states and in such places—and higher taxes on *les dancings,* cinema, and music halls, attendance at jazz venues continued to increase. Another conservative critic, Albert Bertelin, writing for *Le Courrier Musical,* argued that even more governmental action was needed to combat the jazz craze and to save high culture from the distractions of popular culture. He called for higher taxes—over 25 percent—to suppress the cultural contagion. "Hit these *dancings,* cinemas, and music halls with elevated taxes, as they are nothing but places of amusement where intelligence plays no part; by contrast, show consideration to musical recitals and literary conferences, encourage them, and try to inculcate the masses with a taste for the beautiful."[81] If the masses would not adequately support true French culture, which in his mind meant high culture, then the state should uphold *la vraie France* (the true France) without them.

Many who opposed jazz in France diagnosed its presence as a symptom of an internationalism that threatened the sovereignty of true French culture. This concern served as the basis for Louis Vuilleman's sarcastic attack on the shimmy, the newest and most scandalous of the dances associated with jazz. "No one can doubt it anymore, we live in a strange time. The war—since we must call it by its name—has thrown our poor humanity into trouble . . . They [dancers] gesticulate and grimace as if possessed by the Devil [*Ma-*

lin]. They dance a kind of shimmy in which their convulsive shaking obeys nothing but a singular rhythm. Understand what this means: we don't think anymore, we don't act anymore. We dance! We dance all the time. Life today is becoming too pleasant. Modern society, after centuries of evolution, has finally reached its perfect form: it's a *dancing* . . . And all the dancers imitate and resemble one another. There are no more frontiers. Internationalism attains its radiant end . . . In 1921, everything is permitted."[82] Thus, if French civilization was supposed to be the height of evolution, then internationalism at the end of history, symbolized by the shimmy and *le dancing,* was turning France into a culture in which people no longer used their heads. In a world where everything was permitted, Vuilleman feared that French people had forgotten Descartes's warning about the cunning *malin* of the body working its corrupting influence on pure intellect. Rather than following the clear and distinct ideas that he believed were characteristic of true Frenchness, modern society was being led astray by bodies possessed by the kinesthetic rhythms of jazz.

Many French writers dramatized their ideas about the cultural effects of jazz dancing. For instance, Gabriel Timmory's play *Ici l'on danse* (1921) showed manifestations of the dance craze in different strata of French society. The glue for the thirty separate scenes is the theme of *dansomania.* In one scene, the daughter of an aristocrat, Alice, wants to learn jazz dancing, and the dance-master who comes to the house to teach her turns out to be their old servant Adolph. Where he used to serve the aristocracy, Adolph now has better social status teaching jazz dancing. In another scene, set in a courtroom, dance master Monsieur Assuradjam—obviously a foreigner—accuses a former student, Louisette, of owing him 200 francs for lessons. Timmory shows the moral looseness of the times by having Louisette argue to the judge that she had slept with Assuradjam as compensation and that he had certainly gotten more than he deserved. The judge has to call for order when the gallery breaks into laughter and sternly tells her to pay up. One scene, "*École Gagaiste,*" is a send-up of the Dadaists, for whom nothing makes sense except jazz dancing. There are scenes depicting a "jazz buffet, *champagne obligatoire,*" and a "Pajama Ball" where people came to dance ready for bed.

The scene at the heart of the play, "*Les Dansomanes,*" reveals Timmory at his best. The setting is a hospital, where a certain Dr. Arnaud is showing visitors around the halls: "Here are people who had to be hospitalized due to cerebral troubles caused by the recent fashion of dance: we call them *dansomanes.*"[83] When one of the visitors asks why there are not more patients, Arnaud replies that most dansomanes are "free, believe me, they are in the streets. You will be next to them in the metro; they will see you again and you will invite them to dinner. We no longer lock them up until they have reached the state of crisis. That's a strong remedy. Of all the morbid afflictions, dansomania is now the most contagious."[84] Dr. Arnaud takes the group to see some of the patients who have reached the crisis state. "That one is a physics instructor from the Sorbonne," he explains. "He was possessed by the idea of dancing the day he learned his wife had cheated on him with a dance instructor."[85] Another patient is an advanced student at the *École Polytechnique,* who, after a ball, lost his "spirit"; yet another is an old woman who raves on and on about having promised the president of the republic the first dance. At the end of the tour, Arnaud explains to the visitors that he has to leave them in order to go pick up another patient at the police station. In reality, the doctor, too, is a *dansomane* and, taking off his lab coat, goes out dancing. The entire French culture, Timmory seemed to imply, had been infected by the dansomania.

Diagnosis of Dancing

Many of those who opposed jazz in France diagnosed the pervasive desire to dance as an erosion of "true Frenchness. In the conservative *La Revue Mondiale,* José Germain, a right-wing cultural protectionist who had first written on the difference between American and French fashion in 1921,[86] published the results of his inquiry into public opinion about jazz dancing in a series that lasted several months and was later reprinted as a book. Germain amassed opinions from Catholic leaders, writers, politicians, dance instructors, and members of the medical community, each portraying jazz as a threat to France.

From the Catholic perspective, the protests followed the lead of the new archbishop of Paris, Cardinal Dubois, who renewed the condemnation of his predecessor, Cardinal Amette, against "modern dances," particularly the shimmy. Indeed, since France had reestablished diplomatic ties with the Vatican in 1920, it was important to toe the line set by Pope Benedict XV's decree: "Of these exotic and barbarous dances, recently brought into fashionable circles, the one is more shocking than the other . . . There is nothing more proper than banning them all and remaining modest."[87]

This Catholic anti-jazz position was later echoed in a book drawn almost entirely from Germain's work, *Catholics and the New Dances,* wherein F. A. Vuillermet argued the case against jazz dancing succinctly: "Two words sum up all that I have come to say. These dances are nothing other than moral Bolshevism."[88] But it was not only as an anticommunist and a Catholic that Vuillermet condemned jazz as a sign of the godless times. "It is not only to Christian men and women that I address myself, but to Frenchmen and Frenchwomen. Remember that you belong to a country with supreme taste, the country which, over the course of centuries, has given a definitive and often exquisite form to the most beautiful dances in the world! . . . Our ancestral French dances were dances of tact; those that triumph today are those of contact. The former were dances of race; these here are dances of rastas. Preserve the national patrimony, that treasure which has been handed down to you by your grandfathers and grandmothers . . . Be proud of it, impose it on everyone, and, with grace, never concern yourself—you Frenchmen— with the criticism of I-don't-know-which *nègres* from abroad."[89] Accordingly, choosing to be French meant that one should enjoy ancestral dances, the tactful treasures of the patrimony, not the "rasta" dances that he believed were the negation of Frenchness.

Victor Margueritte, a culture critic for the newspaper *Le Peuple,* told Germain that though the war may have set the stage, the dances themselves were the cause, not the symptom, of a cultural degeneration that was particularly dangerous for the young. "The demoralizing dances, the tango, the foxtrot, the shimmy, that's all the young girls dream of now! A dream that, in reality, is nothing but a kind of precocious and dangerous virginal deflowering."[90] Jazz dancing, he argued, had become a kind of collective mania that was destroying the constitution of young Frenchwomen by eroding traditional values. The biggest threat, it seemed, was to traditional gender roles.

Germain further supported his position by including the writing of "objective" scientists from the medical establishment, who stressed the damages that these dances could cause to the bodies of Frenchmen and -women. For instance, the "celebrated hygienist" Doctor Pagès thought that the shoulder shaking of the shimmy and the close contact between the sexes in jazz dancing were something to be feared. "In a time when venereal disease is the most pervasive physical illness in France, we should deplore the fashion for these dances, which increase the excitation of those who are already carried away by the climate of our Latin origins and which threaten the well-being of women and the important role that they play in our daily life. Now, the excitation cannot be denied. The regions of the body that are pressed strongly against one another are extremely sensitive. The skin there is very delicate, and the contact reminds the muscles of the position of sexual actions. This is what makes the movements so dangerous. The contact followed by a strong pressure is certainly a powerful carnal excitation."[91] Instead of performing their traditional roles in daily life, women were performing scandalous dances that incited carnal movements. The need to move, known in French medical circles as "*tasikinésie*,"[92] was natural for primitive peoples, Pagès argued, but completely unnatural for proper Frenchmen and Frenchwomen. This was especially the case when it led to erogenous-zone contact. At a time when venereal diseases were spreading, Pagès believed that jazz dancing needed to be suppressed.

Physiologist Professor Pinard also framed the dance craze as a health problem. The state of sexual arousal, he argued, damaged proper French sensibilities in the young and threatened the future of the race. "In the case of a number of young women, it produces a deplorable excitation. Whereas the ancient and gracious French dances were healthy from all points of view, particularly in preparing and facilitating marriages, these new dances are harmful. In effect, they are detrimental to the perpetuation of the species, and by their excess, they take away from and alter the health of the individual."[93] Again, Pinard's argument followed the standard discursive motif: giving in to an enjoyment that was unnatural took the French body out of its natural equilibrium and led to a degeneration of individual and cultural health.

Another doctor, G. L.-C. Bernard, a specialist in "gynecological and nervous afflictions," echoed this argument and described exactly how jazz dancing threatened cultural health and the "future of the race": "I am able to give you an ensemble of controlled facts, observed impartially,"[94] he wrote. In opposition to the "perfectly sane old dances" once practiced in France, jazz dances, with their "provocative cadences," "bring about interesting pathological troubles in the physiological organism. After a while, these chronic physiopathologic troubles lead to more serious disorders in the peripheral and central nervous system, as well as in the psyche."[95] Like others, Bernard believed that the syncopated rhythms and movements of jazz dancing actually changed the physiology of Frenchmen and -women on the cellular level and led to permanent psychological problems.

In men, Dr. Bernard believed that jazz dancing caused impotency[96] and damaged the innermost part of the brain, the medulla. He noted that dancing caused victims of both sexes to develop insomnia, lack of appetite, circulation troubles, dizziness, migraines, tics, nervous spasm, troubles in arterial tension, loss of speech, anomalies of salivation, and problems with memory. Women who frequented *les dancings,* he warned, developed certain gynecological problems on top of these disorders, including "catarrhal inflammations, irregularities of flow, and spasms of sadness . . . [In these women] procreation becomes more difficult and more rare."[97] But the physical problems were not the only threat to his notion of normal French femininity. "If the excitation seems comparable or closely equivalent, it is an attraction toward lesbianism without limit that holds them. Unfortunately, the number of women who follow that perversity increases from day to day. The preparation for that vice, admired by today's society, is made by dancing."[98] The chronic repetition of dancing weakened the body, broke down gender distinctions, and confused normal sexual attractions. Moreover, it caused "anomalies of the critical sense, increases in flagrant errors of judgment, and incoherence of tone and taste."[99] All of these things, Bernard argued, threatened the future of the French race. In short, he projected jazz dancing and the un-French way of life that it symbolized as the cause for almost every illness that he witnessed in his medical practice.

These anti-jazz pronouncements do more than just dramatize how jazz was used in media debates as a rhetorical opposite through which to define "normal" Frenchness and healthy social order. They reflect grave cultural concerns in the years following the war. Indeed, France suffered from a massive decrease in its birth rate, with the number of births in relation to the surviving population declining by more than 20 percent in 1920 compared to rates before the war.[100] The government did all it could to promote repopulation, passing laws in 1920 that made distributing contraception illegal.[101] Yet something *had* changed. People were getting divorced more frequently: the 32,557 divorces granted in 1921 were double the amount seen in 1913.[102] A new drug, cocaine, had taken the place of absinthe as the intoxicant of choice in the music halls, cafés, and *dancings*.[103] People seemed to be dealing with loss by living it up while they could, and the many traditionalists who believed that it was time to settle down and reconstruct France were worried.

Not all opponents of jazz in France during the first wave were as categorical in their opposition. Some observers believed that the strength of French culture was its republican spirit, its ability to assimilate and civilize. Jazz, from this more moderate perspective, was no different from other foreign influences that had been assimilated into a healthy cosmopolitan culture. For instance, the editor of the conservative *La Revue Française,* Antoine Redier, argued that it was possible to adapt jazz dances and make them French. "I have seen accommodations to French taste, resulting in a relative correction [of the dances] and even, in certain cases, a real aesthetic and even remarkable elegance."[104] Jazz dancing was not intrinsically bad. It was dangerous, he believed, only when unregulated and performed in the *sauvage* state, destructive only when Frenchmen and Frenchwomen tried to imitate *nègres* rather than civilize them. "There is one thing that is impossible for me to consider calmly: these *nègres*, by laughing, crying, and gesticulating, have made whites dance, and these whites dance on command each time the *nègre* conductor whistles. This appears to me intolerable."[105] Who, he asked, was "culturing" whom?

Another example of a critic who wanted to assimilate jazz dances by making them more French was Paul Allain, editor of the short-lived newspaper *Le Radical*. He, too, thought it possible to tone down the wildness of the dance steps through proper instruction. "French taste has corrected the exaggerations of certain gestures and certain attitudes . . . Devil take those without rigor and modesty, if not from the moral point of view, which should be enough, then from the point of view of patriotic morale."[106] As a result of pressure from such voices, dance instructors at the Académie des Maîtres de Danse decided to Frenchify the jazz dances they taught. Indeed, this organization decided to ban the shimmy, the most scandalous of all the jazz dances, as it was just too wild.[107] Madame Lefort, secretary of this *académie* and president of the older Académie de Danse, founded in 1840, announced that "they [dance instructors] will not teach the shimmy because of its too-precise links to idiocy, the *danse de St. Guy,* and other chronic and fleeting infirmities that humanity is, in our days, sufficiently graced with."[108] Instead, members of the *académie* agreed to teach only dances suited to the "French spirit."

The Politics of Dancing

Joseph Jacquin's popular novel *Ici l'on danse* (1923) gave narrative form to the anxieties about jazz dancing in France and raised questions about how to properly respond to it. Should jazz dancing be accepted in France, or should it be condemned and repressed? Constructed as a morality tale with a heavy emphasis on normative gender roles in the face of social crisis, the novel was a warning aimed at the "immutable hypocrisy of fathers and mothers, who at heart are dominated by perilous stubbornness, pride, snobbery, and a stupid fear of ridicule; they are able to watch their daughters dance one of these so-called American dances without a shiver or a blush."[109] Jacquin wanted to open the eyes of naive parents to the many dangers of jazz dancing.

The story begins with protagonist Robert Charmel returning from his travels abroad to be greeted by his old friend Paul, now known as the "king of the foxtrot." Robert also meets two women who, for the author, represent the two female types characteristic of the postwar period. The first is Hélène, who responds to his questions with "the sincerely indifferent tone of a free young woman [*fille libre*], sane and without constraint."[110] The second is Paul's sister, Mary-Anne, "who seemed to him more virile, very elegant and already very much a woman, and who had, in all her undulating and quivering person, a liberty very different than that of Hélène: the recklessness of a perverse cat."[111] Jacquin used the narrative to set up the conflict between the free mind and the free and reckless body. The novel becomes a test of will for Robert—and thus for France—driven by the structural question of which type of woman he will end up with and, consequently, which kind of Frenchness he will choose: will it be the chaste sincerity of Hélène, or the jazz-crazed perversity of Mary-Anne?[112]

Robert soon finds out that he no longer seems to know Paul, who uses dancing as a tool for the conquest and corruption of feminine purity. Paul, a Jazz Age Don Juan, introduces him into his secret society of philanderers, *Les poilus de la paix,* all of whom are dedicated to fulfilling their carnal desires. These men, "swollen with pride," scoff at the idea of marriage, the negation of their dancing creed, which they called "the religion of the future."[113] Jazz dancing, Paul explains, "acts like a wise messenger and restores the irritability to primitive zones," thus restoring people and society "toward that of Natural Man, like in the time of Jean-Jacques!"[114] Framed as a cause and effect of Rousseauian primitivism, Jacquin placed jazz dancing in opposition to the rules of decorum upon which civilization was founded.

Jacquin's device for displaying the tragic effect of jazz on unsuspecting French youth is the character Cécile Vernet. A pure young thing intrigued by the fashionable world of sophisticated adults, she wants to learn the jazz dances. Cécile's uncle, horrified by all music after 1921, forbids her, but Paul convinces Madame Vernet that there is nothing to fear, as Mary-Anne, from the same old bourgeois family as he, is a dancing teacher.

Paul takes Robert to one of Mary-Anne's lessons to show him "the essentials of my theory of pleasure."[115] There, he boasts that he will seduce young Cécile and add her to his "harem." For men, he explains, jazz dancing is a simple and conscious means to an end. The effect of the dances on women, however, is much more powerful. "It's cerebral for us . . . but for women, it's purely nervous."[116] Paul's cynicism—not to mention his mechanistic view of women—seems to arise from one forbidden desire: the taboo of incest. His sister is the one woman he cannot conquer, and he burns with desire as he dances with her to a jazz record. "Do you have a lover?" he asks. "If I weren't your brother, I would ask you to marry me right away."[117] In order to show her students, and especially Robert, how the dance is really done, Mary-Anne begins to dance with another woman, dramatizing the confusing influence that the opponents of jazz in France decried. "And henceforth, they separated no more; each new injunction of the phonograph simply determined a more intimate contact. Mary-Anne, with a feline suppleness, in two contrary movements, acted successfully on the nerves of her partner. Lucie, little by little, closed her eyes, tilted back her pale face, and shivered all over her body . . . The young women for whom she was to serve as an example opened their eyes wide."[118] If Paul is the Don Juan figure, Mary-Anne is the Salomé, whose power of seduction is not limited to men. Robert, however, remains true to his French reserve and skeptical of the cultural benefit of jazz dancing. He quickly recognizes that poor Cécile is in danger.

The conflict in the novel over the future of French youth comes to a head at a ball, set at a Deauville casino dance hall. It is a contest between jazz temptation and French reserve. At the beginning of the evening, Mary-Anne asks Robert to dance the "Monkey Blues" with her. Despite her efforts to seduce him, his resolve hardens. "That's the first and the last time that I dance these dances, Miss. Don't count on me to invite you."[119] The young Cécile, however, cannot withstand the effect of this music on her more susceptible body. Jacquin takes care to describe the music as a "stupid poison reserved for superior classes and for luxurious natures, whose slow ravages on the temperament of nervous girls, in the end, equal those of the popular god alcohol."[120] Cécile has had her first sip. "You know, Mother," she exclaims, "I believe that I have a taste for dancing!"[121] Robert, who now sees jazz dancing as the "evil of tomorrow," warns Madame Vernet that these "dances in vogue, of savage monkeys, are frankly obscene,"[122] especially the shimmy, which he calls the "the quintessence of vertical love."[123] When she ignores his moral warning, he tries to convince her of the medical danger. "It is in innocence, I believe, that almost all those who fascinate themselves with such joy without being suspicious of its origins—or of its consequences on their nerves, or of its medical name. That passion leads quickly to pathology,"[124] causing "neurosis, hysteria, and changes in organic equilibriums."[125] Again, the bad mother ignores him, and even Hélène will not join him in denouncing jazz dancing.

In the end, Robert sees nothing but moral and cultural decay all around him and chooses to leave France once again. For poor Cécile, however, there is no escape. Hypnotized by Paul's powers of dance, she gives in to the movement, "which announced the complete metamorphosis."[126] Naturally, she is destroyed when, after the conquest, Paul turns his attention elsewhere. In a moment of epiphany, she sees that it is too late for her. While her mother glows with the social triumph of the evening, Cécile drowns herself in the sea.

It is too simple, however, to say that there is a direct correlation between

Robert, as the idealistic hero who refuses to rejoin French society, and the author. The dance epidemic and its corrupting influence are only one part of the tragedy. The other part relates to Robert's inability to settle down with Hélène, who, sane, chaste, and refined, represents a kind of pragmatic indifference to the jazz dance craze. Since Robert is able to define himself only *against* the dancing, opposition to jazz becomes central to his sense of Frenchness. In the end, Robert aids only the mythic idea of a pure France by turning away from the present and the possibility of settling down to raise a family. In his quest for the ideal Frenchwoman, he is not that far from Paul, whose Don Juanism is the other side of the same coin. Both perform a kind of search for an ideal woman that, like "true" Frenchness, exists only in their minds.

While Jacquin represented jazz as a symptom of cultural degeneration, some modernist writers felt that jazz was the cure for culture, hearing in jazz music the direct expression they were aiming at in their own writing and a new way of being to be emulated in their daily lives. For Belgian poet Robert Goffin (1898–1984), a participant in the emerging international Surrealist scene in Paris, the simplicity of jazz, in contrast to intellectualized high culture music, made it a cure for what ailed post-war European art and culture. Indeed, since the Surrealists followed Freud in believing that the problem with individuals—and by extension civilization—was that too many innate desires were repressed by restrictive rules, they glorified jazz for being analogous to the unleashing of unconscious instinct that they thought was necessary for the return of psychological health. Jazz, they believed, was good medicine for the discontents of civilization. Writing in *Le Disque Vert*, a Belgian-French journal of poetry, phonograph reviews and critical essays that he edited with André Salmon, Goffin followed this Freudian logic as he compared jazz improvisation to the automatic writing that the surrealists were trying to achieve, one that would be free from the constraints of civilization. "There is nothing like jazz for the impotency of a too-civilized ear, and I would like to postulate *a priori* my auditory inferiority and to take pleasure in it; this might please the herds of intelligent men for whom jazz is nothing but idiotic madness. Yes, it is madness, but it is organized madness and very nice!"[127]

Echoing Cocteau's characterization of jazz as a "domesticated catastrophe," Goffin described how he was drawn to the "organized madness" that he heard in jazz, at least in the *nègre* jazz of Louis Mitchell and the Jazz Kings (which now included Sidney Bechet). "Jazz is not a music of outcome. It does not emerge logically from ten centuries of Europeanization, but, on the contrary, is a music of reaction."[128] Jazz was a reaction to the repressive civilization that had led to war in Europe. European music and musicians suffered from too much logic and too many rules. All the restraint and discipline caused what Goffin described as an impotence resulting from "auto-castration." According to Goffin, "civilized man" was now "only a residue of his brute self." His favorite jazz musicians, on the other hand, still had instinct, passion, and desire, which they freely expressed in their playing. This was where Goffin located the parallel between jazz and surrealism. European music (traditional writing) was an expression of a repressed, intellectualized, and used-up humanity where everything was planned in advance. Jazz (surrealist writing), with all its "spontaneous brutish sexuality and polyphonic perspiration of animality," had an inverse relation to the old used-up forms. Jazz improvisation and surrealist automatic writing were manifestations of thought liberated from intellect and guided by emotion and affect, allowing for an expressive freedom directly related to sexuality. Goffin heard this freethinking in jazz, especially in *nègre* jazz:

> How much I prefer the *nègres,* the beautiful *nègres* who laugh with all their teeth; the banjo player strums the music from his innards, the pianist is feline, the horns are like fields of streams where condensed breaths pursue themselves and explode on arrival. The jazz drummer, a miracle of ubiquity and cohesion, is the counterweight of his comrades. They laugh and play for themselves, with all their vitality, all their memories, all their spontaneous brutish sexuality and polyphonic perspiration of animality. Hoorah! Hoorah! That's everything that one should love in jazz; it's everything that is the expression of a sane race and that should please our flabby Christians. How to be young? Can you read Blaise Cendrars, see the beautiful cowboy films, and not love jazz when the other music is a music of mathematic reasoning, filled with identical curves and predetermined falls? Jazz, itself, is infinity like instinct, its emotions are reflexes and direct, and those who listen to it should not isolate themselves and close their eyes like people do at concerts, where one abstracts oneself and turns one's will [*volonté*] toward a cerebral emotion.[129]

After hearing jazz, the "brute cries" of a sane race, Goffin felt that he had much to "unlearn in order to satisfy myself."[130] Listening to jazz and receiving a dose of its "organized madness" put him on the road to wellness. Goffin later wrote of this self-fulfillment and regeneration in his poem "Liminaire": "And jazz is so great that it contains the future. / The globe turns in my brain / . . . And I dance tonight with the whole world / For these poems which are born at the foundation of my self."[131] Jazz touched him to the core and gave him hope for the future. It exemplified a modern way of being that floated freely above a repressive and corrupted civilization. Such was the freedom that surrealists like Blaise Cendrars, Philippe Soupault, Albert Cohen, and Pierre Mac Orlan were searching for, and they joined Goffin in thinking that the improvisational catharsis allowed for in playing, listening to, and dancing to jazz was exactly what French people needed to heal the wounds of war.

Whereas this chapter examined the explosion of jazz into a French culture that had virtually no rules for judging it except for comparing it to traditional French cultural forms and diagnosing it as helpful or harmful for cultural health, the next chapter centers on the development of a more solid foundation for judging jazz music as it became more familiar. During the second period, as the spaces for enjoying it continued to flourish and it was spread throughout France by way of the radio and the cinema, jazz began to lose its exoticism. Critics started distinguishing between "authentic" jazz and other popular musical forms, and such conversations were used in many different public forums to come to terms with French culture. Thus debate about whether jazz—and what kind of jazz—was appropriate for French culture continued to allow writers a way to define their sense of "true" Frenchness.

3

Jazz and the Modern Public in the Age of Mechanical Reproduction

Mass reproduction is aided especially
by the reproduction of masses.
—Walter Benjamin

As jazz became more familiar to French culture critics, they started
to nuance their thinking about it, moving beyond describing and diagnosing its meaning for cultural health. The period between 1922 and 1926 was
characterized by the emergence of two basic categories for differentiating jazz
along so-called racial lines: "authentic" *musique nègre* and white commercial
jazz. Each had attributes and characteristics that echoed tropes and received
ideas about *les nègres,* Frenchness, and America. Linking the music and its
epiphenomena to these larger categories allowed French writers to convey a
more complete picture of their imaginary notion of true French culture while
coming to terms with jazz's continual presence in France. As it became more
mainstream, the way in which it was spread to a wider audience through
three modern media of dissemination—the phonograph, the radio, and the
cinema—forced observers of modern culture to come to terms with these new
media and what they meant for the French public. The same kinds of debates
over the cultural appropriateness of jazz in Paris were rehearsed in relation
to a new modern sense of popular culture that, by virtue of media technology, was spreading into the French countryside. Critics used the debates on
jazz to make sense of the impact of the new media on national culture, and
of what culture would be like in the age of mechanical reproduction.

An artistic depiction of the new dance culture moving across the ocean by way of electronic media. *La Danse,* no. 26 (November 1922). Reproduced with permission from the Bibliothèque Nationale de France.

Modernist composer Darius Milhaud (1892–1974) was one of the first French observers to both note how quickly jazz was changing and to relate its evolution to the new forces affecting modern culture. In 1922 he took the Tocquevillian approach and left *Le Bœuf sur le toit,* with its Cocteau-style "jazz Parisien," and traveled to Prohibition America in search of answers about American modernity and authentic jazz. He found two Americas and two kinds of jazz.[1] In Boston, he drank whiskey out of a teacup at the Brunswick Hotel and listened to white jazz bands that sounded much like the ones back in Paris. When asked by American reporters about new influences on French symphonic music, he responded with what he thought they would want to hear: "jazz."[2] He was surprised when they frowned at his answer; like many musical purists back home, they thought jazz should be kept in the dance hall, not welcomed into the concert hall. They did not believe that a high-culture composer like Milhaud should be concerned with such lowbrow music.[3] After Boston, he traveled south to New York, where he met Yvonne Georges, a French singer performing on Broadway. First they went to hear the new star of the American recording industry, Paul Whiteman, at the Palais Royal. Here, the mechanisms of modern American cultural production—its slick image management, its star system, and its Americanized symphonic jazz, mass distributed to a public buying phonograph records like never before— were on full display. Then Georges took Milhaud to Harlem and the other America. In search of authentic "Negro folklore," Milhaud met with Harry Burleigh, who had collected and transcribed a volume of Negro spirituals and work songs. After hearing Burleigh's choir sing these songs, he went to a speakeasy at the top of Lennox Avenue for some real cocktails and real jazz. What he heard was, for him, the "creation of a new world." He returned to

Paris with souvenirs of this trip: several Black Swan "race records" (the label and the genre were in their first year of existence) purchased in Harlem, and a new way of conceptualizing "authentic" jazz, which he immediately began to spread.

Milhaud wrote about how the French public had the wrong impression about jazz. The noisy music that the avant-garde played at *Le Bœuf sur le toit* was not really jazz at all. Their "white technique of using false elements"[4] (sirens, horns, etc.) in the service of modern exoticism was based on a misunderstanding of the music. In America, Milhaud reported, mainstream jazz was no longer comic or noisy in this way. White bandleaders like Billy Arnold and Paul Whiteman had begun playing arranged symphonic jazz with a high level of musicality. While many French jazz bands continued to make noise, American jazz bands had "evolved." In the new white commercial jazz, nothing was left to chance; everything was regulated and measured. In fact, Milhaud thought it was appropriate: this symphonic jazz was "absolutely proper" to the white American sensibility. Following standard ideological constructs on modern America, he described how jazz had been "Taylorized" for commerce in the same way that American factories organized material production. "There exists in the United States a series of technical works on jazz . . . There exists equally in New York a school, the Winn School of Popular Music, which has published three method books (*How to Play Popular Music, How to Play Ragtime, How to Play Jazz and Blues*) of a remarkable technical interest, in which all the special elements of this genre of music are studied in a complete and logical manner."[5] If one learned these lessons, one could play such white Americanized jazz and write popular songs. In other words, white America had succeeded in regulating a music once thought to be chaotic and wild. This methodical and rationalized approach to jazz, he argued, allowed the culture industry of Tin Pan Alley to mass-produce "tunes" as commodities. It also allowed white jazz bands—especially Paul Whiteman—to dominate the major record labels and have enormous commercial success.

Yet this was not the only kind of jazz in America, because there was another America. Having visited it in Harlem, Milhaud noted that black jazz had evolved alongside, yet separately from, mechanized commercial jazz, because it was subjected to different cultural forces. "Alongside that mechanized music, rather as precise as a machine, we find the work of the *nègres* of North America. It is a music that, though it issued from the same source, has evolved in a completely different manner."[6]

This "species of jazz," he argued, was still in touch with its "African source."

Segregation had kept it separate and protected from the forces of Taylorized America. Harlem jazz retained the same "taste" and "sentiment" that one heard in the old slave tunes. It had evolved in a different way under different rules.

For Milhaud, who had written to Paul Claudel of his desire to write his *Poèmes juifs* (1916) with the spirit of his own Jewish "blood,"[7] the retention of an authentic diasporic taste was a point of imaginary identification with the jazz of the "*nègres* of North America." "It's the same tenderness, the same sadness, the same faith that animated the slaves who, in their songs, compared their flight to that of the captive Jews in Egypt and who called with all their soul for a Moses who would save them."[8] American culture threatened to conceal this primitive pathos, only for it to be found in jazz "*chez les noirs*" by rationalizing their thought and mechanizing their music. Indeed, modern democratic popular culture, he believed, had a tendency to overwhelm and transform all traditional forms in its endless search for the new. The blacks of Harlem, Milhaud argued, found freedom from cultural Americanization through improvisation. "If in American jazz, everything is put in its perfect place and nothing is left unstudied, in the jazz of the blacks, improvisation plays a larger part. But what formidable musical resources and what power of imagination one must have to realize [such music] without fault."[9] Whereas white Americanized jazz had a sophisticated quality, "authentic" black jazz still had an African or *sauvage* sound. In "the insistence and intensity of its rhythms and melodies," he heard "something tragic and despairing."[10] He testified to hearing the echo of the African spirit of jazz in Harlem: "There, it is not uncommon to hear a *négresse* sing the same melody for more than an hour, an often poignant melody of a design as pure as any beautiful classical recitative supported by a jazz [band] that forms a foundation for these incessantly renewing melodies . . . And so, we touch the source itself of that music, its profoundly human value, which overwhelms one as completely as any universally recognized masterpiece of music."[11] For Milhaud, the retention of authentic African characteristics was a sign of the *nègre* resistance to cultural Americanization. Whereas the standard Taylorized jazz tunes lasted only as long as needed, given the technological and commercial constraints of the phonograph, this "jazz *nègre*" had no limit to its scope or duration. At this secret club in Harlem, the free and "primitive" jazz *nègre* gave Milhaud hope that the vestiges of traditional culture could resist the constant pressure of the modern world.

In Milhaud's description of the authentic Harlem jazz, one can hear how he valued traditional cultural forms that resisted the homogenizing processes of modernization and democratization. In other words, though a modernist,

Milhaud had an aristocratic vision of culture.[12] He valued artists with tastes grounded in tradition rather than those whose musical production merely obeyed the laws of the market and the vicissitudes of public opinion; the best jazz was that which resisted the modern cultural forces that led to homogenized white American jazz. He heard this resistance in the primitive rhythms and pathos of authentic *"musique nègre,"* which, owing to the thriving recording industry in the 1920s, you could now hear on the phonograph.

Milhaud was inspired to create the jazz-inflected ballet *La création du monde,* based on the Bantu mythologies that Blaise Cendrars had compiled the year before in *Petits contes nègres pour les enfants des blancs.*[13] *"La création du monde* finally offered me the opportunity to make use of the jazz elements I had so seriously studied. I composed my orchestra like those in Harlem, with seventeen solo musicians, and I utilized the jazz style without reserve, blending it with a classical sentiment."[14] In other words, Milhaud sought to reenergize French music by making it more cosmopolitan, integrating the powerful jazz idiom into his classical composition. Along with Milhaud and Les Six, more and more young high-culture composers were texturing their music with jazz in an attempt to renew French music and bring it in line with their modern sensibilities.

Whereas Milhaud sought to blend jazz with the spirit of "classical sentiment" and high art, music and film critic Émile Vuillermoz (1878–1960)[15] stressed the benefits of jazz for its democratizing effect on French musical culture. Jazz rhythms, he argued, were a popular and vernacular antidote to the rational classicism that had constrained French music. Over a period of centuries, he argued, Western musicians had rationalized music to the point where it had become too highbrow and aristocratic. Music needed to return to its popular roots. "Music progressively betrayed, from century to century, its high democratic mission. It became, more and more, the secret and confidential language of an aristocracy particularly proud of its privileges."[16] Since social recognition depended on composers learning the rational rules or "secret language" of the elite, musicians lost their connection to the popular sentiment of musical enjoyment that animated the masses. Indeed, Vuillermoz believed that French classical composition had become less and less accessible to the majority of people. Jazz, on the other hand, was a smorgasbord of *vox populi* for the crowd. Jazz returned the democratic element of the "joy of pure rhythm"[17] to popular culture so that anyone could enjoy it, regardless of class background or education. Vuillermoz knew that jazz obeyed a specific "organizing force," that it, too, had its obscure laws and "secret techniques." But these laws were rooted in primitive musical sensibility, not music theory. "The *nègre* race possesses a musical sense of a rare subtlety and an instinct for rhythmic suppleness that we have the right to be jealous of."[18]

That jazz syncopation was grounded in racial difference did not mean that French people could not perform it or enjoy it. Jazz was universal, because rhythm was something all peoples and cultures could understand at some level. In fact, Vuillermoz argued that the origin of jazz "resembled the birthplace of our art"; both French music and *musique nègre* sprang from the same universal human enjoyment of rhythm. Though the rhythmic expressiveness of *le nègre* was "enviable," pure rhythm was something anyone could enjoy. Jazz was a democratic popular music that allowed for "universal suffrage." This universal enjoyment of rhythm, he believed, helped explain the "essentially modern appetite"[19] for jazz in France. Jazz, he argued, should be welcomed by critics into modern cosmopolitan culture, because the majority of the French populace had voiced its approval.

Mechanical Dissemination and Modern Culture

For better or for worse, certain proponents and detractors already considered jazz to be part of Parisian mass culture, and it was spreading rapidly to a larger French public through new modern media: the phonograph, the radio, and the cinema. The phonograph was the oldest of these and by the 1920s had already changed the ways in which people thought about and experienced music. Theoretically, if one could afford a record player—and the 25 percent tax on purchase of players and recordings[20]—then it was possible to listen to recorded music of all styles and genres, or at least those around three minutes long, anywhere and at any time. The use of the phonograph meant that music could be enjoyed in private and that musical culture no longer needed to center around public performance.

Even more striking to critics was the possibility for disseminating musical culture—in private and in public—offered by the Télégraphie Sans Fil (TSF): the radio. Radios, though still beyond many working-class people's reach, were cheaper than phonographs, and one did not need to buy records. Moreover, the possibility of cultural synchronicity (one could be listening to the same music at the same time in Normandy or Narbonne) made the radio enormously important for those interested in spreading national culture to the smallest localities. In France, the first radio stations were state controlled and immediately seen as a potential tool in nation building.[21] Leaders saw the radio as a perfect means for transmitting cultural ideology in the form of news, educational broadcasts, music, and political oration. Not surprisingly, the first radio stations promoted high-culture music and programming. Yet many saw radio's potential for extending beyond its early use, in the creation of a centralized national culture, to become an extension of modern democratic *culture populaire*.

In 1922, Maurice Vinot, the host of the first "radio-journal," proposed a new kind of programming that, rather than disseminating news, state orations, and classical music, would try to appeal to the tastes of a wider audience. One of the programs he proposed, along with serial installments of novel readings, poetry, and a variety of musical genres, was the "radio-dancing"[22] program. At first, the French undersecretary of state rejected the idea of disseminating the jazz and lowbrow atmosphere of *les dancings* over the radio. However, after several more requests, Vinot was permitted to go ahead with a single trial broadcast on November 13, 1922.[23] The trepidation caused by Vinot's foundational move reveals an important dilemma for the radio as a nation-building tool. Its usefulness for disseminating ideas and spreading high culture made radio a perfect tool for broadcasting the kind of cultural values that conservative nationalists thought were truly French. However, according to historian Cécile Méadel, this tight control in the first several years of the TSF created an "esprit Jacobin" which set the "radio of listeners," private stations whose programming responded to what listeners in the public wanted to hear, against the "radio of the nation."[24] Jazz would soon be heard on both.

In the journals that grew with and helped shape the radio-listening public in France, the debates about what music was appropriate for French radio echoed media debates about what music was appropriate for French concert halls and theaters. Indeed, the cultural stakes were heightened because the radio audience could be so large and yet so private and personal. A 1924 editorial in the weekly *L'Antenne* reveals some of these anxieties about how trying to appeal to a wide audience led to a loss of musical quality and cultural value. "The programs [of Radio-Paris] contain the best and the worst. It seems that Victor Charpentier says to himself: in order to conquer the vast public, be mediocre. Too often, Radiola tries to compete with it . . . What's more, the orchestra for radio-dance is lamentable. It gives absolutely no idea of jazz. It is without vigor and lackluster. It plays insipid trifles and deforms works. We are far from the performances of Whiteman in New York, or Zez Lonfrey in Chicago. It is all the more regrettable that Radio-Paris possesses a good frequency and has excellent instrumentalists. Alas, it is badly directed and composes its programs too far in advance to facilitate their publications."[25] Thus the problem with Radio-Paris was the same as that of modern democratic culture: it spread itself too thin. By trying to please a wide variety of musical tastes, it had become tasteless. Charpentier, the artistic director of Radio-Paris, mixed all genres, the best and the worst, right next to one another on equal footing. Whereas high-culture venues staged only the best productions, Radio-Paris broadcast anything. Of course, in fairness to Charpentier, even with the resources of Radio-Paris—which were greater than most stations possessed—programming was no easy task. These were the days before the phonograph pickup (not introduced until 1926, when its impact was profound), so all broadcasts had to be live. This required maintaining studio orchestras made up of good sight readers who could perform any music placed in front of them and move on to the next. But for Micromégas, a critic whose nom de plume was borrowed from a character in Méliès's *Le voyage dans la lune,* these radio orchestras, when compared to specialized orchestras, seemed diluted and mediocre. In his opinion, this was not the way to improve French musical culture; rather, he believed that to preserve French cultural values, such democratization needed to be resisted.

Victor Charpentier's response defended his programming choices and sheds light on some of the new factors in popular culture in the age of mass media. "I read an article by Micromégas in *L'Antenne* this morning. It hurt me a great deal and shows an evident effort to anger me. You are not unaware that the enterprising effort for two years has been superhuman: the exigencies of the public, the technical difficulties, the opposition of groups and syndicates of artists have given me excessive tasks to perform. Your collaborator wants me to serve the public concerts of masterpieces. If I calculate correctly, at forty pieces per day, I need to program fifteen thousand diverse works per year, jazz band included. Do fifteen thousand masterpieces exist in the world?"[26] Though this reasoning is a bit disingenuous—the orchestra did not have to fill every time slot in the programming—one can see where Charpentier was coming from. Radio technology had existed for only two years, and just filling the airtime with music, he argued, necessitated this kind of eclecticism. Since radio could still disseminate only live broadcasts, a station was limited by the material its orchestra could play every day. From Charpentier's perspective, necessity and time were the driving forces behind modern mass-media culture.

Writing in the mainstream publication *L'Illustration,* Émile Vuillermoz noted another problem with the dissemination of culture over the radio. Not only was the music mediocre, but the power of the radio imposed a taste for mediocre music on the public. He argued that the creation of music for radio programming had led to the dominance of "la musique légère"—best translated as "easy music"—a new genre of scored music that was neither classical nor popular, neither pure symphonic music nor authentic jazz. Such musical commodities did not respond to the tastes of the masses; rather, such music was forced on them by repetition, and they soon learned to passively accept it. "We know that music imposes itself on the brains and hearts of the crowd by infiltration and obsession. Our editors of easy music are aware that any old melody can be imposed on the public if one has the material means to make it be heard at all hours of the day and night with sufficient insistence. The less musically gifted being would not know how to escape the tyranny of such bewitching. Soon, without being aware of it, the flock of ingénue music lovers swells, defenselessly humming a foxtrot or a refrain from the radio."[27] By being ever-present and ubiquitous, *la musique légère* on the radio worked its way into the hearts and minds of the French public, many of whom were defenseless against its subtle influence. This, Vuillermoz argued, was not radio responding to popular democratic culture, but rather a mass distribution of musical commodities from above. Radio thus had an extraordinary power over public taste and the direction of French culture. Vuillermoz, a cosmopolitan at heart, hoped that the radio would include all types of music, but he especially wanted radio programmers to strive for something beyond Taylorized mediocrity.

Other commentators on the cultural impact of radio noted how the transmission model of communication was beginning to bridge the divide between urban culture and provincial life. Radio brought the sounds of the big city—the politicians, the sportscasters, the easy music, and the jazz bands—to the smallest villages in France. Not all observers saw this spread of modern urban popular culture as a sign of progress in 1924. For instance, an editorial by Gabriel-Joseph Gros in *Radio-Magazine* exemplifies the growing concern about the cultural impact of this new media technology, made even more pressing by the development of speakers (instead of headphones) for radio listening. "The village was assembled in front of a handsome loudspeaker sitting in an open window . . . Finally, a concert was brought to an excited village. There was the noise of the saxophone, the jazz flute, the banjo, and the laughter of a celebrated comic. Instead of this, why not install a TSF broadcasting station in the village? In this way, by a just return, Paris would be able, at the same hour each day, to give itself a good atmosphere [*bon air*]. The voices of the wind, the songs of the trees, and the birds would balance the calling of races and the cries of jazz."[28] Instead of always using radio to bring Paris to the provinces, he argued that France needed to broadcast culture in the opposite direction. The lacuna that needed to be filled was not in a countryside missing out on modern sounds but in a noisy Paris that lacked reminders of France's pastoral past. Instead of following modern Parisian trends, Gros wanted to use radio to return France to its provincial roots by giving it a daily breath of *bon air*.

Like radio, cinema was a powerful medium for the dissemination of modern musical culture. This idea might seem counterintuitive, since film was still technically silent, but the cinema did have musical accompaniment. More importantly, the cinema was a powerful tool in the creation of cultural ideology, as it linked together modern situations and dictated their moral (and musical) resonance through its associative system of montage. Cultural discourse, literally and metaphorically, was being framed at the movies, an immensely popular form of entertainment, especially for the younger generations. "The cinema," wrote the young Jean-Paul Sartre in 1924, "is the sign of the times: those who were twenty in 1895 render it responsible for the inevitable gap that they find between their spiritual state and ours. One reproaches it, like Socrates, for corrupting the youth: one associates it with dancing."[29] Sartre believed the cinema, like jazz dancing, had placed an imaginary wedge between the generations in France. The older generations looked down on dancing and the movies, holding them responsible for the cultural changes that clashed with their imaginary conceptions of the true France. Yet whether one viewed these modern cultural changes as stemming from French or American causes, the music that came to be associated with the representation of modern life onscreen was jazz.

One of the most innovative films of 1924 was Marcel L'Herbier's (1888–1979) *L'Inhumaine*.[30] It exemplifies some of the ways that modernity became associated with jazz on film. With cubist decors by Fernand Léger and Alberto Cavalcanti and a synchronized score by Milhaud—who had just finished his jazz-influenced *Trois rags-caprices*—*L'Inhumaine* offered a striking critique of a modern mechanized culture. L'Herbier structured the film so that the moral fate of society was figured through the tensions in a romantic relationship between two important character types. In this case, Claire Lescot (Georgette Leblanc), singer and slave to fashion, represents the capricious modern woman; Einar Norsen (Jacques Catelain), the scientist genius—a disciple of Einstein with a convertible sports car—exemplifies the modern man.[31] Normally, Einar Norsen inhabits his laboratory, where he utilizes all the latest technologies for studying humanity, including a "télétransmise":[32] a screen upon which he studies films of "African primitives." Wooed by Claire's silk dresses, golden tresses, jazz songs, and disinterested gaze, Norsen leaves his laboratory and sets out in his car for her international salon of artists and poets.

Her modern world is a cubist cosmopolitan jazz reality that has lost its humanity. With all its exoticism, most poignantly symbolized by the Orientalist figure of the turbaned maharajah constantly whispering suggestions in her ear, the salon has a bad influence on her. L'Herbier visualizes the decadence of this world by having Norsen arrive too late for dinner and stand outside for a while to look at the spectacle. His view on this whirling modern world is presented as a symphony of shots and countershots, cutting back and forth between the figures of the salon and the jazz band. The rhythm established by the visual editing is synchronized to the strumming motions of the black banjo player. All this syncopation has a bad effect on the ethos of this world and on Claire's moral bearings, leaving her open to pernicious external influences. Overcome by a sudden sadistic impulse, she cruelly rejects the young scientist and the modern rationalism he represents. So, too, L'Herbier seemed to be saying, had modern France spun out of control.

The brokenhearted Norsen hops in his sports car and flees. The speed is too fast even for him, and he drives over a cliff into the sea. When Claire finds out that she has caused Norsen's demise, she has an awakening of conscience and turns away from this jazzed-up world. Luckily, in movies the hero can survive crashing over a cliff as a kind of baptism. Thus when she "refinds" Norsen, Claire can now recognize him after experiencing the possibility of his loss: the "relationship between the sexes"—and a healthy and humane French culture—becomes possible when jazz and the kind of un-French exoticism it represents is set aside and modern rationalism is embraced.[33]

In a talk at the Collège de France on *L'Inhumaine,* L'Herbier aligned his art with the jazz-loving surrealists, whose "absolute nonconformism" was establishing new relationships between ideas.[34] L'Herbier talked about how splicing "twenty meters of jazz band" to other images in his film allowed him to construct powerful relationships onscreen. In his case, he linked jazz with situations that had already become associated with the music in media discourse and on film: confusion, heightened desire, modernity, and exoticism. The associative links between modern mass culture and jazz music had been established and repeated in French as well as in American films released in France, like *La jeunesse moderne, La petite Annie,* or Robert Z. Leonard's *La folie du jazz.*[35] In other words, jazz already had a certain connotative value in the cinema that almost anyone in France, regardless of class or education, could understand. In four short years, jazz had already become the background music for a speedy modern way of life on film.

Many directors used these semiotic associations to set modern jazz culture in tension with traditional French culture onscreen. For instance, Gaston Roudes's 1923 film *La guitare et le jazz-band,* based on a short story by Henri

Duvernois, visualized the dilemma of choosing between a traditional and a jazz cultural order for audiences all across France. Like many other literary adaptations, the film was designed to attract the bourgeoisie to the cinema. *La guitare et le jazz-band* presented itself as a realist film, insofar as such films purported to be a slice of life, but its message was melodramatic: the film made the resurgence of right-thinking and bourgeois morality the answer to Jazz Age social unrest. As was the case with Joseph Jacquin's novel *Ici l'on danse,* the story's structure dramatized the choice between the two opposing cultural orders through the choice that the hero must make between two types of women. Denis Crancelin (Jean Devald) is the exemplary Frenchman who must choose. Martine Portereau (France Dhélia), a city girl with loose morals and modern tastes, is the jazz band; Estelle Portereau (Violette Trézel), Martine's sister-in-law, born and raised in the country, is the guitar.

The story plays out according to standard cultural anxieties about jazz. Denis is a friend of Martine's husband, Maxime, who has been called away for colonial duties in Morocco. In her husband's absence, Martine asks Denis to come to her father-in-law's country house, where they will pass the time until Maxime's return. Vamping around in one of those silent movie-star silk dresses, she flirts shamelessly with Denis on the train to the country. Stepping off the train, the two Parisians are met by the stern patriarch Monsieur Portereau and by Estelle, whose big-hearted sympathetic character was described by one reviewer as a "humpback without the hump."[36] Like most country folk in the cinematic universe, Estelle is fascinated by city ways—but she is no rube.

The first night, Martine brings out a phonograph player to break up the silence of the country. Modern media technology serves as the agent of cultural corruption, as Martine plays jazz records from the big city for the wide-eyed Estelle and teaches her the newest dances. Martine announces this lesson as a "victory" to Denis and decides to take the two of them dancing at the nearby Casino de Carville. As they dance the foxtrot, she whispers in Denis's ear, "Prepare yourself to conquer my sister-in-law." Estelle, disoriented by the syncopated rhythms, says that she wants to go home. Again, the film frames jazz as a bad influence on the cultural ethos. Estelle finds herself falling in love and, as Martine plots, Estelle dreams all night of Denis and jazz dancing.

Back on the farm, however, Denis finds himself taken by the country air and the authentic French songs that Estelle plays on the guitar. The melodies of her pure heart move him in ways that Martine, with her flirtations and jazz undulations, cannot. For the modern Parisian, Estelle fills some deeper need missing in his life that all the jazz dancing in the world will not compensate for. They exchange words of love, and Denis writes to tell Martine, still in Carville, that he is going to ask Estelle to marry him. Rushing to the scene, Martine ridicules him for his naiveté and convinces him to return with her to the Parisian jazz culture. But in the end, traditional country Frenchness wins. The great modern train stops, and Denis jumps off to join Estelle. "Haven't you realized that my heart is yours?"[37] she exclaims as they embrace. Denis cannot resist her sincerity and her fidelity, the exact opposite of Martine's fickle jazz-band way of being; he chooses the guitar. As with other realist melodramas, *La guitare et le jazz-band* championed the recentering effect of bourgeois morality, in this case grounded in traditional country values. Many in the film industry saw the importance of disseminating of such celluloid cultural ideology.[38] They viewed the cinema as a moralizing agent that could function to bring the bourgeoisie and working class back to their senses by showing the triumph of traditional values and the resurgence of Frenchness in the face of modern cultural influences.

The ideological association between jazz music and the kind of modern situations and amoral behavior Martine personified (as well as the association between true Frenchness and Estelle) was further established by the mechanism of the film's distribution and presentation. Whereas earlier silent films allowed individual establishments to choose the music to supplement the emotional content of the film, by late 1923, companies such as Gaumont and Pathé Frères published "musical adaptations" that they distributed with the films they rented to theaters.[39] The adaptation for *La guitare et le jazz-band* listed all the scenes in the film according to theme and duration and included the music that was to be synchronized with them. The musical performance depended on the resources of the theaters and could range from piano players at the more modest halls to full orchestras at the more bourgeois theaters. For instance, when the film opened on September 15 at the magisterial Gaumont-Pathé *L'Artistique,* a multi-thousand-seat venue, the music was a major concern for the Pathé company. They used one regular orchestra, one jazz band, and a phonograph player to synchronize the music to the shadows onscreen. For example, the opening scene had two pieces of music: "Amour Schimmygues" by De Bizi and "Schimmy Schimmy," the leitmotif for Martine, by Georges Aubry. The music for the entrance scene into the Casino was "Zaza," a foxtrot. Similarly, for the dance scene between Denis and Estelle, the adaptation included the cue from the screen to the orchestra. When "Denis signals for the jazz band to play" on the screen, the pit orchestra was to play the song "C' n'est pas comme ça."[40] Yet during the pastoral scenes with Estelle, the symphony played traditional romantic orchestral music. Moreover, traditional French music, not jazz, backed the film's happy ending. Thus thousands of viewers saw the images, heard the music, and learned the associations.[41] Though the media was modern, the cultural message of most films during this period was nostalgic. In this way, many films framed the conflicts of the day so that "traditional" French morality, one that resisted jazz-inflected modernity, would be seen as the answer to France's problems of cultural unrest.

Americanized Popular Music

As was evident to almost anyone during this period, modern media technology was having an enormous impact on French culture. Many critics made the dramatic change in postwar French musical culture a symbol of the larger cultural trends and a touchstone for cultural debate. In *Le Courrier Musical,* Jean Chantovoine examined the trends by studying the programming of radio stations and concert halls. He believed that shifts in public taste had enormous ramifications for the French music industry. The changes, he argued, were signs of a culture that wanted less art and more diversion. "This musical effervescence," he wrote, "has as a principle the need for diversion and joy that follows all war."[42] It used to be that the elite led musical culture, he opined, where the best products of the academies dutifully promoted music that enlightened the public. Now musicians followed the laws of the market. They used too many styles and tried to please too many tastes. Just like in American culture, he argued, French promoters had given in to the masses and their taste for distraction and now concentrated only on filling the cash register. Musicians, alas, were following right along. As proof, he noted a recent concert of some of the best young French composers. "We had hoped for a symphony with chorus: they gave us jazz . . . The surprise was painful, not only from the artistic point of view, but, if I am able to say, from the moral point of view."[43] In other words, Chantovoine wanted to protect a hierarchical notion of culture in which tastes and values were disseminated from above. The very fact that these composers used the jazz idiom in settings traditionally reserved for classical music, he believed, proved that musical culture was being democratized and was sinking to the lowest, and most base, common denominator.

Indeed, Chantovoine believed there was a direct relation between the moral climate of a society and its musical tastes. Since the period after the war was a period of indulgence, the academies and conservatories had become indulgent, and this general cultural laxity showed in the compositions. "These young eccentric musicians, who are sarcastic and discordant, and who use audaciousness and simplicity to effect being independent, are nothing but the unconscious agents of a sociological phenomenon that Émile Durkheim could write a fat book about."[44] Chantovoine argued that jazz was to musical culture what hysterical laughter was to the troubled individual: a collective nervous laugh that was the first sign of a mental breakdown. Again, it was necessary to prevent further disintegration and promote "pure" music in the face of such moral laxity. The standard cultural riff about jazz being dangerous for traditional Frenchness rang true for Chantovoine. Jazz, he insisted, was the symptom of a sociological phenomenon that needed to be resisted and corrected, not accepted.

As French critics of all stripes continued to assess the impact of jazz on modern French culture, they continued to look to America for a glimpse at what the future might bring. Many warned that the future would soon bring a more Americanized musical culture in which jazz would be heard in settings once reserved for high culture. One New York correspondent for *Le Courrier Musical,* discussing the opening of Gershwin's *Rhapsody in Blue* performed by the Paul Whiteman orchestra, testified that "for the first time, a jazz orchestra has dared to invade the concert hall."[45] Others portrayed Gershwin and Whiteman's symphonic music as an indicator of how "primitive" jazz was being rationalized and civilized by the classical spirit of composition.

One traveling culture critic, Paul Nivoix, argued that symphonic jazz was neither classical nor primitive. Rather, it was an Americanized music that had taken over the music industry, dominated the radios, and even invaded the opera. This music was composed and performed for purely commercial reasons. Writing in *Comoedia,* he described the "renewal" of jazz music through the efforts of the Otto Kahn family in New York, which had enormous control over the New York music scene. As was often the case, America was used as an object study for describing a possible future for modern French culture.

> The jazz band is king. Be it at the *dancings,* the cabaret, and even in the houses of the good bourgeoisie, the caterwauling [*miaulement*] of the banjos, the sighs of the saxophones transform the most passive of humans into dancing machines. The jazz band has entered into our habits [*moeurs*] and with it the screams of *nègres* with their merry faces and inhuman cries. To speak truthfully, we are starting to tire of it. Reassure yourself, the jazz band is going to renew itself. Here, on this subject, is the latest news that comes to us from America: The jazz band is in full reform. Otto A. Kahn's millions—or at least a part of them—are going to push the movement. If everything goes well, the ordinary jazz band will be replaced by "American symphonic syncopation."

> Roger Wolfe Kahn, the youngest son of the famous banker and president
> of the Metropolitan Opera Company, has invented this new name. He has
> promised to devote his life to the glory of the saxophone and all its ersatz
> substitutes [*succédanés*].[46]

Nivoix asserted that, after years of dancing like machines, people in America
and France were tired of jazz. Indeed, that the staid bourgeoisie had embraced
jazz showed how tired the music was. But where one used to be able to get
away from jazz by going to high-culture venues, a new jazz, an "American
Symphonic Syncopation," would now be heard in American concert halls. With
their middlebrow music, these rich bankers' sons were eradicating high culture
in America by blurring the boundaries between cultural forms. Nivoix believed
that high culture (symphony) and popular culture (the jazz band) should be
kept separate. France needed to be on guard against such corruption.

Nivoix's article reveals some fairly conventional tropes and ideological
constructions heard in discourse on modern American culture. For instance,
the refrain about commercialism corrupting artistic purity and threatening
high culture was a standard cultural riff critics used to rail against jazz's effect
on the traditional French cultural ethos. Such commercialized mass culture
was perfectly exemplified by the "Americanized" jazz of Paul Whiteman,
which was neither high-culture music nor authentic jazz.

> In the manner of Paul Whiteman, the young Kahn believes that musical taste
> could be developed by transforming classics through syncopated arrange-
> ments. He and his associates have tranquilly but energetically pursued this
> dancing aim in his Fifth Avenue apartment, which becomes, in a way, the
> battlefield against the Old Masters. The results have been alarming. With the
> collaboration of his conductor, Arthur Lang, the young Kahn has transformed
> some of the most difficult compositions. He has taken the charge theme from
> the *William Tell Overture* and transformed it into a symphony of syncopated
> rhythms destined for tireless dancers. One of the fiercest assaults against the
> classics consists in the transformation of Thaïs's *Méditation* into a foxtrot.
> The theme of the *Méditation* is played on the violin by a young laureate of
> the Vienna Conservatory, while the banjos and the saxophones rage on. The
> result is truly unique. Can we hold the hope that Mr. Kahn will not attack
> all our classical masterpieces? Pity for Gounod and Saint-Saëns! Pity for all
> our great musicians![47]

The Americanized music that issued from Kahn's Fifth Avenue pleasure
dome was appropriating all kinds of musical material and transforming it into
a homogenized *musique légère* that was neither jazz nor classical. American

Symphonic Syncopation was not only an attack on the purity of the masterpieces that Nivoix treasured, but it also spelled doom for authentic jazz. American culture's problem, Nivoix believed, was that musical genres and the borders between high and popular culture were not being respected and upheld. He feared that French culture, too, would become Americanized in this way and that high culture and true "traditional" or "primitive" culture would be replaced by a valueless commercialized *culture populaire.*

Spaces and Places for Jazz

As the media continued to describe the movement of jazz into spaces traditionally reserved for high-culture or traditional music forms, culture critics also indexed the growth of subcultural spaces for jazz dancing. "The *dancings* of today," one observer wrote, "with their black dances, completely change the countenance of Parisian dance halls."[48] One of the most entertaining accounts of the new forms of sociability associated with jazz dancing in postwar French culture was the 1924 column by Michel Georges-Michel (1886–1985) in *Comoedia,* titled "M. G.-M.'s Jazz-Band." The column, which lasted several months, was a weekly impression of scenes witnessed at jazz venues all over France, each of which conveyed larger cultural messages about the modern French public. On February 5, for instance, he described a dance hall with its professional American dancers and "jazz *nègres,*" two standard items for commercial viability. "They danced, belly to belly, back to back, on tiptoes, joined together, lifting their legs like bankers. The woman was wearing a man's hat, and the man was hunching over her like a gossiper under the blue and pink light. The *nègres* of the jazz band, seeming to dislocate their limbs, their faces, their voices, were throwing concupiscent glances at the blond dancer. They are good children, these black instrumentalists. The majority of them are elegant mulattoes and are filled with spirit."[49] Georges-Michel described American flappers, mulatto musicians, and dancers in a stomach-to-stomach dance craze that was the best thing since the cakewalk appeared in 1903. The cultural force behind the movement, the desire to be up-to-date and part of the crowd, was fashion, and the fashion was jazz. Though Georges-Michel was not antimodern nor an anti-jazz critic, the ironic tone of his column often gave the impression of a French public that was close to exhaustion yet continued to dance just because everyone else was doing it. Critic André Warnod noted the shift in tastes as new and old spaces "changed themselves to follow fashion."[50] Jazz dancing, spread by the modern media, had become big business in Paris and elsewhere.[51]

Léon Werth's (1878–1955) book *Danse, danseurs, dancings* was conceived as a sociological analysis of the jazz dance craze as the modern media spread the taste for jazz. It provides an invaluable window on the well-developed culture of *les dancings* at mid-decade. Werth echoed the idea that there was a pervasive "need to dance" in postwar France. Rather than being a sign of decadence, dancing was actually a sign of "loyalism" to the time. For him, the change in cultural habits symbolized by the popularity of jazz was driven by the need for solidarity: the individual dancer felt a visceral need to be a part of the subcultural crowd and take part in rhythms of the present. "More exactly, it gives [the dancer] a real discomfort and intellectual trepidation; it makes him suffer not to dance. All his body suffers for him. The orchestra revealed to his legs an unknown vocation. Under the table, his legs dream of the dance floor. Jazz is neither argument nor doctrine. Jazz is rhythm and noise."[52] The important thing about jazz, Werth argued, was the physical response it provoked. Listeners heard jazz on the radio, and it drew them to *les dancings*. It made their legs "dream of the dance floor"; the passions of the body took control over the mind, and people found themselves feeling an overpowering desire to share in a group dynamic.

Werth argued that male dancers in France had the most trouble being a part of the jazz-dancing culture. This is not surprising, given that existing French gender norms stressed male rationality and reserve.[53] Men had trouble following the rhythm. They conceptualized the steps too much and, as a result, led their partners with "brutality." The amateur male dancer, fresh from lessons, often substituted "arithmetic" for dance. "His error is Cartesian. We recognize the Cartesian dancer, in that he looks at his feet."[54] When too "Cartesian," too concerned with following the method, the dancer was inhibited and awkwardly chased after the rhythm like "a traveler who is afraid to miss his train."[55] In other words, habitual modes of Frenchness got in the way of good jazz dancing for the dancer who could not let go of a restrained sense of self. However, a new "ontological equilibrium," one that followed the rhythms of the body rather than the dictates of the intellect, was not impossible to learn. "It is very simple, but he doesn't know it yet: dancing is an art of movement. That which the dancer communicates to his partner is his own movement . . . There is an exchange, an accord, a secret contact and telepathy. The dancer and his partner receive the music at the same time."[56] Thus jazz dancing made possible what one might call "perfect communication" without rational speech or thought. The male and the female dancer shared the same time and space and communicated through rhythmic body movement. Moreover, Werth argued that the "ontological equilibrium" that jazz dancing helped establish was healthy for the individual and society.

The master of this way of communicating and being, Werth argued, was the professional dancer, a kind of "mysterious priest of dance."[57] But though proficient, the professional was not always the most natural. For "natural movement," Werth much preferred to watch black American dancers who did not have to learn to dance. "A *noir,* who frequents several Parisian *dancings,* attains in that order what the old critics called natural identity and the sublime."[58] While the black dancer, who danced more naturally than he walked—or rather who danced when he walked—was the ideal of this new Epicurian language of the body, most of the French dancers he witnessed were amateurs from the provinces. Having made the pilgrimage to Paris after hearing jazz on the radio, they wanted to take part in the modern rite everyone was talking about.

Werth's book was largely made up of "impartial observations" of various venues in Paris where such people went to dance. Given the taxes on any establishment that played music (between 10 and 25 percent), the numbers of peoples and *dancings* point to the continued commercial viability of jazz dancing. "It seems that the public absorbs the music like a drink. So perfect and so imperious is jazz that it doesn't exert an absolute power."[59] He described the Tabarin, a more working-class *dancing,* and the Moulin Rouge, with its nude dancers, and he depicted several of the new "*Thés-dancings*" (tearooms that featured jazz). At each space, the couples determined how the dancing would be performed. One could argue that Werth was describing the social expression of modern democratic cultural forces at work: not anarchy and disorder, but individual expressions contributing to the whole.

He described this reigning order at Magic City, an "American temple" where champagne was "obligatoire." At Belle-Wagram's, he noted that the shimmy, once the dominant jazz dance, was now out of style. The smaller Colonial did not have an orchestra, so they used a phonograph for musical accompaniment. Bullier's was filled with "young people already animated by a vaguely agitated romanticism."[60] Remembering that night at Bullier's, Werth's own romanticism overwhelmed him in his description of the most sublime of all dancers, the "*femme noire.*" "I am not sure that she did not appear to me from the beginning from a book of poetry . . . she had become an expression of a kind of sexual poetry innate in us . . . Her grace and her nobleness atoned for the hall of faces who did not know how to deliver themselves—pride of the whites—from stupidity and foolishness."[61] This dancer, who seemed to have materialized from a collective French fantasy, was more erotic than Baudelaire's Black Venus and more exotic than one of Pierre Loti's black queens.[62] The "femme noire" in motion was the embodiment of a sublime poetry of rhythm. For Werth, she was the standard against which all other dancers were to be judged. But one could not expect to find such transcendence at the *dancings,* nor was it what most of society wanted from them. Rather, Werth argued that the psychology of the dance craze was not about the quest for authenticity or an aim toward an ideal, but it had much more to do with "the crowd amusing itself with the crowd."[63]

In describing the difference between a "public" and a "crowd," Werth explained how culture changed over time. The "public" was an idealized entity that writers and theater directors claimed to know. But where the "public" was composed of rational individuals concerned with how French culture *should be,* the crowd was something else, something more powerful. "I am horrified by that fabricated entity that we call the public. But this here is not a public. This is a crowd. Adding its movement to that of the music, it stirs itself and it churns itself. One enters. One is in the music, in the storm, and in the crowd. That crowd has no other rule than that of its swirl. One is jostled, tossed about by the innumerable currants of circulation. This is not a public that wants to impose on me its little manners, its rites, or its conventions. Nobody is here to judge me. Here, there are no individuals. The crowd is indifferent, like the wind or the sea."[64] For Werth, the public was the forum where individuals judged one another and society, arguing about which conventions and rites were proper for French culture. One entered this rational public when one made a statement or published a book. Yet this is not where Werth, the dancer, went dancing. People went dancing in order to take a Baudelarian *bain de foule* (crowd bath), to be tossed around and to lose their sense of self to the "imperious" rhythms of jazz. In jazz rhythm, they found solidarity in a shared experience of time and purpose. In dancing there was no judgment about what was appropriate, just enjoyment. "Dance delivered me from logic,"[65] Werth explained. It enabled him to just be. For Werth, the public stifled individualism while the crowd liberated the individual. The direction of French culture, he argued, was being determined by the modern mass-media crowd.

Of course, the idea of liberation and the association of jazz dancing with freedom were quite threatening to conservative French critics, whose sense of cultural identity was grounded in public order and conventional ideas about French reserve. These anti-jazz critics continued to see the popularity of jazz in a wholly different way, especially after the Cartel des Gauches, a coalition of leftist parties, gained power in the legislative elections of 1924. The anti-jazz critics on the right believed the jazz dance craze was disintegrating the French public into an unruly crowd of individuals seeking merely pleasure, not true freedom. A typical example of such an anti-jazz position was Georges-Anquetil's popular "pamphlet novel," *Satan conduit le bal* (Satan Leads the Ball), which put a gloomy spin on the image of French society losing control and dancing its way toward ruin. With the right-leaning Bloc National ceding power to the left for the first time since the war, this polemic by the editor of the satiric journal *Le Grand Guignol* must have touched a core of enjoyment for conservative readers, as it was reprinted several times.

Georges-Anquetil used 568 pages to diagnose and describe France's "nerve sickness": "it is, without a doubt, a physiological disorder."[66] The allegorical figures that spread this sickness to a "cynical, hypocritical, ferociously egoistic, and corrupt"[67] postwar France were "Vice" and "Drogue." Whereas Werth saw *les dancings* as spaces for solidarity, Georges-Anquetil characterized them as dens of iniquity where vice and drugs reigned supreme and where "true" Frenchness was being destroyed. "At *les dancings* today . . . the crowds of rastas, fops, homosexuals, and cocaine addicts who are unable to appreciate any joy but these easy and obscene sways are taught by exotic professors—more or less procurers (pimps)—with fingers glittering from enormous rings. And these modern dances, am I the only one to denounce them? No, doctors, sociologists, novelists, and academicians have called them 'vertical love' or 'cocaine of love.'"[68] In other words, the *dancing* was a distilled symbol of the general poison degenerating the cultural ethos and ruining French society. Radio shows and films piqued people's interest, and jazz dance instructors became rich promoting the culture of *les dancings* and its "vertical love." Georges-Anquetil cited statistics that 150,000 French syphilis-related deaths had been recorded since the war, and he associated these losses with the "crazy love, contests of nude backs, and dances of flagellation"[69] that took place at *les dancings*. He argued that prostitution[70] went hand in hand with the *dancings* and blamed the social phenomenon on President Clemenceau, whom he called a "pimp." To him, the flourishing jazz subculture represented the sadistic death wish that had overcome France. The nation, he argued, was suffering an economic crisis in which 13,758,000 French earned less than two thousand francs a year,[71] making the ostentatious display of bourgeois luxury at the *dancings* all the more distasteful. "Yes or no, are we in Sodom? How much longer is our government, which targets for itself serving the glory and prestige of France, going to tolerate this public display of the most shameful defect of a corrupt civilization?"[72] He argued that the Poincaré government, in power from 1919 to 1924 and not conservative enough for his taste, was to blame for moral laxity toward such shameful behavior in France. There is an evident political design here: paint a picture of a modern democratic culture in ruin, and blame those in power for that degeneration. Georges-Anquetil rallied the far right by promoting a view of France in which the direction of media culture and the meaning of "true" Frenchness could, and should, be controlled from above to protect both from the sway of the democratic masses. To accomplish this cultural cure, he argued, France needed a "true moral revolution." Though French culture seemed to be infected on the surface, change was not impossible. France needed to protect Frenchness and defend the "true" France from the cultural poisons of *les dancings*. The first step would be to eliminate them once and for all.

The Pulse of the Streets

Writer Pierre Mac Orlan (1883–1970) had a different view of the modern French public and the changes in popular culture. He did not believe that French culture could return to any previous or more true state, as culture was always in flux.[73] "The street turns," he wrote, "in a way that cannot take us backward."[74] His collection *Aux lumières de Paris* (In the Lights of Paris) provides his impressions of the changing sounds and tastes of an evolving French popular culture. His essay "Popular Music," first published in 1925, used the image of a boat floating by on the Seine with an accordion playing a "celebrated java popularized by Mlle Mistinguett"[75] to explain the ephemeral quality of music. It showed how the "popular music" of his youth was becoming faint with the passage of time. Though he thought this music best matched the old French sensibility, its sound was slowly fading away.

As the accordion symbolized the old French music, Mac Orlan made the phonograph the symbol of the new. Whereas the accordion player of old could express his sentiment and "make people dance all night,"[76] the phonograph expressed a different kind of musical taste. The phonograph, unlike the accordion, was not animated by the creative energy of the performer playing through his instrument. Rather, one expressed something about one's sense of self by picking out something to play on the phonograph. "The phonograph joins itself closely to the personality of whoever possesses it. Put on your records, I will tell you who you are."[77] The music people chose to play on the machine revealed their tastes and expressed their sense of being. Of course, in its most "vulgarized" form, playing mechanized popular music was not about possessing talent or having taste, but about collecting all available recordings. There were, he believed, people who consumed modern mechanical music for the sake of consumption, who collected for the sake of collecting. Mac Orlan noted that the most popular records in France, along with the cultural practice of listening to records, were from America, where the recording industry had exploded. "The renaissance of the gramophone, or rather its true situation, is only several years old. It dates from the last years of the war, when the soldiers of the United States of America brought the popular songs and rhythms necessary for the days after the calamities in their combat gear: the foxtrots of Irving Berlin and of all the conductors of the scattered jazz bands like joyous birds around a robust blond girl. It was not only a mechanical jig, but something infinitely young dedicated to the celebrated girls who are made beautiful over there in that stunning town of cinema, Los Angeles!"[78] Whereas the old French popular music had been symbolized by the music-hall *vedette* (star) Mistinguett, this new international popular music—whose rhythms were necessary in the postwar world—was associated with the icons of postwar American media culture: its "girls," its cinema "stars," and its "multicolored lights for advertisement,"[79] which brought a new aesthetic sensibility to France. This new sensibility was transmitted by the mechanisms of mass media and had tremendous power over the old. "The new music," he wrote, "killed [the old] without embalming it." Yet, for Mac Orlan, the taste for the new mechanically recorded music was easy to understand given the need for carnival after the war. Times had changed, and culture, too, must change.

Though he looked back nostalgically to the simple songs of the days before electricity, Mac Orlan argued that traditional French music no longer had enough force to move a people and a city that possessed "a much more sensitive nervous network. Its daily life turns more quickly."[80] Now anyone who craved it could listen to the "rhythm and strength of 'Some Sunny Day,' played by the false Whiteman orchestra for a mug [*choppe*] of the neighborhood."[81] Even in its "false"—read white—form, jazz was the consumable music that people with "tired motors" needed "to recharge their batteries." Authentic jazz was even more powerful and even more important for modern France. "If the air that we breathe, the sun that warms us, and the wind that blows are able to give man a necessary stimulant, a music taken in by endosmosis or capillary action as we stand is equally able to act on the essential gears of our organism. The jazz band matches the speed of the blood in our arteries, the quickness that it acquires at the end of the day . . . The banjos give us a rhythm that is the same as the atmosphere machines we have created for ourselves by the force of things."[82] This mechanically reproduced jazz was the music for modern French culture. By 1925, it was common to hear recorded jazz music streaming out open windows onto city streets, where it reached the tired ears of "workers and young professional men of diverse fortunes."[83] After they had worked in an ordered mechanical environment all day, the setting sun sent common people into the "apotheosis of disorder"[84]—*les dancings*—that dominated the carnival of the night.

Still, Mac Orlan acknowledged that it was hard to comprehend the power and ramification of this new international musical culture disseminated by modern mechanized media. He noted, for instance, that Irving Berlin earned more than a million dollars per annum through the worldwide sale and distribution of records, the "crêpes of black flour" fabricated at "stunning musical factories."[85] Mac Orlan wondered if such industrialized and mechanized jazz could be a "true" popular music, "through which life expresses itself with all its strength,"[86] in the way that the great art and music of the past had expressed the "faith" of a people at home in their own culture. Yet whether or not it was a "natural" or "authentic" expression of French sentiment, "sincere" and "non-Taylorized" jazz, in his words, touched people in a way that could not be denied. "It will be, in several years, rather curious to note the special romanticism of our time by its most direct expressions, those that the jazz band communicates by admirable jolts linked to the rhythm of our blood, to our nervous system, which finally begins to separate itself from old desires that have become impotent."[87] He realized that it was hard for anyone "born before the combustion engine" to understand the direct correlation between jazz and the modern mentality. "We can say that a romantic foxtrot, played sincerely by a non-Taylorized orchestra, is an instructive creation that our nerves soak up like a sponge soaks up water . . . It is the collective realization of our least confessed desires."[88] The same "instinctual force" heard in authentic jazz could be found in the poetry of Blaise Cendrars, Paul Morand's nighttime novels, and Cocteau's essays, which were the "local, that is to say French, expression"[89] of the modern mentality Mac Orlan was linking to jazz. The importance of this "popular music," jazz music, for modern French men and women could no longer be denied.

In 1925, *Conferencia* contributed to the media debates on jazz and *culture populaire* by publishing lectures from a conference on "Rhythm and the Popular Song." One of the participants, E. Jacques Dalcroze (1865–1950), who had been teaching his own version of "eurythmics" for years in Paris,[90] argued along with Mac Orlan that the rhythms enjoyed by a culture directly reflected its material and corporeal existence, its present more than its past. "Each people has its particular motor rhythms that translate themselves in everyday life."[91] Further, Dalcroze believed that such rhythms were "the direct product, the spontaneous and instinctive translation of the nervous, muscular, sentimental, and intellectual state of being."[92] Since the war, he argued, jazz rhythms had contributed to a change in the French rhythmic sensibility. "Some envision these new acquisitions as an enrichment of our artistic patrimony, and we cannot deny that these *nègre* rhythms have had a salutary influence on the development of our rhythmic sentiment. For twenty years, our schoolchildren were incapable of singing syncopated rhythms. Now we hear it in the streets, children completely and naturally syncopating these songs from across the sea. The extraordinary part is that the alluring freedom of these jazz rhythms, the extraordinary vivacity and variety of their cadences and their picturesque turns and returns [*voltes et revoltes*], the richness of their diverse accentuation and of their fantastic counterpoints, have certainly infused a new blood into musical rhythm."[93] This rhythmic jazz sentiment, with its "alluring freedom," had been acquired in less than a generation of constant exposure; Frenchmen and Frenchwomen were now enjoying and performing the *nègre* rhythms that had become the basis for the new *musique populaire.*

Yet though it was appropriate for popular music to reflect the rhythms of modern times, Dalcroze warned that an overinfusion of this rhythmic "blood" was not good for the "true" French character. "This artistic progress assuredly accomplishes itself to the detriment of our national qualities. These new acquisitions risk paralyzing our temperament and our character. They risk curbing the natural evolution of our popular songs."[94] The most obvious sign that the evolution of the "authentic" French popular song was being impacted by jazz rhythms was that the most popular songs of the music hall were often promoted as being of "American taste." The exclusive taste for jazz, he warned, was "betraying the elementary instincts of our race."[95]

The only way these acquired characteristics could be subdued, and "true" French sentiment could be expressed, he argued, was if "our singers" consecrated more of their efforts "to the creation of words and melodies for songs where the natural evolution of our thoughts and our acts would respect that which, in truth, is in the practical and sentimental life of all times."[96] Such popular songs, which incorporated new rhythms but were grounded in "timeless" French sentiment, would allow the world to "know the true France."[97] Paradoxically, it would seem, his theory meant that the evolution of popular music was natural only if it remained faithful to timeless characteristics of French sentiment and taste. Though he stressed the instinctual or innate relationship between a people and the rhythms of their popular songs, his remedy against the onslaught of "American taste" in music was to return to a "natural evolution" based on a conscious collective choice to support what he called "true French taste." But whether one believed that this return was natural or even possible, both Mac Orlan and Dalcroze were acknowledging that a culture's sense of rhythmic enjoyment, rather than being innate or ahistorical, was subject to change. Many critics saw this change as reason to mourn the loss of the authentic French song: "It's a fact: melody is dead, sentimentality is no more . . . it's the slow but sure death of *la chanson française.*"[98]

Jazz, Avant or Devant Garde?

Though jazz was popular in 1925, the future of this international music in France was anything but certain. Many questioned whether jazz would fade away as quickly as it had come or if it would leave a lasting mark on French culture. Again, culture critics followed Tocqueville's example and turned their gaze on American culture for a glimpse into the French future. For example, composer and critic Lazare Saminsky did not think jazz would be a primitive, disordered dance music for long in a land that Americanized everything. He described how America had already witnessed an evolution of musical tastes. The syncopated *nègre* characteristics in jazz were being tamed and ordered; the modern forces associated with Americanization were silencing authentic jazz and replacing it with rationalized symphonic jazz. Reporting on the new ballet *Sooner or Later* by American composer Emerson Whithorne, Saminsky declared that the rage for jazz was over in America. "Jazz is dead in America. The joyous enthusiasm of two years ago is no more than a dream."[99] Saminsky argued that whereas in Europe, where exotic appeal and "scholastic zeal" had kept jazz alive, in America the abundance of jazz that characterized the period after the war was nothing but a memory.[100] Once the American public had regained its equilibrium, he explained, the noisy music had naturally faded from culture. Jazz *nègre*, he believed, had been Americanized. Now jazz was no longer a leading force in the modern public; it was no longer determining the direction of cultural evolution.

Of course, in 1925 jazz was not dead in America. Yet Saminsky's declarative act need not be true to be significant. As a speech act, proclaiming "jazz is dead in America" allowed him to convince readers in France that jazz was no longer at the avant-garde of culture. French observers have used analysis of American culture to predict the future direction of French culture, and Saminsky foresaw a future that would, he hoped, soon leave jazz behind. In this case, the theory that mass culture was always searching for the newest thing worked against jazz. Though writers since Tocqueville often portrayed America as an adolescent culture in which hedonistic individuals pursued their own private happiness at the expense of the public good, in Saminsky's variation America was more grown up than France and had more reserve. The process of Americanization, whereby things were rationalized and mass-produced in American popular culture, had taken control of jazz; Tin Pan Alley, Broadway, the recording industry, and Hollywood were homogenizing culture, and he liked the results. It proved that if there was enough resolve from the programmers of modern media culture, the discordant and wild elements of jazz—those associated with jazz *nègre*—could be eliminated in America *and* France. In this view, Saminsky joined a host of French modernists and traditionalists who were calling for the reemergence of aristocratic classicism as a counterpoint to the steady democratic popularity of jazz. Even some of the avant-garde modernists, among whom Cocteau and Milhaud could now be counted, had their ears open for a newer form of expression that would replace jazz. Cocteau was waiting for what he called the "reaction against the cymbal," since "a new order always disengages itself."[101] Milhaud, for his part, now openly talked of the importance of "perfecting" the American music and bringing it into the classical spirit. Both statements are in harmony with Saminsky's hopes for a future musical culture in France that would assimilate and rationalize jazz.

If one focused on names like Whiteman, Whithorne, Gershwin, and Berlin, who were indeed the stars of the American recording industry in 1925, it might have seemed that white symphonic jazz had overwhelmed jazz *nègre* in American culture. Of course, to represent this as the case to French readers back home, French reporters had to conceal Broadway productions like the all-black *Shuffle-Along,* the *Chocolate Dandies,* and the *Plantation Revue,* not to mention hundreds of black jazz bands, blues singers, and solo pianists in Chicago, Kansas City, Washington, and New York.[102] Indeed, the blues industry in America, with labels such as Okeh and Black Swan, had become a multimillion-dollar business selling millions of albums a year to black and white listeners. Yet French discourse on America, when used to speak to cultural conditions in France, is rarely comprehensive; it often tells us more about the pressing issues in France than it does about American culture.

As for the culture industry in France, it, too, was producing more white symphonic jazz in concerts at *les dancings,* in music halls and cafés, on records, and over the radio. But "authentic" black jazz was not dead in France, either. Louis Mitchell's Jazz Kings were still the house band at the Casino de Paris and had recorded many sides for Pathé records. The Tempo Club had been around as a gathering place for Afro-American musicians in Paris since 1920. Singer Florence Embry, who first performed at the Grand Duc (a café where Americans in Paris like Langston Hughes worked), started her own place called Chez Florence; another black American, Ada Smith (aka Bricktop), performed at both the Grand Duc and Chez Florence and felt so at home in the Montmartre café scene that she opened Bricktop's (the first jazz bar to serve whiskey) in 1926. Moreover, French phonograph owners prized their "race records," and, despite the 25 percent import tax, these records became less scarce in France after the American music industry started exporting them there. Yet jazz *nègre,* now characterized as the most authentic jazz, was largely localized around Montmartre, so white French jazz from the French music industry was all that many who heard jazz on the radio knew.

The cultural dominance of assimilated or "civilized" jazz in France was most apparent in the marriage between jazz dancing and the radio in the first age of mechanically disseminated culture. A closer look at audience demand in 1925 shows this trend. Just as, since the war, new studios for teaching and performing dance had continued to open and take up more space in Paris,[103] jazz on the radio continued to occupy more time. Weekly radio guides in magazines like *L'Antenne* or *Radio-Magazine* from 1925 show listings for "radio-jazz" in the programs of almost every station, both state-controlled and private. Indeed, some stations used the new microphone technology to bring live jazz dance music from the *dancings* directly into French homes. Most stations had thirty minutes of jazz a day, usually the last program of the night. For instance, in July of 1925, Radio-Paris ended its broadcast with "radio-jazz" by "Mario Cazes and his Orchestra from the Caucasian Castle." Similarly, every Sunday the Tour Eiffel brought "one hour of jazz by the jazz Helvett" to listeners all over France. After the November 21, 1925, creation of the *Fédération française des postes privés d'émissions radiophonique* (French Federation of Private Radio Broadcasting Stations), which gave more support to private radio, the number and duration of jazz programs increased rapidly. On the radio, white symphonic jazz had become a ubiquitous feature of everyday life. Yet as jazz moved from being the sound of a subculture to being a constant part of mass-media culture, it lost its exotic appeal as an audience draw. Even the recent use of nudity in the music hall could not stir up the kind of public attention that the impresarios were looking for.[104] What was missing?

From 1922 through 1925, French writing on jazz settled into standard tropes and themes for describing the music even as culture critics came to terms with the influence of mechanical media as the means for distributing culture in the modern world. Following the standard ways of talking about jazz, critics separated the music into two varieties, white and black, and drew on standard cultural riffs to describe each type. Each had distinct qualities and appeal and, since they continued to be popular, stimulated debate about the nature and tastes of the modern French public and about how culture was changing in the age of modern media. As the phonograph, radio, and cinema disseminated popular culture through France, the kind of jazz distributed by the culture industry became increasingly white. While some writers believed that modern popular culture merely followed the laws of the market and responded to whatever musical tastes were commercially viable, other writers continued to promote the idea that popular culture was and should be disseminated from above, where educated elites could dictate the direction, uphold traditional values and classical sentiment, and protect "true" French culture. Yet for all the work done to promote reserved and civilized Frenchness in music to counteract the influence of jazz, critics and audiences continued to be fascinated by the music, especially the "authentic" *musique nègre* that was described in opposition to assimilated or Americanized jazz. Protectionist laws and scarcity, however, made this music something that the majority of French people could only imagine by listening to the faraway sounds of scratchy records. Then *La revue nègre* came to town. The dramatic changes in the way French writers thought and wrote about jazz, and the meaning of jazz for French culture, after seeing *La revue nègre* is the subject of the next chapter.

4

La Revue Nègre, Ethnography, and Cultural Hybridity

There is more truth, more vital substance in certain
nègre blues than in all the poems of all times.

—Michel Leiris

The white imagination sure is something
when it comes to blacks.

—Josephine Baker

    No event in the history of jazz in France captured the collective imagination of the nation as much as did Josephine Baker and *La revue nègre* in Autumn 1925. Only perhaps the scandalous Ballet Russes performance of Stravinsky's *Le sacre du printemps* in 1913 upset the French cultural ethos as much as Baker and company's kinesthetic jazz.[1] Baker, who went from an object of exotic strangeness to French *vedette* (star) and finally to cultural hero and *citoyenne* (citizen), has often served as a metaphorical figure for the story of the French embrace of jazz. Indeed, her story has been a focal point of most histories of jazz in France. By far, *La revue nègre* has inspired more written accounts, both in its time and since, than any other group of Jazz Age performers. Many have examined the overwhelming amount of historical evidence surrounding the show's reception and used the excitement Baker generated as proof of the French fascination with jazz.[2] Rather than merely rehashing the standard take on *La revue nègre,* this chapter examines the shifts in the French discourse that resulted from the intense focus on jazz left in its wake. When one takes a closer look at the media discourse on jazz following *La revue nègre,* one sees the manifestation of a kind of strange attraction on a cultural level that could be characterized as a deep ambivalence about jazz. The cultural confusion, both about the nature of jazz as a phenomenon and its meaning for French culture, led to a kind of discursive dissonance, as previously separate characteristics or linguistic signifiers were mixed together in public debates. In response to the new jazz and the discursive dissonance, an innovative group of cultural theorists, the surrealist ethnographers, tried to resolve the contradictions in the discourse by reformulating their thinking about jazz. They sought to develop a mode of writing about jazz that would account for the strangeness of its cultural reception.

By the time *La revue nègre* appeared, the idea that authentic jazz was a direct offshoot of *la musique nègre* had become a standard trope in French debates on the music. It is certain that the show was designed to play on this idea, as well to reify the exotic and primitivist stereotypes associated with *le nègre*. But even as the troupe conformed their otherness to the fantasies swirling in the French imagination, the avant-garde modernness of their art and the ambiguousness of the cultural response they provoked served to deconstruct notions of fixed racial characteristics and led critics to reevaluate the extent to which jazz, or any culture product for that matter, could be considered a pure expression of race. In short, one can see that the cultural ambivalence surrounding the reception of *La revue nègre* and their jazz forced critics to confront the hybridity of jazz *and* French culture.

When the performers from *La revue nègre* arrived in Paris in September 1925, their show was in the process of being altered to fit the sensibilities of Parisian audiences. Music hall producer Jacques Charles, a master of show-stopping titillation and exoticism at the Casino de Paris, began his work of "making the *nègre*."[3] Rolf de Maré, director of the Théâtre des Champs-Elysées, orchestrated the publicity to generate interest in the press. Though the show was only just coming together in its newly exoticized form, select critics were given a two-scene preview a week before opening night to whet their appetites and start the buzz in the media. *Paris-Midi* critic Paul Achard's

Jazz as the link between primitive and modern cultures. *La Danse*, no. 38 (November 1923). Reproduced with permission from the Bibliothèque Nationale de France.

report dramatizes how *La revue nègre* succeeded in conforming to age-old fantasies about exotic *nègre* otherness swirling in the French cultural imagination. "Before a joyous decor, the jazz [band] attacks, soft, splenetic, brutal, lustful, or sad at the same time. And in front of us, that troop of black artists appeared . . . We don't understand their language, and I am not seeking to link together their scenes, but it is all our readings that pass before our excited imagination: adventure novels; pictures of enormous steamships looming over groups of *nègres* loaded with rich bundles; a singing siren in an unknown port with men of color burdened with sacks, the stories of missionaries and voyagers; Stanley, the Thauraud brothers, *Batouala,* sacred dances, the Sudan; the countryside of the plantations; all the melancholy of Creole wet nurses' songs; all the *nègre* soul with its animal convulsions, its childish joys, and its sadness from a past of servitude."[4] Though Achard could not understand the words to the songs, the jazz rhythms combined with the spectacle drew out the many associations that existed as ideological constructs, as ready-made critical language. Other critics quickly followed suit.

Like Achard, *Le Figaro* critic Jacques Patin predicted that French audiences were going to go wild for the "originality of this spectacle, which unrolls to the sounds of a frenetic jazz band."[5] But while the jazz made Achard draw on cultural tropes about primitives, Patin described something supremely modern. "The crowd that will pack itself into the Champs-Elysées Music Hall tomorrow cannot but confirm the brilliant success obtained by that ultra-modern troupe."[6] This discursive dissonance immediately characterized the show's reception, as the standard cultural riffs associated with the modern *and* the primitive would be used to describe this new *nègre*. André Daven used both kinds of language in the publicity campaign, framing the show as both "authentic" and "raw," associating it with the many ethnographic or cultural exhibits brought to the French *métropole* during that era, and as the epitome of avant-garde. The strategy was enormously successful. Audiences poured in to take a peek at *La Baker* and see what the fuss was about. The many accounts of the packed houses with audiences screaming with disdain and delight, sometimes at the same time and sometimes at each other, show the extent to which the show, and the commercial campaign, hit its mark.

Predictably, most critics, like *Comoedia*'s Yvon Novy, used standard cultural riffs on the *nègre* without reservation on first view. "Revelation? Yes, on more than one account. The uncorking of that *frénésie* of colors; the acrobatic epilepsy of tortuous gestures and hallucinatory spirals launched in abrupt disarticulated throws; that pulsating fever and vertiginous movement emphasized by an obsessive, implacable rhythm of a prodigious confidence and metronomic regularity, has never been attempted with an equal intensity."[7] Yet though the ideological stereotypes were used to convey primitive authenticity, new discursive features crept in. On the one hand, it had all the quintessential qualities long associated with primitive *musique nègre* in French cultural discourse: it was epileptic, frenetic, contorted, disarticulate, fevered, and obsessive. On the other, he noted its "metronomic" regularity, a discursive riff associated with American modernity. In other words, one can see an ambivalence manifesting itself as discursive dissonance.

L'Intransigeant's René Bizet also used standard riffs on *nègre* sensibility to characterize *La revue nègre*. Like many critics, he used them as a set of counterpoints to define "true" French sensibility. His ambivalence, however, was related to the spectacle being cynically constructed to produce this exact response in the public. "It is neither naive enough to disturb, nor intellectual enough to arouse a refined pleasure. But it has, with its succession of dances—as it is above all a dance review—a sadness that, in spite of its cynicism, is not without beauty. The '*danse sauvage*' has an audaciousness that none of our directors would have dared . . . The epilepsy of the dances has something animal, which is a bit tired. And the music, with its grunting, contributes to creating the atmosphere of a virgin forest where great beasts frolic about."[8] One can see that Bizet used *La revue nègre*'s otherness to constitute the self, to construct a normative notion of refined Frenchness; though Baker and her dance partner, Joe Alex, had successfully recreated a primitive *danse sauvage* charged with "epileptic animality," there was something wrong with such a "daring" spectacle (with a topless Baker dressed only in a feather belt that barely covered her grinding hips) being performed in a French music hall, which *should be* a place for performances as civilized and sophisticated as their audiences. In this context, though it was an effective distraction, Bizet believed the popularity of the show was symptomatic of a decrease in refined taste within French culture. He enjoyed it, but that sense of enjoyment clashed with his normative notion of what true French people should enjoy.

Bizet used the center-right newspaper *Candide* to work through some of this ambivalence and push his analysis of the show further. He argued that its popularity was directly related to Daven and Charles's calculated exploitation of French fantasies of the exotic *nègre*. Yet the *nègres* in *La revue nègre*, he noted, were anything but pure. He thought the *danse sauvage* was "sad," as it came directly from whites "being allowed to fantasize." "These blacks, who are grotesque caricatures, have rhythm not only in their legs, but in their skin, which shudders from their heels to the roots of their hair. They sing with a very sure sense of harmony, making us think that they remember their native forest . . . They have in their eyes a childish [*puérile*] faith or an instinctive fear. They have in their gestures a disorder that often makes us confuse their frolics with the *danse de Saint-Guy!*"[9] Here, his description of the dissonant non-French elements lapsed into cliché. He reproduced linguistic tropes denoting un-Frenchness that had been used to protest against jazz since 1917, as if these tropes were necessary to convey its racial authenticity *and* its inappropriateness. As anti-jazz writers had done for years, Bizet argued that *La revue nègre*'s kinetic music was directly related to racial physiognomy: the jazz was in their "legs" and their "skin," and the *nègres* had an "instinctive fear" and an innate ability to express their sorrow. Cynically constructed or not, *La revue nègre* reinforced Bizet's belief that jazz and the jungle-like moral world associated with it was wholly un-French and totally inappropriate for French culture.

Like Bizet, *Le Figaro* critic Jacques Patin described how the jazz sounded to him like a long-vanished state of nature. He used all the standard riffs on the primitive African *nègre* to convey the state of mind this "appalling, resounding racket" aroused in modern French men and women. "In a frenetic and devilish movement, the orchestra unleashes the tempest. It seems that this music has captured all the echoes of the jungle and has mixed them with the moaning of the wind, the rustling of the leaves, the melodious songs of the birds, the howls of the beasts and the thousand cries of the *forêt sauvage.*"[10] For him, the troupe's jazz was an echo of the jungle, a "nostalgic and barbaric litany" to a wild state of being lost to modernity. Its syncopated rhythms "possessed" the "black idol" Josephine Baker, transforming her into an exotic beast who seemed perfectly at home in this state of nature. "She bends, undulates, bounces, stoops, and stands up straight, shaken by a kind of rhythmic convulsion and twisted by the most comical contortions."[11] While a critic like Bizet might have linked this string of associations, related to a lack of control, to cultural decadence, for Patin, Baker's "wildness" was a sign of her originality and naturalism, as her singing and dancing expressed a "more sure and delicate taste"[12] than did cultivated and civilized performers. Thus, for him, the cultural uproar surrounding *La revue nègre* was a symptom of an unnatural and repressed French civilization unable to appreciate its "natural" expressiveness.

By the second or third viewing, culture critics began to change their tune on *La revue nègre*'s naturalism. Many questioned the sincerity or authenticity of the music and dance and conveyed an intense ambivalence about the show. *Comoedia* critic Gustave Fréjaville, for example, put the show in historical perspective and related it to its *nègre* precursors: "[*La revue nègre*] is a tiny event in the history of the Parisian music hall. Truthfully, we have already seen almost all of this before in detail, be it in variety shows or revues."[13] There was the cakewalk in 1903, the comic team Douglas and Jones at the Bataclan, and "Princess Bainka" at the Olympia, and the Moulin Rouge had its "Colored Girls." All these other performers, he argued, "prepared our eyes for several of the effects of Josephine Baker and her company."[14] Moreover, the preponderance of jazz after the war had "accustomed our ears to even the most alarming surprises of rhythm and timbre."[15] Yet the crowds packed in to see them. It was the quality of the performance, not merely its exoticism, that made the show a success. "*La revue nègre* may have come several years too late to produce all its effect of newness. But just as possibly, it may be the fault of a progressive assimilation; have we not already tasted it for several years? The true newness of this show is, for us, in the continuity itself of its effects, the rhythm and grooving [*rainant*] of the ensemble and the personal valor of several of the artists, overall of the star, Josephine Baker."[16] This troupe of dancers and musicians gave new life to jazz in France, which he believed had suffered from several years of imitation and commercialization. Yet despite Fréjaville's analysis of its antecedents in Paris and his discussion of how such exoticism was common, he was unable to conceal his "unforgettable" surprise—and his continuity with other writers—at the sight of Baker and the Charleston Steppers. He pointed out the "eminent quality" of the authentic *jazz nègre*, with its "fluid sadness and its heartbreaking stridency, which never ceases to animate the spectacle with its demonic puffs and nuanced *frénésie*."[17] He had never heard jazz with such kinesthetic power, nor seen dancers react with such force. Though he tried to distance himself from the show's calculated exoticism, he actually underlined its continuity with other *art nègre* by quoting standard riffs on *le nègre* to describe it. Again, the discursive tensions in his description were profound. *La revue nègre* was new, but not new; it was stereotypic, yet distinctly original. Baker, though ultramodern, had a primitive rhythmic sensibility that translated into a sexuality that tormented her partner. But if Fréjaville perceived and described the tragic intensity of the "obscure force of desire" at work on the face of Joe Alex, it was because he identified with him; Josephine Baker was, for Fréjaville and many others, the exotic object of desire, and they could do little to contain the tropes of exoticism that gushed forth in their writing about her.

A particularly exemplary case of the automatic nature of some of the writing on *La revue nègre* came from Louis Léon-Martin, who reviewed the show in *Paris-Midi*. Using a kind of surrealist praxis, he copied his performance notes, so that his writing, like the music and dancing, would be more "spontaneous." The notes show the extent to which such free associations reproduced standard cultural riffs on *le nègre*. "This would be the moment to place my images. I copy: 'The jazz weaves a canopy of frenetic sounds—the dancers stir a cocktail spiced with colors—the eyes: white balls stained with onyx in faces of chewing gum—dissonances at which one undulates and which you flex as if someone pulled one of your nose hairs—*nègre* on the flute: modern Tityre pouring on the crowd of smoking jackets and nude shoulders a troubling and hysterical harmony—the movements of hips awakening the idea of a torture *à la Mirabeau,* of bad and dangerous caresses—the public brushed the wrong way, shuddering as if having tasted a lime."[18] Though one hears the standard characterizations of the "frenetic" and plastic sensibility of the *nègre* in this passage, these characteristics were again metaphorically linked to that quintessentially modern American invention: chewing gum. Once more, the revue's modern sensibility clashed with fixed ideas about the primitive *nègre,* creating dissonance and tension. For his part, Léon-Martin was aware that his analysis of the show habitually turned to literary metaphor to describe the jazz: "like that, we are always able to *faire de la littérature.*"[19] *La revue nègre* was fabricated to give audiences and critics the "authentic" *nègre* they wanted and the modern feel of jazz.

Like Fréjaville, ballet critic André Levinson questioned the newness of *La revue nègre.* In his mind, the show, "supposedly unedited, has caused in us an enjoyment *too* exactly predicted."[20] It followed, he argued, a clichéd formula about *le nègre* "ostensibly calculated"[21] for Parisian audiences. "*La revue nègre* is essentially an article of exportation. Its exoticism is adapted to European taste. It is in no way a disinterested work in the philosophical sense of the word."[22] Despite this knowledge, Levinson described being astounded by the "exceptional gifts of the black race,"[23] the improvised music, and the "rhythmic surety" of the dancers, all of which helped the show achieve a sense of communal harmony normally lacking in the French music hall. Though he knew the exoticism was choreographed and staged, Levinson could neither disavow his attraction to Josephine Baker nor keep the standard riffs associated with *la musique nègre* from creeping into his description of it. "The jazz interprets and seizes the flight, pushing and following the fantastic monologue of that crazed body. Music is born from dance, and the plastic sense of the race of sculptors and the fury of the African Eros pull us along. It is no longer some funny dancing girl that we see, it is the *Venus Noire* that haunted Baudelaire."[24] Indeed, just as Baudelaire's mistress was a recurrent figure in his poetry, the memory of Baker's dance would haunt Levinson's ballet criticism for years. In his mind, her "plastic sense," a characteristic of the "*nègre* race," made European dancers seem stiff. Levinson's analysis shows the persistence of racial stereotypes and discursive dissonance caused by applying such standard language to a spectacle that seemed to defy these tropes. As the weeks and months passed, critics continued to search for words to make sense of this ambiguous jazz spectacle.

In a sense, the critical fury surrounding *La revue nègre* paralleled the economic and cultural turmoil of the times.[25] The show quickly became a symbol of the era. The audaciousness of the show and the excited reactions of the audiences provoked the ire of conservative culture critics, who found both an affront to their sense of Frenchness. Albert Flament, for instance, found the public's fascination with the show sad, and he wrote about it in his column for the literary journal *Revue de Paris*. He described its effect as "a violent injection in the blood,"[26] which threatened to undo the peace he had found in the French countryside. Amazed that people could return for a fix again and again, Flament chastised the public for its *"furia Francese"* and noted that many critics had been so carried away with Baker's exoticism that they treated her like a new species. Critics described her "supple torso, with rhythmic arms in which the infantile and comic face offers, by the convex form of the nape of the neck, the pink ash of her color, the immensity of the eye and the shine of the pupil. These are the kinds of perfections that flatter our senses and by which a lion, a rose, a bee, a medusa, or a beaver is described."[27] Such "naturalist" descriptions of *La revue nègre* seemed a bit sad to him, showing the extent to which such music and dance dehumanized its performers. The French public, he argued, should resist such aestheticized animality in order to regain its own sophisticated humanity.

Candide's Pierre de Regnier was also amazed by the disruptive behavior of the audience at the Théâtre des Champs-Elysées. "There are people who have returned two and even six times. There are others who leave abruptly after two scenes and who slam the doors while crying of scandal, of madness, of degeneration, and of the cult of inferior gods."[28] De Regnier argued that Baker, possessed by the same disruptive spirit that animated the jazz, caused chaos in the crowd. With her modern short hair and "banana"-colored skin, she defied traditional categories of race and gender. Despite his ambivalence about *what* she was, he was clear about the ethos she represented and provoked. "That dance of a rarely seen impropriety is the triumph of lustfulness, the return of the morals of the first ages."[29] For de Regnier, Baker's ability to transcend normal categories and to evoke the "primitive" spirit in her provocative singing and dance made her art completely new. "It is pure modern art! It is magnificent!"[30]

Critic Paul Brach also saw a fascinating mixture of primitive and modern and tied this mixture to the durability of racial expression. As such, the popularity of *La revue nègre* said something about the health of true French racial sensibility in "our nervous and disordered time."[31] "Is there a *nègre* influence on our sensibility? No. But our taste for them finds itself in their sonorous poetry as if they were orchestrations of our daily emotions. We no longer live in a time for complicated romances or for psychological debates. Today we see the triumph of instinct."[32] In other words, the *nègres* had seduced the "nervous and disordered" French public by giving them the "instinctive" expression they longed for in their modern lives. This instinct, which he linked again to race, could be seen in Baker's "irreproachably frenetic legs"[33] and heard in Maud de Forrest's voice. Despite their un-Frenchness and the troupe's "innate expression of sorrow," their primitive expression had helped France to come to terms with its fractured postwar sense of self. "You have come to resuscitate, on the banks of the Seine, our gray and tired life. We thank you for having distracted us with your graceful naiveté. Unconsciously and without malice, you parody our commotion and our *déraison* [unreason] with your voices, gestures, and grimaces, covering our present troubles with a quilt of noise."[34] For Brach, the discursive dissonance had something to do with the French cognitive dissonance about modernity, its ambivalence about civilization coming at the expense of natural expression. While Brach praised the exotic otherness of *La revue nègre* for distracting Parisians from the turbulent times with a jazz that took their minds off the strikes, runaway inflation, and food shortages, other critics worried about its long-term effect on the French cultural ethos.

By December, Albert Flament was using his column in *Revue de Paris* to denounce those who believed that *La revue nègre* was good for French culture. It had, he argued, lasted too long to be "charming." Moreover, during this period of economic hardship, when droves of foreigners and Americans gained advantage from the weakness of the franc, he was disturbed by the lasting marks that American jazz had left on French popular culture. While Brach did not think that the French sensibility was under siege, Flament saw signs of foreign corruption everywhere. "As a result of snobbery, we have imitated the music halls of London. Then, with the depreciation of the franc and the exodus of Americans to France, we began to parody those of New York. In this genre of spectacles, which were formerly only Parisian, today's producers worry only about whether the foreigners will come see them or not."[35] Later that month, he again denounced the corrupting effect of jazz on "true" French sensibility and musical taste. "A woman today, after being at the theater, wants to be able to improvise and take a turn at a *dancing*.

Without needing to survey them all, the music that these *nègre-saxon* jazz bands have brought with them has dealt a rough blow to music."[36] The newness had worn off and the continued imitation of the "jazz *nègre-saxon*," perhaps coined both to deflate its status as pure *nègre* expression and to marshal anti-English sentiment, was eroding true French music. Indeed, as *La revue nègre* became more familiar, anti-jazz critics like Flament worked through their initial fascination and settled back into familiar tropes of discourse in which jazz was a foreign influence wreaking havoc on true French culture. If many culture critics were struggling to come to terms with the show, anti-jazz writers rallied their readers with standard rhetorical tropes.

Le Jazz Français

Despite the growing ambivalence about music that seemed to explode traditional notions of sensibility tied to race, conservative critics began to reject the spirit of cosmopolitan inclusion associated with French republicanism. Many thought that the popularity of *jazz nègre* was part of a larger and older problem caused by the degeneration of France's cultural borders. For instance, José Germain, whose 1923 pamphlet *Danseront-Elles?* established many of the tropes of anti-jazz writing, published an "inquiry" on the state of French culture that included opinions from protectionists, like Jean-José Frappa, who argued that jazz was but one of many external influences that continued to eat away at the purity of the French *patrie*. "For several years, France has been invaded more and more by foreigners . . . When you leave home, the taxi driver that you call is Russian; the maitre d' at the restaurant where you dine is English; the waiter who serves you is Italian; the busboy is Polish; the professional dancer of the establishment is Uruguayan; the orchestra conductor is Czech; the jazz band is composed of magnificent *nègres*."[37] The foreign invasion and influence, along with a cultural thirst for the new, Frappa believed, was corrupting the purity and consistency of "true" French culture. Critics might like jazz, he argued, but it was hard to see how they could agree with the destruction of "pure" Frenchness.

Critic Maurice Fursy further extended the case for acknowledging the Janus-faced nature of jazz influence, positing that too much foreign influence had ruined the melodic, rhythmic, and harmonic purity of *la chanson française*. He traced the decay back to before the war, when more and more foreigners settled with their music into neighborhoods like Montmartre. "The tango received its naturalization papers; it came to join the cakewalk, which we had begun long ago at the Nouveau-Cirque (there was already a *revue nègre* then, you see!)."[38] Slowly but surely, he argued, as French singers heard the music and took it to heart, the French song had been transformed, signifying a troubling "change of mentality."[39]

Not everyone saw this change as a sign of corruption. Some saw it as a sign of republican assimilation. Paul Le Flem, for one, began to rethink the implications of jazz's otherness as it continued to be heard in France onstage and on record. He believed the shift in the kind of music French people enjoyed signified something important that critics were missing: jazz was being assimilated and integrated into the modern French sensibility. "Jazz has planted itself almost everywhere. It has itself become national, on the same level as our anthem."[40] Jazz, he argued, reigned as the music of the music hall and the "apéritif-concert"; it had, symbolically, received the "key to the city," transforming artistic style and taste and winning over the masses as well as the elite. Jazz now influenced the compositions of French musicians, the books of French writers, and the paintings of French artists: "it has acquired for itself a world of enthusiastic admirers . . . Dare to deny the social value of jazz, more powerful than our fragile ministers, capable by itself of realizing a paradoxical moral unity and of intervening victoriously in the antagonism between the classes! Jazz is stronger than politics, what a miracle in our country!"[41] Thus jazz, though foreign, was a great social equalizer that only elitist critics could ignore. Why had average French people embraced it so readily? It was true, he argued, that anyone, regardless of class, could "reproduce jazz and *nègres*" with a phonograph. Yet the popularity of *jazz nègre* among Frenchmen revealed a small paradox in the relation between the enjoyment of music and the ontology of culture. Perhaps, he speculated, French people enjoying jazz was not as un-French as it might seem. Though Le Flem believed that musical taste was linked to race and culture, that *jazz nègre* was superior to commercialized *jazz blanc,* and that "European jazz is nothing but a caricature of American jazz,"[42] he also subscribed to American critic Irving Schwerke's theory—published in the Paris edition of the *Chicago Tribune*—that French plantations in America were the "cradle of jazz" and that the word *jazz* came from the French language. Thus if jazz was really not foreign and un-French, as its critics insisted, then maybe the French passion for jazz was not unnatural at all. "*Jazz* would be a simple deformation of the French word *jasé,* but written in English. Long ago, the black French slaves enjoyed reproducing the thousand noises of nature on their little self-made instruments. They chatted, "*jasaient,*" all the while making music. Thus would *jazz* be of French descent?"[43] Yet despite his assertions that jazz had French origins, he nevertheless quoted standard racialized riffs about the slaves' enjoyment and mode of expression in his telling of this origin myth. French plays the middle term between the three languages (the slaves' musical language, French, and English); it is borrowed to describe the function of the original musical luaguage that the slaves creolized in the English of their new masters. Though Le Flem maintained that the term *jazz* itself was derived from the French word *jaser,* one can see that the spirit of the music was hardly French. Nevertheless, Le Flem used *La revue nègre* to assert the idea that jazz *might be* French.

It is interesting to note that at the Empire four days later, on January 29, 1926, Harry Pilcer's band unwittingly put to the test Le Flem's theory about jazz having the same status as the national anthem. The outcry showed that the ambivalence over jazz still had strong anchors on both ends of the spectrum. It was not the first time that *La Marseillaise* had been jazzed up; Jim Europe had done it back in 1918. But given the furor, it was evident that the jazz aesthetic was, for most listeners, still out of tune and sync with deeply grounded French cultural architectonics. "Last night, all at once, we had the surprise to see them dance to the accents of *La Marseillaise!* A *Marseillaise* truly disfigured by the jazz band that played it. Spontaneous and vehement protests arose against it. One must be fair to Monsieur Dufrenne, who, warned right away, appeased the public. Believe us when we say that he took a reprimand from the audience . . . and he assured the audience that it would not be heard again."[44] It appeared that the public, even a public who had come to hear jazz, had limits on what was appropriate material to "deform" with jazz syncopation. The angry reaction of the crowd showed that *La Marseillaise,* at least, remained sacrosanct and off-limits.

Despite the extreme reactions to the music for or against, many critics argued for a middle way that reflected a kind of republican notion of cosmopolitan assimilation. Instead of jazzing up traditional French music, they sought to Frenchify jazz. For instance, Maurice Delage (1879–1961) argued in the Pleyela player-piano-company-funded *Revue Pleyel* that it was wrong to assume that jazz always had a degenerative effect on the French sensibility. To him, jazz was not the manifestation of a "racial spirit." Rather, it was a musical language that could be mastered by learning harmonic formulas and improvising on those formulas. He described how studying jazz forced French musicians into a disciplined search for individual personality. As the musician found his own expressive sound, he would quickly develop a passion for the music. One could hear an appropriately French use of the jazz language, he argued, in the piano roll recordings of Clement Doucet and Jean Wiéner, who had developed a French way of playing jazz. His description of this French jazz employed the standard discursive riffs on Frenchness usually set up in opposition to jazz. "Our time is marked by the invention of a formula that permits an instantaneous group of improvisers who, though unaware, play with the perfection of the best-disciplined orchestra. [It is] a music that sounds like it is written."[45] Whereas words like *frenetic* or *epileptic* were used to characterize *jazz nègre,* Wiéner and Doucet's jazz was an expression of "our polyphonic refinement" and revealed "a measured fantasy."[46] He thought their French approach brought a "surprising clarity" to jazz, taking the music back to its actual roots. "I believe that an unexpected circuit takes us back to Louisiana and the old foundation of the French romantic song, emphasized by its transition onto the strings of the plantation banjos, tinged minor in the touching dusk where the imported *nègres* sang from their childish and so-lively soul. The American takeover is nothing but a stage of evolution."[47] Here, by way of his evolutionary circuit, Delage joined those who sought French origins for jazz. In this case, he argued that there were French harmonies and melodies that remained strong in Louisiana even though they had been transformed by the *nègre's* "infantile soul." Indeed, he wrote that the *nègre's* repeated use of these French harmonies—*les nègres* being resistant to cultural progress— had preserved them. Ironically, he argued that the "blues are the closest, even though deformed,"[48]variant of an old French music barely alive in France. Having been kept alive in America *chez les nègres,* these old French melodies had been revived in France by Wiener and Doucet's "French blues" piano.

By following "several superficial formulas of harmony," Delage believed that other French musicians could also play "authentic" French jazz. True French jazz, he argued, would always value melody and harmony over rhythm, the inverse of the priorities expressed in *jazz nègre.* Yet he felt this preference was perfectly natural. In "truly" French jazz, rhythm would not dominate the melody and harmony but rather would support it. While "frenetic" *nègre* jazz had melismatic alterations or "slides" of tone, which he referred to as "slips" in harmonic clarity, French jazz limited these slips. Moreover, the traditional harmonies used in French jazz could help regenerate French national music. In short, he asserted that jazz, with its flexible formulas and space for improvisation, was closer in spirit to true French music than was classical music, with its fixed rules of composition. As such, he argued that rather than prohibiting jazz in France, it should be assimilated and embraced as a return of an artistic sensibility thought to be lost in the turmoil of modernity.

As we interpret these accounts, it is important to remember that Delage was promoting sales of Wiéner and Doucet's music on Pleyela player-piano rolls. Thus in order to expand the audience for the music, he needed to convince people that French jazz transcended the normal critical binaries separating authentic *jazz nègre* from commercialized white imitation. Moreover, as he constructed rules for evaluating jazz that differed from the criteria used to judge *la musique nègre,* he helped weaken the notion that authentic jazz always depended on authentic *nègre* racial expression. Rather than denouncing jazz for being the expression of an un-French *ethnos* like the *nègres d'Amérique,* he called for an assimilated jazz that expressed the "true" French character. Showing his continuity with other writers, he conveyed the nature of this French jazz and the taste for it by linking it to standard discursive riffs on Frenchness. *Le jazz français,* as he described it, was ordered, sane, and clear, the very opposite of *le jazz nègre.*

Musician Alexis Roland-Manuel (1891–1966) picked up where Delage left off in his promotion of *jazz français,* whittling away at the notion that jazz had to be pure *musique nègre* to be authentic. He described a specifically French pleasure and passion that one got from listening to Wiéner and Doucet's jazz. This tempered and assimilated jazz was incontestably musical and irrefutably French. Not all white jazz, however, was good music. A great deal of commercialized symphonic jazz revealed "bad taste."[49] This was the case with the records of Paul Whiteman, whose music was an example of the "Americanized jazz" that dominated the American cultural landscape. "The Whiteman orchestra represents the last expression of America taste."[50] Roland-Manuel bolstered the received idea that Americanized symphonic jazz was the negation of racially grounded "authentic jazz," a form now almost extinct in America. Yet his critique of aesthetic Americanization was not directed against the mechanization of musical production, of the commodification of jazz, but against the spirit of interpretation. Most importantly, he believed that, as opposed to Americans, with their "ethic of speed and an aesthetic of haste," French musicians were preserving the true spirit of jazz. While he praised those critics who preserved a taste for authentic *jazz nègre* in France and resisted Americanized jazz, he criticized the "maniacs of authenticity" who unwittingly hindered the assimilation of the jazz idiom into the French sensibility. Just because jazz was assimilated to a sensibility that differed from that of *les nègres,* he argued, did not make it commercialized and false. Wiéner and Doucet proved once and for all that jazz could be authentically French. "Jean Wiéner and Clement Doucet have acclimatized the blues to Paris. They have naturalized it French while giving it a very particular allure."[51] This technique for "acclimatizing" jazz and ennobling it consisted of "pruning the American music of anything arbitrary in its *frénésie.*"[52] By trimming the un-French *nègre* characteristics from their music, their jazz satisfied the "double need for lyricism and geometry that is so powerful in us."[53] Their *jazz françisé* was clear and ordered, and melody always took precedence over rhythm. Aping republican riffs on the civilizing mission of France, he described how these musicians had "taught a thing or two to the American music, that beautiful little savage, and had tenderly put it in its place."[54] They had, he argued, "naturalized" jazz and made it French.

For many critics, however, such ordered and clear French jazz was rarely heard and had little to do with the music animating the crowds who danced the Charleston nightly in Parisian *dancings*. The pervasiveness of the Charleston craze even reached the cinema screen, where jazz dancing was seen more and more. The post–*Revue nègre* French public did not seem to want "clarity" and melody in their jazz; they went for rhythmic levity and carnival, and music-hall producers and filmmakers responded to audience demand.[55] Yet the political tide in France seemed to react against the looseness of the times, and, following a monetary crisis in July 1926, the Cartel des Gauches government fell apart and Poincaré's right-leaning Union National reasserted itself.

Conservative critics like *L'Illustration*'s Léandre Vaillat, for their part, continued their crusade against jazz in France, calling on fellow Frenchmen to silence the "*bruit du jazz*" (noise of jazz). Like the shimmy before it, the Charleston negated the Frenchness, based on Cartesian clarity, that he sought to preserve. While the proper French sensibility craved order, jazz, he believed, stimulated "other kinds of thought,"[56] linked to the body rather than the mind. The "nasal saxophone" heard in jazz was like a "*cri de la rue*" (cry in the streets).[57] Now all that Frenchmen and women wanted to do was dance the Charleston. "If you read a book or play bridge in a corner, you are useless in 1926. Thus understand that for the crowd, the Charleston has replaced the blues and the shimmy. What will replace the Charleston? From Touggourt to Transvaal, that dance of African tribes that Iacovleff made a detailed portrait of during the *Croisière noire* [expedition] is exactly like the Charleston."[58] Again, determining if jazz was appropriate for French culture, for Vaillat, came down to whether one thought such a "hallucinatory" dance from African "physical culture" was good or bad for a French culture that, in his view, was grounded in a life of the mind. Vaillat believed it was his duty to speak out about the continued threat jazz posed to the true French way of life. Like those who equated true jazz with *la musique nègre,* anti-jazz critics like Vaillat continued to promote and protect the notion of a traditional French culture grounded in race. But with *La revue nègre* and Baker defying stereotypes of *le nègre* even as they traded on them, and jazz proponents arguing that Frenchmen could play jazz and that assimilated French jazz should also be a legitimate component of French culture, fewer and fewer critics were trying to justify fixed aesthetics based on racial purity.

Rather than evaluating jazz by way of a fixed referent, many critics argued that music was a living part of culture. Critics used one of two basic theories to make sense of jazz as a living music: evolution or hybridity. The first of these—espoused by the majority of critics from Bizet to Vuillermoz—was a variation of the theory of human evolution used to account for cultural change. Imbued with the ideology of the French *mission civilisatrice*, it held that jazz, like other cultural forms, would naturally become more "civilized." Critics who saw cultural change through this positivistic teleological lens asserted that all cultural forms progressed over time away from primitive states toward more civilized and rational forms. These critics stressed that jazz was changing from a primitive *musique nègre* into a more Europeanized and civilized art. Another smaller group of critics thought that the standard evolutionary model for culture was inadequate when faced with a phenomenon like jazz, so they began to develop something new.

Modern Ethnography and Cultural Hybridity

The critics who resisted the standard evolutionary model of cultural development thought that its positivist eschatological vision of culture made it unsuitable for explaining both the variation that existed in contemporary French music and the actual mix of ethnic and cultural influences that one heard in jazz. Jazz performers like Josephine Baker often blurred the lines between categories of music and ethnicities. Moreover, in the amazing cultural responses it had provoked all over the world, jazz showed that it had as much influence on "civilized" forms as they had on it. Certainly, the intensity of the cultural response to *La revue nègre* in France showed that the relationship of jazz to culture was anything but simple. Fascinated by its paradoxical power to provoke critics and the public, a group of surrealist ethnographers used jazz to develop a theory of cultural development that stressed hybridity and dialogic interaction as the driving factors in the development of jazz and, by extension, culture as a whole.

Ethnographers in France had long been searching for answers about the human condition and the nature of modern culture in "primitive" cultures. For instance, Lucien Lévy-Bruhl wrote *The Primitive Soul* in 1923 to depict the mentality of people who existed at the other side of the evolutionary continuum, far away from the civilized West. It was this interest in primitivism, and in the traces of the primitive found in modern life, that first drew many of them to jazz. In 1925, Lévy-Bruhl, Paul Rivet, and Marcel Mauss, three of the most influential proponents of modern ethnography, established the Institut d'Ethnologie de l'Université de Paris[59] and opened their doors to thinkers of all kinds who wanted to study other peoples in new and sometimes daring ways. Mauss had the greatest impact as a teacher, communicating to his students a taste for the irreducible strangeness of the productions of society and history.[60] This interest in the more paradoxical sides of culture attracted a group of scholars, including André Schaeffner, Michel Leiris, Marcel Griaule, and Georges-Henri Rivière, who joined them in their attempt to understand the "strangeness" of culture by confronting the differences between "civilized" cultures and the "primitive" worlds of Africa, Oceana, and South America. In the words of Leiris, who studied with Mauss and whose work would best dramatize the merger of surrealism with ethnography, "what turned me into an ethnographer was the desire to know non-European civilization, out of disgust with our civilization."[61] In 1926, Leiris's disgust for France was heightened by the colonial war raging in Morocco.[62] Yet while it was disdain for an oppressive and repressive civilization that turned this group of ethnographers away from Europe, *La revue nègre* provoked them to think about jazz as a symptom of modern hybrid culture.

Like the general public, the teachers and students at the Institut d'Ethnologie de Paris were extremely susceptible to the pull of *La revue nègre*'s Josephine Bakerized jazz on their imagination. It satisfied many of their interests. Many of the scholars, along with embracing surrealism, were active participants in the modernist quest for an authentic experience of the self through intoxication, which they sought in Montmartre jazz bars like Le Grand Duc and—a favorite with Leiris—Bricktop's, whose owner and namesake served up whiskey cocktails and smoky blues.[63] Georges-Henri Rivière, the curator of the ethnographic exhibitions at Trocadero, also moonlighted as a jazz pianist for the Ciné de la Madeleine. So it was that jazz, a form that could evoke both the primitive and the modern, both the *nègre* and the American, came to provide a perfect example of the "irreducible strangeness" of modern cultural production that Marcel Mauss stressed in his teaching. Like jazz musicians and surrealists, Mauss relied on improvisation and free association during his lectures, riveting his students with "flashes of intuition" and "unforeseen comparisons."[64] As is the case with most of the legendary jazz concerts from these early years, however, his performances went unrecorded and reach us now only through the excited testimonies of his audiences. Inspired by this Maussian "ethnologic," the ethnographers attempted to make sense of the music that had conquered Paris.

Among these ethnographers, André Schaeffner (1895–1980) was the first to turn to jazz in his work. By 1926, the forty-one-year-old Schaeffner was an established music critic.[65] Though less disgusted with European culture than the younger ethnographers like Leiris, Schaeffner shared a concern for the multiplicities and paradoxes of cultural evolution. In his view, cultures and cultural forms—and the positions from which one viewed them—were always expanding, shifting, blending, and evolving. Consequently, he approached jazz by moving back and forth between an analysis of modern Western cultures and of African or "primitive" cultures. He sought to understand how these seemingly different cultures expressed themselves in jazz. Faced with an ambiguous musical form that was neither European nor African, the old racial category *nègre* no longer seemed adequate. As a more precise signifier, Schaeffner coined a new word, *Afro-Américain,* to describe jazz's hybrid ethnos.

In June of 1926, Schaeffner began publishing his ongoing thoughts on "the music of *Afro-Américains*" in the music weekly *Le Ménéstrel.* From the start, his was an entirely new approach to thinking about jazz, and it was clear that his analysis of jazz would not be limited by its subject. He drew from a variety of sources in musicology, literature, philosophy, and ethnography; he wrote against the philosophical idea of "pure music," treating musical figures like Bach, Wagner, and Gluck; he analyzed centuries of excerpts from voyagers' encounters with African and Caribbean natives and de Gobineau's "scientific" writings on racial music; he compared old descriptions of African art to new descriptions of Afro-American jazz; he traced the genealogies of musical instruments as they spread from Africa to America. Throughout it all, Schaeffner continued to link two interrelated stories. On the one hand, there was the diachronic development of jazz. He explored jazz's African musical roots and its "creative evolution" as a heterogeneous cultural form in response to the encounter with Euro-American culture. On the other hand, he laid out what seemed to be a strange continuity among European observers describing *musique nègre* in the seventeenth century and the contemporary descriptions of *La revue nègre,* both of which were characterized by a great deal of ambivalence and ambiguity. "In *La revue nègre,* it was under the accompaniment of the drums that an acrobatic feat came to be performed in the 'turns' of the syncopation itself—the conflict between rhythm and measure—which received a full physical translation in several *tours de force.* That faculty for a music of rhythmic percussion that intervenes in all plastic action, had this not already been glimpsed in the seventeenth century by Richard Ligon in the *nègres* of Barbados?"[66] Schaeffner often based his assertions about the music on semblances that he constructed by way of metaphorical syntax.

This was a very Maussian mode of ethnographic discourse, which used un-likely juxtapositions to create interesting associations. Indeed, Schaeffner often seems to establish a Socratic relationship with the reader by posing a series of rhetorical questions in the conditional tense: "Had this not already been glimpsed?" In this way, Schaeffner asked the reader to consider what was ahistorical in *musique nègre* and what remained fixed in Europeans who heard that music. Moving between these two poles, Schaeffner presented traces of this encounter, both musical and material, which testified to the special sound of jazz as a musical phenomenon.

Along with examining the literature on modern jazz and historical ac-counts of *la musique nègre,* Schaeffner studied the African musical instru-ments on display at the Berliner Museum für Völkerkunde and the Musée Ethnographique du Trocadero. Again, he saw the same formal continuity of the instruments throughout the *nègre* diaspora that writers had "heard" in the music through the centuries. For instance, he showed how the modern xylophone used in jazz had its roots in the "ancient African balafon tradi-tion." Variations on the "same instrument"—one that used multiple blocks of wood shaped to correspond to certain sound pitches—existed in some form throughout the diaspora, and "for lack of being able to bring them along, they endlessly reproduced them with a strange exactness."[67] For him, the persistent existence of this type of instrument was material proof of a certain musical "need" that was retained and expressed by the *nègres* no matter where they were transported. Similarly, drums had been reproduced in each diasporic culture, depending on the material resources found in that culture.

When transplanted onto America soil, *les nègres* reproduced the same kind of instruments, transforming whatever was at hand to correspond to ancient needs. "It seems that in the creation of these *nègre* instruments—and it is there where the work of Africa pursues itself on American soil—one could always predict that marginal detail that permits the exercise of polyrhythm."[68] The best example was the banjo, which had its roots in the many stringed instru-ments created by Africans out of gourds with skins stretched over them as a sound box for the strings. In America, slaves developed the banjo in this familiar shape out of wood, skins, and steel strings. Though the ancestral instrument had morphed in the new cultural conditions, Schaeffner argued that it materialized the same expressive need. As such, American ragtime was a musical manifestation of this need, as it arose from the way that the slaves plucked and strummed their banjos, lilting the beat with the drone note.

While he was thinking through the influences in Afro-American jazz and the strangeness of the European response to it, Schaeffner got a chance to hear the "white jazz" of Paul Whiteman, who came to Paris in 1927. He felt that Whiteman's symphonic music was "a bit false," that it "repudiated jazz." Unlike the many musical evolutionists who saw symphonic jazz as a logical and necessary cultural development, Schaeffner labeled Whiteman's jazz artificial and unnatural, because it silenced many of the authentic sounds and rhythms that one heard in *La revue nègre.* "Between the jazz of the *Revue nègre* and this white orchestra—except for one 'colored' singer—there was all the difference as between a canoe and a transatlantic liner. Here, several *nègres* looked as if they were hooked to a rough board that the rhythm shook around; there, a supple ease in movement, everything a perfected attraction, the rallentandos and a variety of tempos that no longer respond to that forceful continuity of that singular rhythm that we have always heard in ragtime."[69] The musical opposition provided by the Whiteman orchestra gave him the final conceptual framework he needed to define Afro-American jazz and determine what made it authentic.

With the help of *La Revue Musicale* editor André Coeuroy, who contributed the last chapter (a compilation of the results of an inquiry the two had undertaken the year before in *Paris-Midi*[70]), Schaeffner published the first monograph on jazz in French: *Le jazz.* He immediately set himself apart from previous writers by giving up the search for jazz's exact origin or ontology, as both were "too covered with legends for us to uncover them."[71] Schaeffner's mode of exposition was to place different "traces" of *musique nègre*—musical instruments, rhythmic patterns, harmonic modes, and dance steps—next to centuries of European writing on such music. Jumping back and forth in this way as it works its way to the present, *Le jazz* serves as a perfect example of what James Clifford has called "polyphony and counterpoint" in ethnographic writing.

In *Le jazz,* Schaeffner argued that each ethnic group had forms that corresponded to its spirit: its songs, its musical instruments, its dances, or its philosophies. Yet no group sang, played, or danced only its own "inventions" or used them for only one purpose. For Schaeffner, "pure music," as a phenomenological category or as a Kantian ideal for music criticism, was philosophically untenable, having nothing to do with the actual cultural practice and production of music, which always involved cultural exchange and interaction. Rather than describing jazz in relation to pure music, be it European or *nègre,* Schaeffner hinted at an ambiguous quality that made jazz authentic. As an antidote to such Kantian idealist criticism, his exposition, like the surrealists', was Nietzschean in its emphasis on the metamorphosis of form and the genealogy of cultural values[72]: "For this 'purity,' is this not on the whole the negation of what would, in music, make one believe in an expression of sentiment? So is it not more about the mark of an ambiguous or *amphibiological* quality of the means of musical expression—the unceasing ability of each to be itself and to respond contradictorily to our questions and needs?"[73] Like the surrealists, Schaeffner abandoned the distinction between high and popular culture and portrayed jazz as a perfect example of a hybrid art that exploded these categories. *Le Jazz Afro-Américain* had that *amphibiological* quality, both "a baggage of expression" with "strangely little variation" and, at the same time, an appropriation of modern Western musical forms blended together by rhythmic enjoyment. "Born in the torrid air of Africa," the syncopation driving jazz was guided by physiology (body) rather than by ideas (mind). "We ask ourselves if the pleasure of beating a drum is born of the need not only for marking the rhythm, but of participating still in some manner in a general gesticulation."[74] Schaeffner asserted that this African musical spirit came from a racially determined physiological need to participate in collective rhythm. Theirs was a kind of polyrhythmic language that had conquered three continents with its simple expression of sentiment. Yet just as the jazz musicians found their rhythm by pushing one another along, so, too, did Schaeffner, the ethnographic subject, locate himself through the push and pull, the constant provocation provided by the object of criticism. In so doing, Schaeffner was developing a way of understanding the self and other that was, itself, amphibiological in its attempt to understand the plastic evolution of both sides of the phenomenon: the music, with its double nature, and the Western critic's ambiguous relation to that music.

Schaeffner confronted the ambivalent nature of European responses to the strangeness of *la musique nègre* with his bold syntax of assertion and association: "We can ask ourselves if the same encounter between animal and vegetable, between art and an always latent fetishism, is what troubles us: it escapes us how a music can exist that remains physiological at base and, in some way, is engaged in nature or mixed with the practice of magic."[75] Was this, he asked, not the reason why one always seemed to hear the same kind of Western description of the music as an echo of this encounter? Like the music itself, the defining characteristics of European writing on it were ambivalence and ambiguity. If anything, Schaeffner posited, the most striking similarities between the accounts of the music were the strange attraction it provoked in the occidental observer. "Maybe the discovery of *la musique nègre* coincides *for us* with the dominance of an abusive gaze before which minute divisions between genres are created in the consideration of musical phenomena?"[76] The music was strange for French listeners because it did not fit into Western categories and seemed to defy traditional musicological analysis. Yet for the *nègre*, the music was perfectly natural, as his body carried "the ideal itself of all his music."[77] The uncanniness of the music could thus be attributed to the reception and categorization of the music *"for us."* For the modern French listener, jazz corresponded to a need for simplicity and liberation from "occidental art, saturated with harmony and orchestration,"[78] but the apprehension of this pleasure was constrained by an "abusive gaze," its enjoyment made ambivalent by an occidental taxonomic desire.

Schaeffner tried to avoid echoing the critical traps and stereotypes he had noted in the works of others as he described how African music had evolved into Afro-American jazz. Rather than attributing its origin to one person or one place, he attributed the creation of jazz to a diasporic musical taste[79] and way of using instruments. Jazz was, he argued, rooted in a *"nègre* usage," in particular the ability to "deform" harmony and meter, which was conveyed through several tendencies related to the concept of plasticity, a character-istic linked routinely to race in French writing on art and music. The *nègre*, he wrote, was "happy to mix and manipulate the elements that he seizes or reappropriates."[80] This enjoyment of appropriating things in a way that was expressive of the self underlined the transformation of African music into hybrid Afro-American jazz. As the Western song forms and musical instru-ments were transformed, a new art emerged.

> The music of the *nègres* of Africa and America restores in our eyes the spec-tacle of a properly elementary art, bound more closely to the conditions of their native sun than ours. We discover something plantlike in it, as much through the construction and the timbre of its instruments as by the bold-ness of its push and by the longevity through which its songs carry the mark, in their supple way, adapting themselves indistinctly to all expression, be it of joy or of sadness. From the violent music of Africa to the songs of the fieldworkers in the Antilles or Louisiana, to the spirituals, and finally to jazz, it is never anything other than a musical fact with strangely little variation: a baggage of expression reduced to a minimum, an unsettling simplification that nevertheless has enabled it to conquer three continents.[81]

Thus the metamorphosis of jazz in America, Schaeffner argued, began with the transplantation of the *nègre* into slavery, when all that was retained of Afri-can culture was the bodily memory of music and dance. "He was able to leave Africa naked and to listen to himself in order to rediscover the primordial elements of his art."[82] Schaeffner posited that the "melancholic character of song" and the "subtle and unconscious syncopation"[83] that one heard in jazz could be heard all over Africa. This was because the African song forms and American chord changes had evolved into Afro-American hybrids. Schaeffner "proved" this with another ethnologic assertion: "And the ambiguous character of the dominant major mode, would this not be the origin of those diminished seventh chords that are always found in Afro-American songs, in the blues, in the harmonies of jazz?"[84] These hybrid harmonic forms, he noted, were strongest in America in areas where slaves were the most concentrated, "where the memory of African dances was still alive [and] established a home favorable to the elaboration of jazz."[85] The nature of this amphibiological evolution of jazz, the mixing of African sensibilities and European cultural forms, had much to do with the social parameters that determined how the races interacted with each other after the emancipation of the slaves.

Schaeffner quoted a standard Tocquevillian riff on the condition of slaves in America, arguing that the former slaves, though officially free, were kept on the outside of American culture. Their access to freedom and enjoyment, and hence the basis of their particular hybrid subjectivity, came from taking the Western cultural forms they found around them and making them their own; appropriation was achieved by way of an "unconscious syncopation" that marked everything in *Afro-Américain* life. This innate rhythm, he stressed, altered musical forms as well as instruments, both of which were made to correspond to certain expressive needs.[86] In Schaeffner's view, the African spirit also bent notes and changed harmonies. This melismatic tendency, he argued, was linked to the plastic potential and "inimitable timbre" of the *nègre* voice. It explained how the Afro-Americans had transformed the Protestant hymns of their white masters, bending and blending them to correspond to the African modalities that resonated in their bodies. First the "coon song" and then the Negro spiritual, two of the most distinctly Afro-American forms, issued from this amphibiological expressive need. The blues also resulted from this cultural blend.

Schaeffner believed that jazz really became possible when modern instruments were appropriated, instruments whose precision and range, when played with both the rhythmic and melodic spirit, allowed for the most complete expression of the Afro-American musical sensibility. "Without a doubt, this is the moment at which their great familiarity with our horns, notably with the range of saxophones, began, a familiarity that led to the elaboration of jazz as it is today . . . it is that double superimposition of Protestant hymns and modern instruments that permitted the primitive orchestras of the *nègres* of Africa to reappear in our time under the more civilized, though just as brutal, mask of jazz!"[87] Just as this Afro-American sensibility as expressed by the ragtime banjo had transformed the American musical scene in the nineteenth century, jazz had overwhelmed American music after World War I. Yet Schaeffner argued that its popularity, and the extent to which white America identified with it, was also of an ambiguous nature. "Accepted by whites, that musical form will sometimes seem to turn itself against them, like a soft protest. It knows how to seduce them under a variety of disguises."[88] The "soft protest" of modern *Afro-Américain* jazz, with its "mode of prayer, moaning, and nostalgia,"[89] touched the guilty heart of white America. Yet given the racial division in American culture, it was not surprising that the white musicians who assimilated the Afro-American music back into mainstream culture were more successful than the former slaves who developed it. For instance, Schaeffner paralleled the celebrity and music of Stephen Foster, inspired by "the first troops of *nègre* minstrels, with their banjos and tambourines,"[90] to that of Irving Berlin, who "did not wait for the authentic lesson of jazz to perfect himself and be widely known."[91] In each case, whites commercially reappropriated the amphibiological innovation. Moreover, each time the hybrid music of the Afro-American became the popular music of America, it had had a tremendous impact on France.

Schaeffner postulated that the postwar French public's strange fascination with jazz was due to the rhythmic and sonic links between jazz and the sounds of modern technological culture. When jazz arrived in France, it found a culture still reeling from the rhythmic violence of modern war and industrial society, with its "pulsation of locomotives and the spinning of propellers." The pulsation, he speculated, rendered people susceptible on a primitive or subconscious level to rhythm. This susceptibility to rhythm, "as if invisibly restored in the wrestling of modernity," explained the success of *La revue nègre*. The unleashing of such primitive instinct, he argued, was good for Western art and culture. Indeed, Schaeffner believed that jazz, this new hybrid Afro-American form at "the extreme opposite of our occidental art," could contribute to a "new start" for French music and could teach valuable lessons not only about the complexity of popular music, but also about the hybridity of all modern cultural production. Moreover, the amphibiological spirit behind jazz, ever able to adapt and appropriate any cultural form and lend it meaning, testified to the state of mind that the ethnographer should strive to emulate as he tried to understand culture. Yet it is instructive that Schaeffner's own mode of exposition, with its conditional statements, complex syntax, and constant qualifications, remained ambivalent. His ethnologic intuition told him he was hearing hybrid Afro-American music, but he was still uncertain about its ambiguous nature.

André Coeuroy added the final chapter, or coda, for *Le jazz*, a reprint of his published piece on France's relationship to jazz, titled "La romantisme du jazz."[92] Lacking Schaeffner's ethnographic chops, Coeuroy used an entirely different mode of exposition to present his findings. Yet though he did not share Schaeffner's ambiguous amphibiological mode, Coeuroy presented a French public split in their opinions about the aesthetic value and cultural implications of jazz. He quoted excerpts from the *Paris-Midi* inquiry and analyzed several contemporary literary works that used jazz as a metaphor for modern life.[93] There were those who still considered jazz extremely suspect. Symphony conductor Pietro Mascagni, an Italian in Paris, thought that all "governments should ban jazz like morphine and cocaine; that music does nothing but degrade the taste and morale of the public."[94] Jacques Heugel, editor of the music weekly *Le Ménéstrel*, believed the taste for jazz was a "sign of decadence." He questioned those who called *jazz nègre* "primitive" music, as he believed the *nègre* race was no longer primitive in the Rousseauian sense. "We pretend, I know it well, that by joining ourselves with the *nègres*, we rejoin primitive humanity. I believe nothing of this, having reason to think that the black race is not a primitive race, but a degenerate successor of a primitive race that offers us nothing but a caricature of the first humanity. If we Aryans follow the *nègres* body and soul . . . we risk quite simply falling into a roughly apelike vulgarity, as these apelike forms are also degenerate human forms."[95] In this light, *jazz nègre* was the degenerate music of a degenerate race. In short, Heugel felt that jazz was a symptom of cultural decay in the West that threatened the musical and cultural essence of all pure cultural forms, be they primitive or those representative of "Aryan humanity."

Coeuroy balanced such racist or protectionist denunciations with the words of proponents like Pierre Mac Orlan, who provided an example of a modern French sensibility that embraced jazz. "Mac Orlan," he wrote, "has clearly seen that the rhythms of cerebral pleasure have today descended into the street and that our sentimental and public existence mixes itself closely with jazz."[96] Thus it did not matter where or from what race the music came, only what it meant for people today. Along with Mac Orlan, Coeuroy noted that two short stories, "Surimpressions" by Jean Guermonprez and "Projections" by Albert Cohen, both explained jazz's popularity by linking its "primitive" rhythms to the subconscious rhythms of modern life. As such, many modern artists, including filmmakers, poets, and composers, linked their aesthetics to jazz. Coeuroy's final expressive flurry validated this fascination: "The instruments of jazz are our pipers . . . It is life. It is art. It is the intoxication of sounds and noises. It is animal joy in supple movements. It is the melancholy of the passions. It is us today."[97]

Hybridity as Assimilation

Schaeffner's new explanation of jazz, which made hybridity a mix of cultural influences subordinated to the African spirit of performance, clashed with standard takes on the music, and many writers tried to resolve the discursive and cognitive dissonance. Many critics adopted *Le jazz*'s idea of jazz as a hybrid music but reframed the question of hybridity, sometimes in peculiarly strategic ways. For instance, in his review of *Rhapsody in Blue* at *L'Artistic*, André Tessier panned Gershwin's *composition* because it lacked authentic "Afro-American genius." Because of this lack, he labeled it " hardly anything but the bric-a-brac of sentimental Anglo-Saxon romance."[98] Though Tessier accepted that jazz involved cultural assimilation and that it could be authentic without being pure jazz *nègre,* he frowned upon overly "Anglo-Saxon" assimilated jazz. Some critics continued to use the term *nègre* as a discursive opposite with which to describe French jazz. Even Coeuroy, despite his relationship with Schaeffner's work, retained *nègre* as a qualifier. In reference to Gabriel Pierné's jazz-inflected ballet *Naila,* he called this jazz "transposed into bourgeois style," but the lack of *nègre* characteristics did not cause him to denounce it: "It has neither swaying nor epilepsy . . . The allusions to jazz are softened, and the frenetic drumming of the *nègre* orchestras is supplanted by a calm bass drum."[99] For Coeuroy, eliminating the *nègre* characteristics—again conveyed through standard discursive signifiers like *epilepsie* and *frénésie*— had calmed the affect and the ethos of the music, lending the music a positive salutary value: this jazz was more healthy and more French.

Some critics accepted tacitly the notion of hybridity in jazz but inverted the hierarchies to reflect a sense of republican cosmopolitanism. For instance, André Jeanneret (the brother of architect Le Corbusier) embraced the idea of a mixed cultural form but questioned the extent to which that mix was African. Drawing on stereotypes about fixed *nègre* characteristics, he agreed that the *nègre* had a "powerful instinct"[100] for rhythmic music and dance. Yet he believed that this rhythmic instinct had been Americanized in jazz, where musical time was strictly organized. "That which the *nègre* learned from the American was the value of time; a time secured, organized, and held tightly. Sign of a modern mentality. That is the lesson of America."[101] Like Heugel, who argued that the *nègres* who created jazz were degraded "primitives," Jeanneret argued that American *nègres* were "Taylorized" *nègres* whose modernized mentality enabled them to organize time into effective units. Jazz had, he wrote, conquered the world because of the modern method through which it was produced. Moreover, it was pushed on cultures through the power of mass media and American-style commercial publicity. Yet though he worried about the effect of commercialism on culture, he did not believe jazz was a threat to French culture. Indeed, the lesson he drew from the success of jazz was that French musicians needed to learn to modernize their own music. Joining the "instinctual element" of French music with modern means of organization could "orient our musical creation toward a new sentiment of order and economy."[102]

Even as the notion that authentic jazz depended on racial purity was losing its hold on the French imagination, the court system made a ruling on a case of contract law, relating to the hiring of a jazz band, which gave governmental standing to racially authentic "jazz noir." *Le Ménéstrel* editor Jacques Heugel reported on the case sarcastically: "The tribunals have come to proclaim: a true jazz should be composed of blacks; all the white jazz bands are false jazz, ersatz."[103] The trial related to an incident in 1924, when the Empire theater had booked a band composed of five blacks. On the day of the concert, a white musician replaced one of the black players and the director of the Empire canceled the contract. The tribunal of the Seine took four years to decide in favor of the Empire theater and give standing to the authenticity of "jazz noir."

Yet despite such juridical clarifications, the imaginary picture of the pure *nègre* and of *jazz nègre* became more and more blurry. This blurring is well dramatized by the commercial transformation of Josephine Baker. Everywhere she played, and even where she did not, her increasingly white hybrid image surfaced in poster advertisements. For instance, an advertisement for Chappée Lessiveuse, a soap product, portrayed a dark African figure opening a tin of Chappée and being frightened by the sight of a woman uncannily resembling Josephine Baker, who is so "clean" that all her color is gone.[104] Similarly, by 1927, the Josephine Baker hairstyle was so popular that a product called Baker-Fix was developed so that white French women could achieve Baker's racially ambiguous plastered-down look. Paul Colin, who had done the original poster work for *La revue nègre,* built a career around reproducing various hybrids of the Baker image, culminating in the publication of his portfolio *Le tumulte noir.*[105] Journalist Marcel Sauvage also cashed in on the craze by compiling press reviews of Baker and publishing them with Baker's own account of her rise from the streets of St. Louis to Parisian stardom in *Les mémoires de Josephine Baker.* The tale, which began to sound more and more like the republican story of a French colonial being civilized, included Baker's advice on how to dance the Charleston, fashion tips, and recipes for "authentic" Afro-American cuisine, like beans and rice. Onscreen in the film *La sirène des Tropiques,* which she later claimed to have made without being able to read the script,[106] she played the figure of Papitou, a colonial from the Antilles who, having heard music on French colonial radio, wants to come to Paris to dance. In Paris, a clever promoter sees Papitou in the Jardin des Tuileries dancing uncontrollably to the sound of a jazz banjo. Placed onstage, she conquers the town with her frenetic dancing and exotic good looks. Indeed, the dazzling French colonial who makes the pilgrimage to the *métropole* would soon become Baker's French stage and screen persona, later repeated in films like *Princess Tam-Tam* and *Zouzou*. By 1927, "La Baker" was a bankable commodity, and though she blurred the line between the primitive and the modern, the African and the American, and black and white, she increasingly represented the idea of republican assimilation in the French imaginary.

The idea that hybridity followed the cultural patterns of republican assimilation was a powerful one. Musicologist and composer Arthur Hoérée (1897–1986) took on Schaeffner along these lines and tried to invert the whole notion of racial authenticity and influence in jazz. While Schaeffner thought the Afro-American spirit of jazz was what made it authentic, Hoérée focused on the formal elements of the music that lacked this spirit to get at the essence of jazz. Hoérée examined the "proper laws" of the thirty-two-bar song form and the standard rhythms employed in the majority of French jazz. He agreed with other critics that *la musique nègre* was an important part of the story, but he questioned the importance of the African influence in most jazz as it was actually played. He argued that the overvaluation of jazz's African elements was related to the French love of the exotic and the avant-garde desire to get beyond traditional European music. "Finally, in guise of a conclusion: 'I belong to the white race.' And that is the great grief! But jazz, as I will touch on and demonstrate below, finds itself at the intersection of several races and several cultures. If one counts the heterogeneous elements, only two-sixths of the musical gifts are *nègre*, and, again, one of these two elements, rhythm, is common to Arabs, as well."[107] In fact, Hoérée asserted that if one examined the evolution of the jazz song form, one found that most of its roots were in European music rather than in *la musique nègre*. Thus if one boiled jazz music down to its essential elements, it was a hybrid form in which the European elements were dominant.

Hoérée acknowledged the value of Schaeffner's fine historical analysis, which underlined the "paradoxes" of jazz's evolution, but he disagreed with the racial genealogy that the ethnographer had developed. "The complexity of the problem—the origins of jazz, as I noted above, being considerable— induced Schaeffner to follow a rather special path to arrive at certain highly interesting conclusions."[108] While Schaeffner focused on the syncopated rhythms in jazz, Hoérée argued that rhythm was only of secondary importance, especially in the jazz music and dances heard in France after the war. "It would seem, *a priori,* that the musical history of jazz follows closely the choreographic history of the foxtrot, which to this day remains the archetype of jazz dance."[109] Essentially, Hoérée argued that the dance steps and music forms used by jazz bands and dancers were derived from prewar forms, before the *nègre* influence asserted itself. Though the music was American, and though the *nègre* jazz bands had been the most popular, French musicians like Wiéner and Doucet had demonstrated that they could improvise using these forms, as well. "Jazz today, despite its stylistic unity, is a heterogeneous composite where the rhythmic, harmonic, melodic, and instrumental processes do not come from a common origin but are the result of a fusion of racial elements and different aesthetics."[110] Thus jazz's present-day form—its sheet music and its dance steps—had many origins, and most of them were European. Schaeffner's problem, Hoérée argued, was that he had fixated on the *"usage nègre"* of the drums and on the manner of interpreting jazz music. Rather, jazz was "a *nègre* interpretation of an art of the white race with an European origin . . . Through reason alone, we can see that throughout its evolution, jazz became more seductive when the European elements dominated clearly in its language."[111] In short, his analysis was based on the notion that the musical forms for the foxtrot were around before jazz arrived and had been momentarily *interpreted* as jazz. And as jazz evolved, the fixed *nègre* elements were being eliminated again by the influence of reason and logic. His was, after all, a story of cultural evolution toward "civilized perfection."

Even if the *nègre* "deformation" of rhythm and music brought something new to jazz, Hoérée noted that their rhythmic contributions became standardized through familiarity and repetition. Like the foxtrot, the song forms associated with jazz had come to be dominated by certain rhythmic formulas. The most common formula in sheet music, he argued, was the juxtaposition of a 3/8 measure over the 4/4 measure, but again, this was not a *nègre* trait. "It was Irving Berlin, the father of jazz, who codified the formula. His most reputed spiritual son is George Gershwin, author of the *Symphony in Blue* [*sic*]."[112] Thus, in most jazz, it was not the *nègre* interpretive spirit that dominated, but rather the spirit of American assimilation employed by Tin Pan Alley songsmiths to rein in the heterogeneous elements of jazz. Jazz today, he wrote, was the music of a "white hegemony that had consciously ordered the *nègre* characteristics," a "perfected jazz that was civilized and reached for new heights."[113] In an American culture that was organized and had evolved by way of a logic of order and assimilation, it was no surprise for Hoérée that the language of jazz had been codified by the master songwriters of the "Jewish race, whose power of assimilation we know."[114] Thus jazz form showed a "unity crystallized in the mold,"[115] but this unity resulted from a blending of characteristics through the process of assimilation: "over all those forms that those of Jewish origin used with their assimilating power."[116] In its present form, jazz was a hybrid, assimilated music made up of European harmony, Protestant melodies, and *nègre* rhythm juxtaposed over European meter, all codified and disseminated through Jewish formulas.

For Hoérée, the evolution of such assimilated jazz was not a sign of commercial corruption, but of republican civilization. Since this jazz was no longer *sauvage*, it was now acceptable in a civilized country like France. Importantly, if one followed Hoérée's logic, one could see oneself as a civilized Frenchman and still enjoy jazz. "Those who detest *art nègre* do not have to detest jazz. It has evolved, has perfected itself, and is susceptible to renewal. It is living."[117] As for those who opposed jazz in France despite its civilized evolution, Hoérée believed that "only reactionaries who are in love with the past can detest it."[118] He closed by echoing Coeuroy's phrase on jazz: "It is us today."

Schaeffner quickly responded to Hoérée by affirming his commitment to Afro-American music as the "authentic" jazz. He accused Hoérée of refusing to recognize the importance of "*nègre* elements" in jazz. Hoérée's blindness, he argued, stemmed from his preoccupation with the foxtrot, which marked "the most white and most European period of jazz."[119] In his desire to claim jazz as a largely European music, Hoérée overvalued the European musical form and neglected the Afro-American essence. In short, Schaeffner postulated that it would have been impossible for white culture to create jazz, as its hybrid development depended upon the "*fantaisie du nègre*": "Place a white and a *nègre* in similar conditions of isolation, new Robinsons on a desert isle. It is more probable that the *nègre* would quickly shed these musical objects, which come from his body itself, and surround himself with primitive orchestra instruments to underline his dance and song. Withdrawing into himself, would not the *nègre* discover this sonorous shadow of himself, one over which the white race itself possesses no right of priority?"[120] The *nègre* would always naturally use whatever was available to make the music that resonated in his body. Schaeffner remained convinced that the tendency to appropriate and shape sound was the essential characteristic of jazz. Hoérée, on the other hand, based his characterization of jazz on the outcome of the white tendency to codify and order music, a characteristic that negated the *esprit nègre*. Schaeffner was sure that it was the Afro in Afro-American jazz that made the music what it was: "At the origin, there was always an authentically *nègre* starting point—when there weren't, several times, the *nègre* made a return, thanks to the deformative power of those jazz instruments."[121] Schaeffner argued that the antiformal or deformative "spirit," rather than the form of the sheet music, made jazz music authentic. One needed only to compare Paul Whiteman's jazz to the music of *La revue nègre* to hear this difference. "Between the Whiteman orchestra and the jazz of *La revue nègre*, in their interpretation and their repertoire, have we not perceived an irreducible difference? Everything is there."[122] When Hoérée responded again, he conceded that the *nègre* element was an important one but explained that he had been interested in studying the kinds of arrangements that dominated the sale of records and the performance of jazz in France.[123] He was describing jazz as it was, he argued, rather than jazz as it should be.

Both Hoérée and Schaeffner offered models of hybrid cultural formation through their description of jazz. Schaeffner offered one in which the African spirit blended together the various cultural elements and gave reign to the individual in the moment of performance to make them his own. Hoérée, on the other hand, offered an analysis of the formal properties of sheet music, which David Looseley has argued was the dominant commodity form for consuming French pop music at the time.[124] His notion of hybridity stressed the subordination of disparate cultural elements to a rational order. Schaeffner was intent on capturing the elusive amphibiological qualities of the authentic jazz performance; Hoérée wanted to show that this spirit could be, and had been, assimilated in the commodity song form.

Yet though many critics and musicians adopted Schaeffner's thesis that *la musique des Afro-Américains* was the most original and authentic jazz, they continued to argue that the French jazz they played was authentic *for them* as they were improvising according to their own sensibilities. For instance, Jean Wiéner (1896–1982), the most famous French jazzman, believed that his French jazz was liberated from the "tyranny of the metronome" that constrained European music. Jazz improvisation set him free. He explained the pleasure of jazz improvisation in *Conferencia*, arguing that his French jazz was "natural" because it was grounded in something supremely human. "And there is all the prestige of jazz: music of heart, music of legs, music of the circulation of blood. Based on a logic and made of the elements of life itself. We savor it without hearing it, we dance it, and we sing it. It has become a part of our existence and will never be able to leave us; it will always help us."[125] As opposed to the strict cadences of military marches, jazz rhythm was subtle and based on a "regularized automatic foundation" grounded in the "movement of the normal walk of man."[126] For Wiéner, jazz improvisation symbolized the freedom of choice, the freedom to choose how to express oneself in the present. More than any particular ethnic or racial rhythm, jazz had a universal "human" rhythm that a cosmopolitan France needed to regain its equilibrium in modern times. Alas, Robert Pepin, who reviewed a Wiéner and Doucet concert at the Pau theater, agreed that hearing jazz in France conveyed volumes about the proper choice of expression. "Inebriation of sound and noise, animal joy of supple movements, as A. Coeuroy said. Without a doubt, and nothing but, it is a strong representative of our unfortunate time."[127] In short, Pepin criticized Wiéner and Doucet for choosing the "disarticulate" jazz idiom over French clarity and order. It was, for a critic like him who still believed that "true" French culture was linked to a homogeneous ethnic ethos, a sad sign of the times.

Yet with commercialized jazz dominating the cultural scene in music halls, clubs, bars, and dance halls, the ethnographers continued to voice their opinion as to what kind of jazz was "authentic." Indeed, it was Michel Leiris (1901–1990) who would bring the ethnographic description of authentic Afro-American jazz to its most complete conceptualization and fullest expression.[128] Leiris shared Schaeffner's interest in cultural hybridity and took this notion in new directions as he mixed ethnography and surrealism in his analysis of jazz and culture. During the mid-1920s, Leiris had played an active role in André Breton's surrealist circle and passionately supported its anarchist politics during the colonial war in Morocco.[129] By 1929, Leiris had broken with Breton and had come into his own as a writer and cultural critic. A jazz fanatic who lived the lush life in a number of Montmartre jazz bars, Leiris returned to jazz as an object for cultural analysis after the arrival of two American imports: Lew Leslie's Blackbirds, a touring musical troupe, and the new sound film *Hallelujah,* by King Vidor. At a time when France was being inundated by "white jazz," like that heard in new Hollywood "talking films" such as *The Jazz Singer, The Singing Fool, Broadway Melody,* and *Fox Follies,* as well as popular phonograph recordings, Leiris's impressions of the June 11, 1929, Blackbirds show reveal his excitement: "That revue has absolutely none of the character of an item for export that there was . . . with Josephine Baker . . . everything is more pure and naive."[130] With this perception that the Blackbirds represented unmediated and authentic artistic expression, they quickly became the new prototype of "authentic" jazz for Leiris and the surrealist ethnographers.

Leiris and the surrealist ethnographers, especially the students of Marcel Mauss, were some of the era's most creative and innovate thinkers about culture. In *Documents,* a new eclectic journal edited by Georges Bataille, their brand of surrealist ethnography would reach its fullest expression and the notion of hybridity in culture would reign supreme. The *bricolage* form of *Documents,* dramatized by its subtitle, "Archeology, Beaux Arts, Ethnography, Variety," was itself an expression of a kind of surrealist polyphony: it brought together articles, fragments, curious collections, and disparate images in the service of an ethnographic confrontation with and between cultures.[131] The value-laden cultural categories most French culture critics used were leveled through metaphoric juxtapositions, sometimes to the point of creating absurd associations that supported an ironic relativism vis-à-vis different cultures; the *Documents* critic's job was to decode, devalue, and displace these categories and the hierarchies they constructed. The writing with which they did so, in the words of contributor Carl Einstein, was to be a "psychogram" of the dynamic confrontation between cultures and genres, a spontaneous writing created "at the speed of the psychological processes."[132] Indeed, it was in *Documents* that the surrealist poetics of free association, which sought to emulate jazz improvisation, were harmonized with the flashes of ethnologic intuition that one hears from many of Mauss's students.

In a piece titled "Civilization," which perfectly exemplifies this spontaneous ethnologic, Leiris theorized about the important function that "limit-experiences"—engendered by overwhelming desire—served as ideological anchors in modern culture. Using Maussian phrasing, he argued that the forms, morals, tastes, and manners through which Western society had civilized itself barely concealed its "*sauvagerie.*" Like the "thin green layer—living magma and varied rubbish—that forms at the surface of calm waters,"[133] these surface conceits were constantly separating and breaking down. The wildness in man was constantly appearing through the interstices, revealing itself through the cracks in this slimy civilized layer. Indeed, one could say that Leiris and the surrealist ethnographers sought to create limit experiences to crack the civilized mask. They wanted the primitive in modern man to show his face. Lew Leslie's Blackbirds dramatized the disruptive force that Leiris sought to capture as they provoked the liberating transgressive desire he had in mind. The scene from the show that best expressed the power of their jazz was titled "Porgy," and it depicted the black population of a southern town gathering to mourn in the wake of a lynching: "When a black man is murdered and he is poor, all the blacks in the village gather in a circle and create, with their songs, a sort of hysteria that pushes the men to rape and the women to sell themselves to whites, in order to get enough money to bury the dead."[134] Leiris believed that the jazz and dancing of the

Blackbirds, when they worked themselves into a frenzy in scenes like this one, caused a similar unleashing of repressed instinct among members of the French audience. Yet the Blackbirds' power over them was not merely a result of the call of the exotic; nor was the temporary identification with the singers and dancers merely the result of transferential guilt from seeing blacks suffer. Leiris had been moved by something more.

> What is beautiful in this art is not its exotic side, nor that it contains the strictly modern (this modernism is nothing but pure coincidence), but rather that it doesn't constitute an Art proper. It seems, in effect, eminently absurd to apply to these clear and spontaneous productions that awful, majestic word . . . certainly, it is evident that jazz, and that which is derived from it, has its rules and logic, but that is not enough to force us to call it Art, Great Art, like this or that work which is known (or believes itself) to inspire . . . Spectacles like the Blackbirds revue bring us short of Art, at the point of human development where it has not yet been overdeveloped like that bastard concept, where it is the fruit of illegitimate love, of magic and free play . . . [Jazz] doesn't sing, as we say, "the eternal regrets that pierce our hearts," but we can say inversely that in listening to it, we suffer a terrible regret: regret of being so dreadfully incapable of such a simple and beautiful expression, regret of being mediocre, of living a mediocre life so flat and ugly compared to these creatures who sway like trees.[135]

For Leiris, then, jazz confronted the occidental listener with the mediocrity of existence; the Western mind, mucked and mired in civilized forms and categories, was capable of producing only "Art" that left one flat and suffered the regret of its inability to touch the same profoundly human source of inspiration. Alas, Leiris seemed to be saying, even really good jazz offered only momentary flashes of the real. It brought listeners only temporary relief from the human condition. Though the emotional charge from such jazz spectacles was powerful, "they are nonetheless unable to vanquish completely our spinelessness and engender a hysteria large enough . . . a hysteria so intense that it would be capable of pushing spectators to immediate realizations of sordid acts or of extravagant debaucheries."[136] In other words, jazz had revolutionary potential only while it lasted. In the act of recollection, this momentary magic was always already lost. After a brief experience of transgressive hysteria, the murky layer of civilization, with all its rules, conventions, and logics, returned to shroud over subjectivity. As Billy Strayhorn later noted after the experience of his Paris trip melted into memory, life was awful again for those who were sad and lonely, too.

Like Leiris, Schaeffner penned a piece on the Blackbirds that glorified their jazz as an antidote to the hegemony of "Great Art."[137] However, no writer at *Documents* was more concerned with debunking cultural hierarchies and revealing the inadequacy of language to describe intense experiences than editor Georges Bataille (1897–1962). Whereas Schaeffner and Leiris had complicated the hybrid cultural evolution of jazz and emphasized the philosophical dilemmas that one encountered as a culture critic when describing such a hybrid cultural form, Bataille's appraisal of the Blackbirds trained his jazz-inspired gaze onto the shifting foundation of the critical subject. In the running column "Dictionnaire," he harnessed the positive emotion of transgressive thinking by exploding official classifications and normative definitions through a surrealist poetics of free association and unlikely juxtaposition. One could say that Bataille took his cue from one of Mauss's profound aphorisms: "Taboos are made to be violated."[138] It was here that Bataille took ethnographic cultural criticism to its extreme limits.

In his dictionary entry on the Blackbirds, Bataille made jazz criticism—and all knowledge, for that matter—more about the inevitable projection of desire onto the object of consciousness than the qualities of the music itself. If the amphibiological procedure of the surrealist ethnographer moved back and forth between the self and other, between the expected and the unexpected, and between the familiar and the unfamiliar, Bataille made everything strange. Here the ethnographic subject was dislocated by an aesthetic of the impossible.[139] Indeed, it is striking, and somehow appropriate, that this entry is all but absent of any reference to the music. Bataille's "definition" was not so much of the Blackbirds themselves, but of the nature of the desire they provoked in those who witnessed them and of the associations that arose in the imagination as a product of that desire. It was a definition of the impossibility of defining the Blackbirds and jazz as something other than a collection of images seduced from the limits of consciousness and projected onto the object of analysis. "Blackbirds—pointless to search any longer for an explanation for *colored people* suddenly shattering an absurd, stammering silence with unseemly madness: we were rotting away from neurasthenia in our homes, the cemetery and mass grave of so much pathetic hodgepodge; thus the blacks who got civilized with us (in America or elsewhere) and who today dance and shout are the swampy smells of decomposition that ignited above this immense cemetery: on a *nègre* night, vaguely lunar, we are thus witnessing an intoxicating dementia of shady and charming will-o'-the-wisps, twisted and screeching like fits of laughter. This definition will evade all discussion."[140] Indeed, he described the powerful transgressive effect of the

Blackbirds on cultural order, which he associated with death and decay. Yet rather than portraying the musicians and dancers as representative primitives, Bataille made the "blacks who got civilized with us" a symptom of the critic, arising in the imagination like a swampy gas of surplus desire seeping from the cracks of subjectivity. By coming to terms with the shattering effect of the Blackbirds' jazz, Bataille was restating his belief that instances of intoxicating dementia engendered by limit-experiences—and jazz provided many of them for him—were cornerstones upon which knowledge and subjectivity depended. These were the moments of transgressive violence in thought, of a certain "blindness" where the critic's desire supplemented the object of analysis and supported it in consciousness. Bataille seemed to be saying that the Blackbirds, with their jazz and dancing, produced an expression that was beyond the capacity of language, or of the critic, to represent.

Yet though Leiris, Schaeffner, and the other ethnographers in the *Documents* group certainly agreed with many of Bataille's ideas about the limits of knowledge and the need for transgression, Leiris, in particular, continued to search for a language to make sense of jazz as a hybrid cultural phenomenon. The arrival of the celebrated American sound film *Hallelujah* (1929), by King Vidor, would give him an opportunity to bring the crosscultural concerns that characterized his writing for *Documents* to bear on the question of authenticity in jazz. In an issue of *La Revue du Cinéma* entirely dedicated to King Vidor, Leiris turned to *Hallelujah*, its jazz, its vision of black America, and its all-black cast, to argue that the notion of authentic jazz was inherently paradoxical owing to the evolution of the music as a mix of different cultural and ethnic traditions. Everything depended upon the mix: "The unique character of music, dance, spectacles, and all other black American production is without a doubt tied to the very simple fact that there are two absolutely contradictory poles that find themselves in the presence of each other: on the one side, a people that one holds fast in the infancy of the moment when it was transplanted from Africa to America; on the other side, a civilization that is at the avant-garde of capitalist development, a civilization of Fordism and rationalism. The incomparable value of everything that black Americans do proves the perfectly unusual reconciliation of these two poles—the one extremely primitive, the other at the head of modern evolution. Each time, we are talking about an extremely unstable equilibrium."[141] These two dueling forces heard in jazz and all black American cultural production, its spiritual parents *Afrique* and *Amérique,* were linked in a surrealist welding of words to become *Aframérique.* As the neologism itself revealed, it was an ancestry fraught with the amphibiological tension of cultural hybridity.

More than Schaeffner's hyphenated category *Afro-Américain,* which testified to a confrontation between two coherent ethnic entities, *Aframérique* signified cultural miscegenation based on the biological model of parentage. On the one side, Leiris described the "mother," that "old foundation of human sentiment,"[142] which he linked to primitive African magic; on the other was the American desire for technical perfection and utilitarian progress, which, "in the spirit of man, plays the role of a mean and rigorous father."[143] One can hear the surrealist influence of Freudian Oedipal harmonics in this passage as Leiris made sense of the family tensions manifested in different types of jazz. Of this dual heritage, the father's characteristics played the greater role in the majority of commercial jazz, "since more and more, the world moves toward mechanization, and utility exercises its paternity in a way that is more tyrannical each day; a monstrous Saturn who devours much more than his own children."[144]

However, in the "most interesting jazz," the mother's characteristics—the magic, the gestures, and the ritual words—were the most recognizable. As Leiris understood it, when the African mother's "racial sentiment" revealed itself, it was expressed as a "passion for a new mysticism, or more exactly for a new kind of saintliness, entirely free if you like, without anything to do with any morality—a saintliness that you fall into at the moment when you least expect it, like poverty in the world."[145] Hybrid *aframérique* saintliness expressed this fidelity to and identity with a natural order and was the perfect antidote for a "rotten" modern civilization. Leiris witnessed such maternal piety in *Hallelujah.* "I know of no other more pure expression of that kind of sainthood than the black film *Hallelujah.* That a man be a gambler, lustful, adulterous, and a murderer ready for all sacrilege and all temptations—this in no way stops him from being a saint."[146] Leiris's notion of the saint, and of the human, was not of the archetypal Christian who held the passions and temptations at bay. Rather, it was a more Dionysian figure who "let himself go" to his all-too-human desires. This was the expression of passion that Leiris heard in authentic jazz, one that irresistibly pulled the Western listener toward it. "It inflicts a hard lesson on the white race, artistically exhausted and wilted, and now uniquely capable of technical progress."[147] Having experienced the song and dance of a sound film that screened this supremely human relation to the world, Leiris now had a theory for determining authentic *Aframérique* jazz and, by extension, for understanding the authentic expression of passion. *Hallelujah* set a fantastic ideal that would continue to inspire him even as it continued to haunt him. "Since *Hallelujah,* I have dreamed of an analogue to that bleeding nun whom we encounter at midnight at the crossroads of frenetic novels, of a saint with a body the color of night, with a veil soiled in mud and a dress stained with blood, shuffling around with torn bare feet in the most lowdown dive, some White Chapel of Harlem, half crazy, shaking with laughter, drinking full glasses of whiskey, and raving marvelously."[148] True, many of the images or characteristics evoked in relation to the jazzy expressivity of African Americans were variations of standard French discourse on *nègre* expression, but Leiris had given voice to the other forces at work in *Aframérique* subjectivity. Though "interesting jazz" always depended upon the dominance of the *Afrique* over the *Amérique*, of the spiritual mother over the rational father, conceptually Leiris still granted standing to the American influences as an integral part of the cultural mix. Yet he believed that jazz, like all cultural forms, was ripe with ambiguity and paradox. Perhaps proving the perspicuity of Bataille's critique, more and more jazz's transgressive potential would fall short of Leiris's fantasy object, the passionate expression of "positive negation" that arose from the wildness of his own thought. By mid-1930, the chief financial backers of *Documents* would pull out. Leiris, Schaeffner, and Griaule turned their attention toward the cultural alterity they had thus far experienced only in museums, written materials, and photographs, and departed for Africa with the Mission Dakar-Djibouti in search of what Leiris once described as the "other who is not entirely other."[149]

And so, the ethnographic moment in French jazz criticism, born from the cultural turmoil and discursive dissonance in the media surrounding *La revue nègre,* faded into silence as its greatest voices left the scene. Certainly writers like Leiris and Schaeffner continued on as important figures in twentieth-century French intellectual history, but jazz no longer served as the quilting point for their thinking about culture. However, the complexity of their writing and their emphasis on hybridity and ambiguity, their desire to approximate the amphibiological expression they heard in jazz, helped close the door on simplistic descriptions of jazz music that followed standard racial stereotypes about the *nègre*. Yet having debunked the old fixed notions about jazz, the ethnographic critics departed for Africa and vacated the position of authority in jazz criticism that they had come to occupy. The space they left open in French jazz criticism was quickly filled by a young critic named Hugues Panassié, whose way of evaluating jazz was called *le jazz hot*. Panassié's method of judging the quality of the music—whether it was hot or straight—set aside questions of ambiguous racial origin or cultural hybridity in favor of applying aesthetic standards to musical sound. Whereas the surrealist ethnographers stressed the importance of cultural influence in jazz and acknowledged their inability to fully comprehend this mix, *le jazz hot,* as a concept and method of criticism, allowed for a certain critical certainty and paved the way for the rise of the professional critic who need not know anything about other cultures. Moreover, by the time Leiris and Schaeffner returned from Africa, jazz had also changed. To them, it was more commercial and less wild. Showing the extent to which the paradigm in jazz criticism had shifted, the ethnographers, too, adopted the new industry-friendly critical frame when they wrote about the new stars of jazz, like Duke Ellington and Louis Armstrong. The Jazz Hot Age had arrived. But now that the men had been amazed, tantalized, and seduced by the diversity of African cultures, jazz had lost much of its otherness for them. They now experienced jazz as a familiar cultural form that lacked amphibiological appeal.

Indeed, by the time Schaeffner wrote his official entry "The Vogue and Sociology of Jazz" for the 1935 *Encyclopédie française,* jazz, for him, had become "ersatz music,"[150] its authentic primitive expressiveness or otherness having been silenced by a saccharine commercialism of mass culture that was everywhere the same. If Josephine Baker's rise from *sauvage* to star charts the ascendance and ambiguous assimilation of jazz in France, there is probably no greater indicator of the extent to which jazz had been domesticated and commercialized than her own changing persona. La Baker, who now spoke French, owned her own Montmartre club called Chez Josephine, and had an Adolf Loos–designed Paris flat, was now regularly featured on French movie screens and music hall stages. Where she once wore "primitive" banana skirts and little else, she now wore jeweled headpieces and sophisticated sequined gowns. In 1932 her show at the Casino du Paris was again the talk of the town. Yet the tenor of the show was very different from that of *La revue nègre,* which had provoked public scandal with its jazzed-up *danse sauvage.* Indeed, Baker's new revue, still billed as a jazz spectacle, was now centered around a song that conveyed the essence of her new mainstream persona and spoke volumes about the state of jazz in the French imagination. Whereas her performances once conveyed an insatiable desire for uncontrolled primitive dance, she now expressed a different sentiment, singing: "I want to be white."[151] The French conversation on what counted as jazz and what jazz meant for France had shifted again.

5

The Jazz Hot Years

One cannot tamper with the rules of music
(that is, of poetry and taste) without disturbing
the fundamental laws of government.

—Charles Maurras

Though jazz had been an object for music criticism for over a decade in France, as a rule it had been judged according to the same criteria used for classical music. This chapter characterizes not merely what happened to French writing on jazz after the waning of the ethnographic moment, but how a new paradigm for jazz criticism was developed by a new species of specialized jazz critic who came to dominate the discourse. These were turbulent times and yet, at the beginning of the decade, there was an explosion of journals dedicated to making sense of a quickly changing French popular culture. The diversity of these journals was reflected in the heterogeneity of opinions they contained. Slowly but surely, however, this pluralism of many journals and critics who wrote about jazz disappeared as one journal, *Jazz Hot,* set itself up as *the* only true jazz publication. As it took control of the discourse on jazz, fewer nonspecialized culture critics in the general press dealt with the significance of jazz for France. Just as the political landscape in the 1930s saw the rise of nationalist and fascist politics symbolized by great leaders who were surrounded by cults of personality, jazz criticism became less democratic in its approach to truth and more autocratic and authoritarian. The same ideological trends that Walter Benjamin so famously described in relation to promoting mechanically reproduced art and mass political movements can also be seen in jazz criticism during the 1930s, as the Hot Club movement leaders constructed cults of personality around their favorite musicians and increasingly politicized their jazz criticism. Over time, the ethnographic critics' ambiguity and problematics gave way to the unproblematic certainty of the professional jazz critics. By the end of the

1930s, these specialized critics, mirroring the logic of the increasingly purist French culture critics on the right, became more and more nostalgic about the jazz they promoted as "true" or "authentic," and more venomous in their attacks on those who disagreed with them.

Hugues Panassié (1912–1974) was the first and most influential of these specialized critics who set themselves and their work apart from that of general critics. His ascendance to power is analogous to the rise of the professional jazz critic and is central to the story of how jazz is understood today in France. Son of a millionaire manganese mine owner, Panassié grew up in a castle in the south of France, steeped in conservative bourgeois ideology. He was a staunch Catholic and active supporter of the right-wing nationalist political movements like Charles Maurras's *L'Action Française,* which saw modern democracy as a corrupting force in French culture and worked to reestablish the monarchy as the centerpiece in a unified French nation. When Panassié started spending more time in Paris in the late 1920s, he participated in demonstrations against the democratic government of the Third Republic and was introduced to jazz.[1] Jazz really took hold of his imagination while he was recovering from polio, when he began collecting rare and expensive jazz records. Aided by his great wealth, Panassié would use his formidable record collection to become one of the most active proponents of jazz in France. Indeed, as becomes apparent from the title he later chose for his autobiography, *Monsieur Jazz,* he often acted as if he alone were responsible for putting jazz on the map in France.[2] His seminal article "*Le jazz hot*" appeared both in *L'Édition Musicale Vivante,* one of the new journals for recorded music, and in the mainstay *La Revue Musicale* in 1930, when Panassié was just eighteen years old. In it, he argued for a new foundation for jazz criticism based on different categories than those used to judge classical music. Panassié argued that jazz was unlike classical music and therefore should not be analyzed in terms of its formal composition. The value of jazz came not from the formal music, but from the strength of individual interpretation. Critics who employed the same formal criteria for judging all music often mistook false jazz for "true jazz." Panassié employed a kind of Kantian approach to criticism that compared the particular to the ideal. He stressed that a jazz critic needed to judge each record by whether it revealed the "true essence" of jazz, which he used the American term *hot* to describe. "We are generally no longer too unaware of the principles of jazz music, of the true, that is to say *le jazz hot.* Even so, it appears to me good to recall them here briefly. I ask the reader to note that it is not my comprehension of jazz that I am expounding here, but that of the most authoritative players."[3] Panassié did not invent the term *hot;* rather, he borrowed it from American musicians and promoters and the recording industry, who used it to classify jazz. There were two styles of jazz: straight and hot. Panassié believed that it was necessary for French jazz critics to learn these culture industry categories, as there was something untranslatable about the music: "one cannot find any exact French equivalent to these terms."[4]

The first term, *straight,* was used to define the *musique légère* or symphonic jazz familiar to French radio listeners. "*Straight* signifies *droit.* To play straight means to play without straying from a line defined in advance, to play the musical text as it is written."[5] Panassié dismissed this arranged commercial music, with its "*airs banals,*" and believed that people who really knew jazz "quickly tired of listening to it."[6] Yet Panassié noted that "*le straight* is almost the only form of jazz we know in France. And when one realizes this, one better understands how the attitude of the adversaries of jazz is logical."[7] Those who opposed jazz in France, Panassié believed, were not listening to "true jazz." *Hot* was the term musicians used to describe the quality of "true jazz." "To play *hot* means word for word to play very *chaud.* One must listen: to play with heat, with heart. That expression was employed primitively to define the execution of a musician who, in the fervor of playing, had modified more or less the initial theme, improvising at random several phrases."[8] Although neither had been used as categories in the first years of jazz, straight jazz had developed as a distinctive school in both America and France. Alongside it, "*le jazz hot* took a suitable form . . . In scarcely four years, the formulas of *le jazz hot* have stabilized almost definitively."[9] Ironically, his foundation for judging "spontaneous improvisation" was based on listening for certain established "formulas . . . *Jazz hot* is not a formula outside of jazz. It is jazz in its unique and true form; it comes directly to us from the *nègre* tradition."[10] As such, a good hot orchestra was one composed of several hot players whose improvised solos were judged by Panassié to be hot. Very few large orchestras could be considered truly hot, as many only had one or two soloists, accompanied by written arrangements and very little improvisation.

Although Panassié argued that hot style was based on "*véritable jazz nègre,*" the hot sound was possible for some "transcendent" whites. As such, his procedure for judging true jazz on record, while founded in fixed stereotypes of racial difference, was theoretically blind to race. "It would be an error to believe that whites are inferior to *nègres.* They play so much in the style of the latter that they take me there."[11] It was only through listening to the quality of the individual playing on record, he argued, that one could distinguish hot from straight and true jazz from false jazz.

The evaluation of records became the key to his critical enterprise, as Panassié believed that 80 percent of the world's jazz musicians were "bad musicians" incapable of performing in the hot style. Moreover, he wrote that "it is impossible to name one good hot orchestra in France, as they never come."[12] Thus, since it was hard to find good live jazz in France, "it is almost uniquely by disc that we reach these magnificent solos of the great *nègre* and American musicians. In that, discs are precious; and also because they are the only means of faithfully preserving these improvisations."[13] He tried hard to define each hot player's unique style as he heard it, but pointing to the records themselves was the most important part of his critical procedure. To really know hot jazz and be able to recognize it, one had to have access to the records, and Panassié, with his great wealth, was one of the few who could afford to buy such hot commodities, still heavily taxed and rare.

The master of *le jazz hot* for Panassié was Louis Armstrong. "His prodigious imagination allows him to play the most rich and varied solos one can hear, and to endlessly renew himself."[14] Like his trumpet playing, Armstrong's singing was extremely hot. "Certainly, he has a rough voice, but it is strong, beautiful, and full of that *sauvage* character."[15] In all, Panassié listed a select group of musicians whose recorded sound was hot: Jimmy Dorsey; Bix Beiderbecke; Frankie Trumbauer; "a *nègre* alto saxophonist with the Duke Ellington Orchestra";[16] Coleman Hawkins; Bud Freeman; Pee Wee Russell; Benny Goodman; Milton "Mezz" Mezzrow; Jack Teagarden; Tommy Dorsey; "Rex, *un nègre*," who played with Louis Armstrong; "Mugsy," who played with Ray Miller; Jimmy McPartland; Joe Sullivan; Lennie Hayton; and Earl Hines.

Although Panassié believed that the true hot sound did not exist in France, he listed the names of several French musicians who, on a relative scale, approached the hot style. Trumpeter Philippe Brun, who played with Grégor et ses grégoriens and who had introduced Panassié to many American records, was the closest. Pianist Stéphane Mougin, trombonist Léo Vauchant (who played with the Mitchell Jazz Kings in the early 1920s and recorded with Jack Hylton), and violinist Stéphane Grappelli (who also played with Grégor et ses grégoriens) all came close. Hot was not normally possible for French musicians, yet Panassié made a recognition and enjoyment of the hot style readily accessible for French jazz fans and critics who had record players or access to a radio. Moreover, since the categories for listening depended on his ear and his taste, he was the authority on hot. Soon, the categories hot and straight, and his rules for distinguishing between them, came to dominate the emerging field of cultural production: French jazz criticism.

In October 1930, a group of critics and musicians launched the first issue of a new specialized journal called *Jazz-Tango*. Along with educating French listeners about the best American record releases, they sought to "honor French tango and jazz orchestras, which the public, be it by ignorance or snobbery, refuses at the moment to recognize."[17] *Jazz-Tango*'s editorial policy was cosmopolitan, in that it included all kinds of jazz, and nationalist, in that it wanted to discuss and promote French jazz. Of course, *Jazz-Tango* was not alone in its promotion of French-style jazz and jazz orchestras. For instance, critic Émile Vuillermoz, now writing on film, drama, and music for several newspapers and journals, praised the Jazz-Pathé-Nathan for "creating, with purely French elements, a symphonic jazz of real value . . . These virtuosos from our country have kept from the technique of Paul Whiteman, Jack Hylton, and Ted Lewis, that which is the most musical and elegant."[18] Yet while Vuillermoz embraced French jazz for its musicality and elegance, *Comoedia* culture critic Gustave Fréjaville, who had always been skeptical about the ability of French culture to assimilate jazz, criticized Gregor and His Gregorians (they Americanized their name that year) for calling their music "*jazz français.*" He questioned the public taste that required them to hide the "characteristics of our race and of our national temperament"[19] behind a commercial, Americanized front. "What's more, we don't accept the principle itself of a jazz français. What does this signify? That French musicians can play syncopated music as well as Americans?"[20] French musicians, he argued, needed to separate themselves from an "exclusively commercial point of view"[21] and let their authentic French characteristics come through. If they did, he was sure they would not be playing jazz.

Jazz-Tango promoted not only a new specialized approach to jazz criticism, but a cultural loyalty to French jazz orchestras, as well. There was good reason for this. In an early article in *Jazz-Tango* on foreign musicians in France, Maurice Bedou-Ermonchy, a representative of the French musicians syndicate, painted a gloomy picture of the labor situation. Two familiar threats menaced the French jazz musician in 1930: mechanization and foreign musicians. Of the jazz orchestras performing in Parisian clubs, theaters, or *dancings*, forty-four were directed by foreigners, and twenty-four were directed by French. Among the foreign-directed bands, there were 277 musicians, 236 of whom were foreign; even in the remaining twenty-four French-led bands, only 101 French musicians were working. At a time of "intense unemployment" (there had been a nationwide general strike again on May 16), this foreign domination was unacceptable to Bedou-Ermonchy. Indeed, the numbers show that the 1929 Parisian municipal law stating that only 10 percent of musicians on French stages could be foreigners was being largely disregarded.[22] He protested against this trend. "Our colleagues, put out on the street, would be able easily, with some effort, to adapt their talents to one of the specialties that invaded with the Huns of music."[23] He believed foreign musicians were certainly deserving of "the laws of hospitality that have always been the rule in our beautiful country," but not at any price. *Jazz-Tango* believed French musicians were capable of conforming to public taste and should be treated with the respect they deserved. Most importantly, they should be given a chance and employed.

Jean Marcland, for one, thought critics should help cultivate an appreciation for French jazz to combat the overwhelming presence of American jazz. "Student yesterday, today rival; tomorrow he [French musician] can be the creator of an absolutely new genre, born of an intelligent synthesis: *le jazz français.*"[24] What was needed, Marcland believed, was more of the "blues" in French music. Not so much by imitating the musical style of Paul Robeson or Louis Armstrong, who brought the "inestimable contribution of the human voice,"[25] but by singing the blues in French. "The French language is sufficiently rich and supple enough to fold itself without damage into a discipline of rhythm and accentuation that, instead of our lame adaptations of the American foxtrot, will give that indispensable homogeneity to the melodic phrase of sung jazz."[26] Showing a similar desire for an assimilated jazz, the editors of *Jazz-Tango* praised Ray Ventura et ses collégiens for their success in achieving a new form: "finally a French jazz, under the direction of a Frenchman from France."[27]

That one heard such promotional language is in no way a sign of jazz's integration into French cultural identity, as critics whose vision of true French culture did not include jazz were appalled by the idea of French jazz. In *Le Monde Musical,* a conservative nationalist music journal, conductor Fernand Mazzi argued that "a people, when it sings, exhales its sentiment under an interior or exterior influence . . . in an almost unconscious and entirely unreflective manner."[28] Thus any performance of jazz in France by Frenchmen was not a welcome sight, but rather a sign of an unconscious decay of "true" French sentiment. Unlike "the most authentic liturgical songs"[29] from France, which expressed only innately felt melodies, jazz would always be a foreign scourge, a rhythmic "animal" music signifying decadence. "It is the negation of spirit, the suppression of all flight of the soul toward superior spheres, the triumph of matter acting for itself and by itself, the loss of all spiritual control and of all ideal conduct. What's more, such activity has lowered not only the actual state of the individual, but our moral level, making it descend to the inferior level of animated being and driving it toward matter in an almost permanent way . . . It makes us degenerate, like certain human races that appear to have lost their ancestral dignity."[30] Using tried and true anti-jazz riffs, he argued that jazz turned human spirit into animal matter. Even a tamed and assimilated French jazz, he stressed, led to such "quasi-destruction of the most noble part of the human being."[31] The popularity of jazz in France, he believed, was proof of cultural degeneration. If people wanted a true French music, they should stop ceding ground to jazz.

Other conservative critics responded to the change in critical language. *Le Musicien Fédéré,* a journal supporting French music syndicates, used standard notions of French racial and cultural difference to characterize hot jazz as un-French and to promote straight jazz. It allowed them to make available a critical position that was conservative and nationalist yet that accepted jazz if it corresponded to traditional French characteristics. "To play straight is to play it like it's written, classically, correctly . . . To play hot is to play with heat, seething . . . Like the drunk who ends up at home but who would be incapable of saying what path he took to get there."[32] The difference between the two styles had everything to do with the difference between the French and the American mentality; only one was appropriate for France. Indeed, the anonymous editorialist for the journal argued that there was historical precedence for banishing such expression from French culture. "Straight is more liked in the old continent; in America, on the contrary, they prefer 'hot.' Charlemagne himself, who did not have the American mentality (but how old it is!), did not confuse minstrels and artists. A Latin document tells us that the great emperor forbade nimble-minded musicians in his palace who did not know how to read music, or even still treated like 'half-wits' (*bestiae*) those who, while singing, played 'hot' instead of 'straight,' that is to say those who vocalized according to their inspiration rather than singing correctly . . . But now there are no more schools, no more rules, no more ridiculous hindrances."[33] Thus the reaction against such music in French culture, the interdiction of "hot," was as old as the first kings of France. Unless French musicians and critics wanted to betray this spirit and completely adopt the American *bestiae* mentality, they should quit sending mixed signals to the listening public and resist the "musical regime of hot, *du hot en haut* (hot held high)."[34]

Hot or Not?

With the absence of the ethnographers and their critical "problèmatiques" from jazz discourse, the work of simplified categorization of jazz as either hot or straight quickly gained standing as the specialized critic's task. Yet the debates over the appropriateness of jazz for French culture continued among writers of all kinds and, in fact, incorporated these terms as part of the ongoing construction of Frenchness. In the November 2, 1930, *Le Télégramme,* Charles Teissier bluntly contrasted the two styles of jazz. "There are now two genres of jazz. The one remains cacophonic. Pounding the nervous system, it revives the senses by imitating the diverse cries of the wild beasts of the jungle on the prowl. The second genre has justly taken the rights of the city. It is a true return toward virtuosity."[35] For Teissier, *sauvage* cacophony—hot—should remain outside the imaginary boundaries of French cultural identity.

The editors of *Jazz-Tango,* despite their loyalty to the three thousand out-of-work Parisian musicians,[36] took a more inclusive, cosmopolitan approach to jazz of all kinds. Thus they continued to publish contributions from Panassié even though his prejudice against straight left little room for many French jazzmen. Yet as a consequence, an internal conflict developed over hot versus straight. In his articles on hot players,[37] Panassié served as a counterpoint to other *Jazz-Tango* contributors, who promoted "elegant" French jazz. In one of the first of his endless musings on Louis Armstrong, Panassié described Armstrong as the "true king of jazz." This idealism was a necessary antidote to the American entertainment industry's promotion of Paul Whiteman in the high-budget colorized musical *The King of Jazz* (released in France as *La féerie du jazz*).[38] Panassié made the acknowledgment of the true king the mark of a good jazz critic. "All the specialists recognize his supremacy."[39] Whereas other *Jazz-Tango* contributors often expressed an appreciation for Whiteman's symphonic jazz, Panassié made Armstrong's jazz the ideal against which all jazz should be judged. Indeed, he raised up Louis by raising the level of his own hyperbole. "The blood of his soul comes to us from each of his solos."[40] Panassié was now projecting the standard characteristics once associated with *la musique nègre* onto *le jazz hot* and making his own taste the supreme measure of jazz.

The critic who surfaced in *Jazz-Tango* as the best counterbalance to Panassié's hot hyperbole was Stéphane Mougin, a pianist who played with many of the early French jazz orchestras. Despite the fact that Panassié had placed him in the "almost hot" category as a musician; as a critic, Mougin slowly turned against Panassié's binary system, as it created a "snobbism" that worked against French musicians. Instead, he remained open to hot and straight. His first article, in April 1931, was a review of a Sophie Tucker concert given at the Empire theater. He compared the reception of her hot singing—audiences had whistled at her—to the warm reception given to Jack Hylton's straight jazz. "When Sophie Tucker made true jazz, they whistled at her. When Jack Hylton bluffs, he is acclaimed."[41] However, unlike Panassié, who heaped scorn on audiences whose tastes did not conform to the ideals of *le jazz hot,* Mougin believed that these responses were signs of deeply ingrained French tastes. Rather than resenting French audiences, as he argued Panassié did, Mougin thought that audiences needed to be understood. "Jazz will never be the popular music of France . . . Jazz is a music for intellectuals, like the Dada of a minority . . . Jazz has never stopped being the patrimony of a minority, a minority of both intellectuals and musicians. And the French public is not ripe to admit it, no more than the Indians on the banks of the Amazon are disposed to familiarize themselves with Einstein's mechanics, which they hardly need to eat, live, and perpetuate the species."[42] Thus it was not surprising that the French public whistled at Tucker's hot singing and acclaimed Hylton's straight "bluffing." Given their innate tastes, it was natural for them to do so. Panassié and those who imitated his criteria for judgment were in the minority.

Certainly, Bernard Zimmer, who reviewed records in *La Revue Hebdomadaire,* believed in innate French tastes and sought to protect them. His tone is exemplary of an anti-hot movement that was gaining momentum in the Depression-era press as critics sought to cast blame for France's hard times. "'I want to be happy' and 'Tea for Two,' dislocated by the syncopation, become two *danses de Saint-Guy.* Only incidentally and from afar do they recall the two dear romances for sentimental hearts."[43] Many conservative critics like Zimmer now revived anti-jazz language from the 1920s to demonize *le jazz hot* for being un-French or dangerous for the French cultural ethos. Critic Jacques Dolor, for instance, used good old-fashioned xenophobia to build the case against *le jazz hot* in the conservative *L'Ami du Peuple.* "These Anglo-Saxon fashions, which unfortunately always collide with good French taste, have found acceptance in certain circles. Good-bye to music and dances of yesteryear. The end of the end in musical matter consists in having an orchestra composed of exotic and barbarous players . . . This music will never calm the morals [*adoucit les mœurs*]."[44] Such anti-hot communicative acts were gaining standing at a time when literature on American modernity was gaining a wider audience. For instance, Georges Duhamel published his *Scènes de la vie future,*[45] which again used America as a negative example of cultural trajectory, and Paul Achard came out with *Un oeil neuf sur l'Amérique.* But while Achard brought back lessons of progress, Duhamel spoke of a noisy mechanized commercial culture led by a hedonistic laziness that was spreading all over the world through cinema, radio, and records and was snuffing out tradition along the way.[46] Duhamel was the most influential of such antimodern voices and used his authority to denounce modern media, like the radio, that threatened his image of true French culture: "The radio [*téhessef*] and the phonograph favor all kinds of confusion. *Phonophiles* can no longer make sufficient distinctions between the divine Mozart and the *sauvages* of jazz."[47]

For less xenophobic and less antimodern critics, reviewing the work of French jazz bands made it possible to highlight the incompatibility between what they believed to be "true" French sensibility and jazz, important work in the ongoing construction of cultural identity. For instance, one critic in *Le Courrier musical* wrote: "Is it voluntarily that Ray Ventura frenchifies [*française*] jazz? Maybe so; in any case this is not a good method. One likes jazz or not! . . . But this is no longer jazz. I believe that 'jazz' and '*Français*' are incompatible words."[48] French bands could play American music, but jazz would never be French. Thus one could be cosmopolitan and conservative by accepting the presence of jazz as an exotic music while rejecting the possibility that it would ever be an expression of Frenchness.

As a certain critical momentum gained against *le jazz hot* for its un-Frenchness, Panassié became more entrenched in his purist promotion of hot-only listening. In *Jazz-Tango,* he argued that if style was the expression of individual thought, then only hot could be considered a style. Straight playing was merely imitation; thus it had no individual style and, consequently, no thought. European musicians were "inferior" to Americans because they lacked individual thought.[49] After a while Panassié began to say, "I listen only to *jazz hot*."[50] For him, everything else was "false jazz."

By the end of 1931, Stéphane Mougin began to satirize polemicists who moralized on both sides of the debates over "true French music" and "true jazz." Of the former, he spoke out against Pierre Giriat, whose article in the *Lyon Républicain* called for a cultural purge of jazz in the name of "French decency";[51] of the latter, he mocked Panassié and the evangelists of hot. "There is a *nègromanie* that one must deplore, like all these manias that snobbery has pushed to excess . . . It must be said: the *nègres* of the U.S.A. are not the sole parents of the form of jazz we know today . . . The infinite varieties of 'hot' are as much the consequences of the influence of whites and their science, established by their civilization."[52] Stressing human equality and pluralist aesthetics, he argued that jazz expression was not the exclusive domain of anyone or any race. "Art has no country";[53] jazz could be played by all. Later, when Robert Goffin, now the leading Belgian jazz specialist, criticized this position in the Belgian journal *Music,* Mougin responded that he was not trying to deny blacks the paternity of jazz. Rather, he was merely saying that for each group of good black musicians there were also a "dozen who are used only because of their color."[54] He agreed that jazz was originally "of *nègre* stock" but stressed that whites had "normalized it to make it more acceptable to the numerous crowds that participate in its life."[55] It was natural for a culture to assimilate a music like jazz, and it was "mania" to believe that without *nègres,* it was impossible to make good jazz. Critics needed to blind themselves to the color of musicians and open their ears.

Whether one liked hot or not, it was certain that, among critics, the distinction between the two types of jazz served some taxonomic desire to order things. It quickly caught on. Critic Pierre Leroi, who now called *le jazz hot* "jazz in its pure state,"[56] triumphantly announced that these categories had been adopted by record companies in their catalogues. "Our campaign in favor of the classification of jazz, until now mixed without any distinction in the catalogues of record companies, has borne its fruit."[57] Yet as these categories became entrenched in the mechanisms of record production and dissemination, cases arose that tested their usefulness for understanding "authentic" jazz and for defining "authentic" Frenchness in relation to them.

Right in the black, brown, and beige of the authentic-jazz debate was Duke Ellington. While Panassié originally placed Ellington's orchestra in the first tier of authentic hot bands, Ellington's approach to music was different from that of Panassié's "jazz incarnate" Louis Armstrong. By 1932, Panassié began to argue that "true hot" improvisation was possible only with a band of no more than seven players: Ellington had around fifteen, depending on the record. Moreover, Ellington used complex written arrangements, one of Panassié's de facto criteria for recognizing straight jazz. Ellington's sophisticated persona confused critics like Panassié who felt that blacks (and their music) were natural or authentic only when playful and naive. In general, the Duke's sophisticated music confounded French critics. In *Documents,* Jacques Fray held up Duke as a symbol of an evolved hybrid culture and identity. His music, with its modernist harmonic innovations, showed the result of dialogue with "serious" Western music, and this evolution marked a loss of primitiveness.[58] Unlike Panassié and the hot critics, the ethnographers thought this loss was part of the dialectic of modernity: of course American blacks would react to being called primitive by writing more complex music to prove critics wrong. Ellington, too, was part of the dialectic that pushed artists to innovate in order to stay ahead of commercial culture.

Ellington's erudite hybrid persona and music also attracted the sensitive ear of the venerable critic Henry Prunières (1886–1942), founding editor of *La Revue Musicale,* who thought that Duke's precise orchestral arrangements defied Panassié's categories. At a time characterized by "the extreme propagation of lamentable *jazz frelaté* [corrupted jazz]," Prunières argued that Ellington's music proved that "true jazz *nègre* is more alive than ever."[59] He thought that, more than Armstrong, Ellington pushed at the formulas of the jazz song form. Thus his jazz was better, more modern and advanced. "He has pushed the system of collective improvisation to the highest point."[60] He believed the orchestra members' ability to express themselves spontaneously as individuals and as a whole was a characteristic of all authentic *musique nègre.* "Collective improvisation, where the musical genius of the *nègre* triumphs, seems contrary to our morals and culture even though it has been practiced here for three centuries."[61] Yet by placing Ellington's music ahead of Armstrong's and bringing up the European tradition of improvisational music, Prunières opened a debate over "true jazz" that Panassié would not take lightly. Hot was not a question of text or no text, as Panassié often argued—it was a matter of interpretation. For Prunières, understanding Ellington's orchestrated music necessitated more than merely situating it in relation to the conventional binary, with hot *nègre* on the one side and straight white jazz on the other. As with the distinction between *nègre* jazz improvisation and Western music, Prunières believed the difference between hot and straight jazz was superficial and had much to do with the listening habits and record collections of specialized critics.

In the midst of this debate on the authenticity question—Panassié was busy denouncing musician Jean Wiéner for daring to place Ted Lewis and Louis Armstrong in the same sentence in an article[62]—Mougin tried to bring the tastes of the French public back into the equation and legitimize French listeners' preference for assimilated symphonic jazz. He wrote that there were two types of jazz listeners: those who liked the rhythms of any jazz for dancing, and those who only liked hot. "In order to understand jazz and to pretend to like it, one must interest oneself in *people* and like *them* from the start. It is extremely difficult to initiate oneself into jazz music without having the support of a clearly materialist philosophy."[63] As such, he believed that *le jazz hot* was just as much a materialization of the modern age as the minuets of Mozart were a materialization of the "Salon de Louis XV."[64] One had to understand the sociocultural circumstances from which a taste for jazz arose rather than base all criticism on a single idealist system.

Mougin agreed with the long-standing notion that jazz syncopation was the "material manifestation" of the black rhythmic spirit. "The *nègres* have it in their belly and it gives them, with the aid of their rudimentary imagination, a certain known physiological pleasure."[65] He argued that the way occidental listeners identified with these songs, and experienced the *nègre* enjoyment in the face of suffering, had to do with a transferential guilt for having caused their suffering. Yet more than any collective psychology, Mougin thought that the control of radio programming, publicity, and availability of records—the material conditions—determined what listeners heard. The combination of these psychological and culture industry forces determined a people's musical tastes. Thus Mougin insisted that jazz critics understand the legitimacy of a culture's particular taste for music and take this into consideration when evaluating jazz. As it was, the complexity of a culture's taste was almost impossible to understand. "I know well that jazz, in its present form, is not entirely the work of the blacks nor of the people of the U.S. It is assuredly not the peasants or workers who daily record the countless marvelous discs we know. But one must note that social circumstances, the psychology of people and the public, and the atavism of present-day dances and rhythms have an important influence on taste. Everything is tied together."[66] In France, straight jazz pleased a lot of people; that was all one needed to know. "Those who construe art in their ivory tower like those who preach morality from Mt. Sinai spread nonsense and allow themselves to follow chimeras."[67] Musicians like Ray Ventura also pleaded with the specialized jazz critics to be more forgiving of French jazz orchestras, who, like popular jazz orchestras in several other countries, tried to play what audiences liked to hear. "At the moment, all the great so-called jazz orchestras simply play the popular music of their country . . . There is thus no reason why we should not be able, in these conditions, to play *la musique légère française* according to the same principles of orchestration."[68] As economic conditions worsened for French jazz musicians, Mougin's "materialism" would take a more Marxist form, setting the long-standing French tastes of *le peuple* and the rights of French musicians to work against Panassié's brand of either/or critical orthodoxy.

Yet Mougin was no laissez-faire champion of mass culture. His Marxist chops made him sensitive to the potential for "false consciousness" among people, caused by culture industry commercialism. For instance, Mougin spoke out against the growing tendency among French jazz orchestras to replace brass sections with strings, a "sterilizing" trend he associated with the Americanization of culture. "One must deplore that *mode* which appears to me like a sign of decadence, of a public spirit that has become more insensitive than ever to art and to jazz music."[69] While he dismissed this commercialized taste in France as a symptom of *le régime capitalist,* he also took some pleasure in ribbing the purist Panassié for being out of touch with the French public. "That the public prefers these disguised and ungrateful orchestras this year will surprise Panassié in his candid and respectable enthusiasm, but nothing is more logical."[70]

The French public's taste for sterilized jazz was a mark of false consciousness, a symptom of the Americanization of culture. The best way to avoid such corruption, Mougin argued, was through French solidarity: "in a word, the corporative and syndicate spirit."[71] French musicians should be allowed to play the kind of jazz they wanted to play and, most importantly, they should be supported as workers.

Le Hot Club

As economic conditions continued to worsen, those whose image of Frenchness excluded jazz continued to link it to the ills that plagued modern France. Antimodernist Jacques Piths, in L'Ami du Peuple, nastily compared jazz to the architecture of Le Corbusier: "It can be said that this barbarous and decadent modernism is to architecture and decoration what jazz is to music."[72] But perhaps no one voiced their disgust as strongly as the aging music critic and essayist André Suarès. For him, jazz was the negation of everything French, civilized, and human. "Jazz is cynically the orchestra of brutes with nonopposable thumbs and still-prehensile feet in the voodoo forest. It is all excess and, despite this, worse than monotone: the monkey is freed to himself, without morals, without discipline, fallen into all the thicket of instinct, displaying his nude meat in all his leaps, and his heart, which is a still more obscene meat . . . Jazz is made of only five or six formulas, two inept and two of ipecac to make one vomit: jazz is the music of stomach and for all those who carry their beautiful soul between the liver and the thigh. There you have it, the music of musicians and men made on assembly lines."[73] In an age when descriptive excess in racialist discourse and anti-American cultural protectionism was becoming less suspect, Suarès's statement was playing on the anxieties of those who saw "true" French culture in decay.

Proponents of traditional high French culture tried to protect their "true" France from the forces of modern popular culture by calling for higher taxes on cinema and music halls to generate funds to support national theater and opera, both of which had suffered at the box office from the depression. As a result, jazz lovers had to pay the higher prices for "spectacles" to hear bands play. One way out of this taxation dilemma was the creation of private listening clubs. The first of these for jazz was the Jazz Club Universitaire, started by Elwyn Dirats and Jac Auxenfans.[74] These two seventeen-year-olds later approached Hugues Panassié, who used his considerable resources to send out the call for a larger private club where hot records could be enjoyed without the heavy taxation placed on live music. *Jazz-Tango Dancing* ran advertisements in January of 1933 for Le Hot Club.

Stéphane Mougin, in the meantime, found himself trapped in the philosophical dilemma characteristic of moderate French jazz musicians and critics in the 1930s. If he followed the critical orthodoxy of Le Hot Club, he would have to turn against his own playing style and that of his fellow French musicians. He would have to admit that they were not playing true jazz. Instead, he argued for pluralism and for acknowledging that French jazz could be its own thing and have its own value. He stressed that fixation on hot jazz was also a materialization of the spirit of the time; the same commercial times and material conditions that had produced the straight jazz had also "materialized" the Hot Club's beloved hot. "What is most difficult—since no one does it—is to elevate oneself and look philosophically at jazz music and the behaviors that go with it in the same glance, to understand its social and moral significance, and in order to determine that which, in the social structure of the United States, for example, constitutes the most considerable neuralgic point of jazz, so as to say what it feeds on. That is what it means to philosophize: to see the context of a thing and to express a value judgment on the whole."[75] Though he did not cross the increasingly powerful Panassié and his Hot Club orthodoxy, he noted ironically that the market forces that produced commercialized jazz were the same forces that had pushed Armstrong and Ellington to the top of the charts. Since market forces determined record production, they also determined what French critics of all tastes got to hear.

At Le Hot Club, one could access the latest records and meet other people who wanted to discuss them. It promoted all media products and publications related to *le jazz hot*. One of the first activities of the Hot Club was an evening at the Cinéma Falguière on January 31, 1933, set up by Jacques Canetti (1909–1997). Hot Club members were shown three "unedited *films nègres*," *Black and Tan Fantasy, St. Louis Blues* (featuring Bessie Smith), and a Betty Boop cartoon featuring the music of Louis Armstrong. The films were followed by a lecture on *le jazz hot* by Panassié that, reportedly, did not go well.[76] Musician Michel Emer reported on this "*Soirée Hot*"[77] for *Jazz Tango*. Along with the continuation of "*Hot Ciné*," the club organized a Hot Club ball and new programs on several radio stations that would broadcast *le jazz hot*.

Henry Prunières, whose expertise on baroque aesthetics led him to compare jazz improvisation to the improvisatory performances of the *Commedia dell'Arte*[78] in Italy, reported on this new subcultural development and its self-proclaimed leader. "*Jazz hot* remains unknown to *le grand public,* but it has little by little spread in the manner of a secret cult. It has its great pontiff: Hugues Panassié; it has its fanatics who listen with drunkenness to the news discs of the marvelous Duke Ellington Orchestra or to the virtuoso of hot playing: Louis Armstrong. A club has founded itself, Le Hot Club, which invites its members to very interesting meetings. In that sympathetic ambience of artists, feeling in common with the listeners, blooming and unleashing themselves, one can truly get an idea of the true *jazz hot* that one can hear in Harlem or Chicago."[79] One can only speculate about how Panassié took the success of the Hot Club, which continued to open regional offices in towns all over France, but Prunières may not have been too far off in his use of the pontiff metaphor to describe how Panassié, who was gaining a vertically integrated hold over all aspects of jazz media and production, was beginning to act. Indeed, Panassié quickly used his swelling critical authority to quell rumors of Armstrong's death after it was mistakenly announced on the radio by Le Poste Parisien. Then he attacked British *Melody Maker* and Belgian *Music* critic Robert de Kers on questions of doctrine.[80] Finally, after fending off claims from John Hammond in America that Satchmo had gone commercial, Panassié began to describe Armstrong as the transubstantiation of jazz spirit, calling him "hot made flesh."[81] Whenever anyone questioned his judgment, Panassié indexed his record collection and the authority vested in him as the great defender of true *jazz hot.* Panassié's authoritarianism and ad hominem style was becoming dominant. Indeed, Prunières could not stem the discursive tide and eventually changed the name of his column in *La Revue Musicale* to "Jazz Hot."

Hot Heroes?

In July 1933, just as the Aryan purity and anti-Semite campaign was picking up in Germany, Duke Ellington's European tour began with several concerts in England. After a short tour of Holland, Duke and his entourage arrived in Paris for two dates at the Salle Pleyel.[82] The Ellington orchestra quickly became a test case for the utility of the hot-versus-straight method for categorizing jazz and for Panassié's growing hegemony. Critic Vincent Breton wrote, "Straight jazz or hot jazz? It is indispensable in 1933 to have an opinion on that serious question."[83] Breton believed the Ellington orchestra laid this question to rest. Although the complexity of the written arrangements seemed to call for its categorization as straight symphonic, there was still something about Ellington's jazz that made it hot. "There is an invention there, a power of orchestration that is simply extraordinary. At all times, the soloists pull from their instruments these unheard-of and always renewing sounds."[84] In *Le Temps,* the more conservative Henry Malherbe agreed with Breton that the music had a kind of "*sauvage* beauty," but more than just properly categorizing the music, he was interested in making sense of the crowd that made *la rentrée* to Paris early for the concert. "We knew that there were devotees to 'hot' jazz. But we never believed that there were so great a number, nor that these worshipers of *musique nègre* practiced an idolatry so superstitious . . . Overall, fashionable men and women are overwhelmed by Americanism, drunk with their *nègromanie.* They have left the beaches, the country, the fresh shade, to rush, in that burning atmosphere, before one of the prophets of hot jazz."[85] The concert was important for these faithful (whom he described as cosmopolitan liberals and avant-garde modernists) not because of the music, which Malherbe himself appreciated, but because they wanted to be seen at this scene promoting their hot idolatry. His concern was that these slavish devotees of *le jazz hot,* owing to the influence of foreign culture, had lost their clarity, their reason, and their love of "true" Frenchness.

Like Malherbe, André Schaeffner was just as interested in the sociology of the crowd and the Hot Club movement as he was in Ellington's music. Although he liked this jazz, Schaeffner did not believe that it had the "primitive energy" to be called hot. "He hardly represents any longer, in the proper sense of the term, 'hot' jazz."[86] For Schaeffner, Ellington's appearance had more to do with French-American relations and depression-era economics than with the *nègre* diaspora. Gone was the excited description of the "amphibiological" quality that had been a leitmotif in his work on jazz in the 1920s. His use of the concept hot rather than the hybrid cultural terms he had coined for *Le Jazz* shows how dominant *hot* had become. Alas, Schaeffner no longer heard the "original violence" or "primitiveness" associated with hot jazz in most of Ellington's new pieces. This music, he believed, seemed to recapitulate the impressionism and older cultural order jazz had overthrown. Although the orchestra played some of the songs recorded before 1930 that "reflected *jazz hot,*" most of their songs left them (and the audience) "sitting in a Ravelian comfort . . . Between Bolero and this, what is the difference, save that which marks several years in the fabrication of automobiles."[87] Yet despite this impressionistic assembly-line analogy, he believed that traces of the "inherent virtuosity of hot jazz" could still be heard in the "incredible play of mutes that lends that musician the most repulsive laryngological quality."[88] It was as if

Ellington's civilized orchestrations tried to repress this "repulsive," voice-like hot sound (which could only be a description of Cootie Williams's trumpet), but sometimes it came through nonetheless.

In the new conservative newspaper *Gringoire,* Georges Devaise also used the Ellington concert as an opportunity to sound off on the new "*snobbisme du hot*" that had taken hold of jazz criticism and the jazz listening public. "That there is actually a 'snobbism' of *jazz hot* is undoubtable after attending the first of two concerts given this last week by Duke Ellington. The Salle Pleyel was packed. There were false stiff collars and tails. The announcement of each of the pieces wrenched rapturous 'ohs' from 1,500 breasts. And when, by chance, several of the profane chuckled at the mewing of the clarinet or with the 'wa-wa' of the muted trumpets, one had to hear the indignant 'shshsh' of the initiated."[89] Devaise agreed with the idea that hot was rooted in "spontaneous immediate invention," but he did not believe that the Ellington players truly "abandoned themselves to the inspiration of the moment."[90] To describe what "true" hot would be, he traced out a history of jazz with Ellington's jazz marking its end. He believed that Ellington's jazz had "ceased to be the national music of the *nègres* of the U.S."[91] Like other critics in the right-wing *Gringoire,* he wanted pure music, not music that represented *métis* mixed-race culture. Yet he revealed his own allegiance to another "true jazz" that was still pure: "Finally Louis Armstrong comes! Virtuoso of the trumpet—without a doubt the greatest that we have ever heard—that black is going to ask other black virtuosos to magnify with him the deformative genius of their race."[92] In the end, the object of Devaise's irony was not those who believed in the racially grounded "deformative genius" behind pure hot, but the "snobs" who mistook the slick Ellington repertoire for "*le vrai jazz.*" Again, coming from a center-right paper, Devaise showed that it was possible to appreciate jazz as a foreign form on its own terms—to be a conservative cosmopolitan—without giving up on the idea that there was a true French music that was pure and, more importantly, not jazz.

Pierre Trevières's review in the centrist-left *Paris-Soir* was also more concerned with the implications of *jazz hot* for French culture than with Duke Ellington. "Do you like jazz? Me, I adore it . . . For jazz has marvelously adapted to our *mœurs,* our dreams, our desires, to the spirit of our time itself."[93] If there was something a little wild in *le jazz hot,* he argued, it was not a reflection of the musicians' primitiveness, but rather of "the state of the contemporary soul."[94] Stéphane Mougin, for his part, believed Ellington's jazz was marvelous, but Mougin was troubled by the mirror-like inversion of right-wing polemics that he heard in the hot reviews. While the conservative cultural purists wanted only true French music, the Hot Club devotees wanted only true *musique nègre,* even if they now called it hot. "But we are well 'compartmentalized' in our heterogeneous society of jazz lovers . . . The youngsters have one fault, a very great fault, an aggravating fault. They see only orchestras from the U.S. They only see (more exactly) musicians from 'over there'; certain of these youngsters have gone to the point of seeing only the black American element. That is a gross error. It is an enormous lacuna in their spirit . . . They forget, among other things, that in France there are a number of musicians who are 'hot,' who have personality, *their personality,* maybe, who have sincerity in their playing, naturalness, in a word, and who would be able to measure strongly against the best from America."[95] He worried that jazz lovers were increasingly elitist and purist in their tastes and critical perspectives. They had developed prejudices that led them to reject French jazz *a priori.* Again, Mougin argued that this loss of diversity in taste was due to the mechanisms of production, promotion, and criticism in the culture industry that pigeonholed music into categories to aid sales and hyped the music to generate interest. Even hot critics seemed to be aware that the hot jazz they called noncommercial was, in fact, accompanied by intense publicity campaigns. Indeed, after witnessing the "grotesque publicity,"[96] Panassié had to explain to those who questioned Ellington's authenticity that this commercialism was an exception, not the rule for *le vrai jazz hot.*

Henry Prunières, too, was amazed by the fanaticism he saw at the Ellington concert and blamed it on the Hot Club. "*Le Hot Club* is composed of young people touched by the hot grace, letting themselves go to an unbridled propaganda."[97] Their ears were so clogged with Hot Club propaganda that they had not really heard the orchestra's refined sensibility, as it defied the simple hot taxonomy. Ellington's music, for Prunières, did not correspond to the notion of "deformative genius" that the by-now-standard jazz discourse attributed to "hot" and *la musique nègre.* Rather, he described a group led by a "great leader" whose ideas so "saturated" the group that he only had to be present for the band to respond. Unlike other hot jazz that sometimes fell into "anarchy," this was a thoughtful, reasoned music that even the most intellectual French could appreciate. Rather than making the critical question whether the music was hot or straight an either/or proposition, as Panassié's brand of criticism did, Prunières sought to explain the music as a synthesis of both. Such an approach, however, went against the grain of Hot Club doctrine.

Émile Vuillermoz, editor of *L'Édition Musicale Vivante,* had heard enough of the hot critics and their Manichean dogma. While his liberal inclusive journal promoted all kinds of recorded music, from classical to jazz, purists, like

Panassié, dismissed this cosmopolitan approach. Eventually the hype of hot led Vuillermoz to declare that jazz, as he and those of his generation knew it, was finished. Whereas openness and cross-class solidarity had characterized the early jazz days in France, a new form of classicism, rooted in divisive fanaticism, dominated the new jazz landscape. "The partisans of straight treat the specialists of hot as *sauvages* enamored with noise and shrieks, while their adversaries scorn the timidity of ear and the too-easy taste of these poor people who look for grace, seduction, and charm in music."[98] Along with noting how different social groups defined themselves and their tastes by opposing the other style, Vuillermoz found the success of hot troubling. He argued that the common jazz of the early 1920s, based on chord changes that anyone could play, had been overshadowed by a highly complex music played by groups of "super-virtuosos."[99] The crowd of Hot Club fanatics had preconceived ideas about true jazz that were so fixed that they were duped by Ellington's carefully choreographed spectacle. Vuillermoz saw this false consciousness as the outcome of the fanatical *jazz hot* criticism that had divided and conquered jazz fans in France.

Critic Jean Wilmés, in the increasingly ultra-right-wing newspaper *Je Suis Partout* (I Am Everywhere), agreed with the writers who heard hot in Ellington but gave a familiar perspective on the incompatible difference between hot and proper French sensibilities. He used the Ellington concert as a pretext to denounce *le jazz hot* for being un-French and described it with standard racist stereotypes. "*Le jazz hot* has and will always have against it its exterior clownesque side, properly intolerable, that essentially *nègre* need for disordered gesticulation, for burlesque and savage pantomime . . . how banal."[100] The aesthetic question for him, and for others in a host of journals springing from the growing influence of the right in France, like the integralist *L'Action Française* and *Gringoire,* was not hot versus straight, but French versus foreign and white versus *nègre.* Manichean thinking on jazz was gaining ground as a feature of cultural discourse. Just as Panassié would hold up "pure" hot as the aesthetic object of his ideology, critics from the right would continue to hold up the image of a "pure" France that needed to have all the foreign blemishes wiped from its face.

It Don't Mean a Thing if It Ain't Got That Swing

In the October issue of *Jazz-Tango Dancing* (the last word of the title added that year), Stéphane Mougin continued to voice his concern about the growing division in jazz criticism. As an antidote, he introduced a new concept into the French critical lexicon on jazz, *swing,* to explain how Ellington's music could be both *sauvage* and refined, and still vital. Like *hot, swing* was an American word used to describe the rhythmic element in jazz that was even more important than Panassié's hot. Mougin argued that jazz, like all music rooted in rhythm, should make people want to dance. Yet the rhythmic tenacity of jazz was only the beginning of what he called the "essence of swing." He believed it was hard for French listeners to hear and understand swing, because French people had problems following syncopated rhythm. "It might seem ridiculous to recall here, but in France, it is indispensable. For the French have no rhythm. It is probably one of the consequences of a too-great civilization. But it's a fact that dance, primitive pleasure par excellence, is retarded when intellectuality mounts . . . Most jazz pianists here have crumpled fingers. Absolutely no regularity, no rhythmic will . . . That is the truth."[101] This was not a sign that Mougin had suddenly cast aside his materialism for an essentialist view of race-bound aesthetics—"the French have no rhythm"—but rather that a cultural tendency, "too much civilization," led French musicians to overintellectualize. Rather than a racial characteristic, swing was a subtle technique. French listeners (or dancers) needed only to open their ears to hear swing rhythm, so essential to authentic jazz. In a sense, Mougin was riffing on a standard Rousseauian theme here, opposing civilization and natural beauty. What French musicians needed to get the balance necessary to swing was not to imitate black musicians, but rather to relax and be natural. "Be natural," Mougin stressed—"that is everything."[102]

At the Hot Club, however, the notion that hot and swing were grounded in race all but took over as Panassié's authority grew. One can see the power of the link between hot and *nègre* in the titles and formats for club events, like the *gala d'art nègre* organized by Jacques Canetti on October 29, 1933, at the Salle Pleyel. Canetti, now Panassié's only rival, booked Freddy Johnson et les Harlemites[103] (Harlem having become something of an imaginary holy land for the Hot Club) as the house band and screened Paul Robeson in *Emperor Jones,* as well as two short animated films backed by jazz. "Some have said that jazz is out of style," wrote one critic; "the success of this event proves that it still has many faithful enthusiasts."[104] Yet though Panassié agreed with the correlation between *art nègre* and hot, this was too impure for Panassié, who was not asked to give a lecture and would never have called Robeson's music hot. In January of 1934, Le Hot Club reorganized itself to look like a national political movement, with officers, national headquarters, and regional offices.

Panassié was elected the first president of the Hot Club de France and took the oath to "propagate true *jazz hot*." Charles Delaunay (1911–1988), son of avant-garde artists Robert and Sonia Delaunay, became its secretary general.

Yet *Jazz-Tango Dancing* was still the only jazz journal, and many of its critics still defended straight French jazz in the spirit of liberal cosmopolitan inclusion. For instance, the same issue that published Panassié's inauguration promise to propagate hot also included Léon Fiot writing on a "new orchestra of French jazz," Raymond Legrand et son orchestre. "He hopes to give a new beginning to national jazz, in a bit more agreeable form, a bit more jazz, let's say the word. He wants equally to demonstrate the qualities and merits of other young French composers in this genre."[105] Such cosmopolitan pluralism in *Jazz-Tango Dancing* was untenable for Panassié, who began to denounce critics who did not adopt his definition of *le vrai jazz*. He lashed out at English jazz critic "Mike" from *Melody Maker* for not proclaiming Louis the king of jazz. "What is unfortunate is that 'Mike's' spiritual state finds itself, and worse, in almost all the English jazz critics."[106] This form of ad hominem attack would become the classic Panassian move against critics with different tastes. Slowly but surely, his orthodoxy took control of the discourse, and critics like Stéphane Mougin stopped writing.

One particular event gave critics the opportunity to show were they stood on the question of hot. In 1934, Cab Calloway came to town and played at the Salle Pleyel on April 23 and 24. Again critics seemed to be just as interested in explaining the behavior of French audience as they were in describing the music. Roger Tulleron in *Le Courrier Musical* noticed the effect of Calloway's jazz on the ethos of the French audience and did not like what he saw. He avowed that it was not his intention to put *le jazz hot* "on trial," as he believed that the existence of pure aesthetic categories was still very debatable. Nonetheless, his descriptions of Cab Calloway reproduced the standard riffs associated with hot, characteristics that, he believed, were unsettling for Frenchmen and -women. The band's hot jazz, he argued, had a dangerous psychological effect on the listener. "The high notes of the trumpets are a terrible ordeal for the sensitive nerves of the listener—burning and tearing the flesh. After an hour of that regime one is under the control of a violent overexcitation. One feels an irresistible need to defend oneself, to kick and bite. For a moment, one feels the need to attack one's neighbor (that would be dangerous, supposing that he finds himself in the same disposition). So, nerves exasperated, hearing tortured by these atrocious vibrations, one gets wise and flees, only to be pursued for a long time by haunting visions of these *nègres* gone mad."[107] Paradoxically, though he was trying to convince his readers that this frenetically wild music was dangerous to the nerves of Frenchmen and the ethos of true French culture, with the reproduction of hot hyperbole he may have legitimated the authenticity of Calloway's jazz for hot fans.

Similarly, Pierre Leroi praised Calloway's "Zah-Zuh-Zaz" in the June 1934 *L'Édition Musical Vivante* for being a kind of "psalm or phrase shouted by the soloist and repeated by a faraway chorus, an echo . . . Cab Calloway is a kind of vocal phenomenon. He pushes human resistance to incredible limits."[108] Comparing his description of Calloway to his review of French jazzman Michel Warlop, one can also see that though he placed Calloway as a unique phenomenon at the limits of the human, he was not advocating an imitation of this style for French jazz musicians. He was using this opposition to construct his sense of a more updated Frenchness. "Here is, in effect, the first hot French orchestra. It is Michel Warlop who has intensified these things for which we can now only congratulate him. Tempered tendencies, certainly, where music is constantly present, even when the soloists free themselves to their personal exploits. Maybe we had to wait for French taste and reserve to give hot a new life?"[109] Thus Calloway was hot at its extreme, a marker of the boundary between *sauvage* and French that was to be noted but resisted in the service of a tempered French hot that, though maybe not ideal, was more appropriate for France.

Predictably, Panassié wanted to have the last word on Calloway's reception in France. "Cab Calloway strongly bored me with his lamentable clowning."[110] He denounced critics who "dared to compare him to Duke Ellington"[111] and attacked the promotional publicity that named Calloway the "king of jazz." Both had had a detrimental effect on the public's ability to recognize "true jazz." "It's ridiculous and intolerable. Advertising should forbid itself from passing certain boundaries of exaggeration. One baptizes the first orchestra to come along 'king' of its specialty, even if it is one of the most mediocre . . . Unfortunately for the coming of Cab Calloway, the harm caused by the disproportionate publicity has not fallen back on Cab Calloway, but upon *le jazz hot* . . . In effect, all the uninformed people—that is to say the immense majority—went to Cab's concert sincerely believing that they would hear the most typical kind of hot orchestra. Naturally, the hollering and clowning [*beuglements et pitraries*] of Cab himself and the mediocrity of half of the soloists have produced a deplorable effect."[112]

Panassié complained that Calloway's concert had ruined the work he had done to propagate *le vrai jazz hot*. "We see that the result is disastrous! Now we must double the effort to interest those susceptible to liking hot interpretation and make them understand it. Will we ever recover from this misunderstanding?"[113] But what exactly, for Panassié, was the correct way of judging jazz threatened by such misunderstanding? Instead of *Jazz-Tango Dancing,* which Panassié would now longer write for, because of Canetti's influence, he used the venerable *La Revue Musicale* to set the record straight about the "true physiognomy of jazz music" and the relation between hot and swing in authentic jazz. As before, he split jazz into two general categories, hot and straight. The latter category was something he detested and often served as a waste bin in his theoretical system for jazz that he did not think had the essence of "authentic *jazz hot.*" First, authentic *jazz hot* had to have "binary rhythm," meaning that one never heard true jazz in waltz time. If it was a waltz, it was not true jazz. Just as a house had a foundation, binary rhythm was the foundation of jazz. For Panassié, however, the "fundamental element of true jazz" differentiating it from other music with binary rhythm was "swing *nègre.*" Without swing, jazz was not authentic. Like hot, swing was an untranslatable concept for Panassié, just as ephemeral as the nature of the "black musicians who spontaneously created it."[114] Without swing, Panassié could not call it "le vrai jazz." It either had the "vital element" or it did not. For jazz to be authentic or true, it had to be hot *and* swing. The public needed to be protected from the misinformation of those who dared to say otherwise.

Just as he used examples of "false jazz" to define "true jazz," Panassié wrote against critics whose views on *le jazz hot* differed from his own. The truth of *le jazz hot* could be indexed only by referring to hot records. For example, when Henry Prunières used the analogy of baroque aesthetics to talk about jazz improvisation, Panassié shot back, "If one could content oneself by defining hot as a series of variations improvised by diverse players in an 'orchestra,' one could legitimately write, like M. Prunières, that jazz is a kind of 'return to the orchestras of the sixteenth century,' which were not confined to playing the written note."[115] While Prunières's analogy emphasized points in common with European improvisational music and searched for cultural similarities between the different musical traditions, Panassié differentiated himself through his rejection of metaphor and commonality and his insistence on "essence" and difference, both of which were manifest in the intonation and style particular to "*la vraie musique nègre.*" This essence "escapes a precise description."[116] Rather than define it, as in all things jazz, Panassié used Louis Armstrong's records, where it was manifest. Armstrong's "personal genius" was the master signifier that explained what Panassié's theoretical system could not. All true hot players, he argued, followed Armstrong's "*nègre* style." Listening to Louis records had even made "hot white style" (read American or

French hot) possible. White musicians could learn to imitate the *nègre* style and approach hot in their playing. Paradoxically, in order to be authentic, one had to imitate this *nègre* style without fault. Panassié's critique of jazz, it would seem, was based on recognition of certain characteristics that made sense only within a system grounded in his own personal tastes. Whereas for years, critics in France had been using "authentic" jazz improvisation to discuss artistic freedom, where the musician expressed his own sensibility and self, Panassié now decreed that the only way to play authentic *jazz hot* was to be his kind of *nègre*.

Saint Louis's Blues

The debate on the essence of true jazz continued in the October and November 1934 issues of *La Revue Musicale,* in which musicologist Blaise Pesquinne offered a theory that, along with discussing *le jazz hot,* focused on the non-*nègre* side of jazz. Like Prunières, he sought to link jazz to other improvisational music in the West. In the fifteenth century, for instance, there had been organ improvisation. Collective improvisation had also been practiced in the eighteenth century, when some kinds of German choral music used rules that allowed the group to improvise together on a given theme. He argued that over time, however, this kind of improvisational freedom had gradually been eliminated in Europe through the dominance of music based on written rules of harmony and counterpoint.

For Pesquinne, who held up a kind of pan-European high culture as his ideal, an essential difference between jazz and classical music was akin to the difference between written and oral culture. In written classical composition there was "organization and architectural clarity" in the score; in jazz, where there were no written rules to guide improvisation, "everything is *liberté.*"[117] Yet there was an undeniable order in jazz, only the harmonic order was subconsciously retained, either as an innate or intuitive sensibility—an "interior *frénésie*"—or in memory. "The sureness of the harmonic ear in *nègres* and in musicians who improvise jazz is highly educated."[118] So where European composition was grounded in the written score, in jazz, the oral rules were deeply rooted in memory. "True" jazz improvisation was based upon this tacit cultural knowledge that Pesquinne linked to "the harmonic tradition of black music."[119] It was possible to have true "collective improvisation" only in a group that shared an intuitive knowledge of a harmonic order and tradition particular to jazz. For Europeans, who lacked this tacit knowledge, this was rarely the case.

Pesquinne argued further that the very harmonic intuition that made good jazz improvisation possible for blacks often made it disagreeable to European ears, more proof that their harmonic order and cultural sensibility differed from *les nègres*. This music was "still often displeasing and ungracious, if not shocking, for Europeans."[120] When jazz rubbed against the grain in this way, it testified to a difference in cultural traditions and sensibilities. "The blacks live their affective and passionate life on the outside and express their most intimate emotions and sensations at the same time as their most violent show themselves in the nude. Sadness, joy, desire, all of that can be translated into music by these combinations. But they are also translated by a cry and a timbre of voice, a howling that is perhaps the expression of its sentiments in life (and fortunately, there are still people for whom moral and intellectual modesty is the first mark of civilized man). In any case, it is certain that in music, one has the right to wait for a transposition a bit more veiled."[121] As opposed to "civilized man"—read the French—who showed emotional restraint in self-expression, *les noirs* let it all hang out in their music.

Pesquinne used Louis Armstrong's sound to show this direct relation between the interior life of *les noirs* and the physical affect of their expression, and to differentiate it from the normative Western aesthetic. While Louis's playing was unrestrained, in "civilized" expression, Pesquinne argued, such affect was "veiled." His abusive way of singing was even more disagreeable to Pesquinne, as it clashed with his own "civilized" French sensibility. "In fact, his sung choruses represent the summoning of the most unsavory expressionism. He never hesitates to resort to purely animal effects, giving the listeners the impression that he resents them and letting himself go to those repugnant explosions. He demonstrates to us clearly that he has, as we say, absolutely no taste . . . By his example, we clearly see the beauty and problem of individual *nègre* lyricism at the same time."[122] Pesquinne believed that Armstrong's jazz expressed an "organic being" rooted in racial memory, an innate harmonic order based on an absence of civilized taste. Moreover, he diagnosed this sensibility as a symptom of "resentment": he believed American blacks *should* resent whites, who had caused all their suffering. In his mind, Louis's "repugnant explosions" were understandable and appropriate for black Americans. Yet he did not "resent" jazz; he merely thought it was the "artistic manifestation of a race different than ours."[123] For him, jazz, and all music, for that matter, was best if it respected and expressed proper racial and cultural difference. Purism of all kinds was gaining the upper hand in music and cultural criticism.

By the time Louis Armstrong finally got to France in late 1934, the cultural scene had changed in a way that led to more unrestrained cultural criticism from the right. A political scandal, the Stavisky Affair, was used by a right-wing coalition to wrestle power from the left. As this political divide continued to grow, jazz became a metonymic symbol of cultural miscegenation and what was wrong with France. So when Louis got to Paris, he was not only the symbol of "true jazz" for Hot Club proponents, but also for jazz's opponents.

In the months before he arrived, the Hot Club warmed up for him with special meetings, radio programs, and the release of Panassié's book *Le jazz hot,* for which Louis wrote the preface. The publicity for Panassié's book in newspapers and journals was intense. Yet Panassié, at only twenty-two years old, did not have total control of the Hot Club. It was Jacques Canetti who booked Armstrong for a staggering 130,000 francs for seven weeks of work and managed him in France.[124] Canetti also wrote an unfavorable review of *Le jazz hot* in *Jazz-Tango,* criticizing Panassié for his "polemical tone." Armstrong was to appear onstage and on the radio, to be a centerpiece for the Hot Club, and support the promotion of Panassié's book. He would be at the center of the struggle for control of the Hot Club and for dominance in jazz criticism.

After the November 10 concert at the Salle Pleyel, Panassié announced that "Louis remained . . . not only the best trumpeter, but still the greatest of all hot musicians."[125] Yet, though musician Mugsy Spanier and jazz critics Albert Wynn and George Frazier Jr. wrote articles praising Satchmo for the November issue of *Jazz-Tango Dancing,* Armstrong received less attention in the general press than had Ellington or Calloway. The articles that did emerge showed just how polarizing Armstrong had become as an icon of *le jazz hot.*

Lucien Rebatet (1903–1972), the culture critic for the right-wing integralist newspaper *L'Action Française* and for *Je Suis Partout* (and officer in his own protofascist purist cultural movement), used Armstrong as the "essential figure of jazz-hot" to denounce the music and the movement as being signs of the mixed-race (*métis)* cultural influences that were, in his mind, destroying the true France. He agreed that Armstrong was a "trumpet virtuoso" and that he played with a "*sauvage* magnificence" that had a "surprising effect."[126] However, this also served as the basis to his objection to Armstrong and to *le jazz hot.* "Hot, if one believes the *hotisants,* is an improvisation on some American melody, an improvisation that is valued for the playing, the fantasy of the player, and the technical cleverness that permits him to freely abandon himself to his demon."[127] It was important for Rebatet to solidify the "*hotisant*" view that Armstrong was "integral hot," for by criticizing him, Rebatet was also making a statement about the beliefs of the "fanatics" who idolized him. "We much admired his way of using his shadow. This barbarian, all while gesticulating and sounding his horn with his mouth, cast a fantastic silhouette on the walls of the Salle Pleyel, an apparition from prehistory, a primate possessed by the devil. Physically, this is truly the pure *nègre*, with hairy knees and simian suppleness in the legs [*jarret*] and in the spine. But to have to listen to it and see it for two full hours, that is very quickly a puerile monotony."[128] One hardly needs to point out the pernicious racist language and stereotypes at work here, with their "scientific" overtones. Rebatet argued that, given its associations with *nègres* and all their exotic physical difference, he could understand how French listeners would have been drawn to "authentic" jazz after the war. But in the late 1920s, jazz, too, had been corrupted by American commercialism, which for Rebatet was always the fault of the Jews. The jazz today, neither musical nor primitively authentic, smelled of this decay. "That was the time when the commerce of dance tunes corrupted the primitives. Over the assembly-line rumbas and foxtrots that saturate the atmosphere of our time, we would very much like to hear a clearly tropical music, which is cutting in its rawness. This is not 'hot,' but simple jazz, of course."[129] Jazz performers always had a commercial exterior whereby "trances of panic . . . and an almost unvaried jolt" were used to connote authenticity. Indeed, Rebatet thought that this affect was merely an "unrefined pretense that Armstrong himself cannot avoid." After fifteen minutes with the mediocre orchestra, Armstrong sounded like "an angry automobile horn."[130] If Louis was the king of *jazz hot*, Rebatet argued, then he wanted no part of it. Rebatet had begun his all-out campaign to drive hot and other symptoms of modern *métis* culture out of his "true France."

Yet despite some opposition in the right-wing press, Hot Club partisans embraced Armstrong. He took an apartment in Montmartre, where he held court and slept long into the afternoon after being wined, dined, and toasted everywhere he went. He was made honorary president at the Hot Club general headquarters in Paris and taken on a tour of the growing number of regional clubs. Armstrong also played a short concert over the radio during the now regular "Hot Club" broadcast on Le Poste Parisien, in which he, as was his fashion, began with "When it's Sleepy Time Down South."[131] Yet the all-out promotion of *jazz hot* orthodoxy accompanying his performance caused a backlash among proponents of French jazz. The writers in *Jazz-Tango Dancing*, for instance, seemed to be tiring of the Hot Club hype, as a report on Fred Addison et son orchestre indicated. "Here is an orchestra that finally does honor to our corporation. What's more, despite its foreign-sounding name, the orchestra is composed exclusively of Frenchmen . . . always in a moderate style."[132] As Armstrong traveled south to play at the Marseilles Hot Club in January of 1935, critics started to turn their resentment of the hot-only critics onto poor Louis. For instance, Herman Klosson, in the solidly cosmopolitan *La Revue Musicale*, wrote that the Hot Club faithful continued "to make good people believe that jazz is the supreme form of modern music. The mysticism of the devotees of hot is one of the most comic things there is. They speak to you at length of Armstrong's trumpet but haven't the least idea that there was a time when someone named Bach existed."[133] André Coeuroy, who reached the apex of his authority on jazz in France when he associated himself with Schaeffner's 1927 *Le Jazz,* and who now published his criticism in the right-wing newspaper *Gringoire,* reported on the publication of Panassié's *Le jazz hot.* "Very interesting. Very narcissistic, as well. The author complacently sees himself in the reflection of his black idol Louis Armstrong's trumpet."[134] Coeuroy criticized Panassié's "copious bible on *jazz hot*"[135] for being a mere collection of his journal writings and offered his own analogy for understanding the "essential element of jazz: swing. Until now, no one has furnished a precise definition . . . To give a vague idea, we could say that it is a sort of balance in rhythm and melody that always induces a great dynamism. That embarrassing search for a definition is very interesting."[136] In addition to the bobbing and weaving of boxing, he offered the analogy of the shifting from side to side that one performed while skiing, which depended upon the course and the speed of the skier. What true jazz did not depend on, Coeuroy believed, was Panassié's approval.

The Defenders of *le Vrai Jazz Hot*

In March 1935, Panassié and Charles Delaunay created *Jazz Hot,* "the official organ of the Hot Club de France." With an array of international collaborators and articles in both English and in French, *Jazz Hot* was a journal that finally satisfied Panassié's need for editorial purity. The journal, whose layout was established by Hot Club secretary general Delaunay, was something of a cross between the photographically illustrated cinema journals, which cultivated the personas of movie stars, and Catholic journals like *Études.* There were interviews and biographies of jazz stars supported by photos, pieces on critics who spread the word, and news from the missions, where new local Hot Clubs were opening every month. Most importantly, everything in *Jazz Hot* underscored Panassié's authority as *the* leader of the movement.

The composition of the first issue of *Jazz Hot* reveals this ideological function. It began with Panassié's promotion of the latest performer to come to

France, Coleman Hawkins, who was also the first American musician to record on Panassié and Delaunay's new record label, *Swing*. Panassié had heard Hawkins with Sam Wooding's band and had gone out and "bought every record by Fletcher Henderson"[137] in order to hear more Armstrong and Hawkins. Of course, Panassié maintained the hierarchy of his jazz pantheon by stating that Hawkins did not "find his stride" until he was touched by grace, or rather "impregnated with the spirit of Louis."[138] As he did with other musicians he liked, Panassié constructed a cult of personality around Hawkins. Just as Panassié continued to define "authenticity" and defend his authority by associating himself with the jazzmen and records that he alone truly knew, other critics in the journal grounded their criticism in Panassié's expertise and persona. By doing so, they reified his status as the authority on jazz.

For instance, John Hammond added to Panassié's cult of personality with a "letter from America" stating how happy he was to write for a journal "controlled by people who really understand and appreciate swing music."[139] To build up Panassié, Hammond criticized *Jazz-Tango* and *Melody Maker* and promoted the belief that Panassié possessed an incomparable ear. "I'd like to say right now that Hugh's [*sic*] book *Le jazz hot* is marvelous from start to finish. His taste is always of the best, and the details and definitions in the book make it by far the most important single event that has ever befallen swing music."[140] Similarly, Georges Hilaire declared all pre-Panassian criticism to be the work of "snobs" who were ignorant of the "true principles" of jazz. It was Panassié's "courageous objectivity and attentive argumentation of the phenomenon of hot,"[141] he argued, that transformed the jazz scene. Hilaire bashed Ferroud, Rebatet, Malherbe, and other culture critics for their French "prejudice." He wrote that only Panassié, with his Cartesian eye for detail (and who now owned over three thousand jazz records), actually had the true French critical spirit. "Panassié, with his spirit of properly scientific investigation and, all said, with his instinctive application of Cartesian method, can identify any American musician after hearing the record once. He, who can cite by heart the principle choruses of hot, has done it better that Robert Goffin, with his personal, esoteric, and hermetic work. He would not be satisfied to write his theory of jazz! Not at all! He wrote *the* theory of jazz. The normative character of his study displays a methodological will to elucidate all the obscure zones for other critics of jazz. Work of reason, 'discourse on method' for the critic that we recommend for all the amateur critics who wander on unknown ground."[142]

Panassié displayed an "instinctive" Cartesianism; although rather than being the Cartesian eye, he was the "instantly identifying ear" upon which certainty rested. But instead of giving a discourse on method for jazz analysis that allowed for ontological certainty, the book *Le jazz hot* was an external authority, a kind of bible whose words had a moral status that any critic who wanted to be published in *Jazz Hot* had to accept and index in their criticism.

Although Panassié now controlled the criticism and had his own jazz label, Jacques Canetti was still a threat to his authority. In the second issue of *Jazz Hot*, Panassié lashed out against Canetti, the unbeliever, for promoting the idea that Louis did not like to play with musicians who might steal his spotlight. Rather than addressing the issue, Panassié immediately went after Canetti himself in an ad hominem attack that would later be known as the Canetti Affair. "I know that M. Canetti is not a Frenchman and that, for a foreigner, he is to be commended for knowing of our language what he knows. But when one is incapable of writing without likewise massacring the French language, there is a certain tone that one should not be allowed to adopt."[143] This tone was the authoritative tone that, by now, only Panassié and those who submitted to his orthodoxy of taste could employ without reproach. Panassié described Canetti's criticism as a "tissue of lies"[144] that revealed "very bad taste." "*Jazz-Tango* and *Melody Maker* dishonor themselves by publishing the indignant attacks by M. Canetti against a nice musician and one of the most loyal men I have had the luck to know."[145] Like the growing number of protomilitary organizations on the cultural right, the Hot Club faithful were closing ranks around their charismatic leader.

There was little that the remaining critics at *Jazz-Tango Dancing* could do to compensate for Panassié's Hot Club propaganda except double their own epideictic efforts by following the Hot Club example. In May of 1935, the proponents of French jazz at *Jazz-Tango Dancing* began the "jazz club de France" for "the defense of *jazz français*" and began to have their own "Jazz-Tango" cinema events.[146] As a result, the rhetoric in *Jazz-Tango Dancing* became a nationalist counterpoint to that in *Jazz Hot*, as critics dedicated themselves almost entirely to the promotion of French musicians like Ray Ventura, Roland Dorsay, Grégor et ses grégoriens, and a number of lesser-known groups who were having a hard time finding work. The *Jazz-Tango* writers pleaded for theater directors to hire French musicians, but the box-office power of the "*hotisants*" made it difficult for establishments that did not exclusively support "true jazz." It was already illegal for directors to have fewer than 30 percent of their musicians be French, but *Jazz-Tango* continued to sound the syndicate protectionist "*cri d'alarme.*"[147]

It was amid these critical battles that André Schaeffner was asked to contribute a section on the sociology of jazz in France for the 1935 edition of the *Ency-*

clopédie française, edited by Lucien Febvre. Schaeffner's entry was in a section on the relation between "collective needs and music." According to the preface, jazz testified to the "contamination of the arts by one another," which was the mark of a hybridized modern civilization. "Whether we enjoy or deplore it, jazz is a characteristic, the characteristic of our musical civilization."[148]

Schaeffner argued that jazz had filled the need for exoticism in all European countries as a kind of "vogue." In France, the jazz vogue had been part of the reaction against the "false orientalism of the Debbusyists."[149] Owing to the popularity of its "eclectic international style,"[150] jazz had stimulated a nationalistic reaction. This reaction (and counterreaction) was the sociological force behind the changes in jazz music and criticism. The current critical debates on hot and straight, he proposed, were merely a way to "reassure ourselves"[151] of the authenticity of a music that had lost its original character. Jazz, like the rest of culture, had become an eclectic mixture of different influences. "Purity," whether in regard to "true" jazz or "true" French culture, he argued, was merely a chimera that critics tried to conjure through a dogmatic insistence that concealed a lack of certainty.

Ontological certainty was indeed the trademark of the Hot Club and its *Jazz Hot* critics, who continued to denounce those who dissented. Henry Malherbe, after Panassié named him an "adversary of jazz-hot,"[152] responded to the attack in *Le Temps.* "For six years I have tried, on my part, to inform you of the essential elements of what I have called the *musica dell'arte* of the black instrumentalists."[153] He was the enemy of no music or musician, he argued. He had merely tried to describe jazz metaphorically and more precisely than Panassié, whose hyperbole and string of superlatives were equaled only by his disdainful words for other critics. "We would like for the frenetic expert in *Jazz Hot* to use a mute—if only a 'wa-wa' mute—on his enthusiasm and be more calm in his pronouncements. He courts the risk of passing for one of those 'amateur' critics who, in their little country papers, excite themselves over the clumsy exhibitions of amateur societies."[154] He mocked Panassié's overvaluation of Ellington and Armstrong's genius that placed them above all other music and all art. "One would not talk otherwise of Homer, Virgil, and Shakespeare. Does Hugues Panassié understand the terms he employs? I doubt it. Let us not engage in discussion with a fanatic who is victimized [*en proie de*] by such flights."[155] The greatest irony of all, Malherbe argued, was that after 363 pages of *Le jazz hot,* Panassié was unable to translate and describe the essence of hot. In the end, Panassié's dogmatism succeeded in turning Malherbe away from hot altogether. Along with his more calm and reasoned French criticism, he now preferred assimilated and civilized French symphonic jazz.

Yet in the increasingly combative world of French cultural criticism, negative portrayals of Panassié often proved beneficial for the movement, as *Jazz Hot* critics used them to show how the "enemies of hot" were a force to be reckoned with. Bolstered by this external threat, Panassié became the crusader, the critic who spoke the truth no matter the odds. Consequently, he retained his title as president of the Hot Club de France with virtually no opposition. Indeed, when the International Federation of Hot Clubs was founded by Marshall W. Stearns in New Haven, Connecticut, he called the book *Le jazz hot* "the Bible of Swing Music," and Panassié was named the first president. Panassié's authority on jazz was now international.

Nationalist Rhythms, Socialist Times

As France's economy continued to stall, the government had to reduce its role in promoting French music. The increasingly radicalized right wing in France held up Germany as an example of how nationalist cultures should be constructed. In Germany, the National Socialists grabbed control of culture with an iron fist and allowed only the dissemination of "Aryan culture."[156] Critics on the far right cheered when news came that the new Reich director of Berlin Radio, realizing the importance of radio in the dissemination of information and culture, had forbidden the broadcasting of jazz and all "Negro music."[157] Anti-parliamentarian voices in France thought that this was a path to follow. Like the Hot-Clubbers, they took their aesthetic politics to the concert halls. For example, a report in *Le Monde Musical* described an incident that occurred when Madeleine Grey gave a concert of several of Kurt Weill jazz songs in November 1933. "Members of the audience began shouting: '*Vive Hitler! Vive Hitler!*' And then the explanations added: We have enough bad musicians in France before one sends us all the Jews in Germany."[158]

The most pernicious of the right-wing journals, *Je Suis Partout,* highlighted the successes of National Socialists in Germany by comparing them to the degeneration of culture in America. Reporter Marcelle Prat—probably inspired by Louis-Ferdinand Céline's tropic dystopia[159]—wrote of Harlem's ghettos, the holy land for the "*hotisants*" in France who had lost sight of their true Frenchness. "*Les blacksmen et les blackswomen* have brains guided only toward gaiety; a hysterical gaiety of morose and sensual coquetry . . . a mix of sexuality, melancholy, and joy that hits you like a slap. From the *nègre* baby to the *nègre* father, they think of nothing but *jouissance.* They burn life with the senses. In that neighborhood, it appears, they are constantly arresting someone for rape. A race spellbound by vices and music. Each throat here is, itself, a jazz band."[160] With this racially impure American dystopia in mind,

Je Suis Partout called for a nationalist cultural politic that would combat and purge the jazz influence in France.

Even in the new centrist-left Popular Front created in 1935 as a coalition of socialist, radical, and communist parties, jazz was becoming politically dangerous. As the notion of pure cultural forms became more prominent and persuasive owing to the tenor of the times, they, too, supported national cultural politics. Though the anti-Semitic voices from the right were already busy trying to cast aspersions on Minister of Posts Telegraphs and Telephones Georges Mandel, who was reorganizing national radio programming, linking him and the rest of the Blum cabinet to the Jews of Tin Pan Alley and Hollywood, Mandel unequivocally declared, "I don't like jazz."[161]

Musician Raymond Legrand wrote in *Jazz-Tango Dancing* that French national music needed more sincerity to regain its strength. Too much concentration on commerce had led musicians and critics astray. When they chased after the market's tastes in music, their innate Frenchness no longer came through. "We must guard ourselves from pursuing the beaten path. We have, happily, a wholly other spirit . . . Could we not take what is good, prune the bad, and replace it with the innate quality of our Latin race?"[162] In March, he argued that each nation in Europe had adapted jazz to "the soul of the country" and had created a national style, "more or less derived from *le jazz hot* of an American importation."[163] The Italian style was essentially melodic. "The compositions are obviously feeble, the taste of the country going toward slow songs, melodies, tangos, and voluntarily simple harmonies, for which we cannot blame them."[164] Spain, on the other hand, owing to their "innate rhythmic sense," most evident in flamenco, had created a "magnificent replica of *le jazz hot.*"[165] In England, where many local governments manifested a protectionist spirit and had admirably "supported the great jazz orchestras,"[166] all kinds of jazz were heard. England, Legrand wrote, had "a professional consciousness at the base of everything." The French national style, naturally, was "purely musical."[167]

Even at the Hot Club, the promotion of the new Quintette du Hot Club de France, featuring Django Reinhardt and Stéphane Grappelli, gave way to nationalist positioning. Panassié, now promoting his own record label, Swing, to French listeners, declared the group to be a perfect adaptation of hot characteristics to French style. Of their recording of "I'se a muggin'," which featured the expatriate Freddy Taylor—the owner of the bar Harlem, in Montmartre—he wrote: "Stéphane's first chorus, just after the first passage sung by Freddy Taylor, is of a unique beauty, in a perfect style. The melodic development of all the choruses is of an admirable logic. And in the last, the intonations of Grappelli are extraordinarily hot."[168]

Yet even as Panassié consolidated his power as president of the Hot Club movement by winning elections year after year, jazz evolved in ways that set him at odds with new musicians. To defend his own authority, he attacked critics who championed the new. He used American critic George Frazier to condemn *Jazz-Tango Dancing* for the Canetti Affair and to label *Die Jazz-Welt* "dull and tasteless." The magazine "*Jazz Hot* is, of course, the best thing of this kind ever attempted . . . Hugues Panassié is an incredible guy and *Le jazz hot* an incredible book."[169] Panassié himself panned *Melody Maker* critic Hilton Schelman's book *Rhythm on Record* and picked a fight with John Hammond and *Down Beat*. "Even competent critics allow themselves to be fooled by preconceived opinions and, next to correct judgments, sometimes write stupefying things. In regard to the public, its taste and its admiration are above all guided by current events. It excites itself with new musicians or new orchestras to which the praise of critics or the new recordings have given a kind of vogue. It is generally pride and admiration without control."[170]

Again, Panassié's tirade was set off by a readers' poll in *Down Beat* that had dared to place Roy Eldridge on par with "Saint" Louis. He blamed the American voters' "incompetence" on John Hammond, who had, he wrote, stopped defending "true jazz." French jazz critics, he decreed, had a duty to uphold true jazz in the face of such madness.

Just as Panassié dismissed American and French jazz orchestras for being false, critics from the right also condemned non-*nègre* jazz for being untrue to the sensibilities of its performers. For example, after hearing a concert of the Orchestre National, Robert Bernard echoed Panassié's purism from the other side of the cultural spectrum, arguing that jazz could never be assimilated into French music: "Our orchestras are incapable of rivaling specialized orchestras . . . [Jazz] cannot be assimilated by our symphonic *phalanges* [armies]."[171] That it was a bad performance was actually satisfying for Bernard, who did not believe Frenchness and jazz were compatible. His use of the military term to describe the orchestra tells us something about the stakes of the culture wars swirling around jazz. Certainly, French symphonic composers' had written works aiming to assimilate jazz, such as Alfred Roussel's *Jazz dans la nuit*, Ravel's *Concerto* for piano, and Marcel Poot's *Jazz music*. Yet these composers had merely used jazz idioms as an effect blended into the larger symphonic tapestry of sound.

According to Bernard, jazz should be used only in a true symphonic composition, as it was in Amfitéatrof's *Panorama Américain*, to create "a hallucinatory evocation of a civilization based on the machine."[172] It was legitimate to use jazz to represent the modern American dystopia described by writers like Mauriac and Duhamel, an "artificial paradise . . . intoxicated by alcohol or drugs."[173] Thus, if the jazz tones were used sparingly in a representational sense to characterize the "reality" of the civilization they came from, they would fit well onto the palette of colors for French composers. But jazz should never be used, he argued, to express the truth of French civilization.

As the cultural right in France became more violently anti-Blum, anti-Semitic, and anti-American, especially in regard to the Hollywood presence in France, Panassié, too, became more openly anti-Hollywood in his rhetoric. After the release of the *Big Broadcast of 1937*, which featured Benny Goodman as the "King of Swing" and which dubbed the music of Teddy Wilson over the image of white musician Jess Stacy, Panassié cried "scandal" and denounced Benny Goodman for "dishonoring" jazz by being a part of a production guided by such commercially motivated racial prejudice.[174]

Yet as nationalistic rhetoric gained favor in the general press, Panassié's own criticism began to change, partially for commercial reasons. Whereas he had once denounced French jazz musicians for not being "truly hot," he now began to fudge his categorical imperatives, admitting several French musicians into hot's happy few. Along with pronouncing that "once and for all, Grappelli has proven that he is equal to the best American soloists,"[175] he named André Ekyan one of the few white sax players who could use the instrument well. "There have not been many great altos of the white race. Truly, Ekyan is one of the white race capable of drawing from his alto a full, incisive, and robust sound. Ekyan possesses a flame in his sound, his hot and vibrant intonations, which is lacking in almost all the altos of the white race."[176] Ekyan's intonation was hot in a way in which Goodman's was not. More importantly, this French hot was different from the hot of the "black race." This racial and cultural difference and nationalist mode of categorizing jazz sound was institutionalized at the Hot Club with the Hot Club prize for the "Disc Hot 1936": French Hot was given its own category.

A Piece of the Real

The biggest threat to Panassié's total authority on jazz in France continued to be his dogged attachment to Louis Armstrong as the symbol of *le vrai jazz hot*. The more he defended Louis, whose records were dropping in sales and who had recently been hospitalized with a split lip, the more he turned against new jazz players and styles. When critics used words like *commercialized* or *dried-up* to describe Armstrong's evolving style, Panassié denounced the criticisms as "lies" signifying that the accusing critic had, himself, sold out. In the pages of *Jazz Hot,* there were photos almost every month of Satchmo captioned with statements declaring him the "Real King of Jazz." Why did Panassié cling so hard to Louis as "incarnated jazz"? In a piece titled "From 1 to 1000," Panassié set out to count the reasons why Louis was the master, despite the criticism from others with corrupted ears. "If one listens with an impartial ear to the records, one quickly realizes that Louis has lost none of his interior flame, none of his pathetic accent."[177] He argued that Louis's style preserved "true" jazz and the "time before the effects of commercialism."[178] Louis was still the foundation of truth in matters of hot. "Thus I have the right to believe that, in this conflict, I alone have conserved the correct equilibrium."[179] Like culture critics on the right who looked back to the "true France" before the onslaught of modernity, Panassié the royalist had become nostalgic. As the leaders of the nationalist political movements did with their message, Panassié recognized the symbolic importance of raising a great man to stand for the essence of jazz.

To understand the importance of Louis Armstrong in Panassié's critical framework as a foundation for authority and as an access to truth on jazz, Kierkegaard's materialist theology provides a helpful analogy. In Hegel's idealism, truth was found through spirit reflecting upon its own notion. Kierkegaard reversed this. He made the body of the savior the absolute nonabolishable condition of all access to truth. As such, eternal truth for Kierkegaard was directly contingent upon the materialization of the Holy Spirit.[180] The savior, in his system, was the word made flesh, a piece of the real, a historical fact that existed. For Kierkegaard, without the savior's body occupying that place within the theology as incarnated spirit, the system crumbled and access to truth disappeared. In Panassié's *jazz hot* orthodoxy, Armstrong functioned in a similar way. The word was recorded jazz, inscribed on discs, and Louis was "jazz made flesh." This made access to the truth of jazz dependent on Louis and the relationship to Satchmo's jazz an essentially transferential one. With his records as "sacred texts," if one found fault, it was a sign of one's own faulty critical approach and bad faith.

Moreover, the language and rhetoric of Panassié's zealotry has striking similarities to the discourse that right-wing nationalists in Germany and France used to promote their ideology and leaders. (Indeed, Panassié now had a radio audience on stations like Radio-Cité and Le Poste Parisien.) For each movement, the body of the great man was the hyperbolic center of its political rhetoric, serving as a materialization of truth that fixed and concealed the essentially tautological construction of the commentary. One could say that the national government was looking to ground itself in a similar way when it brought back Maréchal Pétain, the "father of victory" in World War I, to head the French military in 1934.[181] By shifting further to the right, Édouard Daladier had defeated Blum's Popular Front in 1938, but protofascist thinkers like Robert Brasillach and Lucien Rebatet believed that France desperately needed a truly great leader—preferably a king—to unify the French people and stimulate them to redress a degenerate culture. They thought they had such a leader in Jacques Doriot, whose Parti Populaire Français was on the rise. Though they wanted a French form of fascism, they patterned their thinking on Germany, where Goebbels built the cult of personality around Hitler as the truth incarnate of National Socialism. It is thus no surprise that *Le Monde Musical, Journal des Débats,* and other antiparliamentarian newspapers published the Führer's speeches on restoring "true Aryan culture," and advocates of National Socialism and cultural purity in France often pointed to Germany as a model for cultural *redressement.* What the movement leaders demanded of their respective followers was not fidelity to some theoretical position (to the general notion of hot or to the abstract principles of National Socialism) but fidelity to "the piece of the real." Importantly, since the great man in each case sets the unquestionable criteria for truth, the ideology of such movements was fundamentally at odds with the Enlightenment aim to render truth independent of authority. This helps explain why Panassié demanded fidelity not only to Louis and the sacred records, but also loyalty to his own authoritative listening and his own person. At the Hot Club, any deviation was an act of bad faith worthy of censure.

Yet the body and face of jazz *had* evolved in America beyond Louis Armstrong. Swing jazz was now the most popular music, and the dances that its followers loved were rapidly becoming popular even in France. For instance, the Hot Club itself used their increased revenues to open a new bar called Swing Time in early 1937. Indeed, by June 1937, when the Cotton Club review came to the Moulin Rouge with a new dance, the Lindy hop, other dances, like the jitterbug, had already caught on. Even Madeleine Gautier, Panassié's loyal follower, praised the "ability of their legs and their arms, and the dynamism of their movements, the expression of their faces. It is all of a purity of swing that makes their dance the 'hottest' in the world."[182] Surely Panassié was assuaged when the results of the first *Jazz Hot* reader referendum showed that the faithful in France were still following his lead. Far and away, Louis was the favorite of *Jazz Hot* readers.[183] But though his reign as president continued year after year, Panassié was losing his command over a new generation of Hot Club members, teenage musicians like Boris Vian, Hubert Rostaing, and future Gaullist minister François Missoffe, who were fonder of the jam sessions and the camaraderie than of toeing the line in the critical debates.[184] To make matters worse, Louis appeared in the films *Pennies from Heaven* and *Artists and Models,* which made it hard for Panassié to divorce Armstrong from Hollywood's commercial stain. There was little for Panassié to cling to except the records from the good old days.

Cultural purists on the right held a similar nostalgic position on their own music and culture. For instance, Raoul Brunel argued in *Le Ménéstrel* that French radio, with a larger-than-ever influence on French culture,[185] needed to seize the moment to regain control of its programming and help the public shake the confusion and rediscover their taste for music of times past. "The public, which is incapable of that effort of reconstitution, habitually pleases itself with these corrupted sounds that completely falsify its tastes. The ease with which, by turning a dial, one can indefinitely procure for oneself this genre of distraction makes it difficult to redress this state of affairs by listening to true music in a good lyrical theater or a great concert . . . In reality, it is the public that adapts itself to raucous and nasal records rather than true music. The banality of offered programming, at least in France, works to demolish the musical sense. In reality, are not the discs that attest to the lowest taste those that meet with the best favor of the public? How many discs of café-concerts and jazz-band tunes are sold compared to the *Prelude of Tristan?*"[186] He pleaded for French programmers to repair the damage done by commercialized mass-media culture. Constant pandering to the public's taste for distraction, he argued, decayed French musical taste and disrupted traditional French values. Yet it was not too late to restore "true" French culture; the public could, he argued, rediscover its taste and orientation in a time of chaos by fixing on true high-culture music. If only France, like Germany, had the will to protect itself from modern mass culture's corrupting influence and reassert traditional high culture.

Jazz Hot also seemed to yearn for a return to "true" music before mass-culture corruption. Madeleine Gautier, who continued to translate song lyrics and write her own poetry on jazz in *Jazz Hot,* offered the case of Bessie Smith as a sign of the troubled times and as a possible antidote to the commercial "crooners"[187] and "big bands" that now dominated the radio. Due to such commercialism, she argued, even blacks were losing their taste for the blues. "The decline of the phonograph and the crisis on the one hand, and on the other, the believed popularity created by the radio, which everywhere serves the awful repetitious refrains of Broadway, have perverted the taste of the blacks and lured them away from their magnificent blues voices. The records of Bessie stopped being sold and, after 1931, they stopped recording her. The tone of her voice is seizing: grave, full, with the ringing of metal mixed with pure accents of sound; that voice is so natural that she could repel, right away, those who like the 'cultivated' organs too much!"[188] Whereas the commercial crooners sang with a cultivated vocal style, Bessie's bluesy moaning was completely natural. Panassié had few kind words for those who did not immediately recognize this authentic quality: "Bessie is a perfect example of swing, and only those imbeciles altogether imbued with the 'modern spirit' would never perceive it."[189] To further differentiate true swing from commercial swing, *Jazz Hot* also began to run a column in which Louis Armstrong recounted stories (presented in English and in translation) about growing up in New Orleans with other musicians, giving a nostalgic idea of the "authentic" precommercial cultural matrix from which jazz arose.[190] For Panassié and *Jazz Hot,* true jazz had none of that "Puttin' on the Ritz" flash; there were no sophisticated ladies eating with Satchmo; this was the real stuff of hot: simple, down-home naiveté straight from La Nouvelle Orléans. Panassié lamented that "since 1930, you will find no new musician comparable to [the musicians of] the great epoch. There is lots of talent, but no more of these geniuses like Louis, Bix, Duke, and Bessie Smith."[191] Indeed, at this time Panassié got the idea for organizing a "New Orleans Revival," the first of its kind, which eventually was recorded in New York in 1938 for his Swing label.

Critics at *Jazz-Tango Dancing* saw this nostalgia as a sign that Panassié (who was now lecturing on *le jazz hot* at the Sorbonne, appearing on film in *March of Time,* a short on the development of swing, and offering correspondence courses on *le jazz hot* through the Centre d'Études de Jazz) and the *Jazz Hot* critics had become stagnant. Émile Laurent, for instance, thought that the fixation on one kind of hot was based on a distant relationship to a living, evolving music. "Time has marched on and hot has stayed in the same place, which is to say that it has remained stagnant in that swamp where it was thrown even by those who had been its greatest defenders when it appeared, and who pinned a definition on it without even knowing how it was defined in its country of origin."[192] Panassié, of course, now responded to such comments by speaking only of the accusing critics' prejudice or "*mauvaise foi.*"[193]

Yet as the *Jazz Hot* critics became more dogmatic in their claims about the essence of a "real" jazz threatened by contemporary mass culture, critics on the right began to vilify jazz using language that had rarely been heard since the early 1920s. Robert Bernard, for instance, argued that jazz was a cause and sign of the degeneration of French culture and called for a return to music that was calm and ordered and followed a timeless French logic. He linked the "true characteristics of French music" to a mythic time and French way of life rooted in the *grand siècle* (seventeenth century) and the spirit of the great academies. "We are talking of French art, notably, which is the reflection of a civilization and a thought that are profoundly human, the foundations of which are ancient and solidly established."[194] A return to this foundation of clarity and order in thought was what was needed in these chaotic times. *Le jazz hot,* which Bernard characterized using standard anti-jazz riffs, was to be resisted in the name of calm and order. "The states of trance, delirium, drunkenness are morbid excitations of which our artists—fortunately—are suspicious. Intellectually, French music is marked by its submission to the exigencies of reason, to multiple qualities that are primordial in us: tact, measure, conscience, the taste for the true, for simplicity, and for naturalness."[195] These were, in his mind, the natural qualities of the "true" French race, characteristics that had been degenerated by the influence of foreign music like jazz. "The French musician has a primordial desire to play with style, a style in the literary sense of the word, which is to say conformity of thought and its expression . . . Logical and ordered, French music is intellectual by its discipline, and by the external and internal constraints that it sets for itself."[196] This set of standard discursive tropes was, for Bernard, the "psychological truth" of the French way of life, the essence of civilization captured in the form of true French music that, rather than recording the present, brought listeners in touch with another, truer time from the past.

By 1939, jazz rarely made headlines amid the saber rattling and rumbling of the Nazi war machine to the east. When it did, it was most often used as a tool for ideological positioning. In these unsure times, *Jazz Hot* continued to stay out of overt political alliances. In an article on the similarity between poetry and hot, Georges Herment reversed the long-standing notion that jazz was an expression of black America's socioeconomic suffering at the hands of white American culture and argued that jazz now was a purely existential expression, arising from a confrontation with being rather than with material culture or politics. "Hot and poetry are neither the beginning nor the end. They have no other struggle but than TO BE . . . Hot is the negation of opinions . . . Hot, today, partial collective communion, hot communion of tomorrow."[197] Like Herment, who linked jazz to the apolitical side of existentialism, Michel Manoll recommended a communion in hot, divorced from the problems of the day, as a relief from the desperate situation in politics. "Walking too constantly in reality enfeebles the step."[198] For the modernist hot critic, these momentary withdrawals into hot brought perspective and meaning to an increasingly rigid and lifeless political world. While Herment and Manoll urged aesthetic withdrawal into existential hot, *Jazz Hot* editor

Charles Delaunay (whose own upcoming book *De la vie et du jazz* was about to go to press) argued that almost everything in the world was out of control. Human notions of beauty and human value in cultural production had been replaced by struggles for profit and power. As a result, after a mere twenty years, jazz was now guided by specialists, commercial monopolies, and referendums. "Why? Because today more than ever, one sole thing seems to count: Money! Art, industry, groceries are nothing but means to earn money. To win money one must 'win' the public. This consists notably in buying the press, either by the critic and his power to persuade or more simply, by buying it."[199] This capitalist system and its incessant publicity in service of its own musical commodities had "killed swing," by associating it with Benny Goodman and the jitterbug. In the end, the popular music industry turned the masses against true jazz. "Jazz is Armstrong, Bechet, Bix, Ellington . . . They are so great that it seems that they have disappeared before the eyes of the dwarves who represent jazz today."[200] Only Panassié, Delaunay faithfully declared, had been able to remain pure of this commercial corruption. "Hugues Panassié, with his enthusiasm and his impulsive prejudices, only he is pure of all compromises and from the lies of advertizing that seem today to direct even jazz music."[201] Like almost every mass-media movement, the partisans at Le Hot Club now placed all their faith in their great leader.

The reality of the politicized racism and displaced aggression that plagued the Continent seemed to be inescapable even for the greatest jazz leaders. Duke Ellington embarked on a European tour under new management with the cargo holds of his ship, the *Champlain,* filled with crates of bombs. As their train passed from Sweden through Germany, they saw signs of the Nazi machine everywhere. The musicians were glad when Germany was behind them.[202] In Paris, Duke was met by crowds at the train station and was welcomed as the "aristocrat of jazz." Playing in tails for audiences at the new Palais Chaillot, the world's only bombproof auditorium, Ellington even did an arrangement of Rachmaninoff's Prelude in C-Sharp Minor. This was not a concert to satisfy the orthodox at *Jazz Hot,* but the more cosmopolitan straight jazz critics raved. In *Le Ménéstrel,* Denyse Bertrand, reviewing the April 3rd and 4th concerts, held up Ellington as the "uncontested champion of jazz . . . The jazz, be it 'hot,' 'swing,' or 'straight'—and we will not enter into the quarrels of the schools, for the bulkheads barriers between them are much less watertight than the defenders of each style imagine them to be—has certainly evolved."[203] Duke, the great leader and "arranger of talent," transcended any of the petty arguments between critical schools. This was an "evolved" form of symphonic jazz that dazzled a sophisticated audience.

In the centrist culture magazine *Paris Qui Chante*, Pierre-Jean Laspeyres upped the ante further. He raised Duke from great leader to demigod. "He is like a god imprisoned by his stature, better chained by his bronze, better petrified in his marble . . . Children follow him."[204] Importantly, Duke's characteristics were now a mix of the best of both jazz and classical traditions. For Laspeyres, Duke was a modern "Prometheus" bringing a universal "flame that is all music, all heaven and all hell,"[205] to save a Europe darkened by division. For many, Duke, with his art representing the civilized richness of modern French cosmopolitan republicanism, symbolized a kind of last hope for an inclusive society.

Panassié, who did not like anyone stealing his critical fire, was not impressed by Ellington. From his perspective, Ellington had "degenerated" since his 1933 appearance in France. In this concert, Panassié heard only "strictly commercial pieces"[206] and no *jazz hot*. Nevertheless, he conceded that, though not *le vrai jazz hot*, these scraps were good for a public starved for jazz. In the meantime, Panassié had other fronts to defend. He denounced John Hammond in America for his comments on Ellington and called Hammond, *Melody Maker*'s "Mike," Leonard Feather, and Paul Miller "shameful" for saying that Satchmo had declined. "What decline? Are your ears blocked, or are you prejudiced?"[207]

As the events of summer 1939 heated up, the headlines were ominous in the polarized French press. With the Daladier government tacitly approving the annexing of Czechoslovakia, the *Je Suis Partout* crowd on the right was smug and increasingly vocal, aping Nazi calls for cultural purity through more stringent racial hygiene; the antifascist voices in France spoke out against appeasement and inaction. Fifty percent of young people between ages of twenty and thirty believed that war was inevitable.[208] In *Le Ménéstrel*, Robert Le Grand warned about the "abuse of jazz" criticism that was following the rise of the cultural right. The reactions against jazz, he argued, were merely a residue of the antimodern and anti-American literary movement exemplified by Georges Duhamel's *Scènes de la vie future*.[209] Le Grand thought critics on both sides took their jazz criticism and their sense of true culture too seriously. They had become polemicists who did little more than cast dispersions on each other. In the heat of battle, those debating about jazz and its relation to true French culture made people forget that jazz was a useful tool for "initiating" people to music that everyone could enjoy. Instead of building bonds of solidarity through shared aesthetic enjoyment, the critics erected barriers between Frenchmen. Now, with more pressing and real political problems, moderation was needed from critics on the right and from Panassié. "We should never fall into such excess and should avoid the contagious epidemic that M. Duhamel signaled for us. We should also guard ourselves from following certain 'up-to-date' critics who, in order to serve their idol, would like us to burn all that is not jazz."[210] Elsewhere, the burning of disapproved art and literature had already begun.

Nazi minister of information Josef Goebbels, when he got whipped into a frenzy in front of a roaring crowd, was fond of calling jazz "Americano nigger kike jungle music."[211] In July, the Nazi's powerful war machine began to realize Hitler's desire to eliminate these hybrid influences from European culture and attacked Belgium. As the summer turned to fall, Parisian taxis were mobilized to carry millions of Frenchmen to the front. Everything changed. The next chapter tells the story of the ultimate battle over the legitimacy of jazz in French culture during the German occupation.

6

Zazou dans le Métro

Occupation, Swing, and the Battle for la Jeunesse

Joy lifts you up, joy makes you strong.

—Maréchal Pétain

Making sense of how French culture changed under Nazi occupation remains a difficult task for the historical observer. The shock of the daily violence, the fear of denunciation, and the control of the public dissemination of information make existing traces from the Vichy period hard to decipher. Retrospective accounts of life under occupation help close the gaps in public discourse left by the forces of censorship, coercion, and terror. Memory, however, has an amazing power to change the significance of traumatic events retroactively. The one-sidedness of media discourse during Vichy is matched only by a retroactive need to temper the memory of collaboration with the Nazi regime, a tendency known as *Vichy syndrome*[1] and that testifies to the necessity of forgetting for getting on with the present. These kinds of stories are very important for understanding the ongoing need to make sense of life under the occupation. So as not to be pulled into this Vichy mnemonic disorder, a kind of heightened example of the Casablanca complex discussed in the first chapter, I try to reconstruct the public debate about jazz and swing from the existing traces of Vichy media sources more than from retrospective attempts to come to terms with this complicated past. Viewed through this corrective lens, one can see how the struggle to define the meaning of jazz and swing served as the final step toward the integration of jazz into French cultural identity.

Jazz was never completely forbidden under the occupation, either by German military dictates, known as the Otto list, or by Vichy law. In fact, though American cultural products were banned, French jazz flowered like never before. Nevertheless, perhaps because those opposed to jazz felt they were losing the fight, anti-jazz writing and sentiment reached a feverish pitch that had never before been achieved. As such, during the occupation, debates about "true" French culture converged upon the swing subculture as a quilting point in the struggle for ideological authority. The youth and what the youth enjoyed took on supreme importance for Vichy propagandists. They wanted the public to believe that "la vraie jeunesse française" supported the Vichy revolution with all their hearts. For the generation of right-wing writers who found their voice during the occupation, jazz, that *judeo-nègre-américain* hybrid, symbolized the influence of the mixed-race or *métissage* forces they wanted to eliminate from their imagined community. But as the debate over jazz and swing became a site for political battles over the meaning of "true" Frenchness and the future of the "true" France in the censored press, listening to jazz records, dancing to swing tunes, and wearing the clothes that signified an allegiance to the swing subculture became a public way to express an alternative view of that future. So while Vichy writers argued that jazz and swing represented degenerate and un-French forms of enjoyment, that a "true" Frenchman would not like swing jazz, and that its popularity was a symptom of the poisonous cultural forces responsible for the fall of France, the refrains of "being swing" or "being Zazou" came to symbolize resistance to the Vichy moral order. While French fascist youth groups marched in parades and worked in the country to aid the Vichy cause, other, defiant French youths hung out at jazz cafés and sneaked out after curfew to do the jitterbug in basement dance halls. In extreme conditions, the positions on jazz's meaning for France became extremist. As the Vichy media's hyperbolic denunciations of the jazz-loving public became more venomous and caricatured, the Zazous emerged as an extreme version of the jazz lover, publicly flaunting their opposition to the voices of Vichy authority. The battle over jazz and swing music during the occupation would mark the ultimate ideological struggle between those who felt jazz was a legitimate part of French culture and those who believed it was a symptom of cultural decay.

"Being swing" during the occupation had a much broader meaning than it did in the orthodox pages of *Jazz Hot* in the late 1930s. A segment of the French youth had appropriated the hegemonically encoded language of jazz criticism and had submitted it to alternate decoding. In a *Candide* article from March 1939, Robert de Thomasson explained how young people who frequented dancing clubs like Le Club, just off the Champs-Elysées, or Jimmy's in Montparnasse used the language of jazz criticism to describe their dancing and way of life. Dramatizing Stuart Hall's thesis that "subcultural response" represents a synthesis of the ritualized forms of adaptation, negotiation, and resistance elaborated by the parent culture,[2] one can see how the semantic content of the forms of language or signs had shifted. One could be "hot, that is to say very pulsating and jumpy, or swing, that is to say more balanced."[3] *Swing* and *hot* in this context meant the way one expressed oneself at a *dancing* with one's body language. For these youth, dancing was about communication: "It's a way of talking."[4] Each gesture, each step was a way of expressing oneself to the other dancer, of entering into a conversation where the language was based on a knowledge of jazz steps and songs, like the jitterbug or the Big Apple. To be swing—to know all these American songs and dances—was to be light on one's feet, to be alive, to be young and carefree. The identification with American culture enacted through this dancing was a form of generational solidarity whereby a subculture of French youth distanced themselves from the political turmoil in Europe wrought by their elders.

After the order for French mobilization was issued on the second of September 1939, writers frightened by the Nazi menace began to use America as a rhetorical counterpoint. The ambivalent relation to American culture quickly shifted in the French press. Now America represented protection from the real threat to their imagined community. A good indicator of this shift comes from *L'Illustration,* described by the great chronicler of the occupation, Henri Amouroux, as the "bible for the average French bourgeoisie"[5] during the Vichy period. In the September 30 issue, culture critic Henry Malherbe glorified "the American soul of today" that might offer defense against "the events that threaten the death of our civilization."[6] Whereas the great inspiration for French literary fascism, Louis-Ferdinand Céline, looked at America through its sewers, Malherbe's America was viewed from the skyscrapers of Manhattan. America, he argued, had taken the French spirit of rational positivism and had adapted it to the work of creating a new world. Whereas in France, the older generations pushed their notion of culture on the young, in America, "all confidence is placed in the youth."[7] For Malherbe, the "young dancing girl" was the symbol of the energy and spirit of America. "She affirms that intellectual progress should go together with mechanical progress . . . In the folds of her short and easy dress, she carries perhaps the destiny of her nation, fierce, intrepid, and diligent."[8] It was this American destiny, which combined Old World rationality with youthful dancing energy, that Malherbe tried to link to France and rally to its aid. "America knows the hellish and insane plot that has been woven for the fall and massacre of the inhabitants of the Old World."[9] Not all those who looked to America for hope embraced its rationalism, but many embraced the spirit heard in jazz and swing as a necessary component for cultural health. Charles Delaunay's brief existential manifesto *De la vie et du jazz,* penned just before mobilization, used the orthodox language of *Jazz Hot* criticism to try to understand how the world had spun out of control and humanity had lost its way. "Man has lost his equilibrium. He has believed in vain in 'intelligence,' in the infallibility of reason. He has scorned his body: a monstrous atrophy against nature translated by his actions. A deregulated being, an automaton, a dangerous monster who has made a world in HIS image, according to HIS reason and has bit by bit detached himself from the real world. 'Disequilibrium' by excess of reason."[10] Jazz was, "despite those who oppose it," the antidote to this disequilibrium and excess of reason; it gave a "lesson in life." It could negate the learned "habits" of reason that worked "against life" and put things back into balance. Jazz, for Delaunay, was an expression of the vitality of life and of the importance of forgetting the past and living in the moment. By the time *De la vie et du jazz* was published, the National Socialist political forces opposed to jazz had sent the world into disequilibrium. Though already outdated by events, Delaunay's manifesto would be republished several times during the occupation and become important underground literature for *les Swings,* the youth movement that embraced jazz in opposition to the Vichy vision of culture.

De la vie et du jazz would be one of the last publicly pro-jazz writings in France until 1942. For on the other side of the ideological divide, right-wing periodicals like *Gringoire, Candide, L'Action Française,* and *Je Suis Partout* were rallying their readers to fight against communism and other "mixed-race" cultural influences and calling for an end to the struggle against the Nazis.[11] The *SFIC,* the communist party in France, went underground and launched the clandestine journal *L'Humanité.* France was at war not only with Germany, but with itself.

Je Suis Swing

Several very popular songs during this early period were part of a growing public consciousness tied to swing jazz. The most significant of these was Johnny Hess's "Je suis swing." Hess had begun his musical career playing with Charles Trenet at the College Inn, a cabaret in Montparnasse. During the long winter of 1939–40, with Trenet now working as a solo act, Hess took the job as the artistic director of Jimmy's.[12] The release of the "Je suis swing" broadcast this anthem for the swing culture of the *dancings* over Radio Paris. A new movement was born and grew around it:

La musique nègre et le jazz hot	La musique nègre and hot jazz
Sont déja les vielles machines.	Are already old machines.
Maintenant pour être dans la note	Now in order to be hip,
Il faut du Swing.	You've got to swing.
Le Swing n'est pas une mélodie.	Swing is not a melody.
Le Swing n'est pas une maladie.	Swing is not a malady.
Mais aussitôt qu'il vous a plu	But as soon as it pleases you,
Il vous prend et ne vous lâche plus.	It takes hold of you and won't let go.

Along with defusing the entrenched media clichés of anti-jazz criticism, the song does several things. The first stanza is itself a kind of declarative act. *La musique nègre* and *le jazz hot* are declared to be things of the past, "old machines." Now, to be up-to-date, one had to swing. The singer flaunts what others denounce and thus appropriates the negative characteristics ascribed to jazz by its critics. Yet it was the chorus, with its final rhythmic onomatopoeia, that made the song a hit.

Je suis swing, je suis swing.	I am swing, I am swing.
Da dou da dou da dou da dou dé	Da dou da dou da dou da dou dé
Je suis swing, oh je suis swing.	I am swing, I am swing.
C'est fou, c'est fou	It's crazy, it's crazy
C'que ça peut me griser.	That it can get me high.
Quand je chante un chant d'amour	When I sing a song of love,
J'le pimente d'un tas de petits trucs autour.	I spice it up with a heap of little things.
Je suis swing, je suis swing.	I am swing, I am swing.
Za zou za zou, c'est gentil comme tout.	Za zou za zou, it's nice as can be.

The song continues in this vein. Swing, in the grand Baudelairian tradition, was a way to get drunk in order to escape the weight of time. In short, the song creates a rhythmic identification with a character carried away with joy, who amuses and relieves himself despite the reproach of anti-jazz voices. Significantly, using the literary figure of the fool who amuses himself with his own antics was a way to defuse criticism before it arose and would be a persona adopted by several singers during the occupation. The last line of the chorus would become the most significant, with its "Za zou za zou," which, according to Hess, was inspired by "Zah Zuh Zaz," the Cab Calloway scat song from 1934. It would become the name of a subculture and the rallying cry of a generation.

Even as the Nazi war machine worked its way through Belgium in May 1940, Raymond Latour wrote in *Candide,* a center-right culture newspaper, about how the dancing continued at Le Club, "the temple of pure swing,"[13] despite the coming storm. "The dancers thrashed about as if it was the hour of the final judgment. We had the curious impression of being in an oasis."[14] This protective "trance" would not last for long. Two weeks later, Georges Mandel, minister of the interior in a doomed government, closed the *dancings.* Ironically, though appointed by the Union National government, *Je Suis Partout,* which had raged for years against jazz dancing and all that it represented, criticized "the Jew Mandel" for the action. "With one stroke of the pen, Mandel, who took control of the Ministry of the Interior yesterday, fired a panicked police chief, dismissed an incapable functionary, and closed *les dancings.*"[15] For them, it was too little, too late.

On May 27, 1940, the Belgian army capitulated, and on the 30th, the evacuations of French troops at Dunkerque began. On June 3, the attack on Paris began from the air. During the next week, the streets were filled with men, women, and children in cars, on bicycles, or on foot, fleeing the city in long, silent columns. Two million of the inhabitants of Paris and its suburbs abandoned the capital with the government. On June 14, the Reich army marched through the Arc de Triomphe. They filled the deserted city with the sounds of boots on stone, marching to the rhythms of a military band installed at the Place de L'Étoile.[16] On June 22, an armistice was signed between France and Germany in the Compiègne forest. During the next week, over a million French soldiers were taken hostage and transported to prison camps.[17] On July 10 the National Assembly was dissolved and power was ceded to Pétain, *père de la victoire* (father of victory) in World War I. The propaganda began immediately: "Abandoned populations, have confidence in the German soldier."

On June 28, the *Staffel Propaganda* (Propaganda Detachment) was established in Paris. Under the control of Goebbels in Berlin, its mass media spin doctors were charged with inundating *Frankreich* with tracts and posters designed to manipulate the public perception of events and crush the spirit of resistance. As it had done through the control of mass media in Germany, the Nazi propaganda machine tried to direct the resentment of the French public toward preexisting scapegoats, cynically simplifying the cause of the war and defeat by shifting the blame and attention elsewhere. The bad influences and causes of defeat needed to be cleansed from French culture, and the writers for a host of now dominant rightist journals set to work to do just that. On September 16, the *Militärbefehlshaber* (regional military commander) law made it illegal to take photographs outside, in public, without permission. What the public saw in the media of life under occupation would now be from the eye of Vichy.

Most people's response to occupation was public silence and staying indoors. Yet remarkably, by December of 1940, jazz began to resurface in the public. Jazz cabarets like Ciro's were given permission to reopen, but Jews and blacks were forbidden. Charles Delaunay, now the head of the Hot Club de France—Panassié having retreated with his records to his estate in the nonoccupied zone—organized the first Festival du jazz at Salle Pleyel.[18] The December 19 concert featured French jazz, including accordionist Gus Viseur, and was so successful that another was organized for February. During that winter, the Hot Club membership soared as five thousand new members joined the fold in Paris.

With the press under thumb, the anti-Vichy writers went underground and formed clandestine journals. Many of the voices that joined in open collaboration were the cultural purists who had been most fervently opposed to jazz in France from the very beginning. P. A. Cousteau, Robert Brasillach, Lucien Rebatet, and the other writers in the Association des Journalistes Antisémites worked hand in hand with the Nazis to associate resistance with the "vengeance of Israel."[19] Yet despite the purist vision of a jazzless culture, and despite the fact that singing "La Marseillaise" was forbidden, the Staffel Propaganda continued to allow French jazz to be performed in public. Perhaps, as Ludovic Tournès argues, this was because the editors at *Jazz Hot* had effectively depoliticized jazz in the year before the war.[20] Perhaps the Germans reasoned that the public needed some pop-culture distraction and that to ban it would open the door for bigger problems. Perhaps, as Charles Trenet would later argue, "one occupies like one loves,"[21] and the German army wanted to preserve this *verboten* vestige of an exotic Paris. On January 16 and 18, Alix Combelle et le Jazz de Paris gave concerts at Gaveau. More cabarets were reopened to the public in February, such as Chez Jane Stick, Le Monte Cristo, and Le Bœuf sur le Toit, where Clément Doucet played without his exiled Jewish partner, Jean Wiéner. The subculture of clandestine *dancings* began to grow.

By the end of 1940, the Vichy media powers began to see the problems with this growth: French youth were dancing instead of collaborating. The eighty-four-year-old Pétain, speaking over radio from Toulouse on November 5, 1940, showed the symbolic importance of the youth: "It's the youth that I count on the most. It is for them that I will pursue my work with all my heart and all my energy."[22] These words became the masthead for *Jeunesse: organ de la génération 40,* a fascist journal filled with illustrated articles about the

sturdy collaborative youth like the Jeunesses Populaires Françaises (JPF)—
the French version of the Hitler youth—who were hard at work for the Vichy
cause. Headlines read, "Students, work with enthusiasm," or "Young people,
let's obey the Maréchal!"[23] Pierre Laval, the new head of the Vichy government, announced that all twenty-year-old men were required to *faire un stage*
(do an internship) of eight months in a "youth camp," where they would
experience a more pure form of "physical culture" as they cut firewood and
baled hay. Posters on Parisian walls read: "It is time to work" (C'est l'heure
de travail).[24]

The response to this propaganda campaign came from the songs of popular
culture. During spring 1941, a singer named Georgius, with a thick country
accent, countered the slogan "C'est l'heure de travail" with his song "Mon
heure de swing" (My Time to Swing).

C'est mon heure de swing.	It's my time to swing.
Oui, mon heure de swing.	Yes, my time to swing.
Zu zazou zazouzazou zazou	Zu zazou zazouzazou zazou
Un accent avant	An accent to begin
Ça fait un tremblement.	Makes for a tremblin'.
C'est charmant, quand ça	It's charmin' when that takes
le me prend.	me in.
C'est mon heure de swing.	It's my time to swing.
Je fais des boums et des bings.	I go boom and bing.
Zu zazou zazouzazou zazou	Zu zazou zazouzazou zazou

The song continues along these lines. One can see that *zazou,* quoted from
Hess's "Je suis Swing," had already caught on as a marker of subcultural group
identification. In each verse, Georgius repeats it. The singer describes about
not caring what the neighbors think—"*zute* for the neighbors"—or what the
collaborators think about wartime duty. His sense of duty lies elsewhere; he
is going out dancing. "I don't give a damn about anything, da dou da dou
da dou." Along with "Je suis swing," the song is filled with coded lines that
index other popular swing songs, a way of quoting that comes from the
world of jazz. The line "I go boom and bing," for instance, quotes the Charles
Trenet song "Boum." Rather than working, the song's protagonist "goes out
to swing." Georgius sang how "all my brothers are swing," showing how the
word *swing*—which could be a verb, adjective, or noun—had now become a
marker of solidarity describing the mentality of the noncollaborating youth.
The final verse of the song stressed that swing dancing was not just superflu-
ous enjoyment, not just a leisure activity to flaunt in the face of the occupi-

ers, but was important political work. "We work for everyone (*tous*) / Pity us (*nous*). / We heal at home (*chez nous*), Zazu zazu zazu zazu zu." A popular Charles Trenet song from 1941 echoes Georgius's sense of the importance of performing the swing persona in the face of the Vichy propaganda for these public figures. "Swing! Troubadour" is a somber song that "swings" only insofar as it is about swinging to get over the occupation blues. The verses tell of the loss of friends, lovers, and youth. The chorus of the song explains the destiny of the singer and his duty during this sad time.

> Swing Troubadour
> Your destiny, Swing Troubadour,
> Is to sing of happiness
> Even if your little heart is heavy,
> Swing Troubadour.

The Swing Troubadour—and Trenet was by far the most popular singer of the day—is bound by duty to sing of happiness even though he has lost his joy.[25] His duty is to resist the fascist organization of enjoyment by using his swing songs to bolster the spirit of resistance. For the swing youth who used the song as a creed, they kept up this joyful facade as an oppositional duty to show that they were not collaborating.

The Vichy media machine launched an ad hominem campaign against this resistant subculture in the pages of *Jeunesse* and *Je Suis Partout*. In *Jeunesse,* columnist Edith Delamare singled out the youth who frequented the clandestine *dancings* in the Latin Quarter and the terraced cafés around the Champs-Elysées as personifications of the cultural forces responsible for France's demise. She denounced them for corrupting the spirit of the true French youth. The nasty, hyperbolic tone of the essay was typical of the Vichy response to French jazz lovers.

> There are prisoners, there are the unemployed, there are young people in the youth centers, and then there are the others . . . The useless, the harmful do-nothings. For in this moment, he who is not useful is harmful . . . They are the well-fed daddy's girls—still and always well fed . . . And so, no, no, no, *la jeunesse française* is not that boundless stupidity, that appalling egoism, that always harsh desire for *jouissance* [enjoyment] . . . They do this to destroy confidence in *le Maréchal,* symbol of a new life, of a life where there will be no more of the little outfits and miserable pleasures that only they know . . . For sure, we cannot purely and simply suppress them (though for my part, I see absolutely no inconvenience in destroying these parasites, these useless socialites), but it is inadmissible that a category of people continue to live like

before and even better than before . . . Let's go quickly and make clean sweep of all that. Send the boys to a rural center and the girls to a youth center . . . and close the Pam-Pams.[26]

The "useless" swing youth, Delamare argued, destroyed public confidence in Pétain with their extravagant quest for pleasure. The most threatening of these "parasites" were those between the ages of seventeen and twenty-one who avoided the *service civique rural,* obligatory agricultural work instituted that spring. The slackers and their meeting places, she argued, should be eliminated. Yet the Pam-Pam, a terraced café on the Champs-Elysées, and other jazz cafés stayed open and remained places where like-minded youth could meet, be seen, and plan future events.[27]

As Germany began to rain England with a daily tonnage of bombs, the clandestine newspapers and the BBC radio (known popularly by its "Ici Londres" opening line) talked of the inevitability of America entering into the war. The swing movement, by which one would express one's identification with America, continued to grow. To compensate for the injection of optimism, the anti-swing discourse became more pronounced. The word *atteintism* was coined to describe the "lazy" sector of the public waiting to be liberated by de Gaulle and the Americans. *Jeunesse*'s Magsy Dauru described this optimism among the swinging students of the Latin Quarter with disdain. "These pretended free spirits, who have no other care than how to do their makeup each morning so they can look like Miss Hollywood star number X, are they even students? . . . Fanaticized by Judéo-American cinema, they are all admirers and imitators of the morals of the Far West: anglophiles every one of them . . . In one word, they are unconscious gallophobes. That is the microbe, the virus of decadence in the neighborhood! It is localized around blvd. St Michel. The plague is imminent. Quickly, we need energetic remedies."[28] The "gallophobic" students were not collaborating because they had been manipulated by the Judéo-American cinema. Drawing on anti-jazz medical discourse not heard since the 1920s, Dauru diagnosed their public appearance and identification with America as symptoms of an un-French sickness that needed to be fought with fascist mass-media antibodies.

Two days after Pétain's June 1941 appearance in Paris, where large, welcoming crowds were organized to capture the illusion of popularity on camera, Edith Delamare once again denounced the useless snobs who performed the very public swing persona instead of their proper racial identity.

"He is swing"—"I am swing." When a well-determined category of our contemporaries announces this, they have said it all . . . Our "swing" youth are literally beings who dangle, oscillate, or balance themselves. Certainly, these clueless youth feel this foreign qualifier while being unaware of its exact significance . . . The swing being has the largest ideas (listen: the absence of intelligent and constructive ideas). He is generally found propping up bars. Physically, he has all the characteristics of a snob. His moral sense is almost nonexistent. . . He has a heightened sense of strange, dissonant rhythm, not disagreeable, but too new, too unheard-of for the countrymen of Gounod or Chopin, that miracle of Aryan sensibility . . . To be swing implies a lot of things: egoism, an I-don't-give-a-damn-ism, the absence of effort, and the total disinterestedness in *redressement,* which is for us a question of life or death.[29]

Here, the problem with jazz and swing was not an aesthetic one, but a problem of publicly personifying cultural ideology. If one displayed a love of the un-French rhythms, one was openly defying the Vichy cause of *redressement.* A real "readdressing" or "recovery" of true culture in France would mean embracing Aryan music and conservative dress. Yet the idea of pure racial sensibility here operates according to the Vichy logic of concealment. Indeed, the "miracle" of Chopin's Aryan sensibility was that he was not Aryan at all. But for the Vichy writers, swing was the negation of the sensibility to be found in their imagined community. Anyone who enjoyed it was—de facto—egotistical, lacked moral sensibility, and displayed an absence of thought. Anyone who publicly flaunted this oppositionality was an enemy of the true France.

Since swing had a significant media presence on the radio, in clubs, and at the cinema, it inspired torrents of venomous ink in the Vichy press. After seeing the new Charles Trenet film *Romance de Paris,* François Vinneuil (Lucien Rebatet) denounced it and members of the audience as suffering from the same cultural illness. Even though Trenet was hugely popular, he was to be condemned. "M. Trenet has against him all his smug admirers, those little 'swing' lumps so ignorant that they believe to have discovered jazz, and who would be stunned if one taught them that these mechanical syncopations upon which they thrash about are nothing but the degeneration of the old that has gone on for over twenty years."[30] But even more than the jazz-influenced songs in the film, Rebatet, aka Vinneuil, denounced the persona that Trenet cultivated. Rebatet argued that Trenet was too happy-go-lucky. A more serious public face was necessary in these times. More damning, however, was that Trenet's blond locks peeking out from under his ever-present hat made him look like the Jewish American movie star Harpo Marx and encouraged French youth to mimic his love of Judeo-American swing jazz. "There is an excessively abominable resemblance between M. Trenet and his play and a certain number of Judeo-American clowns. Fortuitous resemblance? Does he cultivate it voluntarily? Of this, there is no doubt. M. Trenet has contributed as much as possible to the judaification of French taste."[31] But despite the Vichy resentment of those who were not part of the active collaboration and their cartoonlike characterization of them, swing—the hybrid French popular music—continued to be commercially successful at a time when little else could. Songs like "Êtes-Vous Swing?," "Swing, Swing Madame," and "Swing à l'École" would be big hits for the French record industry.

Though more moderate voices, like that of an anonymous *Candide* columnist, sought to defuse the resentment against swing by stressing its association with "flexibility" and "balance,"[32] most of the Vichy press performed the role of the righteous and inflexible racist collaborator, an identity formation that they linked to being a "real patriot" or a "true Frenchman." Indeed, David Carroll has described this type of active denunciation of cultural difference as the basis for fascist solidarity.[33] As such, the collectivity becomes a people or a race not through blood or birth, but rather through the struggle to rid itself of anything foreign to its imagined community. But as the Vichy voices denounced swing music, dances, and people for being un-French, they also risked alienating their countrymen. The cartoon nature of their rhetoric, with its pernicious stereotypes and below-the-belt humor, could cut both ways,

Cartoon rendering of the Charles Trenet type. "To each his preoccupations." *Le Petit Parisien* (May 20, 1942). Reproduced with permission from the Bibliothèque Nationale de France.

and more and more it seems to have worked against itself in the struggle for cultural authority.

The Rhetoric of Cultural Purity
and the Emergence of the Zazou

In September 1941, Vichy's *L'Institut d'études des questions juives* opened to the public the "Exposition anti-juif," where they portrayed the gradual disintegration of cultural purity in France since the emancipation of the Jews following the French Revolution. The exhibit looked back nostalgically to a pre-Enlightenment order when European cultures had more "sane" racial hygiene.[34] This was the time before the influx of mixed-race or *métissage* influences on culture. Yet even as this exhibit was mounted, Charles Delaunay and the Hot Club organized a series of jazz festivals at Salle Pleyel. The first was on September 21, and the next was announced for three weeks later. The Hot Club's "Swing" record label had grown significantly in the absence of American competition,[35] and the Hot Club festivals were quickly becoming events that swing fans looked forward to as a way to publicly display their solidarity with other like-minded people. It was evident that the music was reaching a wide audience.

The October 14 concert raised the anger of the columnist Rojan in *Jeunesse*. He was disturbed by the sight of a new, more exaggerated version of the swing fan. "Stunning spectacle: more in the hall than on the stage! Here is the specimen of the ultra-swing 41: hair to the neck twirled in a knowing disorder, little mustache *à la* Clark Gable, knitted coat, loud pants, shoes with thick soles, and a syncopated walk . . . That specimen goes to the *le festival swing,* nervously throws paper airplanes, and howls Sioux Indian cries while several idols of *jazz hot* display their virtuosity. . . . For those who, like us, taste jazz music but don't make it a way of life, it is truly torture to see them massacre the talent of the artists this way."[36]

It is interesting that Rojan was not denouncing jazz *qua* jazz here but rather the people who supported and populated these concerts. In particular, he hated the "specimen"—read subhuman—of the "ultra-swing" who made acting out in public a "way of life." The swing fan's dress, which mimicked that of the great Harlem jazzmen, showed a *métissage* influence and American identification that was anything but French. These "ultra-swings" were part of a growing subculture of dissonant dandies who flaunted their noncollaboration and refusal to participate in the *service civique rural* for the Vichy "revolution."

In December 1941, with Hitler's Reich army moving on the Soviet Union, America officially declared war on the Axis. At the heart of it all in Berlin, Heydrich, chief of Reich security, announced "the final solution of the Jewish problem."[37] With the labor shortage caused by two fronts and an intensification of internal policing, Hitler began making more demands on Pétain and Pierre Laval to provide the labor necessary to carry on the war. The winter was cold, but the ideological battle for authority and control was heating up.

America, whose isolationism during the first year of the war was portrayed in the Vichy media as a "betrayal," was now an ideological presence to be dealt with. Many French men and women still remembered being liberated by American troops twenty-four years ago and the jazz of the celebration. It was imperative that Vichy writers control the public's perception of America, and the techniques for manipulation remained the same. For instance, P.-A. Cousteau launched a series of articles on "*l'Amérique juive*" (Jewish America) in *Je Suis Partout*. To harness his readers' resentment and prejudice, Cousteau used all the tropes of anti-Americanism. The forces that had corrupted America, he argued, were the same as those that had caused of the defeat of France: a mixture of the consequences of democratic ideas left over from the 1848 Revolution and the influence of the Jews. Indeed, all modern cultural forces were labeled Jewish. Present-day American culture, he hissed, with its leader, "the Jew Roosevelt (Rosenfield),"[38] was the materialization of this corrupt spirit. "They have discovered everything in America, elevators, *les frigidaires, les chewing-gum, les five and ten cents,* the Taylor system, and *les petting parties.*"[39] The Americanisms on this dirty laundry list were all consequences of the Jewish influence. "That which we call Americanism is nothing but the Jewish spirit, which has found its definitive expression."[40] Jews ran Hollywood, the radio, and the government; thus anti-Americanism was, in reality, sane racial hygiene. "The same microbe provokes under all scopes the same organic disorders. That which has almost killed France could not make a sane nation out of America."[41] Worst of all was New York, which he described as a "ghetto" run by "its Jew mayor La Guardia," filled with gangsters like Dutch Schultz and corrupt Yankees. "The standard Yankee of New York is a little thick-lipped Goodman . . . He dresses like Clark Gable and tries to wear that little imperceptible mustache of the Romeos of Hollywood."[42] In other words, comparing the similarity of the description of the dandy to its Parisian counterpart, the Yankee and the new "ultra-Swing" or Zazou, as several Vichy cartoons attest to, were symptoms of the same disease. Thus the America entering into war was an extension of the same Jewish peril that had already poisoned France and was to be resisted by any means necessary.

Star-crossed Zazou. "The Silhouette of the Swing." *L'Oeuvre* (March 4, 1942). Reproduced with permission from the Bibliothèque Nationale de France.

Nevertheless, the hybrid swing music that the Vichy media associated with blacks, Jews and other racially "impure" groups continued to pull in listeners. After Johnny Hess's concert on January 29 in the music hall A.B.C., *Le France-Socialist* columnist Jean Guigo noted two significant developments in the swing public and their implications for the national revolution. The first was its growth, which he explained away as a mere product of the bizarre capriciousness of youth. The second was increased usage of the word *Zazou* to signify the youth who liked swing music. "It is, I believe, incontestable that a part of our youth has been, until now and of its own admission, 'Swing.' Why? And first, why this form, which signifies nothing in itself? A case of fashion, a case of snobbery on the part of these youths who attempted to prove themselves by screaming, 'Zazou zazou,' by waving their index fingers around like flyswatters, and, above all, by the disheveled mop of hair."[43] This way of explaining away acts of public opposition as mere whims of fashion, as opposed to a movement with political resonance, would continue to be

The decadent Zazous in their native environment. "Zazou Bar."
Au Pilori (June 11, 1942). Reproduced with permission from the
Bibliothèque Nationale de France.

the standard method for defusing the importance of *les Swings* and the new
flamboyant Zazous. However, in the second part of the article on the change
in the public, one sees the remainder of this disavowal at work as Guigo announced that the new direction of fashion was returning toward "true" French
tastes and the "Revolution." So while fashion, when directed toward American jazz, was only a superficial trend with little cultural importance, when it
moved toward traditional Frenchness, it was the return of an authentic racial
and cultural taste. "I should avow that, until now, I had held Johnny Hess to
be the spiritual father of the 'Swings' (in France, at least) . . . All that I have
come to reveal of Johnny Hess has changed the score. He, the creator of the
genre 'swing,' is the first to abandon it and return to works that, though they
depend on the rhythm, allow his natural fantasy, sense of humor, and infectious ardor to find a more stable ground where they are more in agreement
with good French taste."[44] Thus the "spiritual father" of swing, Hess, was re-

straining himself, becoming more natural, just as culture should in the service of Vichy *redressement*. Guigo, like his fellow collaborators, wanted people to believe that public taste, though "mere fashion," was moving back toward the stable ground of *"le vrai goût français"* (true French tastes); the influences of mixed-race forms were being wiped away. Yet this was more an example of a declarative act than a statement of fact, as swing music continued to remain popular, and the Zazous became more and more visible.

As the popularity of hybrid French swing music grew, many critics made swing the antithesis of Vichy's "revolution ideals" of cultural and racial purity. For them, swing took on special significance in the Manichean logic of collaboration and was associated with those who did not collaborate. A front-page article in *Au Pilori* by Jean Lestandi, titled "GAULLISM = BUSINESS AS USUAL, or STUPEFACTION," shows this false causality at work. Published right above a cartoon titled "Eclipse of Race: Les Swings," it gave an easy-to-follow model of totalitarian logic and reason. Following the equation, those whose sensibilities were the antithesis of French "generosity, heart, and spirit"[45] were responsible for the fall of France. This part of the population, its "spirit anesthetized by a politic of lies, tall tales, incoherence, and stupidity [*sottise*]," had helped create a "specifically inhuman system."[46] Lestandi argued that this system would have been unimaginable for "our great ancestors."[47] This corrupt mixed-race spirit, which had led to the deaths of over 30 million Europeans since 1914, was embodied in *les Swings*. "It is that future evolution of a race that is synthesized today on the spiritual plane by gaullism and on the physical plane by the degenerate type called Swing. Why gaullist? Because quite simply, in the spirit of the unfortunate sufferers of that malady, the triumph of de Gaulle and of England would represent the return of their little material lives."[48] One can see the vital importance of the "possible future" here as the ideological object at stake in the culture wars. Lestandi addressed this future in relation to the question of cultural health. Gaullism, which led toward sickness, was diagnosed as a form of "craziness rather than as a form of idealism."[49] The same "craziness" that allowed people to believe in the political movement caused them to enjoy swing jazz. The Vichy revolution and its "essential truths," Lestandi continued, was an antidote against this corrupt spirit that had to be eliminated at all costs to help restore France's racial health and its "true" French spirit. "We will battle gaullism with nothing but an iron fist . . . We must fight it and not forget that certain sicknesses sometimes necessitate a surgical intervention. If we want to give the magnificent qualities of our race back to our people, it's by being unpitying."[50] The logic at work in this passage is, of course, a cartoon version of reason driven by an "unpitying" resentment. Thus the key to the ideology is to be found in the cartoon that illustrated the piece.

This portrait of the "degenerated type" causing the "Eclipse of Race" shows the caricature version of *les Swings* emerging in the Vichy media. There are well-heeled, stylish young women with short skirts (above the knee for dancing), tailored jackets, and angora sweaters. There are rich men with suits made from stylish fabric and sporting little Clark Gable mustaches. Many of the figures visibly flaunting their style at an outdoor café are smoking, proving that they had access to the black market. In other words, *les Swings* were portrayed as a privileged class who identified with Hollywood at the expense of their Frenchness. They were publicly enjoying the life of leisure, waiting for the return of the old, corrupt symbolic order while the rest of France suffered.

Lucien Rebatet, who now wrote for several newspapers and was briefly the voice for the Vichy *Journal de la Radio,* also denounced the degenerate jazz lovers for being privileged and un-French in an article titled "Jazz, Hot, Swing and Co." The "and Co.," in English, was a Vichy riff used to allude to the presence of a commercial trust, and Rebatet lumped all things jazz into the same teeming mass of *métissage.* In order to create the appearance of public outcry, the piece was framed as a response to letters from his readers about "these little swing imbeciles." "One of them even accuses jazz of a quantity of evils of which democracy and *juiverie* figure as white columns . . . Others ask, Why not defend true jazz against these little swing cretins?"[51] To explain his position on "true jazz," Rebatet recounted a history of jazz in France.

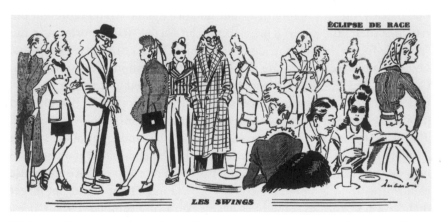

"Eclipse of the race: les Swings." *Au Pilori* (June 29, 1942). Reproduced with permission from the Bibliothèque Nationale de France.

Originally, when it was in its pure *nègre* form, he admired jazz like he admired all pure racial art. Indeed, he appreciated all forms that emanated from some nostalgic premodern source. However, this pure racial spirit was hard to find in jazz music, which had been corrupted like most modern cultural forms through commercialization and the influence of the Jews. The problem with jazz began in 1929, with the rise of hot jazz in "reaction against the merchandising of the adulterated fox[trot]."[52] Though jazz was already a racially impure form, the *jazz hot* movement had quickly turned into a form of snobbery designed to market music. "Hot had its disciples, and their pope was Hugues Panassié."[53] Since it was not pure race music, Rebatet argued, there was no longer any "true jazz" in French culture. The prewar "mania" for hot, a mixed-race music, was the real foundation for the "Swings of 1942," the "new vogue of jazz." This youth movement, embracing *métissage* jazz and swing, deserved his full scorn. Their lack of imagination, though understandable in youth, was a sign of the same sickness of racial impurity that had plunged France into catastrophe. Thus the costumes and outlandish behavior of *les Swings* were symptoms of racial degeneration and the decay of "true" Frenchness. "In making the physiology of the integral swing, one should place it as the aftermath of gaullism and pro-Judaism, as a way of saying that one is with Roosevelt and the different archbishops of Canterbury! . . . It would justify the somber diagnosis as the incapacity of a new generation to leave the ape house of times gone by . . . I want simply to repeat to these swing infants [*Benjamins*] what I have already said: 'But my poor children, you are appallingly late. Your swing, it is imitation hot, the most abominable, worn-out crap there is. You are enamored with syncopated music when it is out of breath, fallen to the rank of the flattest, most commercial and banal repetition. Your jazz of 1942 is miserable industrial ersatz of drum machines and the 'blues' dragged in grenadine syrup."[54] One can see the rhetorical trap that Rebatet was constructing. Panassié, once the protector of "true jazz," who had spoken out against Rebatet's criticism of *nègre* music in the 1930s, had allowed his commercial trust to be overwhelmed by the "ersatz" of French swing. Now Rebatet was baiting Panassié and trying to use the rhetoric of "pure jazz" against *les Swings*.

Though Panassié, in his estate in Montauban, did not respond, *Candide,* more moderate in its tone than other newspapers, subtly defended the swing movement with an article exposing the intolerance of *"les Anti-Swings"*: "In the newspapers of Paris, a rather precise campaign is being formed against swing. Not against musical swing, if you will, which restored, so say its informants, the dynamic variations of black jazz—it is still bad taste to confuse swing and hot—but against these young people who call themselves 'swing" and who are not."[55] In one sense, this statement sounded much like the denunciations of *les Swings* in the more extreme papers. Yet the irony defused the hardened realism of the collaborators by questioning their certainty. The anonymous editorialist questioned the extent of the swing movement and the threat it posed by arguing that it was more imaginary than real. "The rally cry of *les Swings*, is it really 'Zazou-zazou!' like we pretend? The young Swing, does he really distinguish himself from others 'by wearing a false high collar, by waving his index finger' like the good spirits affirm, going too far with his too exterior dadaism? Is it always what we think, in this difficult time? 'Swing' is not disarticulated, yet we dream, very seriously, of forbidding it—the music, evidently . . . The interdiction of 'swing' will not change that unfortunate state of spirit that, one says in Paris, wins over the youth of all classes."[56] The function of the rhetorical questions in this passage is twofold. On the one hand, the article solidifies the notion of the essential difference between being swing and being a dutiful collaborator; on the other, it questions the characterization of *les Swings* by the collaborators and the cultural impact of interdiction. The *Candide* editorialist argued that forbidding the music, corrupt though it was, would serve only to make its appeal more powerful for the French youth. The "anti-swing" movement, he seemed to say, needed to think over the implications of its propaganda against the increasingly popular music, as it was dividing people along these lines.

What music was pure enough for cultural purists like Rebatet? At high-culture venues, like L'Opéra, the occupiers made sure that plenty of German symphonic music, like Beethoven, was played. Among French compositions, Vincent d'Indy's anti-Semitic *La légende de Saint Christophe* was a favorite.[57] As for *musique populaire* on the radio, Vichy stations like Radio Jeunesse, tasked with regenerating French culture—giving it a "powerful ear rinsing" in the words of its founder Pierre Schaeffer— in an era of moral decay, played choral music sung by French Scouts (a protomilitary youth group), fascist texts spoken en masse by large choirs, and various forms of collective address.[58] Many Vichy critics expressed a love for accordion music (a move that later inspired the explosion of accordion jazz[59]) and a desire to hear the return of pure French folk music.[60] A telling example of this nostalgic desire came from impresario Raymond Asso, who fantasized about the perfect medieval musical joy that one would experience in heaven in the newspaper *La Gerbe*. It would be the opposite of that expressed by the Zazous with their swing music. "And those who dance above, I have a vague idea that they will dance while firmly holding hands with one another, that they will dance a true human round-dance, their feet well placed on the ground, heads straight, hearts calm and in joy . . . but surely not with their fingers in the air, mouths open, and butts tight!"[61]

Yet despite the official protests and the all-out campaign against mixed-race swing music in the press, Radio Paris played French jazz and even American jazz songs that had been popular on the radio during the 1930s. They were desyncopated as *musique légère* and renamed, but the melodies remained the same. For instance, "Some of These Days" became "Bébé d'amour," "China Boy" became "Petit chinois," "Honeysuckle Rose" became "Rose de miel," and "Lady Be Good" became "Les bigoudis."[62] Announcers were not allowed to utter Jewish names like Gershwin or Berlin over the radio, but the music was, nevertheless, on the air for those who knew jazz. Radiodiffusion Nationale de Vichy even broadcast a radio concert ranging from the "Jazz Fred Addison to the orchestra of Jo Bouillon."[63] The critical campaign against jazz in the Vichy media seems not to have been concerned with the private enjoyment of music on the radio, but about the denouncing of *les Swings* for publicly defying the national revolution.

Raymond Asso's critique of Charles Trenet provides an example of this subtle distinction, which could be read as a sign of just how assimilated jazz-inflected music had become on an unconscious level, even for those on the right. Asso, known for turning Édith Piaf into the queen of *la chanson française,* liked some of Charles Trenet's songs but criticized him for calling his music "swing," dressing like a Zazou, and misleading the "great crowds of patriotic Swings."[64] Now, these Swings were free to "copy you, to wear the uniform! And yes, my friend, there is a Trenet uniform."[65] Swing, though the majority of it made him "sick," if played by a Reinhardt or a Rostaing "could be very beautiful." But Trenet belonged to another category of music. Asso knew the "real" Trenet, whom he addressed in the *tu* form. "You are not Swing, Trenet: not at all."[66] Asso wanted him to stop with this false persona and rejoin his true semantic category. "Come on! "Y'a d'la joie." "La Polka du Roi!" "Je Chante! . . ." That is clean! It's honest! It's Franc! Franc! As for the true 'swing,' let those who know how do it. Let those in the 'patriotic swing club' take the prize, fingers in the air. They will tire out quickly, go on! In a word, let those who know try to make us understand. But don't you mix with it! Remind yourself that there is a past, THAT THERE CANNOT BE 'SWING' FRENCH SONGS. Make us only the beautiful songs that you will sing simply, to the rhythm of your heart, and not to the rhythms of the sick arteries of all these poor saps."[67]

Thus if his output was called "French popular music," Trenet was tolerable, but labeled as a resistant form of "swing," the popular singer was to be denounced using all the standard anti-jazz riffs.

Yet the more the Vichy press denounced *les Swings* and the Zazous, the more public they became, colonizing terrace cafés all over town. Yves Ranc's ad hominem condemnation of the "young patriots Swings" in *L'Oeuvre*, another collaborationist newspaper, shows how their growing visibility was becoming a political problem. This problem was again framed as a problem of race. Whereas *les nègres* had long been represented in anti-jazz writing as being evolutionarily equal to monkeys, Ranc portrayed *les Swings* as an even lower form of species. "That species, which timidly made its appearance in 1941, tends to multiply. The problem of swing thus has moved to a higher level. Until now, the work of our researchers has had only few results . . . The young swing girl is not a myth . . . one only has to look around to figure this out. The subject stretches considerably in this way toward the subject of race. It is a preview, in effect, of what the swing household would be and, plausibly, of the swing children who will be born crying Zazou-zazou . . . A race is in the process of forming, and if man still descends from the monkey, the next generation will descend from swing, which is hardly more despicable."[68] Again, the decay of French family values and traditional French gender identities is the main cause behind the growth of the Swings. Strangely enough, Ranc was describing a kind of Lamarckian transformation of racial characteristics—where change in behavior slowly changes the physiology of the species—that seems to go against the rhetoric of racial purity he was defending, in which characteristics are immutable. Yet this is telling, since he drew on a strain of literary fascism inspired by Maurice Barrès, in which a race and "true Frenchness" are always formed through an opposition to otherness.[69] Ranc argued that the behavior of the degenerate Swing, whose home and hearth habits threatened the true characteristics of the French race, could be understood by examining their fashionable way of describing themselves. "To be swing: don't take anything seriously; do nothing like the others; do nothing in general; frequent bars assiduously; be unaware; hold on to one's own faded personality; be immoral; be incapable of drawing a line between that which we *could do* and that which we *should do;* have absolutely no respect for the family, nor for love; love nothing but money; and overall, appear disgusted and, with all that, try to pass for an intelligent 'type.'"[70] Being swing, he posited, was the opposite of *Travail—Famille—Patrie* (Work—Family—Fatherland); it meant that one liked to drink all day, dance all night, and ignore duty. Further, being swing was a sign that one had lost touch with "reality," that rhetorical object so important to fascist propaganda. "The swing people make no difference between fiction and reality. So we could think that they are a matter for psychiatric medicine and do them a great honor. Go tell a young swing that he is crazy: he will be excited."[71] Again, Ranc's denunciation quoted the standard discursive riffs established by thirty years of anti-jazz media discourse. It was the swings—this new degenerate race—who had divided France. He hoped that people would adopt his scornful tone against *les Swings* to halt the advance of this un-French species, "because it's advancing, gaining . . ."[72]

"One Becomes the Man of One's Uniform"—Napoléon

At the end of March 1942, the Vichy government *Conseil National* created a commission to "study the problems of organizing the youth."[73] One strategy they employed to combat the popularity of swing was reviving mythic French heroes in the age-old struggle against the English. The most prominent of these was Jeanne d'Arc, who symbolized the anglophobia, total obedience, and sacrifice that Pétain called for in a number of radio speeches.[74] Yet the lesson of Jeanne d'Arc's appeal also taught the Vichy forces that they could not martyr *les Swings* or the flamboyant Zazous. To compensate for the attention on *les Swings*, the Vichy media gave the *Jeunesse Populaires Françaises* and the French Scouts a more central role in propaganda spectacles for Vichy cinema and official photo opportunities.

While fascist youth groups were lauded, some of the denunciations of *les Swings* and the Zazous began to take a different tone. In the glossy pages of *L'Illustration,* for instance, an article by Roger Baschet, titled "Nouveaux Dandys," followed the by-now-standard form but softened its condemnation. Baschet began by describing the Zazou: long hair, short pants, outrageous suits, the syncopated walk, and the index finger in the air, muttering, "Zazou zazou." His description quoted all the tropes of anti-jazz writing to characterize the Swings as un-French. "That is the uniform that these young people have come up with to cooperate in the reconstruction of France, in order to talk of the future between two epileptic and clandestine dances . . . between two swings."[75] But whereas other critics had diagnosed the Zazous as having a specifically modern disease related to the influence of mixed-race culture, Baschet opened the closets of history to explain and relativize these new dandies, who took their role seriously. "Successors of the Muscadins, the Merveilleuses, the Charlestons, and all those happy-go-luckies [*insouci-antes*] born out of great troubles, they imitate these traditional characters by talking with emphasis and by waving around their arms."[76] Thus, rather than being a historically situated political movement, Baschet argued, the Zazous' outrageous behavior was merely a normal accompaniment to all troubled times. Like these other dandies from the past, the Zazous had the "pretension of orienting tendencies"[77]—they believed they moved public opinion. However, Baschet thought the enthusiasm for swing presented in the press was the extreme case, not the expression of the true French public, which remained ambivalent about swing.

Such ambivalence was not the case in the pages of *Jeunesse,* where an "inquiry" was undertaken to construct the idea that public opinion was against the swing movement. Letters from readers were published with commentary from the columnist Rojan. Yet few of those interviewed were interested in the music. Rather, they were concerned with the behavior of *les Swings.* Jean Lambertie, a reporter for *Paris-Soir,* answered: "*Le Swing?* It's a very pretty music. Alix Combelle, Barelli, Warlop, and Django Reinhardt are great artists, sensitive, human, and true. But what is inadmissable are those crackpots-of-those-bars-around-the-Champs-Elysées for whom every day is carnival and whom we should spank publicly once and for all."[78] Jean Lambert, "a singer of tender songs," gave Rojan's favorite answer: "I don't like Swing . . . It's not music. I can tolerate two or three hot, but not more."[79] In short, *Jeunesse* was trying to spin the idea that public opinion was against these jazz lovers because their behavior was contrary to the aims of the Vichy revolution.

Just as the inquiry in *Jeunesse* constructed "real" public opinion by quoting people found in the streets, *Candide* writer Pierre Lancien used the reporter-in-the-streets genre to show the true nature of *les Swings.* Lancien went to the Rive Gauche, the hotbed of Zazou activity, and infiltrated a subcultural swing café filled with young people with "long hair . . . much too long."[80] He described how, after entering the café, he was approached by a young man and woman of the same age, a "mix of bohemian and the free girl, brought up English style."[81] Faintly touching Lancien, the young man uttered the clandestine pass phrase: "*Je suis swing.*"

Sitting down, he explained to Lancien that all the young people in the café were swing. As Lancien surveyed the group, he noticed the peculiar behavior of one youth. "Not far away, in the middle of a group, a young, absent-looking boy was rhythmically moving his shoulders as if he was keeping time."[82] Lancien then engaged the young man, who explained that being swing was more than a fashion; it was more than just having long hair and enjoying jazz. It was about being "direct" and political.

"Well! Monsieur, he said, to be swing is to have certitude that there is a world to offend. And then, certitude that it is us who will make it disgusted. Do you understand? He made several rapid gestures in the air where I recognized the lines of the political architecture of which he dreamed."[83] When Lancien tried to explain his position against the dangers of such a "direct" swing and the need for *redressement,* the young man ended the conversation. "He looked at me with a sovereign contempt. I see what it is. Monsieur is an Anglophobe. He went Peuh! got up, and, very dignified, turned his feet and left."[84] In Lancien's view, it was the *Swings,* not those who supported the Vichy cause, who were intolerant of difference. Snubbed by the "petit Swing," who was following the preferred method for dealing with collaborators,[85] Lancien left the café. If this was the intolerance with which Swings treated Frenchmen whose tastes and opinions were different, Lancien wanted nothing of it. Even if the fashion was only to show one's youth: "You don't need to slouch in your oversized jacket to affirm your youth. Nor wear long hair in opposition to the shaved necks of the military, who shave the napes of their necks and even their heads because of lice and typhoid. Is it death that you want, the death that prowls in Europe? 'I am swing'—that signifies: 'I am alive and want to live.' And also: 'Get out of our faces with your heroes.' And finally: 'Look at me, don't I look rather Anglo-Saxon?' I am looking at you, but without pleasure. I knew young men like you in 1919. There is nothing new under the sun."[86] Not only had this type of jazz dandy existed in 1919, but Lancien joined other critics who compared *les Swings* to other dandies who appeared in times of crisis. He compared them to Les Incroyables under the revolutionary terror of the Jacobins. Les Incroyables had dressed differently, he argued, but they had the same loose morals and the same lack of concern for the future of France. "Les Incroyables were ridiculous, for sure, like you and your comrades and, for a moment, they imposed their ridicule. In the rottenness of their time, they affirmed themselves as the masters of the Parisian streets like you affirm yourselves."[87] He believed it was possible to suppress these dandies as they had done then and to eliminate this "*snobisme anglo-saxon.*"[88] Yet despite his protests, Lancien had lent credibility to the political nature of being publicly swing.

By May 1942, the JPF, with its three essential principles of "Work, strength, and joy," redoubled its efforts to perform their role as "true *jeunesse française.*" With 35,000 members,[89] they organized sporting events, well-publicized retreats and lots of on-camera work in the country for *la patrie.* The *Conseil National* also staged many events where the collaborating youth got to wear their uniforms and be filmed in the presence of leaders like Laval, Admiral Darnal and Pétain. Pierre Lancien described the kind of joy that this activity gave the "true youth" whom he described as the hope for the French future. "The presence of the Maréchal electrifies them, we are all electrified."[90] Off camera, the JPF were also getting a charge out of their own version of acting out their fervent belief in the national revolution through increased acts of violence toward the enemies of the "true" French youth. The conflict between the Zazous and the JPF, a kind of left-side-story gang fight for the future of French culture, would reach its apex during the summer of 1942.

The Hunt for the Zazous

At the end of May 1942, the Parisian police decided to send a message to the Zazous. *France-Revolution,* another Vichy broadsheet, reported that the police rounded up seventy-two men and women "practicing *le swing* and avowing to be zazous!"[91] "Interrogated in the police stations, it appears that the new Incroyables, long of hair but short of ideas, were all gaullists! So this is where de Gaulle recruits his followers: among these outsiders [*métèques*] and the little weaklings [*crevés*] who frequent fashionable bars and cafés! That's what France calls free? That's gaullism? Yes, that's it: Communists, Jews, Swings, and Zazous! And it's with that clientele of assassins, bad influences, or escaped lunatics that the general would like to regenerate France."[92] Here, the attempt

"Enemies of the true youth." *Le Franciste* (October 10, 1942). Reproduced with permission from the Bibliothèque Nationale de France.

to characterize gaullism and resistance as un-French and abnormal is obvious. Yet, though the Vichy forces cracked down on public cafés and bars, the number of private swing clubs and clandestine *dancings* continued to grow.

The more outrageous the Zazous became, the more violently their critics denounced them in the press. Robert Brasillach (1909–1945), editor of *Je Suis Partout,* called for another crackdown, this time against the clandestine *dancings,* which he called *maisons des jeunes Swings.* While the collaborating youth were dutifully taking part in the *service civique rurale,* he argued, the Swings, armed with their records, were dancing. "One dances there in the afternoon, girls and boys. One smokes English cigarettes. One delves into a little of the black market. One nibbles away at little petit fours . . . The young swing people do not have the fascist spirit, which is first and foremost the spirit of joy."[93] Those who did have the fascist spirit of joy, he argued, volunteered for work in the country. Indeed, if one can believe an article in *Le Cri du Peuple,* the number of "volunteers" grew in May 1942 to somewhere between 66,000 and 67,000 workers.[94] Xavier Pasqier, head of the *Ligue de Jeunesse,* created by the *Conseil National,* praised these "true patriots" and denounced *les Swings,* who had been led astray by "bad shepherds, profiteers, and traitors." [95] He had a plan for *la jeunesse* to help it regain its "true" Frenchness. "It must become calm, voluntary, and disciplined and free itself of that genre 'Swing,' which rings more of dementia than reason. It is necessary that it wake, once and for all, that true patriotism that is within it and persuade itself that only the Maréchal is the living symbol of eternal France, which it should serve more each day, with more fervor and tenacity."[96] He called for the creation of a Union de la Jeunesse Française, which would join the adults in the service of the national revolution and drive out the forces of unreason in the media and in the streets.

In the first week of June 1942, Pierre Ducrocq stepped up the anti-swing rhetoric, following the words of a friend who called for "a public spanking" for the Zazous.[97] His critical "spanking" was designed to ridicule the Zazous for being un-French. "In a jungle born of defeat these sly little beasts, these instigators [*boutefeux*] in short pants and long jackets, these Incroyables of slang language are no more dangerous than lice."[98] These "innocents," whom he saw "mashing their chewing gum between two Yiddish words,"[99] were not entirely to blame. "Their sole excuse? Youth. But that is also their great infamy. In a time when we should be able to count on the youth, they betray our hope."[100] He blamed Hess, Trenet, and "the crown prince" of swing, de Gaulle, in England for leading them astray. The cartoon logic linking swing with Semitic and anti-French elements was inescapable.

"Regionalism: swing is our folklore." *France-Révolution* (June 14, 1942). Reproduced with permission from the Bibliothèque Nationale de France.

Two days later, Abel Clément, member of the *Conseil National,* was assassinated. *Je Suis Partout* declared that this act marked the end of leniency with dissenters. "In one blow, we have entered into the time of assassins. The time of assassins is the time of the jungle, and the law of the jungle remains an eye for an eye."[101] There were reprisal shootings of "spies." The Nazis announced a new reign of order that required all French Jews to wear a yellow Star of David in the occupied zone. Rebatet proudly praised this development: "There is no country that has suffered from the Jews like ours . . . Last winter, I spoke of my joy at having seen the first Jews marked with their yellow stamp in Germany. It will be a much livelier joy still to see that star in our Parisian streets, where, for three years, that execrable race has trampled us."[102] Rebatet's only regret was that the Nazis had called for the law before the French

"Goals of War: For a Swing France in a Zazou Europe." *Je Suis Partout* (June 6, 1942). Reproduced with permission from the Bibliothèque Nationale de France.

could create one of their own. Next to Rebatet's article, a cartoon by Ralph Soupault (1904–1962) illustrated the "Jewish" future for Europe that Rebatet described. Drawing his title from a cartoon called "Ballandard's Dream,"[103] which appeared in *Au Pilori* the week before, Soupault sketched "Goals of War: For a Swing France in a Zazou Europe." It showed the Jewish minions, including Stalin and Churchill, watching a "Swing France," marked by the Gaullist symbol and Star of David earrings, dancing the Big Apple to their beat. The lines drawn in the sand had been set firmly: one was either for the national revolution and the purist vision of "true" French culture, or one was for swing and for a France overrun by the forces of *métissage*. "*Les Swings*," wrote an editorialist in *La Gerbe*, "are not French."[104]

Bernard Isère, in *L'Atelier,* another nationalist daily, echoed Soupault's satiric turn of phrase which, itself, played off the official Vichy slogan: "For a sane France in a new Europe."[105] He began by questioning Johnny Hess's assertion in the song "Je suis swing" that "Swing is not a malady. If one wants, and to each his own idea! . . . In any case, the extension of its epidemic allure

"The Odor of Beasts." *Au Pilori* (June 18, 1942). Reproduced with permission from the Bibliothèque Nationale de France.

makes us believe that it is."[106] In opposition to the Vichy youth who were "in the process of regulating, on the battlefields and in the work camps, the future of Europe,"[107] he argued that these "swing troubadours" did nothing constructive. As anti-jazz writing had done for decades, he associated *les Swings* with vice, loose moral behavior, and a lack of reason. Just as there was no longer a need for leniency with France's Jews, Isère warned that "it is time to make them understand, even if the wake-up could be brutal."[108] Yet despite the danger, some accounts have indicated that some of the more audacious Zazous responded to the laws requiring Jews to wear the yellow star by wearing a yellow star of their own with the word *Zazou* in the middle.

The editors at *Au Pilori,* which had already labeled Radio-Londres "radio Zazou,"[109] brought the popular comic actor Ferdinand to their aid in his column "Fool's Corner." He linked *les Swings* to bad psychological health. "Having observed this year a correlation between an epidemic of certain parasitic insects coming out of the Benita water and the gaullo-swing vibrations of the Zazou-zazous, we thought it necessary to reserve our 'Fools' Corner' this week for a study of Zazoutisme."[110] The Zazous, he argued, had serious "psycho-physiological" problems, something they shared with "other democratic intellectuals."[111] The Zazou had "Gaullist sentiment," and his actions had "nothing to do with real patriotism . . . His patriotism prefers to translate and manifest itself by the least dangerous gestures possible. For example, by laughing when the German guards pass by on avenue des Champs-Elysées. Oh! Not too visibly, because a kick in the a . . . is always possible."[112] Ferdinand described their uniform and how they acted in public. Zazous were easy to identify by their English vocabulary. They said "Hello" when they met, "Bye-bye" when they parted, and "O.K." when they were in agreement. The word *chéri* had been replaced by the word *darling*. They were easy to spot and find.

The remedy recommended by the editors at *Au Pilori* was simple. They called for the JPF to begin the "hunt for the Zazou," which would consist of humiliating the "swing patriots," at least those who flaunted their subcultural style, by a number of means. "The most practical remedy for ridding ourselves of the Zazou consists in using scissors and cutting his jacket off of him . . . There is also the remedy that consists of putting a foot in the a . . . of the Zazou-zazou. But from our point of view, what we are talking about has a useless brutality to it and is liable to give him the halo of a martyr. That is why we prefer the more efficient method of using the scissors and the clippers."[113] The article ended with "advice for those with scissors or clippers desirous of hunting le Zazou-zazou"[114] on where they could find them to begin the violent public humiliation.

On June 18, *Au Pilori* continued the heightened campaign of scorn against swing with a cartoon ridiculing the "swinge judéo-gaulliste" (combining the word for "monkey," *singe,* with *swing*). Drawing off decades of racialist characterizations of jazz's *nègre* origins, the cartoon shows a good French mother protecting her eponymous son, "François," from the smell of these dangerous caged animals. "Let's get out of here, François, they really smell too bad." The hyperbolic rhetoric that accompanied the cartoon announced that "the hunt for the zazou-zazou, that by-product of swing, is already open . . . The battle promises to be fruitful."[115] Yet though the Vichy press denounced them, calling for the police to crack down and the JPF to crack their heads, *les Swings* and the Zazous became more vocal and more visible in the Latin Quarter and on the Champs-Elysées. Swing was becoming more political, more overtly oppositional. *L'Appel* reported on this development. "The Champs-Elysées has been invaded by the Jewish youth from all the arrondissements of Paris. The terrace of the Triomphe, the Colisée, and the Pam-Pam, overflowing with that idle and derisive riffraff."[116] Very quickly, the police descended upon *les Swings. L'Appel* reported the incident with glee. "The grotesque little 'Swing' world was in effervescence. Imagine! Without warning, without crying look out, last Friday evening at the fruit juice hour, the police made a raid on the Champs-Elysées, in all the establishments where the Parisian Zazous are esteemed. The Pam-Pam, the bar at the Colisée, and other preferred sites of that degenerate youth were scoured by the police, who, in a tone like no other, demanded to see their identity cards . . . The purge that has begun should be pursued. Next a descent into the clandestine 'swing' *dancings*. If it is needed, we could furnish a list."[117] Of those rounded up in the raid, *L'Oeuvre* smugly reported that "only the men were invited to spend the night in a rather classic cell, with little hot."[118] They offered a quick remedy for these anti-revolutionaries who did not want to work for the cause. "Have we not already spoken of the *service civique rural* for young people without jobs? Would the Swing resist several weeks of work in the fresh air, in contact with nature, under the sane influence of a rural conglomeration that is conducted for nothing but work?"[119] According to another report of the incident, in *La France-Socialiste,* the arrested Zazous were given no choice. "They will be inscribed at the office on the list of volunteers for *service civique rural.* One cannot applaud enough that spiritual method of battling the young idlers with the Zazou malady. And we hope that the unpitying roundups continue

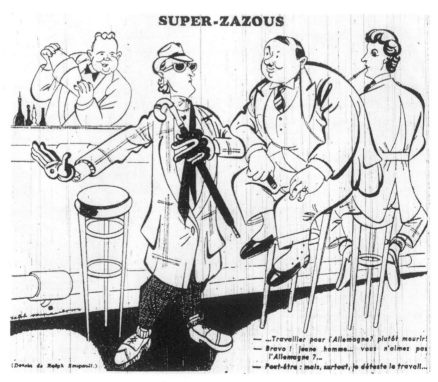

"Super Zazou . . . Work for Germany, I'd rather die . . . Bravo young man, you don't like Germany . . . Maybe, but mostly I detest work." *Je Suis Partout* (July 2, 1942). Reproduced with permission from the Bibliothèque Nationale de France.

SERVICE RURAL

Je suis swing !..   Zazou-zaux champs.   Tu es swing !

"Rural Service: Zazous in the fields . . . I am swing . . . You are swing." *Jeunesse* (June 28, 1942). Reproduced with permission from the Bibliothèque Nationale de France.

until the destruction of the microbe is complete." The *chasse aux Zazous* had begun.

As the anti-swing campaign became more official in the media, the popularity of swing surged. *Les Swings* got their inspiration from several songs in the summer of 1942 that tried to defuse the animus directed toward them in the press, such as Josette Daydé's "Grand-père n'aime pas le swing" or the title song to the Richard Pottier film *Mademoiselle Swing*,[120] sung by its star, Irène de Trébert. "It's happiness that delivers us / Of a youth that wants to live, to live!" The most important parts of *Mademoiselle Swing* were the scat choruses that Trébert performed using the "zah-zuh-zaz" model for no other purpose than enjoyment of the rhythm, a marker of empathy for the Zazous. The end of the song stresses the need to follow this route, "We must brave destiny." However, not only the Zazous were singing in the streets; the JPF also had its songs. One of their favorite marching songs simply repeated the lines "*Rasez* [shave] *le Zazou, rasez le Zazou*,"[121] the rally for the *chasse aux Zazous*.

In fact, this marching song helped motivate the JPF toward violent confrontations with the Zazous. Jean Geslin reported on a series of incidents on May 25 and 26, 1942, against these "young citizens of free France, waiting for the victory of de Gaulle and the return of Coca-Cola."[122] Under the battle cry of "Pétain-Doriot," the JPF tracked down the "decadent Zazous" in the midst of their "reunions of judéo-nègre rhythms and swing alcohol"[123] and dragged them into the streets. Several were beaten and publicly shorn. "These docile lambs who take themselves for savage lions can reassure themselves, the nudity of their heads won't deprive them of any of the excited stupidity that went so well with the looks on their faces when they were given a kick in the behind. The decadence should be stopped and the decadent corrected. That these students, these true French students, cut several wisely curled lockets;

Cartoon depictions of the public shaving of the Zazous. "Volunteer haircutters: Le J.P.F—And if monsieur wants a little friction?" *Le Cri du Peuple* (June 23, 1942). Reproduced with permission from the Bibliothèque Nationale de France.

"The Zazou Hunt: They scalped you! But why didn't you call for help?
I did . . . I called Roosevelt . . ." *Le Petit Parisien* (June 19, 1942). Reproduced with permission from the Bibliothèque Nationale de France.

that they cut off several jackets; that they administered several spankings, all of this will help make the Zazou youth disappear altogether."[124] Words, on this front and others, did lead to action; metaphoric violence in the media led to real violence in the streets. *Je Suis Partout* reported on the success: "Les swings have almost disappeared, but there are still the gaullists . . ."[125]

Several particularly sadistic cartoons that portrayed the *chasse aux Zazous* give a grave reminder of the double-edged sword of laughter under a totalitarian regime. Though thinkers like Milan Kundera have noted the importance of laughter as a way to defuse totalitarian ideology through ironic distancing, humor can also be used to distance people from the actual violence of a totalitarian regime. Creating a public discourse in which oppositional voices are

reduced to their cartoon image allows for acts of cruelty to be aestheticized and overlooked, to be judged according to the rules of the cartoon universe, where people are never really hurt by the atrocities that befall them. In the cartoon universe, when the cartoon exterior of the animal, say Daffy Duck, is shaved off or blown away, there is a real "human" skin that remains underneath and remains intact. This is the same dynamic that we see in the logic of the Vichy cartoon universe: if the cartoon exterior of the opposition, the Zazou's hair and jacket, is flayed off, then the "true" Frenchman will assert itself freely.[126] By framing things in this way, acts of sadistic violence, effectively distanced from the real by portraying them as funny and necessary jokes, become tolerable.

Perhaps the battle to denounce swing and the Zazous in the press had its most telling moment when it linked these dandies, and the violence against them, to the dandies of other revolutions. François Furet has established the importance of linking political action to the spirit of the French Revolution.[127] It was certainly the case under occupation, when the continued battle over the "true" revolutionary spirit in the press was a recurrent theme in the struggle for ideological authority. Those arguing that the Vichy National Revolution represented the "real" restoration of Frenchness claimed that the aims of the 1789 Revolution had been thwarted in the postrevolutionary period. Jean Mericourt, for instance, argued in *Au Pilori* that the spirit of '89 had been betrayed by the Jews. Out of this corruption came first the Incroyable and, now, the Zazou.[128] "The postrevolutionary Incroyable was equally a snob who did not retreat. It became necessary to smack him to make a point, to strike a blow with a club or to string up one of these jerks [*salopards*] . . . The pitiable Zazou is on the same scale for the national revolution, with the same spirit and extravagance . . . Several slaps and several roundups made his ranks retreat."[129] Now, he argued, just as the Jews had corrupted the 1789 Revolution, the masses were in danger of being lured away from the principles of the national revolution by the Zazous with their "anti-French manner." According to Mericourt, there was only one solution: continue these "slaps" and eliminate the lure. "The most practical solution is still to suppress the guilty parties and to eliminate the public lives of these men."[130]

While Mericourt drew the Incroyables out of the closet of history to address the present, literary critic André Billy (1882–1971) tried on the dandies of the Restoration for size. "Someone remarked to me that the dandies of the Restoration and of Louis-Philippe were not eagles, either, which did not keep them from counting among them a certain Baudelaire."[131] In addition to linking the Zazous to a beloved historical figure like Baudelaire, Billy drew attention to the similarities between their methods of public provocation. "To be swing is not to be on the margin of elementary morals, but is to raise oneself against outdated morals and ridiculous principles. It is to break the chains that hold back innovation . . . That is, I believe, very nice . . . The young Swing, is he a distasteful dandy or an available hero? After receiving and reading several letters, I am asking myself the same question."[132] Though his statements were always protectively couched as questions posed by anonymous readers, Billy's logic was inescapable: if the Zazou were the extension of the revolutionary spirit and they opposed the Vichy moral order, then the collaborators were the negation of the spirit of the true French Revolution. Billy questioned the Zazou way of expressing their spirit with their outrageous "inspired air," but he supported their aims of extending that spirit of "true" Frenchness to fight the tyranny of the present. Moreover, his second-guessing and willingness to perform such ideological work shows the extent to which the acceptability of anti-jazz rhetoric had reached a tipping point.

In *Confluences,* a "review for French rebirth" published in Lyon, François-Charles Bauer reported that the "battle waged in the press against swing is beginning to degenerate a bit."[133] The only thing that was clear was the political ignorance of those who wrote against the popularity of swing. He argued that it was understandable, given the lamentable state of culture during the war, that the youth would be drawn to something with enough energy to distract them. The mistake of the Vichy powers was that they had not offered an alternative as powerful as jazz and swing. "It is not, in effect, with boy-scout dances or with renamed activities from the twelfth century that one will give these young people the feeling of grandeur and virtue that they need."[134] He thought the best way to defuse the tension that had Frenchmen fighting with one another was to depoliticize jazz and swing and allow the kids their fashion.

The Twilight of the Zazous

At some point during the summer of 1942, the Vichy press seemed to realize that the viciousness and repetitiveness of the campaign against *les Swings* was working against itself. By focusing so much attention on the Zazous, the Vichy writers had unwittingly helped constitute the movement by creating the impression that the problem was everywhere. This was the opinion of *Journal des Débats* columnist Solange de Bragard, who questioned the efficacy of denouncing jazz and swing dancing. "Swing again! We talk too much of it; we will finish by giving it a true consistency . . . These articles have valorized these Swings by explaining them abundantly. They have made Swing a symbolic image. That is a shame!"[135] He argued that for the confused youth who already liked swing jazz, the critic who denounced their favorite pastime became an enemy no matter what he said. "We must have a more delicate touch, more patience in observation, and more indulgence in order to judge them."[136]

Louis Guibert also called for a change in tactics. He argued that "to check swingmania, stop talking about the *schpountzs!*" The war in the press against the Zazous, which he used the Yiddish word *schpountzs* to describe, had been going on for over a year and "if several juvenile cretins (they are no more than a minority) have not yet understood the ridiculousness and anti-Frenchness of their attitude, it is overall the fault of their parents and their educators."[137] The campaign needed action, not more words. Yet he emphasized that it was important that the counteroffense against the Zazous be done quietly. "There is no need to satisfy the aims of those judéo-gaullists by giving this species of 'schpountz' the large publicity it gets. By now, we know all too well who they are, what they do, and where we can find them. So enough talking about 'swing,' of '*zazouillements*' and '*zazouteries*'! . . . There is one sole means to avoid this: make their parents and professors responsible for these scraps of society. As for the Zazous, in order to make their liquified brains more consistent, require them by pleasure or by force to be employed for useful ends in the fields or in the factories. Or better yet: send them to the 'Stalags' in exchange for prisoners. That way, everyone would be satisfied and it would be for the greater good of society."[138] In his opinion, the best way to combat the Zazous was to take the focus off them in the media and keep them out of the public eye. Their parents should be denounced, and both, if need be, could be sent away to labor camps in exchange for prisoners of war; but the press should no longer publicize their plight. On the walls of Paris, JPF-stenciled words began to appear: "*Les zazous aux stalags.*"[139]

Yet despite attempts to keep the Zazous and the Swings out of the public, the eruption of violence against them drew attention to the Zazous and to the harshness of their Vichy detractors. In *Paris-Midi,* Jean Monfisse took advantage of this tacit silence about the Zazous, announcing that the *chasse aux Zazous* called for by the press had been a success. He tried to justify the violence. "Certainly, it was reasonable to hunt down the Zazou. That thin animal, a villainous figure with unseemly ways, reproduces itself so quickly and so well that it is always threatening to proliferate, like the rabbits of Australia . . . Thus we hunted the Zazou—with the clipper. And the Zazou has taken flight! . . . Not one single Zazou on the platforms of the métro . . .

Those who venture out could be considered zoological curiosities—like the kangaroos in game parks. The Swing peril is gone."[140] The Zazous, he boasted, had been driven from the public. There were still "snobs," he argued, who licked their wounds in the clandestine *dancings* in the suburbs, "those last Mohicans of the *mode syncopée*,"[141] but the majority of the Zazous were now in the country doing their obligatory work for the revolution, helping Pierre Laval meet the ever-growing demand from Hitler for more labor.

As the tide began to turn against anti-jazz discourse for its intolerance, several critical works were published that readdressed the increasingly popular jazz and swing in order to reframe the music in relation to Frenchness. In other words, parts of the collaborationist press sought to modify their definition of jazz and their sense of "true" Frenchness so that the two terms would be compatible instead of antithetical. The most telling was André Coeuroy's *General History of Jazz: Strette-Hot-Swing,* which, as the title suggests, focused on the development of French *strette* jazz. The majority of the book repeated truisms about the history of jazz. However, Coeuroy differed from earlier texts in the imaginative way in which he tried to legitimize French jazz by constituting the notion that jazz was really French by origin. Thus he stated that its assimilation into French culture was really a return. "For a long time, we believed that jazz was specifically *nègre.* The present thesis is exactly the opposite. Jazz was black only by chance. The principal elements that compose it come from whites, and whites from Europe. By its history and by its material, jazz is ours. Its future is in our hands."[142] To complete this tautological explanation of a jazz that was French by origin, he opposed the idea that jazz was originally African. "Its cradle is in Mississippi, and its inventors were the *nègres* already enslaved by Frenchmen, and still today in the service of families who came from Poitou, Saintoge, Aunis, Normandie, and Picardie . . . the French genius, more than the Saxon genius, with the gallant, amiable, and gay spirit of our civilization, more than the puritanical and severe spirit of Old England, was the creator."[143] Thus jazz did not come from African or English sources. Like the rest of "good American culture," jazz had come from the French settlers in New Orleans, the "cradle of jazz." The proof of this was in the etymology of the word *jazz* in the French word *jaser* (to converse) which Coeuroy revived from his 1927 work with André Schaeffner. But whereas Schaeffner had used Irving Schwerke's theory to describe the way slaves appropriated the French term to describe an African musical action or behavior, Coeuroy linked the meaning of *jazz* to its root word in Celtic culture. "Africa dialect? Patois *nègre?* In reality, an old Celtic word, the Provançale form of which is *jasar,* the French form *jaser* (and *ga-*

zouiller), the Italian *gazza* (which designates an itch), the Breton form *geiz.*"[144] New Orleans jazz, he argued, always evoked this "Celtic" notion of a conversation. "Each instrument *jase* in its turn. For in Louisiana, the verb *jazer,* in the form accorded by popular usage, is still alive."[145] Though the rhythm of this musical conversation may have been *nègre,* the language they used—the melodies, the harmonies—were European. "Harmonically, jazz teaches us nothing new. It resonates like it does in Europe, because it is from Europe."[146] Jazz was not to be feared as an un-French cultural force. "[This is the] new profound reason why jazz has a real sense for *la jeunesse,* why by its presence alone, it gives a lesson. There is nothing that could be more commendable at this time. It is curious and sane as can be, this *jeunesse,* supported by swing, where the malevolent want to see nothing but disordered frenzy, and where we could find, simply tonically, a patient life momentum that never gives up hope."[147] By changing the terms of the jazz debate, and making the expression of swing music an expression of European musical ideas and of the French tendency to civilize that which they encountered, Coeuroy managed to accomplish two tasks. On the one hand, he made it possible to enjoy *strette* jazz and be a "true" racist European. Considering that Coeuroy had contributed articles to *Je Suis Partout* and *La Gerbe,*[148] he may have wanted to make sure that enjoying jazz was compatible with collaboration. On the other hand, his thesis legitimized the enjoyment *les Swings* found in their music as a pleasure of European origin that only the "malevolent" could denounce.

Ironically, the hardened purists and critics of the swing movement may have found their best ally in Panassié, who could not let Coeuroy's attack against "true jazz" go without rebuke. In *Le Figaro,* the newspaper of high finance, Panassié lashed out against Coeuroy and the "commercial jazz" that he legitimized. The idea that jazz was fundamentally European, he declared, was "constructed on false premises."[149] The important thing in jazz was not the form, but the style, the improvisation and the way of playing, which were specifically *nègre.* But more important than the content of his criticism is the fact that it was now possible to express a love of jazz in the Vichy public. Swing and jazz were no longer to be denounced and suppressed. Nothing had changed with Panassié, who was back to performing his role as the protector of jazz purity by denouncing the profane, but the rules of culture discourse had changed so that even those sympathetic with Vichy could legitimately enjoy jazz. Panassié continued to protect "true" jazz from *les Swings,* publishing his book *La musique de jazz et le swing* in 1943. In the end, however, Panassié's concern with purity and his own personal authority as jazz fan number one made him, however unwittingly, part of the critical arsenal against the Zazous and the Swings, who, in his eye, had "transfigured" pure jazz into a "mediocre" vox populi. It was a position for which he would later pay.

Sur le Pont d'Avignon, On y Danse, On y Danse

Despite the attempts to ignore the Swings and the Zazous and to depoliticize the now ascendant French love of jazz, the Zazous did not go away. Henri Amouroux recounts a story from September 1942 that exemplifies their continued presence as an oppositional force. After a mass at the Hôtel Invalides for 211 fallen members of the Légion (those who voluntarily joined the German army[150]), the legionnaires, some of them wearing German uniforms, marched down the Champs-Elysées. The Zazous reversed their chairs and launched their "war cries, more effective in Paris than on the Russian steppes."[151]

Though concealed in the press, public manifestations of Zazou solidarity continued after the institution of the *Service Travail Obligatoire,* mandatory work in Germany for those born between the years of 1920 and 1922. The clandestine paper *La Terre* called for noncompliance, warning: "Frenchmen, to leave for Germany is to forge your chains!"[152] When Zazou sightings were made by denouncers, the police would quickly descend on the scene, and anyone who was caught would find themselves on the next train to Germany. The Zazous, for both ends of the political spectrum, continued to symbolize the refusal to work for Germany.

Yet despite the general change of tone in relation to swing, the most hardened of the cultural purists on the right did not give up their campaign against jazz, even when it was apparent that they had lost the battle to prevent its acceptance into French culture. David Carroll has argued that for many of the true believers like Rebatet, the ultimate marker of their own political correctness was, in fact, the defeat of their cause.[153] One book, *Swing and Morals,* by Henri Vémane, tried to use statistics to stack the deck of public opinion against jazz, claiming that over 70 percent of the French were "hostile to swing."[154] He explained their response. "They are scandalized, indignant, and tend to lash out at these violent maledictions against today's morality . . . One phrase best reveals their sentiments: It's stupid."[155] But for all his sociological "objectivity," he quickly lapsed into the tropes of anti-jazz writing, the standard discursive riffs used since the 1920s, to denounce swing and its effect on the ethos of French culture. It caused "nervous excitation";[156] the "swing mentality," like the "modern mentality, neglected the dictates of the past";[157] swing led to cultural degeneration, a moral break from the past, and the "defeat of reason by passion."[158]

The Vichy authorities, for their part, continued the systematic police campaign to eliminate the *dancing* because it had become a locus for resistance solidarity. Though *les dancings* had been *verboten* since the onset of the war, dance schools had grown systematically. *Je Suis Partout* first called attention to this legal technicality in July of 1942. "The number of Parisian dance schools, which were no more than several dozen before the war, is now more than a thousand today. So we truly have the impression that if the public powers would really like to take the trouble, it would not be hard to limit the spread of the scandal."[159] Once again, *Je Suis Partout* was at the avant-garde of collaboration and the media war against the influence of jazz in French culture. In 1943, the Zazous found their way back into the press. The emboldened *Candide*, which *Je Suis Partout* had few kind words for, candidly announced, "Yoo-hoo, there they are!" "We believed to have finished with the fearsome tribe of Zazou. But it appears not. Several characteristic types made their reappearance in the past few days in the bars of the Champs-Elysées . . . The Zazou 43 is characterized by his tuft of hair, his white shoes, and his 'giraffe' tie in a minuscule knot. He carries a starred handkerchief . . . There were a number of Zazous at the Étoile au Rond-Pont, but the alarm was given; a hunting party was organized. Fortunately, it will not be serious."[160] *Candide* continued to make sure that its readers knew that the Zazous—and their spirit of defiance—had not disappeared, nor had they lost their sense of style, even though the stakes for appearing were higher. But as the risk of violence continued, the fervent anti-jazz discourse began to recede in the press.

In July 1943, *Candide* announced that the campaign against jazz dancing in Paris had taken a new turn with more active policing. "It is now no longer the Zazous who raise the eyebrows of our representatives of order, but the dancers. One can be a dancer and a Zazou, but one can have the taste for dance and not wear one's hair in a little tuft."[161] Heavy with irony, the story mocked the seriousness of the anti-swing voices and explained how the dancing schools had been used as a way for average dancers to get around the law against *les dancings*. "Naturally, the police were alerted. They made raids . . . But these measures have proved insufficient. One always finds locations, one always finds musicians, and, what is more serious, one always finds dancers."[162] Tacitly, the writer was letting people know that the partisans of swing were numerous, everywhere, and committed. Later his sarcasm toward the authorities and collaborators who profited from the Vichy laws that allowed "Aryans" to become the "trustees" of property left "vacant" by fleeing, deported, or imprisoned Jews and resistors[163]—and it is not by chance that the most active black marketeers were the collaborators and the Germans who *had money*—became even more transparent as he reported the subtleties of the crackdown on swing dancing. The police were not going to shut down all dance schools, only the "false schools" that showed contempt for the law. His sarcasm showed his contempt for the intolerant. "The committee for the organization of spectacles will decide. That's not all. After October 1, swing is forbidden. One cannot dance it, teach it, or learn it. It is true that swing can hardly be taught by professors. This is one of those things that one learns from comrades. One is initiated into swing . . . But finally, they must be severe and ruthless. And now, there is nothing to do but discover clandestine balls. Leave it to the police, and to the wisdom of those who will try to organize them and who risk prison . . . Only the scalp-dance around swing, if we can say, is authorized."[164] By the beginning of November, the authorities had decided that out of the fifty-five dance instructors brought in for questioning, twenty-one of them were harmful. Despite the risk involved—and perhaps because of the thrill that risk brought—clandestine swings spread through Paris and its suburbs. These meetings, hidden from the eye of Vichy, were featured in songs like Jacques Pills's "Elle était swing," in which the lyrics describe meeting all kinds of people and creating bonds of enjoyment with them: "I found that charming, without knowing why or how." These clandestine meetings remained an integral part of the youth resistance movement in the remaining years of the war.

Though it was an almost certain way to be caught for *Service Travail Obligatoire,* the Zazous did not all go underground. Johnny Hess, hoping to capture the remaining vestiges of fanaticism, came out with the song "Ils Sont Zazou." Yet like the switch from the first person in "Je suis swing" to the third person in this song, Hess was no longer counting himself among the Zazou dandies. The flamboyant Zazou was becoming passé. The dandy figure that Hess described in the song continued as a leitmotif in the Vichy media among writers and cartoonists, who, even after it seemed certain that Germany would lose the war, wanted to prove that the Jews, and all the symptoms of cultural decay associated with them, were still public enemy number one.

After the Nazis pushed into the nonoccupied zone,[165] Lucien Rebatet explained the move as a reaction to "the Jewish fact" and called for "fidelity" to the anti-Semitic truths of National Socialism.[166] The war against the Jews continued for the hardened fascists, but their battle in the press over whether jazz could be a legitimate form of enjoyment for *la jeunesse* had already been lost. *Les Swings,* now a symbol of the importance of a tolerant and balanced French way of life, had won.

In 1944, Radio National broadcast a concert featuring music "from Debussy to Jazz" all over France. Even *La Gerbe* legitimized symphonic jazz—a

MÉLANGES

— Goûtez mon nouveau cocktail : « F. T. P. » composé de gin anglais, wisky américain et vodka soviétique...
— Vous devriez y ajouter pas mal de sang français.

"Mixing: Taste my new F.T.P. cocktail. It's made of English gin, American whiskey, and Soviet vodka . . . You should add a lot of French blood to it . . ." *Je Suis Partout* (May 19, 1944). Reproduced with permission from the Bibliothèque Nationale de France.

musical form it once diagnosed as a symptom of the Judeo-Americanization of culture—for France.[167] The Vichy media forces were still fighting against the threat of "Judeo-American democracy"[168] in any way they could, but jazz was no longer the public focal point of these battles. At the Hot Club, now in full swing, a young trumpet player named Boris Vian wrote about the end of an era: "*Il n'y a plus de jazz en France*" (There is no longer any jazz in France.)[169] Jazz would no longer be forbidden fruit, and enjoying jazz would never again be a clandestine activity. Now it was a music for everyone.

As the Germans lost more ground to the Allies, a frantic period for Vichy began. The Vichy media warned of the "sacking of France" by the English and the onset of the "democratic virus" from America. People flooded back

QUATORZE JUILLET

— Mais que font donc nos « amis » anglo-américains !! Ils nous avaient pourtant promis de nous faire danser aujourd'hui !!
— Vous trouvez qu'ils ne nous font pas assez danser, tous les jours, ...devant le buffet ?

(Dessin de Ralph Soupault.)

"July 14: But what are our Anglo-American friends doing? They promised to make us dance today? But don't you find that they make us dance enough every day . . . in front of the buffet?" *Je Suis Partout* (July 14, 1944). Reproduced with permission from the Bibliothèque Nationale de France.

to Paris. The Resistance now championed cultural forms and practices that had been opposed by Vichy. Strikes became more numerous, and journals for the Resistance came out in the open. As Joseph Darnand's "maintenance of order" collapsed, a reign of terror and vigilante justice began. Jacques Doriot, collaborator and editor of *Le Cri du Peuple,* was shot in his car. Cousteau and Rebatet left France with the German army. The Allied troops entered in Paris on August 25, 1944, and the celebration began. Once again, jazz was the collective soundtrack for the liberation of France from the forces that threatened it. De Gaulle, profiting from four years of unifying rhetoric from the Vichy press, assumed his role as the figurehead for a heterogeneous resistance movement. Now the forces of resistance paid their respects to the defiant Zazous in the media. The *Francs-Tireurs et Partisans Français* (FTP) used their journal *L'Assaut* to announce the staging of a symbolic funeral for Lieutenant Zazou and called for vengeance against those who had opposed him. "It's here that he takes his final rest, a brave soldier, Lieutenant Zazou . . . Zazou, we are proud of you. You are dignified of our forefathers; your fathers know that you died bravely fighting to liberate your country. You have fallen as others will fall. But nothing will stop us . . . Zazou, all us FTP, we swear to avenge you. We swear as well not to rest until we have avenged all those who fell like you, before having liberated the French people from the Nazi yoke . . . Zazou, adieu."[170] Indeed, the resentment of four years under the Vichy boot gave way to thousands of acts of revenge. Collaborators were now the hunted. Women accused of "*coucheries* [sleeping] with the occupant," like the Zazous before them, were shaved and paraded in public.

In *Le Franc-Tireur,* Marcel Landowski announced a call for rapprochement and calm with a festival of Franco-American music for October 13, 1944. He framed the concert as a testimony to the faith of *la vraie jeunesse française* and of their resistance to anti-jazz and anti-French cultural forces. "For faith, *la jeunesse,* and the people are three forces that absolutely no conservative barrier can ever contain. These three forces are possessed in jazz; and like all passion, it will leave traces: worked, disciplined, and amalgamated finally to the European musical tradition, the new generations, following the traces of Gershwin and Tausman, will have another color for their artistic palette."[171] Where the Vichy cultural order was marked by its resistance to jazz and swing, the resistance to Vichy and "true" Frenchness would now be associated with the love of jazz in post-occupation French culture.

When the trials for the collaborators began, the *Je Suis Partout* writers received life in prison.[172] Charles Maurras, director of *L'Action Française* and author of the essay "Stupidity Is without Honor," was given life in prison and received a kind of *mort civil* by being thrown out of the *Académie Française.* André Delion de Launois, the editor of *La Gerbe;* Abel Bonnard, Vichy secretary of education; Admiral Darnand; and Pierre Laval were all sentenced to death. Robert Brasillach, editor of *Je Suis Partout,* was convicted of "intelligence with the enemy" and was executed.[173] Vichy journalists Suarez, de Puységur, Chack, Béraud and Lucien Rebatet were also convicted of capital crimes, though Rebatet, de Puységur and Béraud all had their death sentences commuted to hard labor, which they served with other collaborators, like cartoonist Ralph Soupault. Finally, Pétain, now the symbol of French collaboration, was brought to trial. Though he, like many others, claimed, "I was the resistor of the métropole,"[174] he was stripped of his honors and sentenced to death. However, "taking into account the great age of the accused,"[175] the court commuted his sentence to prison, where he was to live out the rest of his life in disgrace. José Germain, the editor of *Collaboration* and a tireless opponent of jazz in France since the 1920s, was tried, convicted, and jailed.

In this period of macabre celebration, anti-jazz media activity took on a new significance in relation to these guilty anti-jazz voices. In the new ideological hegemony, the coding of cultural discourse changed. Being swing now meant resisting the forces that these anti-jazz villains had unleashed on France, Europe, and humanity; being swing meant celebrating the return of *Liberté, egalité, fraternité;* being swing celebrated surviving the occupation without collaborating. Having a passion for jazz was a symptom of being swing. The enjoyment of jazz was now tied to an authentically French postwar identity that was suspicious of those who did not love jazz. The old standards of anti-jazz media discourse no longer rang true in the cultural harmonics. After the occupation, they would be forever associated with a time and mentality that many wanted to forget.

7

Assimilation, Absence, and the Liberation of French Discourse on Jazz

> Jazz has too often been considered like a *mode*. But a *mode* that lasts for twenty-five years is no longer a *mode*. It is an epoch.
>
> —Arthur Honegger

Endings always mark new beginnings. This final chapter marks the end of an era when discourse on whether or not jazz should be accepted as part of French culture served an important function for the negotiation of cultural identity. After the liberation, public debates about jazz and its meaning for French culture were marked by the absence of anti-jazz voices. After three decades of critics asserting that jazz was un-French and dangerous for the health of "true" French culture, the unspoken ideology in media discourse now made public opposition of jazz—and the identity formation linked to such opposition—next to impossible. Jazz was no longer portrayed as un-French or as a threat to "true" French culture in the media; it had been embraced as a legitimate part of French culture and assimilated into French cultural identity. This shift of forces within discussions of French popular culture speaks to a radical shift in discursive paradigm and the emergence of a new unconscious hegemony.

Jazz was still an important cultural phenomenon, and public debate on it flourished after 1945, but the discourse served a different function. Writing on jazz reflected the intellectual and cultural mentality of the postwar era. It was marked by a turn toward irony, relativism, and pluralism as a new generation of disillusioned critics, wary of totalizing arguments about culture, came to terms with an uncertain world. Whereas jazz critics in the late 1930s found their voices and purpose struggling against the violently anti-jazz rhetoric of the right, postwar jazz critics were faced with a new problem: what was left to say about jazz now that its legitimacy for France was no longer contested?

Certainly, French critics had to make sense of the incredible changes in jazz that had happened during the five years when France was at war and American records and movies had been forbidden. During the war, a new style of jazz, bebop, had emerged, and it shocked the ears of older French critics just as it shocked those of many of their American counterparts. Moreover, the new jazz was hardly the only American cultural product flowing into France in the postwar era. Indeed, whereas anti-jazz voices faded out in French discourse on culture, the number of critics warning of American cultural hegemony grew exponentially. Anxiety about Americanization, which the French communist party called "Marshallisation" and "Coca-colonization,"[1] intensified as America-the-superpower pushed the American way of life on France and much of Europe through export of culture and capital.[2] Yet in postwar debate on popular culture, jazz was separated from discussions of America-the-superpower in the French imagination. Embraced as a part of a shared cultural heritage, jazz now floated above the question of national origin and became congruous with postwar notions of Frenchness and representative of a "true" France grounded in the wartime experience of resistance. To be sure, critics used certain kinds of commercialized jazz to represent the kind of American culture that should be resisted, but the absence of anti-jazz discourse and the unavailability of the subject position associated with it signified a dramatic shift in the French sense of self.

Things Ain't What They Used to Be

Just as the French press in 1945 looked much like it had before the war, so, too, did the old critical guard try to reestablish its authority in jazz criticism. It is telling that the first major work of postwar jazz criticism came from André Hodeir, a twenty-four-year-old musicology and violin student at the Conservatoire de Paris,[3] who had come of age reading *Jazz Hot* before the war. His book, *Le jazz, cet inconnu,* moved the debates about jazz to the apolitical realm of art discourse as it tried to reassert the prewar order for jazz criticism. During the war, he argued, the proponents and enemies of jazz spent too much time arguing over swing and, as a result, the "valuable youth of the country" were misled by "those detestable and ridiculous 'Zazous,' whose futility and bad taste were evident."[4] Aping his hero, Hugues Panassié, and the older critic's purist categories, Hodier asserted that "true jazz," despite what the Zazou-influenced public might have *felt* during the occupation, was not a hybrid French music, but the music of black Americans. "We have altered the diamond that the black made sparkle . . . and we have made of it an 'affair,' a 'business.'"[5] In America and France, swing had been "swollen by publicity"[6] and pumped up by massive commercial campaigns that fooled the public into believing that it was hearing "true jazz." This false jazz caught the ears of the confused wartime public and displaced real jazz in their imaginations. "The music made us forget. One was 'swing' or not. There was a way of dressing 'swing,' a 'swing' mentality, a 'swing' haircut."[7] While he believed that the wartime Swings had been "inoffensive in their stupidity,"[8] Hodeir made it his mission to reaffirm the conceptual difference between the real thing—now flowing back into France in recorded form—and the music of the majority of "white orchestras called 'jazz' who are, in reality, commercial orchestras."[9] Yet the hybrid swing jazz that Hodeir disliked had been fondly embraced by French culture. French swing and *jazz manouche* (Gypsy swing) were now interpolated into the national popular culture. Moreover, American swing bands like those of Glenn Miller, Harry James, and Tommy Dorsey dominated the Armed Forces Radio and set the backbeat for the postwar celebration. Hodier hoped that Panassié could restore order to the now chaotic critical scene in which everyone was a jazz fan.

Indeed, the Hot Club in Paris quickly reestablished itself, and its membership surged. In the fall of 1945, with swing dancing dominating the postwar jubilation and the American performers Fred Astaire and the Glenn Miller Orchestra playing to Parisian crowds, *Jazz Hot* announced its mission to propagate "true jazz." Editor Charles Delaunay claimed that the Hot Club was one of the only places in the mixed-up postwar world where true jazz was protected. Significantly, the rhetorical foils were no longer the "enemies of jazz" in France, but rather the presence of *too much jazz* in France. While other jazz journals around the world were "guided more by commercial necessities than by a rigorous musical aesthetic,"[10] *Jazz Hot* remained pure. Yet Delaunay acknowledged that the times had radically changed in France in regard to jazz: jazz was no longer opposed for being un-French. "Today, the question is very different. Our ideas have triumphed. During the occupation we maintained the ideal of jazz, and the cause has won the day. At the same time, we see the appearance of a swarm of parasites . . . *Jazz Hot* reappears today after a five-year hiatus. It has become again THE BEST—we can no longer say the only—specialized international review . . . It thanks the Hot Club Français, which maintained the flame and hope of spirits taken with jazz, thus of liberty."[11] As the last sentence makes clear, jazz and liberty were now linked in the French imagination. Yet there were many definitions of *freedom*, and there were many definitions of *jazz*. The Hot Club critics sought to bring order to the chaos of the liberation period by reasserting their definition of "true jazz." Panassié, writing from his estate in Montauban, where he had weathered the war, asserted himself as the head of the Hot Club restoration and affirmed his dedication to *le vrai jazz*. The "real jazz" he proclaimed, was the antidote to the commercial swing that glutted the market. Despite the immense popularity of Alix Combelle, Django Reinhardt, Léo Chauliac, Hubert Rostaing, Charles Trenet, and many other stars of French swing, Panassié argued that jazz culture needed to be purified. "Bad jazz music has completely supplanted sincere jazz music in the eyes of the public. The admirers of this bad jazz have proved to have such stupidity that rare are the musicians, critics, or listeners of good music who care to know that new branch of musical art in its true light. We have, today, with that '*frénésie* of Swing,' a new example of the ravages that snobbery can cause."[12] In a country that was now jazz-crazy, it was time for the return of true jazz and for the restoration of an art-music discourse in place of popular conceptions about the music. Yet despite the initial reflex to restore the Hot Club orthodoxy, there were now new—and old—critics who expressed a certain concern about the return of a prewar hierarchy. A fracture was growing in the Hot Club's critical foundation. In the postwar period, Panassié's firebrand criticism seemed dated, recalling an era of culture wars that most French men and women wanted to leave behind.

One of the most significant changes in French culture criticism in the postwar paradigm was skepticism toward all forms of dogmatic or purist cultural criticism. Jean-Paul Sartre, the most influential public intellectual of the day, used his new journal, *Les Temps Modernes,* to assert that realist, purist, and historicist thinking had led to the rise of fascism and the fall of France. Linking "realism" with "collaboration," he sought to bar such thinking in the postwar world. "That tendency of dignifying themselves under the name of 'realism' has profound roots in the ideology of our times."[13] The collaborators justified their stringent fascist vision of pure or true French culture because they based their thinking on a "reality" about the meaning of French history and culture that they alone had access to. Filled with the daily resentment of life under occupation and fixed upon this future return to a "real" or "true" French culture, collaborators developed an inferiority complex that caused a reversal of values and a hatred of self and others. "The favorite thesis of the collaborator—as well as the fascist—is realism. We must profit from our victory by confirming the defeat of all realist politics. Certainly, it is suitable for underlying the facts and for drawing lessons from experiences. But that suppleness, that political positivism was only a means toward realizing an end whose existence did not depend on the facts. By making an example of all politics based on these principles, we will contribute to the disappearance of that species of 'pseudo-realists.'"[14] Pseudo-realists and collaborators acted *as if* they knew the facts about "true" culture, *as if* they knew the "reality" through which the present state of culture was to be condemned. Sartre argued that authors, politicians, or culture critics who used such language, and who manifested this pseudo-realist mentality in regard to art, music, and culture, were suspect. Such cultural discourse was to be engaged and resisted.

Yet while Sartre and France's leading intellectuals called for existential engagement, relativism, and restraint in cultural criticism, Panassié wrote about jazz as if nothing had changed. He set the critical tone at the Hot Club by refusing to accept bebop, the new postwar style, as real jazz. Along with denouncing this new "modernist" style, he lashed out at postwar American jazz critics who, he argued, had lost sight of true jazz. "If jazz music maintained itself living well in the U.S. during the war, the jazz critic, of which the level has not always been very elevated, has become, in the majority of cases, scandalously idiotic."[15] It is easy to see the trajectory of Panassié's criticism from this point as he became more hardened in his pseudo-realist rejection of the new. In an almost humorous repetition of a now outmoded prewar Hot Club propaganda style, when Panassié made his return to Paris for the first time since 1939, promising to bring order to the critical realm, his coming was written about in *Jazz Hot* as an "event."[16] With his anti-jazz foils like Rebatet now silent or in prison, Panassié became a caricature of his prewar self. He attacked critics who did not fall into line and maintained that he alone was a moderate and objective judge of jazz. "Readers who have confidence in me, listen a bit . . . Be large of ear and you will be rewarded."[17] However, both in style and in content, the *Jazz Hot* editors and critics found that their fidelity to Panassié was alienating the increasingly large listening public in France. Many of the *Jazz Hot* critics *were* opening their ears to what the new musicians had to say. Like Sartre and much of the postwar public, they wanted to engage with the complexity of the present. Critics like Frank Ténot and Boris Vian were starting to question Panassié's nostalgic pseudo-realism.

Despite the internecine tension at *Jazz Hot,* Panassié churned out two quick retrospective works designed to bolster his authority and debunk the interlopers. The first, *Douze années de jazz* (1927–38), souvenirs, traced his own personal experience of *le vrai jazz.*[18] He used the anti-jazz critics, now silent and hardly a threat, as straw men and cast himself as the tireless crusader against them. The second book, *La véritable musique de jazz* (The Real Jazz), defined what he was defending. "We have talked a great deal, several books have been written on the subject, and, nevertheless, the public still hasn't the least idea what that music *really* is."[19] Almost perfectly dramatizing Sartre's characterization of the pseudo-realist, Panassié argued that the word "'jazz'—it is an indisputable historical fact—served from the beginning to designate the music of black orchestras from the south of the U.S.A., a music radically different from the commercial forgeries of which I allude to."[20] Significantly, he excluded bebop, which he did not consider to be true jazz.

In October 1947, Boris Vian, a Sartre protégé who also played trumpet at the famous jazz cave Le Tabou, began a jazz column in *Combat,* the leftist daily created underground in 1943 and now edited by Albert Camus and Pascal Pia. His first piece described the current state of French jazz criticism and marked the beginning of Vian's practice of mocking Panassié in a critical style that he described as "jazzistique." In the 1930s, Vian recounted, the Hot Club faithful had followed the opinions of their president. "Around 1940, tired of changing his mind every year, Panassié retired completely to the country and Charles Delaunay assumed alone the responsibility for the defense of jazz during the occupation."[21] After the war for jazz and France was over, Panassié returned to reclaim his rightful position, and a struggle for power began. "Estimating that the moment had come, after seven years of inertia, to assert his royal prerogatives, Huges le Montalbanais left his retreat, indoctrinated the valiant presidents of the regional Hot Clubs, infiltrated the Hot Club de France . . . and attacked Charles Delaunay under pretexts no less ridiculous than fallacious."[22] Indeed, Delaunay returned the snub, and when he put together a successful edited volume called *Jazz 47,* he included articles by Sartre and Belgian critic Robert Goffin but passed over Panassié. This, Vian wrote, led the furious Panassié to declare a schism in the Hot Club movement. While some of the regional Hot Clubs sided with the "Grand Hugues," the Hot Club in Paris sided with Delaunay. The split had begun, not over whether or not jazz was a threat to "true" French culture, but over critical authority and the commercial control of a now immensely popular and marketable form of mass culture. Vian asked readers not to let jazz, the music, be drowned out by the "indifference, ignorance, and impotence of the physical pontifications of the bearded moral pontiff."[23] More and more, Vian used irony and satire to liberate French jazz criticism from Panassié's pseudo-realist authoritarianism, signing his articles with satiric pen names like the Pannasié sendup Hugo Hachebuisson.[24]

In the November 1947 *Jazz Hot,* Delaunay, Hodier, and Ténot formally declared the journal's independence from Panassié. Panassié responded by attacking the *Jazz Hot* critics in his new *Bulletin Panassié* over questions of doctrine and reporting how various regional Hot Clubs were aligning themselves. Unable to move beyond the old prewar propaganda style, Panassié decreed that Delaunay was "disapproved of by an overwhelming majority"[25] of members in France. Panassié attacked Ténot, Avon, Boulogne, Grosos, and other critics who had sided with Delaunay, and he declared that "the true Hot Club de Paris is going to be immediately reformed."[26] In *Arts* magazine, whose regular jazz columnist was the repatriated Jean Wiéner,[27] Marc Pincherle wondered where this schism would lead French jazz criticism. His remarks are poignant because they come from someone outside the struggles at the Hot Club. "I know that jazz is not only an art, with its annexed branches, an industry, and a form of commerce, but also, for thousands, even millions of young people, a kind of religion that is periodically reinvigorated by schisms and fanatical oppositions."[28] Jazz was, he argued, firmly established in France, which now ought to accept all types of jazz. For instance, though he preferred symphonic jazz, which he thought more European, he also accepted bebop. Despite what the critics might argue in order to conjure up public concern, jazz was no longer new, no longer scandalous, and no longer considered foreign; it had been assimilated into the French sensibility. One could prefer one kind of jazz to another, but to do so was merely a matter of taste.

Boris Vian had begun to argue the same point and quickly felt Panassié's wrath: "The stupidity and the self-importance of Vian is inexpressible."[29] Vian ignored the attack of the aging critic and used his *Combat* column to categorize different types of jazz listeners. For many, he wrote, jazz was only dance music, equal to any old waltz by Strauss. For others, jazz was a kind of "materialization of the good life."[30] For others still, it was a way of differentiating themselves, "like a method of reaction, a way of 'upsetting the parents.'"[31] Finally, there were those who were touched by "the sense, by the intelligence, by who knows what . . . a memory, an association of ideas, but who don't search to delve into them, to know, to understand; who don't want to remain there . . . And it is precisely these people who stay faithful to jazz and follow its evolution, which, for others, will be nothing but a moment in their life, the folly of youth from the time when they were 'Zazous.'"[32] Vian noted that as wave after wave of jazz heroes arrived in postwar France, critics seemed to divide into these camps. More and more, French culture critics used the kind of jazz they liked as a way to indicate their relationship to the present and the past.

As Ludovic Tournès and Colin Nettelbeck have shown, the postwar period was a blessed time for jazz culture in France.[33] Along with a flourishing club and concert scene, a new format was developed, the beloved Festival de Jazz, which gathered musicians and listeners of all kinds together for weeklong concerts in various locations all over France. As a sign of their importance as cultural events, these concerts were often broadcast nationwide over state-run Radio France. Many of the performers who came to these festivals, like Louis Armstrong or Dizzy Gillespie, often toured throughout France afterward. After playing at the International Festival de Jazz, Armstrong played at the Salle Pleyel, where he had first performed in 1933. Vian described the new fans and old fans "who came to taste a sentimental pleasure."[34] The aging artist no longer rubbed against the grain. Everyone loved him, and he gave fans exactly what they wanted. "The shock is now assimilated,"[35] wrote Vian. Satchmo was now a received master in France, an almost classical figure for older fans. When Dizzy Gillespie played the Semaine du Jazz (Jazz Week) at the Théâtre Marigny in Paris, critics publicly began to take sides in the battle over styles.[36] Importantly, though the battle over bebop was raging among critics, no one in the media was voicing concern about the presence of jazz in France and its impact on cultural health or the "true" France. Though Panassié continued to make his opposition to it the cornerstone of his postwar authority, fewer and fewer jazz critics were denying that bebop was legitimate jazz.

In the fall of 1948, Michel Dorigné summed up the critical battles over bebop in a retrospective book called *La guerre du jazz*. "The postwar world was a world still filled with pain and populated by men torn from their illusions; bebop had evolved to reflect that world. Some critics wanted to preserve their rosy view of the world where musicians were simple and naive and blamed the dissonance on a new generation."[37] Dorigné argued that Panassié needed to evolve. Just as the French media needed to become (and had become) more pluralistic, French critics should accept the necessities of new styles and schools of jazz. It was a mistake to claim that one knew the essence of jazz and to declare that only one style expressed its true sense. Such purist pretension, he argued, was nothing but "intellectual masturbation."[38] Dorigné accepted that there were different styles of jazz for different tastes, and to condemn someone else's taste in jazz as false was to act in bad faith.

Just as the jazz concert scene flourished in postwar France, jazz journalism also exploded with different types of criticism designed to appeal to different kinds of readers. To promote his pseudo-realist style, Hugues Panassié founded his new, true "organ du Hot Club de France," called *La Revue du Jazz,* in January of 1949. This was not the only publication that followed Panassié's jazz dogma, but it was the most official. Armstrong was still the basis of Panassié's critical authority, where he was to criticism what Satchmo was to "true jazz," and only those who followed him were true "friends of jazz." A critic either agreed with Panassié, which meant that he could publish criticism in *La Revue du jazz, La Casserole, Le Bulletin du Hot Club du France, Hébdo-Latin, Jazz Panorama, Le Point,* or any of the other avenues for publications or radio programming that Panassié controlled, or he was an enemy of jazz.[39] The efficacy of this approach, and perhaps the reason why Panassié's logic worked, was that when the "false prophets"[40] defended themselves, Panassié used this defense as proof of the necessity of his own quixotic position.

Jazz Hot, which Panassié began to refer to as *Zazzote* so as to link its editors to the "ignorant Zazous,"[41] had a very different style. As Charles Delaunay turned more of his energy toward battling Panassié and toward other editorial projects, André Hodeir took over the reins of the journal, and his philosophical and musicological approach to jazz discourse characterized its pages. If Panassié's criticism was as formulaic as Dixieland standards, Hodeir was like Charlie Parker with strings. He was the most erudite critic in *Jazz Hot,* often writing on the "unknowable"[42] or paradoxical topics in jazz criticism, like race and genius.[43] Though he often apologized for his philosophical digressions, he linked his work to contemporary trends in philosophy, such as existentialism and Husserlian phenomenology.[44] As they no longer needed to defend jazz against anti-jazz critics who opposed its presence in France, the majority of articles in *Jazz Hot* merely let the public know who was releasing what and who was touring in France. Significantly, in an attempt to eliminate the propagandistic style that had characterized the prewar era, the editors provided a variety of perspectives on key issues in jazz criticism. Thus articles with a strong position were often contrasted with alternative perspectives on the issue. Critics Lucien Malson, Frank Ténot,[45] and Georges Daniel[46] provided the theoretical apparatus to situate the articles and opinions in *Jazz Hot.* Malson tried to explode the myth of racial determinism as the sine qua non of jazz expression by placing jazz critics who based their truth claims on the "authenticity" of race in the same camp as Gobineau and other racists. Like other humanists in the postwar era, he stressed the importance of culture and environment over race. "Where the aesthetic sensibility is concerned, the 'racial' factor cedes the way to the cultural factor."[47] Each jazz style was an "authentic" expression of its particular milieu, "because the cultural atmosphere favors aesthetic choices."[48] Perhaps in reaction to Panassié's repeated attacks, the *Jazz Hot* critics stressed that the lingering mission to convince the French public of the existence of a single true jazz was merely a stunt designed to trump up commercial interest. They sought to turn the public's attention toward understanding questions of evolution of style in relation to changes in culture. As the final ingredient to the *Jazz Hot* gumbo, from 1948 to 1958 Boris Vian wrote his famous column "Revue de la presse," in which his tireless intellect and wit made sense of the international critical scene and ridiculed critics, especially Panassié, who were too dogmatic in their assertions about jazz or French culture.

Michel Dorigné's *La Gazette du Jazz* marketed itself as an independent jazz journal, and sought to reform the debate on jazz, which had become too marked by prejudice and polemics: "We are not chauvinists . . . All opinions of good faith are commendable."[49] Like other jazz journals, the *Gazette* primarily responded to the concerts and records. Its contributors, many of whom also contributed to *Jazz Hot,* included Michel de Villers, Jacques Jauffret, Xavier Clarke, and Stéphane Golmann. They were encouraged to use the qualifier "for me" when making claims about the essence or truth of jazz. Despite the rigorous critical spirit of its contributors, the journal did not fare well commercially. The market for jazz criticism was oversaturated, and the public seemed to be more willing to spend money on records and concerts than on criticism. The *Gazette* tried to drum up interest by joining the fight against Panassié and his journals and ridiculing his preference for "Uncle Tomism."[50] Dorigné even went so far as to link Panassié, in spirit, to Pétain.[51] Xavier Clarke proposed a series on the Luter Affair, over the critical appraisals of clarinetist Claude Luter, to draw attention to the prejudice against French jazz by purist critics.[52] The *Gazette* critics even entered into the postwar retrospective on the Zazou.[53] But with the vast array of journals to choose from, *La Gazette du Jazz* lasted only a little less than two years.

Jazz News was another short-lived industry journal, started at the end of 1948 by Eddie Barclay and funded in part by Blue Star Records. The journal was internationalist by design, including not only French critics like Hubert Fol, but an international array of critics like Carlos de Radzitsky and Yannick Bruynoghe, from Belgium, and Walter "Gil" Fuller from America. They not only reported the jazz news in France, but included news from America, Belgium, and Germany.

Of the many journals in postwar France dedicating space to jazz criticism, Boris Vian was the common link. The public was already aware of his talent as a writer, not only from the books *L'écume des jours* and *Vercoquin et le plancton,* which he published under his real name, but also from the "pornographic" novels that he wrote under the name Vernon Sullivan: *J'irai cracher sur vos tombes, Les morts ont tous la même peau,* and *Et on tuera tous les affreux.* In addition to *Combat, Jazz Hot* (where he joined the editorial staff in November 1951), *La Gazette du Jazz,* and *Jazz News,* he also wrote the jazz column in *Radio 49, Radio 50, Spectacles,* and *Arts,* and he contributed to *Les Cahiers du Disque, Opéra, Hébé, Relais, Midi-Libre, La Parisienne,* and, later, *Jazz Magazine.* More than any other writer—and many have tried to imitate him—he captured the sense of postwar thinking about jazz in his *jazzistique* writing. Like the great musicians he admired who created new riffs over old chord changes, he refused to be categorized and was always quoting phrases that matched the sound of the words he was alluding to. He once wrote that jazz music was "regarded by some as the most appropriate vehicle for conveying their emotions—their affective being—to others."[54] Thus he stressed the importance of listening for jazz and placed the humanity of the player first and the critical debates second. He ruthlessly mocked dogmatic critics who were more concerned with bolstering their categorical certainty than acknowledging the joy or sorrow expressed in jazz. Consequently, the role he played in postwar jazz discourse was something like that of a referee: he reminded critics and jazz fans that there was a difference between the language of jazz music and the language of jazz criticism, and he kept them from going too far with their hyperbole.

More than anyone else, Vian dedicated himself to combating dogmatic jazz criticism. When Panassié began to retroactively speak out against the Zazou for debasing the "truth" of jazz doctrine, Vian countered by putting the Zazou back into jazz parlance. Stylistically, this meant replacing the letter S with the letter Z whenever possible. He began to translate the word *cat* (as black American jazz musicians referred to one another) as "Zazou"[55] and always referred to Charlie Parker as "*Zoiseau*" (*oiseau* = "bird" + Z). He also invented verbs like *gillespizer*[56] to describe the bebopper's fast improvisational runs.

In an article from the March 1949 *Jazz News,* Vian ironically listed the motives that led one to become a jazz critic in the postwar era, when jazz was thoroughly accepted in France and when people should spend more time listening to it than writing about it. There was a little something about the different motivations for all the critics he knew, "because there is absolutely no reason that anyone not be a jazz critic."[57] In order to be persuasive, he argued, one needed to find a style in which to write. The easiest method, and the most common, he wrote, was to "know how to count." One just put on a record and described how and when the sound changed. For example, when the saxophone took over from the trumpet in the fourth chorus, one should describe it with a flourish of superlatives like "the terrifying return of horns."[58]

There were several critics who went beyond such formulas and differentiated themselves. Ténot, Vian wrote, was one of the few who had a personal writing style and "frequently has extremely interesting results."[59] One could also "write in America to find out about it. That is the Delaunay method, a bit simple, but sure."[60] There was the "Hodeir method, dangerous but brilliant": "One invents tales of the 6th-9th diminished with a backpedaling in a broken line [*retropedalage en ligne brisée*]."[61] One could, like Panassié, declare that "the others are wrong." Vian paraphrased his "master," Sartre, to describe Panassié's method. "When one no longer knows what to say, it is enough to pretend with a strong conviction that your interlocutor (one can always create one) is an imbecile, for it is absolutely impossible for him to prove the contrary."[62] Finally, "one can talk of other things. That is my method."[63]

Writing against Panassié, for Vian, was like sitting in with a good rhythm section: it brought out some of his best choruses. He named the dogmatic critic on different occasions: "Gugusse Peine-à-scier," "Hugues le Matalbanais,"[64] "Le clown de Montauban," "Le Grand Hugues," "Pope Hugues," "Papenassié,"[65] "Panapapassié,"[66] "le Pana,"[67] "Père Pana,"[68] and, of course, "Père Hugues Panne d'Acier."[69] As many of the names suggest, Vian focused on the way in which Panassié operated his critical realm according to a papal hierarchy based on moral dictums and decrees. He ridiculed him not because his tastes differed, but because of the "bad faith" in which Pope Hugues attacked other critics.

Though it is hard to choose the most representative of his articles mocking Panassié's dogmatism, the most systematic was one written for a special number of *Jazz Hot* in 1950, titled "Papal Bulls: Collective Improvisation in a Sacred Style on the Themes of M. Panassié, Known in Criticism under the Name of S. S. Hugues I, Pope of Jazz."[70] The article was designed to twist Panassié's own words to make him unwittingly accept bebop as "true jazz." Vian constructed a "Catechisme du Saint-Père Hugues I," in which he provided the call and used Panassié's own words as the response, all the while revealing the extent to which Panassié's position on key issues, such as bebop, changed like the weather. Throughout, Vian criticized Panassié for his lack of personality and dubbed him a knight of bad faith. "*Peine-à-sciere* is like don Quixote. It is necessary that he spend his time battling against windmills [*les moulins à vian*]."[71]

When Panassié later began to play for conservative jazz audiences in *Vie Catholique Illustrée*—and jazz had become *that* assimilated and safe for the conservative French establishment—and began calling Vian a "pornographer,"[72] Vian threatened to stop acknowledging him altogether. "Let him fall, that sad sire who works elsewhere and who destroys himself more surely than anyone else could ever do."[73] Yet despite himself, Vian continued to combat Panassié's *mauvaise foi* and defend himself from Panassié's attacks, as this was the last cause that a French jazz critic could serve in good faith. Following the Duke Ellington concerts of 1950, when Duke was awarded the medal of the French Légion d'honneur, and which met with much more success than his '49 concerts, since the musician syndicate blockades had been dropped and Duke was allowed to play with his orchestra, Vian wondered in print what was left for the French jazz critic to do, save serving as a publicist for jazz musicians. Perusing the patented press reviews, which had nothing new to say about Duke save to repeat the standard riffs of jazz hyperbole, Vian wrote in his *Jazz Hot* column: "There is very little to sink your teeth into, as we have said before, literally, seeing that it's soiled, and figuratively, seeing the minimum interest introduced by those who write on jazz. The longer that continues, the more I consider that it is much better to listen than to comment—one will answer that propaganda is necessary, but when we do it, we should do it well, without *blabla,* without literature—and that we should leave it to good publicity agents."[74] Vian continued to fulfill his professional duties to *Jazz Hot* and to meet other journals' requests to do jazz criticism, but he also moved into other genres of criticism and expression, from screenplays and short stories to popular songs. Times had changed, and France's military assertion in Indochina and the polemics of the Cold War made other issues more pressing than debating the finer points of jazz criticism. His jazz-influenced songs like "J'suis snob" and "Je bois" are now considered classics in the tradition of *la chanson française.* In others, like "Le Déserteur," about a draftee writing to the president of his refusal to go to Indochina to "kill those poor people," it is hard to tell where the jazz influence blends with the traditional word orientation of the realist *chanson.* A new music, rock 'n' roll, was gaining popularity in America and was becoming fashionable in France, and Vian embraced this new sound in classic songs like "Fais-mois mal, Johnny." The times were changing.

Coda

When Charles Trenet died in February 2001, political leaders, media spokesmen, and public intellectuals all mourned his loss for French culture. President Jacques Chirac praised him as "the very symbol of a happy and imaginative France."[75] That jazz was a major influence on this hero of *la chanson française* was a given, passed over without comment. From French swing to *jazz manouche,* the existence and persistence of jazz in French popular culture is now taken for granted; that "the French love jazz" is now a statement held at the level of normal common sense. Ideology, to paraphrase

Althusser, may have no history once it has been naturalized, but the process of this naturalization does.

This book has shown how a foreign cultural phenomenon once opposed by the dominant ideologies within French cultural discourse came to be taken for granted as part of French culture. First heard as the expression of racial and cultural otherness, jazz slowly worked its way into the national unconscious so that its presence as a feature of everyday life was no longer felt as anything but natural.

To be sure, right-wing cultural protectionism exists in France today. Just look at Jean-Marie Le Pen's Front National (FN), which continues to use xenophobic and protectionist media rhetoric to define a "true" France "menaced" by immigrants, globalism, and "Big Brother America." As part of their platform, the FN pushed for more stringent regulation of the French media to ensure the promotion of French music over the radio. Protectionist laws that went into action in 1996 limit the airtime of foreign music like American jazz, hip-hop, and rock. By statute, 40 percent of music on the radio has to be French. But jazz and jazz-influenced popular music sung or performed by French performers is now considered French by law. Even the FN seems to be okay with that; they have other bones to pick. Times have changed, indeed.

Notes

Introduction

1. On the importance of the "ongoing argument" on cultural identity, see Natalie Zemon Davis, "Towards Mixtures and Margins," *American Historical Review* 97, no. 5 (December 1992): 1415.

2. See Raymond Williams, *The Long Revolution* (London: Chatto and Windus, 1961), 10.

3. For an analysis of this imaginary invention in relation to historiography, see Eric Hobsbawm and Terence Ranger, eds., *The Invention of Tradition* (Cambridge: Cambridge University Press, 1983).

4. On the importance of living with cultural difference in the modern nation-state, see Stuart Hall, "Culture, Community, Nation," *Cultural Studies* 7, no. 3 (1993).

5. On the installation of jazz into the French cultural patrimony, see Ludovic Tournès, *New Orleans sur Seine: histoire du jazz en France* (Paris: Fayard, 1999), 363–420.

6. For a general account of this phenomenon, see Bill Moody, *Jazz Exiles: American Musicians Abroad* (Reno: University of Nevada Press, 1993). See also Mike Hennessey, "Europa Jazz," *Jazz Times* (June 1986).

7. See, for instance, Richard Kuisel, *Seducing the French: The Dilemma of Americanization* (Berkeley: University of California Press, 1993).

8. Indeed, it might help explain the meaning of a subject position that has become available in French debate on globalism and the nature of the post-9/11 world order, the "anti-anti-American."

9. For example, see Roland Barthes, "The Grain of the Voice," *The Responsibility of Forms: Critical Essays on Music, Art and Representation,* trans. Richard Howard (Berkeley: University of California Press, 1985), 267. Barthes argues that the act of

listening involves translating musical sound into language that has no one-to-one referentiality with musical language and, by nature, is always already arbitrary. This makes music criticism necessarily highly personalized "adjective criticism." "Music is, by a natural inclination, what immediately receives an adjective. The adjective is inevitable: this music is *this,* that execution is *that."* For a post-structuralist psycho-analytic theory of psychic projection as it manifests itself in jazz criticism, see Francis Hofstein, *Au miroir du jazz* (Paris: Éditions de la Pierre, 1985).

10. See Simon Frith, *Performing Rites: On the Value of Popular Music* (Cambridge: Cambridge University Press, 1996), 16.

11. See Claude Lévi-Strauss, *The Raw and the Cooked: Introduction to a Science of Mythology,* trans. John Weightman and Doreen Weightman (New York: Basic Books, 1964), 16.

12. See Jane F. Fulcher, *French Cultural Politics and Music: From the Dreyfus Affair to the First World War* (Oxford: Oxford University Press, 1999); and Jane F. Fulcher, *The Composer as Intellectual: Music and Ideology in France, 1914–1940* (Oxford: Oxford University Press, 2005).

13. Frith, *Performing Rites,* 19.

14. Ibid., 272.

15. David Hesmondhalgh, "Audiences and Everyday Aesthetics: Talking about Good and Bad Music," *European Journal of Cultural Studies* 10, no.4 (2007): 508.

16. Here I am alluding to Stuart Hall's semiotic system through which meanings, both hegemonic and oppositional, are generated as a feature of cultural identity. See Stuart Hall, "Encoding/decoding," in *Culture, Media, Language: Working Papers in Cultural Studies, 1972–1979* (London: Centre for Contemporary Cultural Studies, 1980).

17. This concern with the ethical dimension of music performance in society dates back to Plato and the Greeks. It is closely linked to ontological presuppositions about the nature of the person and of society and the connection of music with emotion. Because certain modes of music were thought to evoke characteristic movements of the soul, thereby affecting the emotions and character of individuals, Plato urged the careful monitoring of musical activities out of respect for the ability of music to inspire both order and lawlessness. See Philip Alperson, "Music as Philosophy," in *What Is Music?* Philip Alperson, ed. (University Park: Pennsylvania State University Press, 1986), 195–210.

18. See David L. Looseley, *Popular Music in Contemporary France: Authenticity, Politics, Debate* (Oxford: Berg, 2003), 4.

19. On this concept in relation to popular music, see Lawrence Grossberg, *Dancing in Spite of Myself: Essays on Popular Culture* (Durham, N.C.: Duke University Press, 1997). See also Grossberg, "The Media Economy of Rock Culture: Cinema, Postmodernity and Authenticity," in *Sound and Vision: The Music Video Reader,* Simon Frith, Andrew Goodwin, and Lawrence Grossberg, eds. (New York: Routledge, 1993).

20. On this notion see, for example, François Furet, *Penser la révolution française* (Paris: Gallimard, 1986).

21. On the theme of the *mission civilisatrice,* see Theodore Zeldin, *France, 1848–1945* (Oxford: Oxford University Press, 1977); see also Alice L. Conklin, *A Mission to Civilize: The Republican Idea of Empire in France and West Africa, 1895–1930* (Palo Alto, Calif.: Stanford University Press, 1997).

22. See Homi K. Bhabha, "The Other Question," in *The Location of Culture* (New York: Routledge, 1994), 66–84.

23. For an analysis of the French fascination with *nègre* cultural production in the early part of the twentieth century, see Gérard Le Coat, "Art nègre, jazz nègre, revue nègre: esthétique primitiviste et syndrome raciste en France (1905–1935)," in *Carrefour de cultures: mélanges offerts à Jacqueline Leiner,* Régis Antoine, ed. (Tübingen: G. Narr, 1993). For an account of the popular fascination with Africa in the latter half of the nineteenth century, see William H. Schneider, *An Empire for the Masses: The French Popular Image of Africa, 1870–1900* (Westport, Conn.: Greenwood Press, 1982); Christopher Miller, *Blank Darkness: Africanist Discourse in French* (Chicago: University of Chicago Press, 1985); and William B. Cohen, *The French Encounter with Africans: White Response to Blacks, 1530–1880* (Bloomington: Indiana University Press, 1980). On the theme of cultural and racial othering throughout the West, see Edward Said, *Orientalism* (New York: Vintage Books, 1979).

24. For an analysis of the rhetorical importance of "America" for French writers, see Jean-Philippe Mathy, *Extrême-Occident: French Intellectuals and America* (Chicago: University of Chicago Press, 1993); Denis Lacorne, Jacques Rupnik, and Marie-France Toinet, eds., *L'Amérique dans les têtes: un siècle de fascinations et d'aversions* (Paris: Hachette, 1986); Jacques Portes, *Fascinations and Misgivings: The United States in French Opinion, 1870–1914,* Elborg Forster, trans. (Cambridge: Cambridge University Press, 2000); and Richard Kuisel, *Seducing the French: The Dilemma of Americanization* (Berkeley: University of California Press, 1993).

25. For an account of the power of an "imaginary" tradition in the construction of cultural identity, see Benedict Anderson, *Imagined Communities: Reflections on the Origin and Spread of Nationalism* (London: Verso, 1983).

26. On the importance of this construction for twentieth-century cultural identity in France, see Herman Lebovics, *True France: The Wars over Cultural Identity, 1900–1945* (Ithaca, N.Y.: Cornell University Press, 1992).

27. Mathy, *Extrême-Occident.*

28. Charles Baudelaire, "Exposition Universelle, 1855," *Baudelaire as Literary Critic,* L. B. Hystop, trans. (University Park: Pennsylvania State University Press, 1964), 83. This quote appears in the *Petit Robert* under the definition of the word.

29. See Claude Lévi-Strauss, "The Structural Study of Myth," *Structural Anthropology,* Clair Jacobson and Brooke Grundfest Schoepf, trans. (New York: Basic Books, 1963), 206–31.

30. For an analysis of the importance of this concept as it relates to arguments about cultural purity from the right, see David Carroll, *French Literary Fascism: Nationalism, Anti-Semitism, and the Ideology of Culture* (Princeton, N.J.: Princeton University Press, 1995).

31. Jeffrey H. Jackson, "Making Enemies: Jazz in Inter-war Paris," *French Cultural Studies*, 10 (June 1999): 179–99. See also Colin Nettelbeck, "Jazz at the Théâtre Graslin: A Founding Story," *French Cultural Studies* 11 (2000): 201–17.

32. See Colin Nettelbeck, *Dancing with de Beauvoir: Jazz and the French* (Melbourne: Melbourne University Press, 2004).

33. See Michael Haggerty, "Quand la France découvrait le jazz," *Jazz Magazine*, special issue, no. 325 (January 1984); and A. David Franklin, "A Preliminary Study of the Acceptance of Jazz by French Music Critics in the 1920s and Early 1930s," *Annual Review of Jazz Studies*, 4 (1988). See also William H. Kenney III, "The Assimilation of Jazz in France, 1917–1940," *American Studies* 15, no. 1 (Spring 1984).

34. See Tyler Stovall, *Paris Noir: African Americans in the City of Light* (Boston: Houghton Mifflin, 1996); Michel Fabre, *From Harlem to Paris: Black American Writers in France, 1849–1980* (Urbana: University of Illinois Press, 1991); William A. Shack, *Harlem in Montmartre: A Paris Jazz Story between the Great Wars* (Berkeley: University of California Press, 2001); T. Denean Sharpley-Whiting, *Negritude Women* (Minneapolis: University of Minnesota Press, 2002); and Brent Hayes Edwards, *The Practice of Diaspora: Literature, Translation, and the Rise of Black Internationalism* (Cambridge, Mass.: Harvard University Press, 2003).

35. Jody Blake, *Le Tumulte Noir: Modernist Art and Popular Entertainment in Jazz-Age Paris, 1900–1930* (University Park: Pennsylvania University Press, 1999).

36. Charles Rearick, *The French in Love and War: Popular Culture in the Era of the World Wars* (New Haven, Conn.: Yale University Press, 1997).

37. See James Lincoln Collier, *Duke Ellington* (London: Michael Joseph, 1987), 159. Collier is referring to critic Constant Lambert.

38. See Tournès, *New Orleans sur Seine;* and Jeffrey Jackson, *Making Jazz French: Music and Modern Life in Interwar Paris* (Durham, N.C.: Duke University Press, 2003).

39. Richard Terdiman uses this riff from Pierre Bourdieu to look at the construction of identity in nineteenth-century French culture. See his *Present Pasts: Modernity and the Memory Crisis* (Ithaca, N.Y.: Cornell University Press, 1993), 12.

40. See Whitney Balliett, *American Musicians: Fifty-Six Portraits in Jazz* (New York: Oxford University Press, 1986), 3.

41. James Lincoln Collier, *The Reception of Jazz in America: A New View* (New York: Institute for Studies in American Music, 1988), 56.

Chapter 1: Vamp on the Meaning of Jazz

1. On the changing cultural landscape in fin-de-siècle Paris, see Jerrold E. Seigel, *Bohemian Paris: Culture, Politics, and the Boundaries of Bourgeois Life, 1830–1900* (New York: Viking Press, 1987); Roger Shattuck, *The Banquet Years: The Origins of the Avant-Garde in France, 1885 to World War I* (New York: Random House, 1967); Stephen Kern, *The Culture of Time and Space, 1830–1918* (Cambridge, Mass.: Harvard University Press, 1983); Modris Eksteins, *Rites of Spring: The Great War and the Birth*

of the Modern Age (New York: Anchor Books, 1989); and Eugen Weber, *France, Fin de Siècle* (Cambridge, Mass.: Harvard University Press, 1986).

2. See Charles Rearick, *Pleasures of the Belle Époque: Entertainment and Festivity in Turn-of-the-Century France* (New Haven, Conn.: Yale University Press, 1985).

3. On this notion see Eugen Weber, *Peasants into Frenchmen: The Modernization of Rural France, 1870–1914* (Palo Alto, Calif.: Stanford University Press, 1976).

4. See Weber, *France, Fin de Siècle.*

5. Rearick notes that the gross receipts for entertainment more than doubled between 1893 and 1913. *Pleasures of the Belle Époque,* 29.

6. *L'Instransigeant* (November 1, 1902): 2. For further perspective on Saint-Saëns's traditionalist views of music and culture, see Camille Saint-Saëns, *Outspoken Essays on Music,* trans. Fred Rothwell (New York: E. P. Dutton, 1922).

7. Rearick, *Pleasures of the Belle Époque,* 83–115.

8. For further analysis of French discursive tropes about American mass culture, see Jean-Philippe Mathy, *Extrême-Occident: French Intellectuals and America* (Chicago: University of Chicago Press, 1993).

9. Rearick, *Pleasures of the Belle Époque,* 28.

10. Ibid., 95.

11. Ibid., 111. Toulouse-Lautrec's poster art helped make central Paris the new center of popular culture. See also Franc-Nohain, *Les mémoires de Footit et Chocolat* (Paris, 1907).

12. Rearick, *Pleasures of the Belle Époque,* 50, 91.

13. For further explanation of the origins of this genre of entertainment, see Robert C. Toll, *Blackening Up: The Minstrel Show in Nineteenth-Century America* (New York: Oxford University Press, 1974). See also William T. Leonard, *Masquerade in Black* (Metuchen, N.J.: Scarecrow Press, 1986).

14. Addé, *Le Gaulois* (October 28, 1902): 3.

15. Ibid.

16. Ibid.

17. Nicolet, *Le Gaulois* (November 1, 1902): 3.

18. Triboulet, *L'Intransigeant* (December 7, 1902): 3.

19. *Le Rire* (February 7, 1903).

20. The Floridas were reviewed in the *Petite Parisien* (January 24, 1903): 4; *Elle est rien bath!* was reviewed in the *Petite Parisien* (February 1, 1903): 5; *Le nègre continue* was reviewed in *Le Matin* (February 7, 1903): 4; *Le cakewalk* at the Théâtre des Nouveautés was declared "tout à fait amusante" in the *Petite Parisien* (February 17, 1903): 4; and the *Petite duchesse du Casino* was reviewed in the *Petite Parisien* (February 22, 1903): 5.

21. Rae Beth Gordon, "Natural Rhythm: La Parisienne Dances with Darwin, 1875–1910," *MODERNISM/modernity* 10, no. 4 (2003): 636.

22. Abel Hermant, *Les transatlantiques* (Paris: P. Ollendorff, 1909), 12.

23. Ibid., 30.

24. Discussion of the "race problem" in discourse on America is a theme that dates back at least to Tocqueville. In 1903, French readers were kept up-to-date about its latest manifestations in America. For instance, on February 28, 1903, *L'Illustration* ran the article "Lettre d'Amérique," by F. Valmigere, which denounced the "scandalous" race conditions in the South that led seventy blacks to "return" to Liberia. "Why that general hatred? It must have reasons. The men of the South have brains like ours, and they live in contact with the *nègres*. We see it from very far and we are indignant against what we call prejudice of color." *L'Illustration,* no. 3131 (February 28, 1903): 139.

25. Jacques Redelsberger, "Pavane et cake-walk," cited in Rae Beth Gordon, "Natural Rhythm: La Parisienne Dances with Darwin, 1875–1910," *MODERNISM/modernity* 10, no. 4 (2003): 640.

26. C. C. B., "Le Cakewalk," *L'Illustration,* no. 3124 (January 10, 1903): 29. Though he is usually remembered for his military marches, Sousa's bands also played "ragtime" until 1908, when the popularity and corruption of ragtime caused him to declare it "dead."

27. Jules Michelet, *The People,* trans. John P. McKay (Urbana: University of Illinois Press, 1973), 47.

28. C.C.B. "Le cakewalk," 30.

29. Ibid.

30. Ibid.

31. Ibid.

32. Ibid.

33. Ibid.

34. Ibid.

35. See Jean-Jacques Rousseau, "Essay on the Origin of Languages Which Treats of Melody and Musical Imitation," trans. John H. Moran, in *On the Origin of Language* (Chicago: University of Chicago Press, 1966).

36. Henri de Rive, "Danses d'autrefois, d'aujourd'hui, de demain," *L'Illustration,* no. 3128 (February 7, 1903): 90.

37. Ibid.

38. Žižek uses Lacan's dialectic of desire to argue that desiring a certain kind of enjoyment is always reflexive in this way; it is always a *desire of a desire:* "desire is never directly aimed at some object but is always desire squared—the subject finds himself with a multitude of heterogeneous, even mutually exclusive desires, and the question with which he is thus faced is: which desire should I choose? Which desire should I desire? . . . What we call valuation thus is always based in this reflectivity of desire, which is of course possible only within the symbolic order; the fact that desire is always already symbolically mediated means nothing but that it is always the desire of a desire." See Slavoj Žižek, *For They Know Not What They Do: Enjoyment as a Political Factor* (London: Verso, 1991), 131–32.

39. See the description of the disappearance of such traditional dances as social rites and the influx of "American dances" in Weber, *Peasants into Frenchmen,* 451.

40. Žižek, *For They Know Not What They Do,* 132.

41. Maurice Chevalier, *Ma route et mes chansons: soixante-quinze berges* (Paris: René Julliard, 1963), 8. "Thanks to the Americans," he remarked, "I had my style."

42. See Richard Abel, *The Ciné Goes to Town: French Cinema, 1896–1914* (Berkeley: University of California Press, 1994).

43. Méliès's Star-Film studios produced *La danse de feu, Danse serpentine,* and *La danseuse microscopique.* In the Pathé catalog, along with the films on the cakewalk, there were *Valse excentrique* (1903) and *Valse Apache* (1906), among many others that documented the rhythms of different dances.

44. See Jacques Malthête et al., *Essai de reconstitution du catalogue français de la Star-Film* (Paris, 1981), 120. For Méliès's own description of this period, see Madeleine Malthête Méliès, *Méliès, l'enchanteur* (Paris: Ramsey, 1995). See also Jean Mitry, *Histoire du cinéma: art et industry,* vol. 1, *1985–1914* (Paris: Éditions Universitaires, 1967), 208; and Georges Sadoul, *Histoire du cinéma mondial* (Paris: Flammarion, 1972), 36.

45. The Pathé brothers, Charles (1863–1957) and Émile (?–1937), founded the phonograph company Pathé Records in 1894. In 1896 they moved into cinema production. Their companies would be a dominant force in both industries.

46. See Andre Gaudrealt, ed., *Pathé 1900: fragments d'une filmographie analytique du cinéma des premiers temps* (Québec: Les Presses de l'Université Laval, 1993), 106–8. See also Richard Abel, *The Ciné Goes to Town,* 81.

47. Lussan-Borel, *Traité de danse, avec musique* (Paris: Lionel Labrousse, 1909), 240.

48. Ibid.

49. Ibid., 242.

50. Louis Laloy, "To Dance or Not to Dance," *S.I.M.* (June 1914): 57. Golliwog was a popular European storybook caricature of the American minstrel, a caricature of a caricature that Debussy, who had seen the figure in one of his daughter's books, linked to the new dance.

51. With Jim Europe and the Castle-Walk, Victor became the first company to record a black dance orchestra. See Samuel B. Charters and Leonard Kunstadt, *Jazz: A History of the New York Scene* (New York: Da Capo Press, 1962), 36–40. See also Reid Badger, *A Life in Ragtime: A Biography of James Reese Europe* (New York: Oxford University Press, 1995).

52. Walter Lippmann, *Drift and Mastery: An Attempt to Diagnose the Current Unrest* (Madison: University of Wisconsin Press, 1985), 118.

53. French jazzman Fred Adison, for instance, spoke of a soldier named Jimmy who had introduced him to jazz. See Fred Adison, *Dans ma vie y'a d'la musique* (Paris: Éditions Clancier Guénaud, 1983).

54. Both Ernest Ansermet, traveling in America as the conductor of *Les Ballets Russes,* and Gabrielle Buffet-Picabia are known to have brought back "ragtime" phonograph records to Paris in 1916. See Erik Satie, *Écrits,* Ornella Volta, ed. (Paris: Éditions Champ Libre, 1981), 305n262.

55. Ibid., 262.

Chapter 2: The First Wave

1. "Les soldats de l'Amérique aclamés par les Parisiens" *L'Intransigeant* (July 4, 1917): 1.

2. "Nos échos," *L'Intransigeant* (July 4, 1917): 2.

3. See Charles Rearick, *The French in Love and War: Popular Culture in the Era of the World Wars* (New Haven, Conn.: Yale University Press, 1997), 28–29.

4. Le Wattman, "Nos échos," *L'Intransigeant* (September 13, 1917): 2.

5. See Rearick, *The French in Love and War,* 28–29.

6. See Jean Touzot, *Jean Cocteau* (Lyon: Manufacture, 1989); and Neal Oxenhandler, *Scandal and Parade: The Theatre of Jean Cocteau* (London: Constable, 1957).

7. George Hugnet, *Petite anthologie poétique du surréalisme* (Paris: Éditions Jeanne Bucher, 1934), 2. Though Cocteau often named *Parade* as the point of departure for surrealism, Apollinaire coined the term in 1916 to describe *Les mamelles de Tirésias.*

8. See Eveline Hurard-Viltard, *Le groupe des Six, ou, le matin d'un jour de fête* (Paris: Méridiens-Klincksieck, 1987). See also Frederick Brown, *An Impersonation of Angels: A Biography of Jean Cocteau* (New York: Viking Press, 1968); and Roger Stéphane, *Portrait souvenir de Jean Cocteau* (Paris: Tallandier, 1964). Poulenc was the first to add the new musical idiom in his work *Rhapsodie nègre,* first performed at the Vieux-Colombier in December 1917.

9. Jean Cocteau, *Le coq et l'arlequin, notes autour de la musique, 1918* (Paris: Stock, 1978), 41.

10. Ibid., 50.

11. Ibid., 43.

12. Ibid.

13. Ibid., 53.

14. Ibid., 53.

15. Cocteau finally used the term *jazz-band* in *Paris-Midi* and directly linked it to the new Dadaist sensibility. "If one accepts the jazz-band, one must welcome as well a literature whose spirit tastes like a cocktail." Jean Cocteau, "Carte-blanche," *Paris-Midi* (May 19, 1919). For Cocteau, the most important aspect of the jazz aesthetic, like the unrestrained expression of the Dadaists, was the shock potential contained in the mechanical trap set of the *"barman des bruits,"* the symbol of the new music. Indeed, Cocteau later identified himself as the "jazz trap drummer" of the Dada jazz-band at Le Bœuf sur le Toit and the Gaya Bar.

16. Ibid., 64.

17. See Hayden White, "The Burden of History," *Tropics of Discourse: Essays in Cultural Criticism* (Baltimore: Johns Hopkins University Press, 1978), 27–50.

18. "La multiplication des cafés-concerts," *Le Courrier Musical* (November 15, 1918): 34.

19. See David L. Looseley, *Popular Music in Contemporary France: Authenticity, Politics, Debate* (Oxford: Berg, 2003), 13–15.

20. "Métamorphe," *Paris-Midi* (March 13, 1918).

21. See "Les noirs aux États-Unis," *Paris-Midi* (January 12, 1918); and "L'américanisation au camp d'Uplon," *Paris-Midi* (February 24, 1918). In 1921 the journal of "comité France-Amérique," *L'Amérique,* ran a story on the wartime segregation of black troops. "Les troupes noires," *L'Amérique,* no. 39–40 (March–April 1921), 2.

22. See Michel Fabre, *From Harlem to Paris: Black American Writers in France, 1840–1980* (Urbana: University of Illinois Press, 1993), 46–61. Fabre, in describing the presence of black troops, points out the contradictory response to race shown by the French populace. Despite what many early jazz musicians thought, the French were not colorblind. While they did embrace the black American troops, often more than their white countrymen, French African troops, especially Senegalese, were considered "animals" who could not be trained. The Senegalese "shock troops" were often treated as cannon fodder. See also Tyler Stovall, *Paris Noir: African Americans in the City of Lights* (Boston: Houghton Mifflin, 1996), 16–26.

23. See Reid Badger, *A Life in Ragtime: A Biography of James Reese Europe* (New York: Oxford University Press, 1995). Europe and his Hellfighters recorded thirty-two record sides in Paris for the Pathé record label, under names like the Scrap-Iron Jazz-Band, including songs like "On Patrol in No Man's Land" and "All of No Man's Land Is Ours."

24. "A Negro Explains Jazz," *The Literary Digest* (April 26, 1919): 28. In fact, La Garde Républicaine asked for sheet music from Europe. But when they played it, perfectly, it lacked the "effect" of Europe's band. On this initial moment see Colin Nettelbeck, "Jazz at the Théâtre Graslin: A Founding Story," *French Cultural Studies* 11 (2000): 201–17.

25. Arthur W. Little, *From Harlem to the Rhine: The Story of New York's Colored Volunteers* (New York: Covici Friede, 1936). Cited in Samuel B. Charters and Leonard Kunstadt, *Jazz: A History of the New York Scene* (New York: Da Capo Press, 1962), 68.

26. Badger, *A Life in Ragtime,* 176.

27. Francis Poulenc, *Correspondence 1910–1963,* Myriam Chimènes, ed. (Paris: Fayard, 1974), 61.

28. Charters and Kunstadt, *Jazz: A History of the New York Scene,* 70.

29. *The Literary Digest* (April 26, 1919): 28. Tragically, on May 9, 1919, Herbert Wright, a drummer in the band, ended the Hellfighters' reign as the most popular jazz band. Europe, who had been having trouble with Wright during performances,

had called him to his dressing room to discuss the problems. Before anyone could come to Europe's aid, Wright stabbed him in the neck with a pocketknife and severed his jugular vein. Europe died within several hours.

30. "Mily jouait du trombone," *Jazz Magazine,* no. 325 (January 1984): 56.

31. Emmanuel Bourcier, "Après la guerre . . . maisons de danse," *Paris-Midi* (February 14, 1919).

32. Le Semainier, "Courrier de Paris: jazz-band à vendre," *L'Illustration* (June 21, 1919): 621.

33. Ibid.

34. Ibid.

35. See Rearick, *The French in Love and War,* 43. See also Daniel J. Sherman, *The Construction of Memory in Interwar France* (Chicago: University of Chicago Press, 1999), 143–214. *Poilu,* normally an adjective meaning "hairy," was a nickname for French soldiers during World War I.

36. Jacques Florange, "Coulisses: jazz-band," *Paris-Midi* (May 18, 1919).

37. Jean Cocteau, "Carte-blanche," *Paris-Midi* (May 19, 1919).

38. Lazarille, "Échos de partout," *La semaine littéraire* (February 1, 1919): 56.

39. Jean Chantovoine, "L'anarchie musicale," *Le Courrier Musical* 21 (November 1, 1919): 257.

40. Ibid., 258.

41. Maurice Ravel, *A Ravel Reader: Correspondence, Articles, Interviews,* Arbie Orenstein, comp. and ed. (New York: Columbia University Press, 1990), 188. Letter to Colette de Jouvenal, February 27, 1919.

42. Ernest Ansermet, "Sur un orchestre nègre," *La Revue Romande 3* (October 1919). Reprinted in *Écrits sur la musique* (Neuchâtel: Éditions à la Baconnerie, 1971), 171.

43. Ibid. It is important to note here that by "popular music," Ansermet did not mean "popular" in the statistical sense that it has taken on in contemporary American culture, but rather as a synonym for the "folk music" of a culture.

44. Ibid., 172.

45. Ibid.

46. Ibid., 174.

47. Ibid.

48. Ibid., 175.

49. Ibid.

50. Ibid., 176.

51. Ibid.

52. Ibid.

53. Ibid.

54. Ibid.

55. Ibid., 178. This passage may be familiar to readers of American jazz critic and biographer Whitney Balliett, whose section in *American Musicians: 56 Portraits in Jazz* on Bechet, "Le Grand Bechet," cites Ansermet's article. However, Balliett's

translation—as well as his retrospective claims that French writing on jazz originated with Panassié—is marked by the post-swing paradigm, as he translates *s'engouffrera* with the phrase "will swing along." Though this makes sense to post-swing jazz fans, the word *swing* did not enter into jazz discourse until 1930. See Whitney Balliett, *American Musicians: 56 Portraits in Jazz* (New York: Oxford University Press, 1986), 27. The same "swing time" translation is used in John Chilton, *Sidney Bechet: The Wizard of Jazz* (London: Macmillan Press, 1982), 40.

56. Under the name of "The Most Famous American Syncopated Orchestra," the S.S.O. played at the Théâtre des Champs-Elysées in May 1921. The band, when necessary, would break down into smaller combos, like pianist Elliot Carpenter's Red Devils, and drummer Benny Peyton's Jazz Kings, which played in Paris dance halls and bars during the early 1920s.

57. Section from an article in *L'Action Française* (November 1919), cited in Paul Douceur, "Danseront-elles?" *Études* (April 20, 1923): 200.

58. Georges Auric, *Quand j'étais là* (Paris: Bernard Grasset, 1979), 173. The "negro Vance" was American banjoist/saxophonist Vance Lowry.

59. Ibid. Auric would later look back on this time when Cocteau, "with an inconceivable assurance," led them to believe that they were playing jazz "rather long before finally hearing a true and authentic jazz!" (164). What they had believed to be "*jazz Parisien*" was far from the real thing: "Sixty years after, was I wrong to bother myself with those horns, those boards, with those triangles, and those bells? I have since learned to know and judge jazz and give credit to the admirable jazz that has been performed for so long, by those black Americans whom we were unaware of except by name" (171).

60. Le Semainier, "Courrier de Paris," *L'Illustration*, no. 4008 (December 27, 1919): 526.

61. Le Semainier, "Courrier de Paris," *L'Illustration*, no. 4026 (May 1, 1920): 274.

62. Paul Sollier, *Traité clinique de neurologie de guerre* (Paris, 1918), 526.

63. Ibid, 529.

64. Mme Daussane, "Chronique music-hall: Ba-ta-clan," *Le Film* (February 1920): 23.

65. Mme Daussane, "Instants de Paris," *Le Film* (March 1920): 19.

66. Charles Tenroc, "L'actualité musical," *Le Courrier Musical* 22 (March 1, 1920): 80.

67. Ibid.

68. Ibid.

69. Reported in *Le Courrier Musical* 22 (June 15, 1920): 210.

70. See Jeffrey H. Jackson, "Making Enemies: Jazz in Inter-war Paris," *French Cultural Studies* 10 (1999): 183.

71. Louis-Charles Bataille, "Les Phylloxeras de la musique," *Le Courrier Musical* 22 (November 1920): 286.

72. Ibid., 287.

73. Le Semainier, "Courrier de Paris: parlons-en," *L'Illustration*, no. 4042 (August 28, 1920): 156.

74. Bataille, "Les Phylloxeras de la musique," 286.

75. Gabrielle Choubley, "Sur la musique nègre," *Le Courrier Musical* 22 (January 15, 1920): 30.

76. Ibid., 31.

77. Ibid.

78. Albert Leclère, "Contribution à l'étude des 'régressions psychiques,'" *La Revue Philosophique* (September–October 1920): 203.

79. Ibid., 257.

80. Ibid., 262.

81. Albert Bertelin, "Misère du temps présent," *Le Courrier Musical* 23 (January 15, 1921): 21.

82. Louis Vuilleman, "Les dieux à la foire," *Le Courrier Musical* 23 (June 1, 1921): 175.

83. Gabriel Timmory, *Ici l'on danse* (Paris, 1921), 111.

84. Ibid., 112.

85. Ibid.

86. See José Germain, "Les élégances et la mode: chic Americain et chic Français," *La Revue Hebdomadaire* (January 1, 1921): 95: "It is by taste and taste alone that we in France can save ourselves from all exaggerations. Since foreigners tell us that our influence dominates in foreign fashions, it is hard to believe that foreign fashions can influence us."

87. F. A. Vuillemet, *Les Catholiques et les danses nouvelles* (Paris: P. Leitelleux, 1924), 34. In *Le Temps,* the column "Vie parisienne" asked: "We are curious to know if the cardinal will have more success than Monsignor Amette and if his flocks will renounce these unseemly dances." Pope Benedict XV died in 1922.

88. Ibid., 34. Vuillemet also published two other books that followed this theme: *Le suicide d'un race* and *Les sophismes de la jeunesse.*

89. Ibid., 49.

90. José Germain, "Les danses modernes: grande enquête sur la danse," *La Revue Mondiale,* (March 1, 1922): 10.

91. José Germain, "Les danses modernes: suite," *La Revue Mondiale* (March 15, 1922): 149.

92. See M. De Fleury, "Démembrement de la neurasthénie," *Bulletin de l'Académie de Médicine,* no. 13, 1923.

93. José Germain, "Les danses modernes: suite," 149.

94. José Germain, *Danseront-elles?* (Paris, 1923), 34.

95. Ibid.

96. Ibid.

97. Ibid., 35.

98. Ibid.

99. Ibid., 37.

100. "Y aura-t-il encore une France dans 50 ans?" *La Revue Hebdomadaire* (May 1922), 284. Certain popular songs of the period argued that the shimmy was hardly to blame for France's population problems. For instance, Suzanne Valroger's 1922 "Dansez le shimmy" made knowledge of the dance a prerequisite for being a young woman's suitor. Whereas many social problems are associated with the shimmy in the song, in the end the problem of replenishing France's population comes up: "Do you want to repopulate France? / Dance the shimmy, but yes, dance the shimmy." See Rearick, *The French in Love and War*, 55.

101. See J. F. MacMillan, *Dreyfus to de Gaulle: Politics and Society in France, 1898–1969* (London: Edward Arnold, 1985).

102. Fernand Auburtin, "Le quatrième congrès national de la natalité," *La Revue Hebdomadaire* (December 1922): 483.

103. For instance, Jeanne Lemoine, in an inquiry in *Le Ménéstral*—a weekly arts and culture magazine—on the decline in theater attendance, declared: "If the clientele diminishes, it is the immorality of the spectacles that the directors should blame. If they lower the price of seats, if they present fine, elegant pieces that shock neither the ear nor the sight, they will fill their theaters and make a fortune. But, for the love of God, enough of these nude men and women, of beds and night tables, of cocaine and drugs! All that moves no one and disgusts everyone!" *Le Ménéstrel* (August 25, 1922): 35.

104. Germain, "Les danses modernes: suite," *La Revue Mondiale*, (April 1, 1922), 276.

105. Ibid.

106. José Germain, *Danseront-elles?* (Paris: Éditions J. Povolosky, 1923), 21.

107. See "Declaration de l'académie des maître de danse de Paris" (January 11, 1921).

108. José Germain, "Les danses modernes," *La Revue Mondiale* (March 1, 1922): 12.

109. Joseph Jaquin, *Ici l'on danse* (Paris: La Renaissance du Livre, 1923), 2.

110. Ibid., 20.

111. Ibid.

112. For an analysis of the important debates about "normal" femininity and gender identity during this period, see Mary Louise Roberts, *Civilization without Sexes: Reconstructing Gender in Postwar France, 1917–1927* (Chicago: University of Chicago Press, 1994).

113. Jaquin, *Ici l'on danse*, 30.

114. Ibid., 145.

115. Ibid., 63.

116. Ibid., 64.

117. Ibid., 68.

118. Ibid., 78.

119. Ibid., 96.

120. Ibid., 82.

121. Ibid., 91.

122. Ibid., 133.

123. Ibid., 143.

124. Ibid., 137.

125. Ibid., 191.

126. Ibid., 171.

127. Robert Goffin, "Jazz-Band," *Le Disque Vert* (June 1922): 72.

128. Ibid.

129. Ibid.

130. Ibid.

131. Robert Goffin, "Liminaire," *Jazz-Band* (Bruxelles: Éditions des Écrits du Nord, 1922).

Chapter 3: Jazz and the Modern Public in the Age of Mechanical Reproduction

1. Darius Milhaud, "Impressions d'Amérique," *Le Courrier Musical* 25 (March 15, 1923): 115.

2. Darius Milhaud, *Notes sans musique* (Paris: René Julliard, 1949), 140.

3. Though they did not use the terms, the debate about authenticity and cultural hierarchy in France often mirrored the debate over highbrow and lowbrow culture in America. See Lawrence Levine, *Highbrow/Lowbrow: The Emergence of Cultural Hierarchy in America* (Cambridge, Mass.: Harvard University Press, 1988).

4. Darius Milhaud, "L'Évolution du jazz-band et la musique des nègres d'Amérique du nord," *Le Courrier Musical* 25 (May 1, 1923): 164.

5. Ibid.

6. Ibid.

7. Darius Milhaud and Paul Claudel, *Cahiers Paul Claudel 3, correspondance Paul Claudel–Darius Milhaud* (Paris: Gallimard, 1969), 86.

8. Milhaud, "L'Évolution du jazz-band," 164. On Milhaud's point of identification between blacks and Jews as oppressed people, see Jane Fulcher, *The Composer as Intellectual: Music and Ideology in France, 1914–1940* (Oxford: Oxford University Press, 2005), 180.

9. Milhaud, "L'Évolution du jazz-band," 164.

10. Ibid.

11. Ibid.

12. Here I borrow Hayden White's characterization of the Tocquevillian differentiation between democratic and aristocratic culture. See Hayden White, *Metahistory: The Historical Imagination in Nineteenth-Century Europe* (Baltimore: Johns Hopkins University Press, 1973), 191–215.

13. Blaise Cendrars, *Petits contes nègres pour les enfants des blancs* (Paris: Jean Vigneau, 1946). For an analysis of Cendrars's use of the *nègre* in relation to myths of

primitivism, see Jean-Claude Blachère, *Le modèle nègre: aspects littéraires du mythe primitiviste au XXe siècle chez Apollinaire, Cendrars, Tzara* (Dakar: Nouvelles Editions Africains, 1981).

14. Milhaud, *Notes sans musique,* 152.

15. Vuillermoz was a student of the composer Gabriel Fauré. He helped found the Société Musicale Indépendente in 1910. Along with his work in music criticism, he was the film critic for the centrist newspaper *Le Temps.*

16. Emile Vuillermoz, *Musique d'aujourd'hui* (Paris: Les Éditions Georges Crés, 1923), 196.

17. Ibid., 207. For another treatment of the universality of "pure" rhythm during this period, see René Dumesnil, *Le rythme musicale: essai historique et critique* (Paris: Mercure de France, 1921).

18. Ibid., 210.

19. Ibid.

20. Jeffrey H. Jackson, "Making Enemies: Jazz in Inter-war Paris," *French Cultural Studies* 10 (1999): 183.

21. The first station was established at the Eiffel Tower in 1921. This was followed by the creation of Radiola–Radio Paris in 1922 and Paris PTT in 1923; all were funded and controlled by the undersecretary of state of the PTT (*Poste, Télégraphe, Téléphone*).

22. René Duval, *Histoire de la radio en France* (Paris: Éditions Alain Moreau, 1979), 35.

23. Ibid., 39.

24. Cécile Méadel, *Histoire de la radio des années trente: du sans-filistes à l'auditeur* (Paris: Anthropos/INA, 1994), 6. On the impact of radio on French mass culture, see Jean-Pierre Rioux and Jean-François Sirinelli, *La culture de masse en France: de la Belle Époque à aujourd'hui* (Paris: Fayard, 2002), 315–19. See also Caroline Ulmann-Mauriat, *Naissance d'un média: histoire politique de la radio en France (1921–1931)* (Paris, L'Harmattan, 1999).

25. Micromégas, *L'Antenne* 81 (October 14, 1924): 6.

26. Cited in Duval, *Histoire de la radio en France,* 55.

27. Émile Vuillermoz, "La T.S.F. et la musique," *L'Illustration* (March 10, 1923): 235.

28. Gabriel-Joseph Gros, "Une lacune," *Radio-Magazine* (September 7, 1924): 3.

29. Jean-Paul Sartre, *Écrits de jeunesse,* Michel Contat et Michel Rybalka, eds. (Paris: NRF, 1990), 403.

30. See Noël Burch, *Marcel L'Herbier* (Paris: Seghers, 1973).

31. "L'inhumaine," *Mon film* 3 (December 5, 1924): 8.

32. This is the word for the contraption used in Christian Lebrot's translation of Standish D. Lawder, *Le cinéma cubiste* (Paris: Éditions Paris Experimental, 1994). The link between film and the scientific study of humankind was not only of academic interest, because such movies as *En Afrique equatoriale* and *Au coeur d l'Afrique sauvage,* both Svenslea films distributed by Gaumont, were commercial hits, as well, in 1923.

33. I am alluding to the theory of the "Remarriage Comedy" established by Stanley Cavell in *Pursuits of Happiness: The Hollywood Comedy of Remarriage* (Cambridge, Mass.: Harvard University Press, 1981).

34. For analysis of the ethics and aims of surrealism, see Patrick Waldberg, *Surrealism* (New York: Thames and Hudson, 1997); and Wayne Andrews, *The Surrealist Parade* (New York: New Directive, 1990).

35. For further discussion of jazz on film, see Jean-Roland Hippenmeyer, *Jazz sur films: ou, 55 années de rapports jazz-cinéma vue à travers plus de 800 films tournés entre 1917 et 1972* (Yverdon: Éditions de la Thièle, 1973). In relation to the use of jazz in American cinema, see David Meeker, *Jazz in the Movies* (New York: Da Capo Press, 1982). On French film during this period, see Richard Abel, *French Cinema: The First Wave, 1915–1929* (Princeton, N.J.: Princeton University Press, 1984).

36. "La guitare et le jazz-band," *Ciné-Journal* (October 19, 1923): 20.

37. "La guitare et le jazz-band," *Ciné-Journal* (September 21, 1923): 20.

38. See Susan Hayward, *French National Cinema* (London: Routledge, 1993), 88–115.

39. For a discussion of musical accompaniment, see Emmanuelle Toulet and Christian Belaygue, *Musique d'écran: l'accompagnement musical du cinéma muet en France, 1918–1995* (Paris: Réunion des musées nationaux, 1994).

40. "Adaptation musical de la guitare et le jazz-band," *Ciné-Journal* (October 26, 1923): 2.

41. "Une présentation soignée," *Ciné-Journal* (September 28, 1923): 7. Of course, not all theaters could afford such a massive production amid the recession. During December of 1923, the musicians' syndicates for cinema and the music hall were again on strike for more job security and better pay. The problem for owners, and audiences, was exacerbated when taxes were raised again in 1924. Again, the response to the strike seemed to expedite the very forces that the unions were trying to halt, as many theaters replaced the striking orchestras with piano players and phonographs in order to cut costs from declining revenues during the strikes.

42. Jean Chantovoine, "Y a-t-il musique d'après guerre," *Le Courrier Musical* 26 (February 15, 1924): 95.

43. Ibid. As an example of the kind of commercially motivated programming in classical settings that Chantovoine warned about, in April 1924 Louis Vuillemin put on a concert of dance music "*de la gavotte au shimmy*" (from the gavotte to the shimmy). The spectacle, which used dancers to illustrate the dances, was designed to show the evolution of dance music from "the two initial steps of Adam and Eve," to the graceful French gavotte and quadrille, and finally to the latest dances *à la mode*, the cakewalk, tango, and shimmy. It was a huge success.

44. Ibid., 96. See also André Clement-Marot, "La crise de la pensée musicale," *Le Courrier Musical* 26 (April 15, 1924).

45. Avery Claflin, "Étranger, New York: le jazz band," *Le Courrier Musical* 26 (May 15, 1924): 257.

46. Paul Nivoix, "Gounod, Saint-Saëns et Chopin en fox-trots," *Comoedia* (April 1, 1924): 2.

47. Ibid.

48. Henry Lyonnet, "Les bals publics de Paris," in *Les spectacles à travers les ages,* Claude Berton et al, eds. (Paris: Aux Éditions du Cygne, 1932), 356.

49. Michel George-Michel, "M.G-M.'s jazz-band," *Comoedia* (February 5 1924): 1.

50. André Warnod, *Les bals de Paris* (Paris: Les Éditions Georges Crès, 1922), 296.

51. See Jeffrey H. Jackson, *Making Jazz French: Music and Modern Life in Interwar Paris* (Durham, N.C.: Duke University Press, 2003), 40–45.

52. Léon Werth, *Danse, danseurs, dancings* (Paris: F. Reider and Cie, 1925), 9.

53. See Mary Louise Roberts, *Civilization without Sexes: Reconstructing Gender in Postwar France, 1917–1927* (Chicago: University of Chicago Press, 1994).

54. Werth, *Danse, danseurs, dancings,* 48. While overly intellectual men did not take readily to dance, Werth believed that women were natural dancers. "Women have more suppleness, more animal nobility than men."

55. Ibid., 49.

56. Ibid., 25.

57. Ibid., 36.

58. Ibid., 51.

59. Ibid., 97.

60. Ibid., 110.

61. Ibid., 118.

62. For an analysis of this recurring trope in French literature, see Léon-François Hoffmann, *Le nègre romantique: personnage littéraire et obsession collective* (Paris: Payot, 1973).

63. Werth, *Danse, danseurs, dancings,* 107.

64. Ibid., 98.

65. Ibid., 184.

66. Georges-Anquetil, *Satan conduit le bal* (Paris: Georges-Anquetil, 1925), 23.

67. Ibid., 28.

68. Ibid., 30.

69. Ibid., 32.

70. On prostitution in interwar Paris, see Alain Corbin, *Women for Hire: Prostitution and Sexuality in France after 1850,* trans. Alan Sheridan (Cambridge, Mass.: Harvard University Press, 1990); and William Wiser, *The Crazy Years: Paris in the Twenties* (London: Thames and Hudson, 1983).

71. Ibid., 132.

72. Ibid., 246.

73. For a discussion of Mac Orlan's life and work, see Bernard Baritand, *Pierre Mac Orlan: sa vie, son temps* (Genève: Proz, 1991).

74. Pierre Mac Orlan, "Aux lumières de Paris: musique populaire," *Oeuvres complètes, La lanterne sourde* (Paris: Éditions Gallimard, 1971), 90.

75. Ibid., 87.

76. Ibid.

77. Ibid.

78. Ibid.

79. Ibid., 89.

80. Ibid., 91.

81. Ibid.

82. Ibid.

83. Ibid., 94.

84. Ibid.

85. Ibid.

86. Ibid., 95.

87. Ibid.

88. Ibid., 96.

89. Ibid.

90. See Irwin Spector, *Rhythms and Life: The Work of Émile Jacques-Dalcroze* (Stuyvesant, N.Y.: Pendragon Press, 1990).

91. E. Jacques Dalcroze, "Le rythme et la chanson populaire," *Conferencia* 19 (January 1925): 138.

92. Ibid., 139.

93. Ibid., 142.

94. Ibid.

95. Ibid., 143.

96. Ibid.

97. Ibid.

98. "Est-ce l'agonie de la chanson française?" *Comoedia* (November 15, 1926): 1.

99. Lazare Saminsky, "États-Unis: le ballet de Whithorne, le déclin du jazz," *La Revue Musicale* 11 (October 1925): 251.

100. As an example of the kind of articles that supported such assertions, one correspondent in *Paris-Midi* reported that in America, the authorities were studying the impact of jazz. "Competent authorities force themselves to analyze and define in detail the effect of musical intonation on the nerves of husbands, to the point of placing ideas of inconstancy in their heads. This problem of moral purification is not easy to resolve. Some think that the tunes favored by the circus stages deafen the listeners to the sentiment of duty. Others accuse the slow waltz or the devilish wiggling of jazz. Vain discussion . . . Music excites only those who have the need to be excited." As is often the case in French commentary on America, this statement about the effect of music on the cultural ethos was addressed to those in France who were still entertaining such a "vain discussion." "Est-t-il une musique indecente?" *Paris-Midi* (August 1, 1925): 1.

101. Jean Cocteau, *Le rappel à l'ordre,* in *Oeuvres complètes de Jean Cocteau,* vol. 9 (Genève: Marguerat, 1951), 136.

102. See Samuel B. Charters and Leonard Kunstadt, *Jazz: A History of the New York Scene* (New York: Da Capo, 1962).

103. By 1925, jazz dancing was a profitable cultural institution in France. Since 1923, the newspaper *Comoedia* had offered a five-thousand-franc prize for the Paris championship of modern dancing—both in "style" and for "stamina" in the marathon contest. That sum was twice what many Frenchmen made in a year.

104. See Maurice de Waleffe, "Paris offre le plaisir des yeux aux étrangers: mais l'abus au music-hall du deshabillé total est une erreur de goût et du propagande," *Paris-Midi* (September 1, 1925): 1. The Parisian shows that publicized their nudity as a draw in 1925 included the famous Lawrence Tiller Girls at the Casino de Paris; the review *Mieux que nue,* at the Moulin Rouge; *Archi-nue* at the Concert Mayol, and *La revue super-nue* at the Gaity with their Girls and the King Jazz Band.

Chapter 4: *La Revue Nègre,* Ethnography, and Cultural Hybridity

1. On the reception of the Rites of Spring, see Modris Eksteins, *Rites of Spring: The Great War and the Birth of the Modern* (New York: Anchor Books, 1989).

2. Examples of this narrative include Jody Blake, *Le Tumulte Noir: Modernist Art and Popular Entertainment in Jazz-Age Paris, 1900–1930* (University Park: Pennsylvania State University Press, 1999); Tyler Stovall, *Paris Noir: African Americans in the City of Light* (Boston: Houghton Mifflin, 1996); William A. Shack, *Harlem in Montmartre: A Paris Jazz Story between the Great Wars* (Berkeley: University of California Press, 2001); and Bennetta Jules-Rosette, *Josephine Baker in Art and Life: The Icon and the Image* (Urbana: University of Illinois Press, 2007).

3. Jacques-Charles, *Cent ans de music hall* (Paris: Éditions Jeheber, 1956).

4. Paul Achard, "Tout en noir ou La revue nègre," *Paris-Midi* (September 27, 1925): 2.

5. Jacques Patin, "Spectacles et concerts," *Le Figaro* (October 1, 1925): 4.

6. Ibid.

7. Yvon Novy, "La revue nègre," *Comoedia* (October 4, 1925): 3.

8. René Bizet, "Champs-Elysées," *L'Intransigeant* (October 4, 1925): 2.

9. René Bizet, "Le music-hall: La revue nègre," *Candide* (October 8, 1925): 8.

10. Jacques Patin, "Figaro-Spectacles." *Le Figaro* (October 7, 1925): 7.

11. Ibid.

12. Ibid.

13. Gustave Fréjaville, "Chronique de la semaine," *Comoedia* (October 8, 1925): 2.

14. Ibid.

15. Ibid.

16. Ibid.

17. Ibid.

18. Louis Léon-Martin, "*La revue nègre,*" *Paris-Midi* (October 10, 1925): 3.

19. Ibid.

20. André Levinson, "Paris ou New York," *Comoedia* (October 12, 1925): 2.

21. Ibid.

22. Ibid.

23. Ibid.

24. Ibid., 2.

25. One must stress the turbulent social context surrounding *La revue nègre*'s reception. It was being performed every night to packed houses at a time when France's economy was in ruins. Among other things, the payment on the war debt to the United States was overwhelming the government budget, and the American government would not budge. Moreover, inflation was racing, and on October 12, a general strike (excluding only the métro in Paris) began and lasted two days.

26. Albert Flament, "Tableaux de Paris: Le Rose et le Noir," *Revue de Paris* (November 1, 1925): 197.

27. Ibid., 198.

28. Pierre de Regnier, *Candide* (October 20), cited in *Josephine*, 72.

29. Ibid.

30. Ibid.

31. Paul Brach, "La nuit noire," *Comoedia* (November 12, 1925): 4.

32. Ibid.

33. Ibid.

34. Ibid.

35. Albert Flament, "Tableaux de Paris," *Revue de Paris* (December 1, 1925): 694.

36. Albert Flament, "Tableaux de Paris," *Revue de Paris* (December 15, 1925): 753.

37. Quoted in José Germain, "Enquêtes modernes: où va le roman," *Conferencia* (January 1, 1926): 81–82.

38. M. Fursy, "Enquêtes modernes: où va la chanson," *Conferencia* (June 1, 1926): 573.

39. Ibid.

40. Paul Le Flem, "Le jazz, serait-il français?" *Comoedia* (January 25, 1926): 4.

41. Ibid.

42. Ibid.

43. Ibid. Perhaps it was the implication of linking the French legacy to the dark history of plantation slavery that kept Le Flem's speculations in the form of a question. Schwerke published his theory about the French linguistic origin of jazz again in *Le guide du concert*. See "Le jazz est mort! Vive le jazz!," *Le guide du concert* (March 12 and 19, 1926), in *Jazz et David Rois* (Paris: Les Presses Modernes, 1927). This linguistic-origin myth was disseminated to a larger public over radio in September of 1926. See Camille Ducray, "Propos avant l'écoute," *Radio-Magazine* (September 5, 1926).

44. "Le jazz et La Marseillaise," *Comoedia* (January 30, 1926): 1.

45. Maurice Delage, "La musique du jazz," *Revue Pleyel* (April 1926): 19.

46. Ibid.

47. Ibid.

48. Ibid., 20.

49. Roland-Manuel, "Wiéner et Doucet, ou les plaisirs du jazz," *Revue Pleyel* (July 1926): 10.

50. Ibid., 11.

51. Ibid.

52. Ibid., 12.

53. Ibid.

54. Ibid.

55. For instance, the American Paramount film *Jazz* was a commercial success when it was released in France in June 1926. French production companies tried to cash in on the craze, and two short films that summer used *Le Charleston* as their title. The first was by the young Jean Renoir; the second was by the Erka production company and was designed to teach the motions and rhythms of the Charleston in six easy lessons.

56. Léandre Vaillat, "Terpsichore en 1926," *L'Illustration* (August 21, 1926): 175.

57. Ibid.

58. Ibid., 176.

59. For an account of the opening in relation to the ethnographic movement in France, see Lucien Lévy-Bruhl, "L'Institut d'Ethnologie de l'Université de Paris," *Revue d'Ethnographie et des Traditions Populaires* (July–December 1925): 16.

60. See James Clifford, "Ethnographie polyphonie collage," in *Revue de Musicologie* 68, nos. 1–2 (no. spécial André Schaeffner, 1982): 45–48.

61. See the Michael Haggerty interview of Michel Leiris in *Jazz Magazine* 324 (January 1984): 35.

62. James Clifford recounts a telling story about Leiris, Mauss, Breton, and other surrealists getting into a shouting match with French patriots from Leiris's window. In front of a huge crowd, Leiris denounced France and was about to be lynched when the police arrested and detained him. See Clifford, "Ethnographie Polyphonie Collage," 45. See also Michel Leiris, "45, rue Blomet," in the same number of *Revue de Musicologie*, 61.

63. "In the first of these bars where I have lived for a while sang a mulatto named Bricktop . . . [with] a mouth that one must depict as full of spirit. She possessed that extraordinary intelligence of movement that reached its height in Josephine Baker and is more than just gymnastic acrobatics: a delicious grace in the movement of arms and fingers, the play of the eyes, the lips, the twitching of the feet, all that united by a voice the likes of which I have never heard, a voice like heavy fabric, torn by shakes from the hip, or like an expansion of flooding water that floods over the eagles." Michel Leiris, "Paris-Minuit," *Der Querschnitt* 9 (September 1926): 685–88. Cited in Michel Leiris, *Journal, 1922–1989* (Paris: Gallimard, 1992), 846. See Tyler Stovall's description of the Montmartre jazz life in *Paris Noir*, 68–81. He stresses that Bricktop's club reflected and re-created the world of Harlem nightlife, offering black jazz to affluent white patrons in search of adventure. The surrealist writer Louis Aragon claimed to

be an intimate with Bricktop and later wrote about the scene in his novel *Aurélien*. See also William A. Shack, *Harlem in Montmartre: A Paris Jazz Story between the Two Great Wars* (Berkeley: University of California Press, 2001). See also Bricktop, with James Haskin, *Bricktop* (New York: Atheneum, 1983).

64. See Claude Lévi-Strauss, "Introduction à l'œuvre de Marcel Mauss," in Marcel Mauss, *Sociologie et anthropologie* (Paris: PUF, 1950), xi. Lévi-Strauss wrote of Mauss's improvisational style and its influence on his students: "In his work and even more in his teaching, the use of unforeseen comparisons flourished. While often obscure because of the constant use of antithesis, shortcuts, and apparent paradoxes that one recognized later as the fruit of a more profound intuition, he compensated his listeners, all at once, by these flashes of intuitions that, over the months, would give rise to fruitful inflections."

65. For a variety of perspectives on Schaeffner's many projects, see the special edition of the *Revue de musicologie* dedicated to his work. *Revue de musicologie* 68 (January–February 1982).

66. André Schaeffner, "Notes sur la musique des Afro-Américains," *Le Ménéstrel* 88 (August 6, 1926): 299. The citation from Ligon was from Richard Ligon, *Histoire de l'îsle des Barbades, dans le recueil de divers voyages en Afrique et en l'Amérique qui n'ont point été encore publier* (Paris, 1674).

67. Ibid., 44.

68. Ibid., 63.

69. Ibid.

70. They asked writers, composers, actors, and other public figures three questions: "1. For you, is *le jazz band* music? Of what order are your impressions about jazz? 2. Does it exert an influence over contemporary aesthetics and, more particularly, over musical forms? 3. Do you think an original and independent jazz music can be created that would obey its own laws?" André Coeuroy et André Schaeffner, "Enquête sur le jazz-band," *Paris-Midi* (July 1, 1925): 3.

71. André Coeuroy et André Schaeffner, *Le jazz* (Paris: Éditions Claude Aveline, 1926), 101.

72. Schaeffner, along with writing on African music, later wrote extensively on Nietzsche. In relation to the "Nietzschean front" of the surrealist movement, see Jean-Michel Besnier, *La politique de l'impossible: l'intellectuel entre révolte et engagement* (Paris: Éditions la Découverte, 1989), 25–37.

73. Schaeffner, *Le jazz*, 10.

74. Ibid., 23.

75. Ibid., 42.

76. Ibid.

77. Ibid.

78. Ibid.

79. On the question of diasporic music as an analytical category and community praxis, see Brent Hayes Edwards, *The Practice of Diaspora: Literature, Translation,*

and the Rise of Black Internationalism (Cambridge, Mass.: Harvard University Press, 2003).

80. Schaeffner, *Le jazz,* 42.

81. Ibid.

82. Ibid.

83. Ibid., 82.

84. Ibid., 70.

85. Ibid., 94.

86. Ibid., 63.

87. Ibid., 67.

88. Ibid., 89.

89. Ibid.

90. Ibid., 106.

91. Ibid, 107.

92. See André Coeuroy, "Le romantisme du jazz," *La Revue Musicale* 11 (October 1926): 221–25.

93. In addition to the publication of this article in *La Revue Musicale,* Coeuroy published a version of the piece, including a summary of Schaeffner's thesis, in *L'Art Vivant.* See André Coeuroy, "Le jazz," *L'Art Vivant* (August 15, 1926): 615–17.

94. Schaeffner, *Le jazz,* 115.

95. Ibid., 133.

96. Ibid., 144.

97. Ibid., 144.

98. André Tessier, "Concerts Morin à l'Artistic," *La Revue Musicale* 8 (December 1, 1926): 161.

99. André Coeuroy, "Impressions de music-hall: ballet de Gabriel Pierné," *La Revue Musicale* 8 (May 1, 1927): 180.

100. André Jeanneret, "Le nègre et le jazz," *La Revue Musicale* 8 (July 1, 1927): 25.

101. Ibid., 26.

102. Ibid., 27.

103. Jacques Heugel, "Échos," *Le Ménéstrel* (July 13, 1928): 324.

104. See Raymond Bachollet and A.C. Lelieur, *Negripub: l'image des noirs dans la publicité* (Paris: Somogy, 1992).

105. See Karen C. C. Dalton and Henry Louis Gates Jr., "Josephine Baker and Paul Colin: African American Dance Seen through Parisian Eyes," *Critical Inquiry* 24 (Summer 1998): 903–34.

106. See Marcel Sauvage's second Baker book, *Voyages et adventures de Josephine Baker* (Paris: M. Seheur, 1931), 135–37.

107. Arthur Hoérée, "Le jazz," *La Revue Musicale* 8 (October 1, 1927): 215.

108. Ibid., 218.

109. Ibid., 216.

110. Ibid., 220.

111. Ibid., 221.

112. Ibid., 228.

113. Ibid., 237.

114. Ibid.

115. Ibid.

116. Ibid., 239.

117. Ibid., 241.

118. Ibid.

119. André Schaeffner, "Le jazz," *La Revue Musicale* 9 (November 1927): 74.

120. Ibid.

121. Ibid., 76.

122. Ibid.

123. See Arthur Hoérée, "Le jazz et la musique d'aujourd'hui," *Le Courrier Musical* 20, (December 1, 1928): 672.

124. See David Looseley, *Popular Music in Contemporary France: Authenticity, Politics, Debate* (Oxford: Berg, 2003): 14–17.

125. Jean Wiéner, "Le jazz et la musique," *Conferencia* (June 5, 1928): 623.

126. Ibid., 630.

127. R. Pepin, "Pau: Wiéner et Doucet," *Le Ménéstrel* 48, (November 30, 1928), 509.

128. See Marc Blanchard, "Pour une ethnopoétique: hommage à Michel Leiris, 1901–1990," *Modern Language Notes* 105 (September 1990): 641; and Anna Warby, "The Anthropological Self: Michel Leiris' 'Ethnopoetics,'" *Forum for Modern Language Studies* 26 (July 1990): 250–58; see also Marc Blanchard, "N Stuff . . . : Practices, Equipment, Protocols in Twentieth-Century Ethnography," *Yale French Studies* 81 (1992): 111–27.

129. See Joëlle de Sermet, *Michel Leiris: poète surréaliste* (Paris: PUF, 1997).

130. Michel Leiris, *Journal, 1922–1989* (Paris: Gallimard, 1992), 190.

131. See James Clifford's account of the *Documents* project in relation to "ethnographic surrealism." James Clifford, *The Predicament of Culture: Twentieth-Century Ethnography, Literature, and Art* (Cambridge, Mass.: Harvard University Press, 1988), 122–34.

132. Carl Einstein, "André Masson, étude ethnologique," *Documents* 1 (January 1929): 100.

133. Michel Leiris, "Civilisation," *Documents* 1 (June–September 1929): 221.

134. Ibid.

135. Ibid.

136. Ibid.

137. André Schaeffner, "Les Lew Leslie's Blackbirds au Moulin Rouge," *Documents* 1 (June–September 1929): 223.

138. This aphorism was reported by fellow Mauss student Alfred Métraux. See Clifford, *The Predicament of Culture,* 126.

139. See Jean-Michel Besnier, "Georges Bataille in the 1930s: A Politic of the Impossible," *Yale French Studies,* 78 (1990): 169–80. For a good reading of Mauss's influence on Bataille, see Michele H. Richman, *Reading Georges Bataille: Beyond the Gift* (Baltimore: Johns Hopkins University Press, 1982).

140. Georges Bataille, "Dictionnaire: Black Birds," *Documents* 1 (June–September 1929): 215.

141. Michel Leiris, "Saints noirs," *La Revue du Cinéma* 11, (1929): 30–33. Page citations given here are from the reedition of the article in Michel Leiris, *Zébrage* (Paris: Gallimard, 1992), 21.

142. Leiris, *Zébrage,* 22.

143. Ibid.

144. Ibid.

145. Ibid.

146. Ibid.

147. Ibid., 24.

148. Ibid.

149. *Jazz Magazine* 324, (January 1984): 35.

150. André Schaeffner, "Vogue et sociologie du jazz," *Encyclopédie française,* vol. 17, chpt. 11 (Paris: Larousse, 1935), 11–13.

151. See Phyllis Rose, *Jazz Cleopatra: Josephine Baker in Her Time* (New York: Vintage, 1989), 148–49.

Chapter 5: The Jazz Hot Years

1. Jeffrey Jackson, *Making Jazz French: Music and Modern Life in Interwar Paris* (Durham, N.C.: Duke University Press, 2003), 169.

2. See Hugues Panassié, *Monsieur jazz: entretiens avec Pierre Casalta* (Paris: Stock, 1975).

3. Hugues Panassié, "Le jazz hot," *La Revue Musicale* (June 1930): 481. The article appeared in *L'Édition Musicale Vivante* in February 1930.

4. Ibid., 482.

5. Ibid.

6. Ibid., 483.

7. Ibid.

8. Ibid.

9. Ibid.

10. Ibid.

11. Ibid., 488.

12. Ibid., 487.

13. Ibid.

14. Ibid., 489.

15. Ibid.

16. Ibid.

17. "À nos lecteurs," *Jazz-Tango* 1, no. 1 (October 15, 1930).

18. Émile Vuillermoz, "Un jazz français," *Excelsior* (October 6, 1930): 3.

19. Gustave Fréjaville, "Les attractions de la quinzaine," *Comoedia* (May 21, 1930), 5. Grégor (Krikor Kelekian) was actually Armenian by origin.

20. Ibid.

21. Ibid. *Paris-Midi* critic Louis Léon-Martin thought that the problem with Grégor (even after he made the name of his band more French) had little to do with the "nationalism" that the audience had manifested. Though he thought that Grégor's intentions were good, he declared that it was simply a question of talent. "Grégor is a mediocre musician and an even worse comic." See "À l'Empire: Grégor et son jazz," *Paris-Midi* (May 21, 1930): 3.

22. Jeffrey Jackson, "Making Enemies: Jazz in Inter-war Paris," *French Cultural Studies* (June 1999): 193.

23. Maurice Bedou-Ermonchy, "La main-d'oeuvre étrangère," *Jazz-Tango*, no. 2 (November 15, 1930): 3.

24. Jean Marcland, "Singing the Blues," *Jazz-Tango*, no. 2 (November 15, 1930): 11.

25. Ibid.

26. Ibid.

27. "Ray Ventura et ses collégiens," *Jazz-Tango*, nos. 3 and 4 (December 25, 1930): 8.

28. Fernand Mazzi, "Le rythme et la musique," *Le Monde Musical*, no. 12 (December 31, 1930): 409.

29. Ibid.

30. Ibid.

31. Ibid.

32. "La saine doctrine en jazz," *Le Musicien Fédéré* (May 15, 1930): 1.

33. Ibid.

34. Ibid.

35. Charles Teissier, "Jack Hylton et son orchestre," *Le Télégramme* (November 28, 1930): 3.

36. See "Échos," *Le Courrier Musical*, no. 2 (January 15, 1931): 46.

37. These articles in *Jazz-Tango*, which would later form the bulk of the book *Le jazz hot*, were by and large collations of the information from the catalogues and record jackets. See Hugues Panassié, "Le Jazz et la critique" nos. 3 and 4; "Jean Cocteau et le jazz," no. 5; "Definitions" and "Les grands cornets hot," no. 6; "Les grands trombones hot," no. 8; "Milton Mezzrow," no. 9; "Les grands saxophonistes hot," no. 10–11; "Bix Beiderbecke," no. 13; "Un disque des Chicago Rhythm Kings," no. 14; "Frank Teschmaker," no. 20; "Duke Ellington et son orchestre," no. 22; "Les meilleurs musiciens hot étrangers," no. 27; "Les grands pianistes 'hot' Américains," no. 32; and "Le premier concert hot," no. 33.

38. See also the review by Léo Dubois, "Dans le noir," *Paris Music Hall*, no. 229 (January 15, 1931): 16.

39. Hugues Panassié, "Louis Armstrong," *Jazz-Tango,* nos. 3 and 4 (December 25, 1930): 7.

40. Ibid.

41. Stéphane Mougin, "Faisons le point," *Jazz-Tango,* no. 7 (April 1931): 4. In an example of how retrospective biographical accounts often clash with the issues important for French observers, Tucker, from the post-Nazi perspective, later claimed that the unrest at the Empire came from her singing *My Yiddishe Momme* to a crowd of anti-Semites. See Robert Dawidoff, "Some of Those Days," *Western Humanities Review* 41, no. 3 (Autumn 1987): 269.

42. Ibid.

43. Bernard Zimmer, *La Revue Hebdomadaire* (February 21, 1931): 490.

44. Jacques Dolor, "L'infortune des musiciens," *L'Ami du Peuple* (May 19, 1931): 3.

45. See Georges Duhamel, *America, the Menace: Scenes from the Life of the Future,* trans. Charles M. Thompson (Boston: Houghton Mifflin, 1931). Few French writers show as much disgust for America as Dr. Duhamel. For an account of this vision within the context of French writing on America, see, for instance, Jean-Philippe Mathy, *Extrême-Occident: French Intellectuals and America* (Chicago: University of Chicago Press, 1993), 52–86. See also Pascal Ory, "De Baudelaire à Duhamel: l'improbable rejet," in *L'Amérique dans les têtes,* Lacorne et al., eds. (Paris: Hachette, 1986), 57–69; and David Strauss, *Menace in the West: The Rise of French Anti-Americanism in Modern Times* (Westport, Conn.: Greenwood Press, 1978).

46. For contemporary reviews of Duhamel's work, see A. Mangeot, "Georges Duhamel et le bruit," *Le Monde Musical* (November 30, 1931): 351; J. Bouissounouse, "Revue des revues," *La Revue du Cinéma* 2, no. 12 (July 1930): 77–78; Georges Petit, "Duhamel et la civilisation américaine," *La Revue Nouvelle,* no. 67 (April 1931).

47. Georges Duhamel, *Candide* (October 29, 1931): 3.

48. G.H.P., "Le Jazz Ray Ventura," *Le Courrier Musical* (December 15, 1931): 598.

49. Hugues Panassié, "Remarques sur le style hot," *Jazz-Tango,* no. 12 (September 1931): 5.

50. Hugues Panassié, "La situation actuelle du jazz," *Jazz-Tango,* no. 17 (February 1932): 7.

51. See Stéphane Mougin, "Coup d'épée dans l'eau," *Jazz-Tango,* no. 14 (November 1931): 7.

52. Stéphane Mougin, "Nègremanie," *Jazz-Tango,* no. 15 (December 1931): 7.

53. Ibid.

54. Stéphane Mougin, "Article incompris," *Jazz-Tango,* no. 19 (April 1932): 3.

55. Ibid.

56. Pierre Leroi, "Instruments divers," *L'Édition Musicale Vivante,* no. 48 (February 1932): 16.

57. Pierre Leroi, "Instruments divers," *L'Édition Musicale Vivante,* no. 51 (May 1932): 18.

58. Jacques Fray, "Duke Ellington," *Documents* 2 (1930): 370.

59. Henry Prunières, "La musique par disque," *La Revue Musicale* 12, no. 116 (June 1931): 72.

60. Ibid.

61. Henry Prunières, "Les tendances de la jeune école française," *La Revue Musicale* 12, no. 117 (July–August 1931): 101.

62. See Hugues Panassié, "Autour d'un article de M. Wiener," *Jazz-Tango*, no. 18 (March 1932): 5.

63. Stéphane Mougin, "Éloge du peuple," *Jazz-Tango*, no. 18 (March 1932): 8.

64. Ibid.

65. Ibid.

66. Ibid.

67. Ibid.

68. Ray Ventura, "Non, le jazz ne meurt pas! Il évolve," *L'Édition Musical Vivante*, no. 43 (September 1931): 7–9.

69. Stéphane Mougin, "Quelques mots entre nous," *Jazz-Tango*, no. 21, (June 1932): 5.

70. Ibid.

71. Ibid. One could detect the rise of such a protectionist spirit through the advertisement of jazz orchestras like those of Roland Dorsay and André Ekyan, who were declared "a triumph of French Industry and a victory for *jazz français.*"

72. Jacques Piths in *L'Ami du Peuple*, May 3, 1932, cited in *Jazz-Tango Dancing*, no. 21 (June 1932): 11.

73. André Suarès, *La Revue Musicale*, March 1931, cited in Hugues Panassié, *Douze années de jazz (1927–1938)* (Paris, 1946), 60.

74. Hugues Panassié, *Douze années de jazz* (Paris, 1946), 96.

75. Stéphane Mougin, "Le jazz et le context," *Jazz-Tango Dancing*, no. 29 (February 1933): 5.

76. Jackson, *Making Jazz French*, 184. On the Hot Club scene, see also Ludovic Tournès, *New Orleans sur Seine: histoire du jazz en France* (Paris: Fayard, 1999), 50–51.

77. Michel Emer, "Soirée hot au Cinéma Flagière," *Jazz-Tango Dancing*, no. 30 (March 1933): 5.

78. The *Commedia dell'Arte* used an improvisational method in which actors played stock figures, like the hunchback or the nun, who were then placed in situations together. The actors would then improvise scenes based on the fixed character types interacting with one another.

79. Henry Prunières, "Le Hot Club," *La Revue Musicale* 14 (June 1933): 50.

80. See Hugues Panassié, "La revue de la presse," *Jazz-Tango Dancing*, no. 32 (May 1933): 11.

81. Hugues Panassié, "Louis Armstrong," *Jazz-Tango Dancing*, no. 34 (July 1933): 11.

82. Since it was a concert hall, Duke played Pleyel on July 27 and 29 without being subject to the laws announced on March 13 by the *ministre du travail* (minister of la-

bor), François Albert, which set the legal proportion of foreign musicians who could be employed in cafés, hotels, and restaurants. See *Comoedia* (August 4, 1933): 5.

83. Vincent Breton, "Duke Ellington," *Paris-Soir* (July 30, 1933): 6.

84. Ibid.

85. Henry Malherbe, "La musique: à la Salle Pleyel Duke Ellington et son orchestre," *Le Temps* (August 2, 1933): 4.

86. André Schaeffner, "La musique: Duke Ellington," *Beaux-Arts* (August 11, 1933): 5.

87. Ibid.

88. Ibid.

89. Georges Devaise, "Le snobisme du hot," *Gringoire* (August 4, 1933): 6.

90. Ibid.

91. Ibid.

92. Ibid.

93. Pierre Trevieres, "Jazz Hot," *Paris-Soir* (August 14, 1933): 2.

94. Ibid.

95. Stéphane Mougin, "Après Duke Ellington," *Jazz-Tango Dancing*, no. 36, (September 1933): 3.

96. Hugues Panassié, "Duke Ellington à Paris, " *Jazz-Tango Dancing*, no. 36, (September 1933): 5.

97. Henry Prunières, "Les concerts de Duke Ellington," *La Revue Musicale*, no. 14 (September–October, 1933): 208.

98. Émile Vuillermoz, "Duke Ellington et son orchestre," *L'Édition Musicale Vivante*, no. 67 (September 1933): 8

99. Ibid.

100. Jean Wilmés, *Je Suis Partout*, cited in *Jazz-Tango Dancing*, no. 36 (September 1933): 7.

101. Stéphane Mougin, "Le swing," *Jazz-Tango Dancing*, no. 37 (October 1933): 4.

102. Ibid.

103. Both Panassié and Delaunay later stated that Johnson helped plan events at the Hot Club. See Whitney Balliett, *American Musicians: 56 portraits in Jazz* (New York: Oxford University Press, 1986): 7.

104. D. B., "Gala nègre," *Le Ménéstrel*, no. 44 (November 3, 1933): 428.

105. Léon Fiot, "Raymond Legrand et son orchestre: un nouvel orchestre de jazz français," *Jazz-Tango Dancing*, no. 40 (January 1934): 9.

106. Hugues Panassié, "Les errors de Mike," *Jazz-Tango Dancing*, no. 42 (March 1934): 7.

107. Ibid.

108. Pierre Leroi, "Les disques," *L'Édition Musicale Vivante*, no. 76 (June 1934): 13.

109. Ibid.

110. Hugues Panassié, "Cab Calloway," *La Revue Musicale*, no. 146 (May 1934): 355.

111. Ibid.

112. Hugues Panassié, "À propos de Cab Calloway," *Jazz-Tango Dancing*, no. 45 (June 1934): 13.

113. Ibid.

114. Hugues Panassié, "La vraie physionomie de la musique de jazz," *La Revue Musicale*, no. 146 (May 1934): 361.

115. Ibid.

116. Ibid., 366.

117. Blaise Pesquinne, "De l'improvisation dans le jazz," *La Revue Musicale*, no. 149 (October 1934): 178.

118. Ibid.

119. Ibid., 179.

120. Ibid., 181.

121. Ibid.

122. Ibid., 182.

123. Blaise Pesquinne, "Le blues, la musique nègre des villes: naissance et avenir du jazz," *La Revue Musicale*, no. 150 (November 1934): 278.

124. See N. J. Canetti, "Mon expérience Louis Armstrong," *Jazz-Tango Dancing*, no. 53 (February 1935): 11. Canetti described how Armstrong, after taking an apartment in Montmarte, had spent much of his time drinking with Alpha Smith. Armstrong, Canetti argued, was "guided by his bad instincts" in a way that made his performance suffer. For Panassié, this criticism was scandalous.

125. Hugues Panassié, "Louis Armstrong à la Salle Rameau," *Jazz-Tango Dancing*, no. 50 (November 1934): 3.

126. Lucien Rebatet, "Les concerts: Louis Armstrong," *L'Action Française* (November 16, 1934): 3. On the origins of Rebatet's violent aesthetics, see David Carroll, *French Literary Fascism: Nationalism, Anti-Semitism, and the Ideology of Culture* (Princeton, N.J.: Princeton University Press, 1995), 196–221. Interestingly, both Rebatet and Panassié were inspired by Charles Maurras's "vigorous realism" and his aestheticized vision of cultural purity, according to which he saw the integral nation as a work of art that could be improved by wiping out ugly stains on the "real" France as part of an ongoing culture war. Both also shared Marraus's nostalgia and his sense that modern culture was decadent. "The decadence of all the humanities shows that the future, the future of French intelligence and of Occidental spirit as a whole, is still foundering." Charles Maurras, *Romantisme et Révolution* (Paris: Librarie Nationale, 1922), 24.

127. Ibid.

128. Ibid.

129. Ibid.

130. Ibid.

131. See Charles Delaunay, "Louis Armstrong au Poste Parisien," *Jazz-Tango Dancing*, no. 51 (December 1934).

132. G. P. M., "Fred Adison et son orchestre," *Jazz-Tango Dancing*, no. 51 (December 1934): 17.

133. Herman Klosson, "Décembre," *La Revue Musicale* 16, no. 152 (January 1935): 63.

134. André Coeuroy, "Le jazz hot," *Gringoire* (January 4, 1935): 13.

135. André Coeuroy, "Swing, jazz et ski," *Gringoire* (January 11, 1935): 13.

136. Ibid.

137. Hugues Panassié, "Coleman Hawkins," *Jazz Hot*, no. 1 (March 1935): 3.

138. Ibid.

139. John Hammond, "Lettre d'Amérique," *Jazz Hot*, no. 1 (March 1935): 5.

140. Ibid. Panassié later returned the favor: "John has a marvelous ear." See Hugues Panassié, "John Hammond," *Jazz Hot*, no. 5 (September–October 1935): 7.

141. Georges Hilaire, "Hugues Panassié," *Jazz Hot*, no. 1 (March 1935): 14.

142. Ibid.

143. Hugues Panassié, "L'affaire Armstrong–Canetti," *Jazz Hot*, no. 2 (April 1935): 7.

144. Ibid., 9.

145. Ibid.

146. See *Jazz-Tango Dancing*, no. 56 (May 1935). One interesting development in the modern dissemination of nationalized jazz at the cinema was the way in which the sound of French jazz orchestras took the place of American bands during the dubbing process. See R. B., "Comment Ray Ventura et ses collégiens ont doublé *42nd Street*," *Cinémonde*, no. 263 (November 2, 1933): 900.

147. See E. Laurent, "Cri d'alarme," *Jazz-Tango Dancing*, no. 59 (September 1935): 8.

148. P. A., "Introduction Chapitre III —les besoins collectifs et la musique," *Encyclopedie Française*, vol. 16, chapter 72 (Paris: Larrouse, 1935), 11.

149. André Schaeffner, "Vogue et sociologie du jazz," *Encyclopédie Française*, vol. 16, chapter 72 (Paris: Larrouse, 1935), 11.

150. Ibid.

151. Ibid.

152. Henry Malherbe, "La musique," *Le Temps* (September 18, 1935): 3.

153. Ibid.

154. Ibid.

155. Ibid.

156. In February 1935, *Le Monde Musicale* reported that the budget for French radio was increased to 26 million in 1935. It compared these resources to the amounts apportioned by the Nazis, who in 1935 spent over 400 million francs (equivalent) to promote Aryan culture over the radio. Along with banning Hollywood cinema, the Nazis promoted classical music competitions limited to "Aryan musicians." Indeed, 1935 laws in Germany made it illegal for foreign musicians to perform without Goebbels's permission. See Michael H. Kater, *Different Drummers: Jazz in the Culture of Nazi Germany* (New York: Oxford University Press, 1992).

157. *L'Intransigeant*, March 6, 1933, cited in "Review de la press," *Jazz-Tango Dancing*, no. 31 (April 1933): 11.

158. The incident was reported in *Le Monde Musicale* (November 30, 1933): 339.

159. For his vision of America, see Louis-Ferdinand Céline, *Voyage au bout de la nuit* (Paris: PUF, 1985). On his treatment of America, see Alice Kaplan and Philippe Roussin, "Céline's Modernity," *SAQ* 93, no. 2 (Spring 1994).

160. Marcelle Prat, "Les quartiers noirs: hot-cha-cha," *Je Suis Partout* (June 2, 1934): 6.

161. "Échos," *Jazz-Tango Dancing*, no. 64 (February 1936): 9. When Mandel took over the ministry of Posts, Telegraphs, and Telephones, he divided the two sections of the superior council into administrative and artistic. Most musical programming decisions were made by the artistic panel, which included Jules Romain, Florence Schmitt, Darius Milhuad, and Paul Valéry. See George Wormser, *Georges Mandel: l'homme politique* (Paris: Plon, 1967).

162. Raymond Legrand, "De la sincérité dans la chanson," *Jazz-Tango Dancing*, no. 63 (January 1936): 15.

163. Raymond Legrand, "Les styles nationaux," *Jazz-Tango Dancing*, no. 65 (March 1936): 13.

164. Ibid.

165. Ibid.

166. Ibid.

167. Ibid.

168. Hugues Panassié, "Disques," *Jazz Hot*, no. 10 (July 1936): 19.

169. George Frazier, "Swing Critics," *Jazz Hot*, no. 10 (July 1936): 5.

170. Hugues Panassié, "Rappel à l'ordre," *Jazz Hot*, no. 11 (September–October 1936): 4.

171. Robert Bernard, "Le jazz dans la musique symphonique," *La Revue Musicale* (March 1936): 208.

172. Ibid.

173. Ibid., 209.

174. Hugues Panassié, "Jazz-hot . . . une scandale," *Jazz Hot*, no. 11 (September–October 1936): 18.

175. Hugues Panassié, "Disques," *Jazz Hot*, no. 11 (September–October 1936): 20.

176. Hugues Panassié, "André Ekyan," *Jazz Hot*, no. 13 (Christmas, 1936): 7.

177. Hugues Panassié, "De 1 à 1000," *Jazz Hot*, no. 15 (February 1937): 9.

178. Ibid.

179. Ibid.

180. Slajov Žižek, *Enjoy Your Symptom: Jacques Lacan in Hollywood and Out* (New York: Verso, 1992), 101. Žižek sees this clinging to the materiality of the authoritative "body" as the same condition for truth that one sees in psychoanalysis—that is, there is no transferential knowledge without the presence of the analyst. This is then a point in common with different "authoritarian" discursive fields, Lacanian psychoanalysis, Marxism, Leninism, and so forth, which all demand loyalty to the founder in this way.

181. I am not claiming here that Pétain being called to the position of minister of war by Daladier and Doumergue in 1934 was the same as Hitler's ascension to power at a similar time. Yet though Pétain's backers did not espouse fascist principles in the same way that Hitler's proponents did, they did try to use him as a symbolic quilting point for their political rhetoric. Thus it is the organizational logic and rhetorical function of the discourse around a "great man" and his authority that links the National Socialists, the national government, and the Hot Club.

182. Madeleine Gautier, "Revue du Cotton Club à Moulin Rouge," *Jazz Hot,* no. 18 (June–July 1937): 5.

183. See the results of the reader polls in *Jazz Hot,* no. 19 (August–September 1937): 5.

184. See Philippe Boggio, *Boris Vian* (Paris: Flammarion, 1993), 19.

185. Most estimate the growth of the number of radios in France from around 500,000 in 1930 to over 5.2 million by 1939. The number of listeners, correspondingly, grew from an estimated 1,875,000 in 1930 to over 19.5 million in 1939. Music constituted about 60 percent of the programming.

186. Raoul Brunel, "Où va la musique," *Le Ménéstrel* (April 2 and 9, 1937): 114.

187. See, for example, Maurice Dumesnil, "Radio Américaine," *Le Monde Musical* (February 28, 1938): 53. "Then, there is jazz and the crooners . . . all that occupies ninety percent of the time."

188. Madeleine Gautier, "Bessie Smith," *Jazz Hot,* no. 22 (Christmas 1937): 4.

189. Hugues Panassié, "Disques: Bessie Smith," *Jazz Hot,* no. 23 (February–March, 1938): 20. Much of Panassié's bad humor, even though *Hollywood Hotel* had just been released featuring Louis Armstrong and Mae West, may have come from his continued battle with *Downbeat.* This time he accused *Downbeat* of "mauvaise foi" (bad faith) for commending the breakup of Mezz Mezzrow's Dixieland revival band. See "La parti-pris de *Down Beat,*" *Jazz Hot,* no. 23 (February–March, 1938): 16.

190. Louis Armstrong, "Les Hite," *Jazz Hot,* no. 22 (Christmas 1937): 7.

191. Hugues Panassié, "Jimmy Lunceford et son orchestre," *Jazz Hot,* no. 21 (November–December 1937): 4.

192. E. Laurent, "Hot?" *Jazz-Tango Dancing,* no. 90 (July 1938): 5.

193. Hugues Panassié, "Le parti-pris de *Down Beat,*" *Jazz Hot,* no. 23 (February–March 1938): 16.

194. Robert Bernard, "Les caractéristiques de la musique française," *La Revue Musicale* (February 1938): 123.

195. Ibid., 124.

196. Ibid., 126.

197. Georges Herment, "Poème et chorus," *Jazz Hot,* no. 29 (January 1939): 8.

198. Michel Manoll, "Hot gramaire du ciel," *Jazz Hot,* no. 31 (April–May 1939): 8.

199. Charles Delaunay, "Jazz 1939," *Jazz Hot,* no. 31 (April–May 1939): 3.

200. Ibid., 4.

201. Ibid., 5.

202. See James Lincoln Collier, *Duke Ellington* (London: Michael Joseph LTD, 1987), 192.

203. Denyse Bertrand, "Concerts divers: Duke Ellington," *Le Ménéstrel* (April 14–21, 1939): 108.

204. Pierre-Jean Laspeyres, "Duke Ellington," *Paris Qui Chante* (May 1939): 5.

205. Ibid.

206. Hugues Panassié, "Duke à Paris," *Jazz Hot*, no. 31 (April–May, 1939): 10.

207. Hugues Panassié, "Impressions d'Amérique," no. 31 (April–May 1939): 6.

208. Henri Amouroux, *La grand histoire des français sous l'occupation: le peuple du désastre, 1939–1940*, vol. 1 (Paris: Robert Laffont, 1976), 123.

209. Robert Le Grand, "L'abus du jazz," *Le Ménéstrel* (June 23, 1939): 169.

210. Ibid., 170.

211. See Mike Zwerin, *La Tristesse de Saint Louis: Jazz under the Nazis* (New York, 1985): 6. On jazz and the Nazis, see also Michael H. Kater, *Different Drummers: Jazz in the Culture of Nazi Germany* (New York: Oxford University Press, 1992).

Chapter 6: *Zazou dans le Métro*

1. On this complex relationship to the Vichy legacy, see Henry Rousso, *The Vichy Syndrome: History and Memory in France since 1944*, trans. Arthur Goldhammer (Cambridge, Mass,: Harvard University Press, 1991).

2. See Stuart Hall, "Subculture, Culture and Class," in Stuart Hall et al., eds., *Resistance through Rituals: Youth Subculture in Post-war Britain*, (London: Hutchinson, 1976). On the larger meaning of style for subcultural groups, see Dick Hebdige, *Subculture: The Meaning of Style* (London: Routledge, 1979).

3. Robert de Thomasson, "Êtes-vous swing? Êtes-vous hot?" *Candide* (March 1, 1939): 5.

4. Ibid.

5. Henri Amouroux, *La grande histoire des français sous l'occupation*, vol. 3, *Les beaux jours des collabos* (Paris: Robert Laffont, 1978), 204.

6. Henry Malherbe, "L'âme américaine d'aujourd'hui," *L'Illustration* (September 30, 1939): 189.

7. Ibid.

8. Ibid.

9. Ibid.

10. Charles Delaunay, *De la vie et du jazz* (Paris: L'Echiquier, 1939), 15.

11. See Jean M., "Combattre le communisme et collaborer," *Je Suis Partout* (November 3, 1939).

12. Jean-Claude Loiseau, *Les Zazous* (Paris: Le Sagittaire, 1977), 59.

13. Raymond Latour, "Swing-Cocktail," *Candide* (May 1, 1940): 6.

14. Ibid.

15. "Les dancings fermés," *Je Suis Partout* (May 24, 1940): 4.

16. Pierre Bourget and Charles Lacretelle, *Sur les murs de Paris et de France, 1939–1945* (Paris: Hachette, 1980), 21.

17. Henri Amouroux, *La grande histoire des français sous l'occupation*, vol. 1, *Le peuple du désastre* (Paris: Robert Laffont, 1976), 494.

18. Delaunay fled Paris at the onset of the war and went straight to the U.S. consulate in Marseilles. But since he was not Jewish, he was not granted asylum. He got the idea for the concerts while making his way back to Paris. See Charles Delaunay, *Delaunay's Dilemma* (Mâcon: Éditions W, 1985), 149–51.

19. See "Le coup de force du juif Mandel contre *Je Suis Partout*," *Je Suis Partout* (February 7, 1941); and Charles Lesca, "Quand Israel se venge . . .," *Je Suis Partout* (February 14, 1941).

20. See Ludovic Tournès, *New Orleans sur Seine: histoire du jazz en France (Paris: Payard, 1999)*, 83.

21. See Pierre Saka, *Trenet par Trenet* (Paris: Éditions Premiers, 1993), 55.

22. See *Jeunesse* (December 21, 1940).

23. See *Jeunesse* (January 10, 1941).

24. *Bourget* and Lacretelle, *Sur les murs de Paris*, 88.

25. This ironic duality is discussed by David Looseley in relation to Trenet. Beneath the merry exuberance of the *fou chantant* (singing fool), "a private universe of sadness was intimated with a lightness of touch which the realist song was seldom capable of." See Looseley, *Popular Music in Contemporary France*, 18.

26. Edith Delamare, "Le snobisme à la vie dure," *Jeunesse* (May 18, 1941): 4.

27. It was at the Pam-Pam that Boris Vian locked eyes with the Michèle Leglise and, after breaking off his engagement with his fiancé over an argument about Duke Ellington, came to invite Michèle to several "Swing thés" and record parties. They signed love letters to one another with "bizous." She gave Boris a Selmer trumpet, like Satchmo's, which he used in a jazz band made up of several friends. The two were married on July 5, 1941. Patrick Vian was born on April 12, 1942. See Philippe Boggio, *Boris Vian* (Paris: Flammarion, 1993).

28. Magsy Dauru, "Le quartier atteint," *Jeunesse* (April 6, 1941): 3.

29. Edith Delamare, "Méfaits du swing," *Jeunesse* (June 22, 1941): 3.

30. François Vinneuil, "Spectacle très swing," *Je Suis Partout* (October 14, 1941): 9.

31. Ibid.

32. "L'air de Paris: swing," *Candide* (October 22, 1941): 5.

33. See David Carroll, *French Literary Fascism: Nationalism, Anti-Semitism, and the Ideology of Culture* (Princeton, N.J.: Princeton University Press, 1995), 26.

34. See, for example, Alphonse de Chateaubriant, "Le National Socialism et nous," *La Gerbe* (March 5, 1942): 1. Chateaubriant, a royalist more than a fascist, argued that the French Revolution "changed the French," with the imposition of Enlightenment ideas that went counter to traditional social values. National Socialism offered the possibility for "rediscovering" this lost social order.

35. Jacques Chesnel reports that over one hundred records were recorded before

1942 on the Swing label. This number would continue to grow until the end of the war. See Jacques Chesnel, *Le jazz en quarantaine, 1940–1944, occupation/libération* (Paris: Isoète, 1994).

36. Rojan, "Civilisation swing!" *Jeunesse* (October 5, 1941).

37. Bourget and Lacretelle, *Sur les murs de Paris,* 84.

38. Ibid., 51.

39. Ibid., 22.

40. Ibid., 26.

41. Ibid., 119.

42. Ibid., 40.

43. Ibid.

44. Ibid.

45. Jean Lestandi, "GAULLISME = AFFAIRISME, OU AHURISSEMENT," *Au Pilori* (January 29, 1942): 1.

46. Ibid.

47. Ibid.

48. Ibid.

49. Ibid.

50. Ibid.

51. Lucien Rebatet, "La musique: jazz, hot, swing and co.," *Je Suis Partout* (February 7, 1942): 7. Here, placed in relation to democracy, "*juiverie*" is used in such a way that it comes to mean a kind of malicious political or cultural system run by Jews. For a full descent into the depths of Rebatet's fascist resentment, see his book *Les décombres* (Paris: Denoël, 1942).

52. Ibid.

53. Ibid.

54. Ibid.

55. "L'air de Paris: les anti-swing," *Candide* (February 11, 1942): 3.

56. Ibid.

57. See, for example, the defense of d'Indy in the April 23, 1942, *L'Appel* by Pierre Masteu, "Les judéo-maçons contre Vincent d'Indy." "Because all his life, Vincent d'Indy was an adversary and enemy of Jews and Franco-Masons . . . He was the sole French musician to publicly denounce, on all occasions, the destructive influences of the Jews on French music."

58. On Radio-Jeunesse, see Philip Nord, "Pierre Schaeffer and Jeune France: Cultural Politics in the Vichy Years," *French Historical Studies* 30, no. 4 (Fall 2007).

59. This helps account for André Hodeir's extreme hatred of accordion jazz in the postwar period.

60. See, for instance, André Chevallier, "La richesse folklorique française," *Jeunesse* (February 15, 1942): 7.

61. Raymond Asso, "Swing," *La Gerbe* (January 29, 1942): 7.

62. See Chesnel, *Le jazz en quarantine,* 12. See also Mike Zwerin, *La Tristesse de Saint Louis: Jazz under the Nazis* (New York: Beech Tree Books, 1985), 147.

63. René Duval, *Histoire de la radio en France* (Paris: Editions Alain Moreau, 1979), 307.

64. Asso, *"Swing."*

65. Ibid.

66. Ibid.

67. Ibid.

68. Yves Ranc, "Swing ou pas swing," *L'Oeuvre* (March 4, 1942): 4.

69. See Carroll, *French Literary Fascism,* 20–41.

70. Ibid.

71. Ibid.

72. Ibid.

73. Reported in *Le Temps* (March 7–8, 1942).

74. The Vichy spin doctors were most fond of Jeanne d'Arc's words from her trial: "I would rather render my soul to God than to be in the hands of the English." See for instance the "Message du Maréchal à conseil national de la Legion," in *Le Temps* (February 5, 1942): 1.

75. Roger Baschet, "Nouveaux dandys," *L'Illustration* (March 28, 1942).

76. Ibid.

77. Ibid.

78. Rojan, "Notre enquête: que pensez-vous du swing?" *Jeunesse* (April 12, 1942): 2.

79. Ibid.

80. Pierre Lancien, "Swing!" *Candide* (April 15, 1942): 1.

81. Ibid.

82. Ibid.

83. Ibid.

84. Ibid.

85. For instance, in August 1941, *Libération* wrote of the duties of resistance: "1. Boycott the *Signal* and *Gringoire,* journals of lies and German obedience. 2. All French who find themselves in a public place (café, hotel, etc.) when Germans come to sit down should ostensibly leave swiftly. It should be left empty and silent for the invader. 3. Boycott restaurants, hotels, and magazines manifesting an evident compliance in regard to the Germans. 4. All salaried employees in an industry or a business, working for arms or the revitalization of Germany, should cooperate with the Liberation by systematically slowing work and exercising acts of sabotage." Quoted in Henri Amouroux, vol. 4, *Le peuple réveillé,* 190.

86. Pierre Lancien, "Swing!" *Candide* (April 15, 1942): 2.

87. Ibid.

88. Ibid.

89. Loiseau, *Les Zazous,* 153.

90. Pierre Lancien, "Notre espoir: la jeune France," *Candide* (August 12, 1942): 2.

91. "Un nouvel ennemi de l'axe: Les Zazous," *France-Revolution* (May 24, 1942): 2.

92. Ibid.

93. Robert Brasillach, *Je Suis Partout,* May 23, 1942, cited in Loiseau, *Les Zazous,* 148.

94. See Jean Lagarigue, "Le service civique rural réclame des volontaires," *Le cri du peuple* (May 30, 1942): 4.

95. Xavier Pasquier, "Vérités sur le problème de la jeunesse française," *L'Appel* (May 28, 1942): 6.

96. Ibid.

97. Pierre Ducrocq, "Swing qui peut . . ." *La Gerbe* (June 4, 1942): 7.

98. Ibid.

99. Ibid.

100. Ibid.

101. "Le temps des assassins," *Je Suis Partout* (June 6, 1942): 1. To descend further into the hell of the anti-Semitic mentality, see Jean Contaux, "Les juifs commencent à payer," *L'Appel* (June 4, 1942): 2. The first trains of Jews to leave France for concentration camps departed on March 27, 1942.

102. Lucien Rebatet, "L'étoile jaune," *Je Suis Partout* (June 6, 1942): 1. For a thorough account of Vichy racial laws, see Richard Weisberg, *Vichy Law and the Holocaust in France* (New York: New York University Press, 1996).

103. The Ballandard, originally Léon Ballandard, became the name for one of the character types that surfaced in the Vichy media. It signified the weak, degenerate Frenchmen, usually the parents of the Zazous, who through stupidity and self-interest wanted the reestablishment of democracy. Jean Lestandi described the *"pauvre type"* (poor guy) in the text that accompanied the cartoon. "Sad Ballandard! Sinister Ballandard! By-product of a regime of stupidity, lies, tall tales, and blunders! Lamentable Ballandard! Racial outcome composed by Levy, which takes its start from the following principle: Make all French into eating machines, then bleed them periodically to permit Israel to fill its pockets . . . Regime of pigs! No more, no less . . . Ballandard! You [*tu*] will be, in the history of the world, the proof that a race, having received from heaven all the gifts of beauty and spirit, can, in less than a century, fall into nothingness [*néant*] simply because Israel passed by."

104. *La Gerbe* (June 18, 1942). Cited in Loiseau, *Les Zazous,* 145.

105. This was, of course, an echo of the Latin maxim *Mens sana in corpore sano*—A healthy mind in a healthy body.

106. Bernard Isère, "Pour une France swing dans une Europe zazou!" *L'Atelier* (June 6, 1942): 2.

107. Ibid.

108. Ibid.

109. This was another of Ferdinand's belittling jokes published in a column called *Le fou parlant* (the talking fool): "Ici Radio-Londres.—"Zazou-zazou wishes night-night to mother butterfly and says courage to Papa Boum! . . . Allô, Allô, Radio-Londres . . . Mother butterfly is sick of your collars, and Papa Boum prefers cheap wine to joints (*pinard aux pétards*)." See *Au Pilori* (May 28, 1942): 8.

110. "Le coin des fous: qu'est-ce qu'un zazou-zazou?" *Au Pilori* (June 11, 1942): 6.

111. Ibid.

112. Ibid.

113. Ibid.

114. Ibid.

115. René M. Fonjallaz, "La chasse est ouverte!" *Au Pilori* (June 18, 1942): 1. On page 6, there was also an article titled "Les français libres parlent aux zazous," in which a fictional de Gaulle, given the name "General Youplallah" (*Youp* was a name for Jews), called the "Ballandards and the Zazous the sole representatives, for us, of France."

116. "Les juifs aux Champs-Elysées," *L'Appel* (June 18, 1942): 2.

117. "Zazou, Zazou!," *L'Appel* (June 18, 1942): 2.

118. "Les Zazous à l'ombre pour une nuit," *L'Oeuvre* (June 15, 1942): 2.

119. Ibid.

120. The success of the film—about a dancer and a bandleader—and the song raised the dander of the Vichy critics. For instance, Guy Bertret had this to say in *L'Appel*: "*Mademoiselle Swing* is, as the title indicates, a 'swing' film . . . What we can't say is at what point the spectator will leave the cinema completely 'zazou' . . . It is impossible for us to tell you what the theme consists of, having been able to remain for no longer than a half hour of the projection. If you are 'swing'" enough to tolerate more, a bit of advice: Go see your regular doctor quickly!" See "Cinémathèque rose et swingeries," *L'Appel* (June 18, 1942): 5.

121. See *Jeunesse* (June 28, 1942): 1.

122. Jean Geslin, "Des décadents: les Zazous," *Jeunesse* (July 5, 1942): 5.

123. Ibid. Jacques Doriot founded the fascist Parti Populaire Français, for which the JPF were the youth group, in 1936.

124. Geslin, "Des décadents: les Zazous."

125. Loiseau, *Les Zazous,* 160.

126. Slavoj Žižek describes an analogous dynamic at work in all radical revolutionary projects, from Jacobinical revolutionary terror to the Khmer Rhouge. Revolution must erase the body of the people corrupted by the long reign of tyranny and extract from it a new sublime body. "The aim of revolutionary Terror is likewise to arrive at such an undressing: to flay off the animal, barbaric skin of the People, in hopes that its true, virtuous human nature will thus appear and assert itself freely." See Slavoj Žižek, *For They Know Not What They Do: Enjoyment as a Political Factor* (London: Verso, 1991), 261–62.

127. See François Furet, *Penser la révolution française* (Paris: Gallimard, 1986).

128. Jean Mericourt, "De 1789 à Vichy et de l'incroyable au zazou," *Au Pilori* (July 2, 1942): 1.

129. Ibid.

130. Ibid.

131. André Billy, "Swing II," *Le Figaro* (June 10, 1942): 1.

132. Ibid.

133. François-Charles Bauer, "Journal sans date: la querrelle du swing," *Confluences* (July 1942): 89.

134. Ibid.

135. Solange de Bragard, "Toujours le swing," *Journal des Débats* (June 24, 1942): 3.

136. Ibid.

137. Louis Guibert, "Pour enrayer la swingmanie . . . ne parlez plus des schpountzs!" *L'Appel* (July 2, 1942): 7.

138. Ibid.

139. Loiseau, *Les Zazous*, 187.

140. Jean Monfisse, "Épilogue swing," *Paris-Midi* (July 9, 1942): 1.

141. Ibid., 3.

142. André Coeuroy, *Histoire générale du jazz: strette-hot-swing* (Paris: Les Éditions Denoël, 1942), 24.

143. Ibid., 26.

144. Ibid., 29.

145. Ibid.

146. Ibid., 59.

147. Ibid., 221.

148. See André Coeuroy, "Goethe et Werther," *La Gerbe* (June 18, 1942): 7; and "Musique et film," *Je Suis Partout* (July 23, 1943): 7.

149. Hugues Panassié, "Situation du jazz dans la musique," *Le Figaro* (August 11, 1942): 4.

150. The *Légion des volontaires français contre le bolchévisme* was created July 7, 1941.

151. Henri Amouroux, *La grande histoire des français sous l'occupation, vol. 3., Les beaux jours des collabos* (Paris: Robert Laffont, 1978), 284.

152. *La Terre* (March 25, 1943): 1.

153. See Carroll, *French Literary Fascism*, 216–17.

154. Henri Vémane, *Swing et moeurs* (Lille: Éditions de Marchenelles, 1943), 3.

155. Ibid.

156. Ibid., 5.

157. Ibid., 7.

158. Ibid., 25.

159. "Ici l'on danse," *Je Suis Partout* (July 16, 1942): 2. Note the allusion to the Joseph Jacquin title from 1923.

160. "L'air de Paris: Coucou, les voila!" *Candide* (January 27, 1943): 3.

161. "Les rumeurs de la ville: le mal de danses," *Candide* (July 21, 1943): 3.

162. Ibid.

163. On this see Weisberg, *Vichy Law and the Holocaust in France*.

164. "Les rumeurs de la ville: sans swing!" *Candide* (August 4, 1943): 3.

165. The clandestine publication *En Avant: Journal de Combat de la Jeunesse Juive* (Journal of Combat for the Jewish Youth) declared: "Our duty, young Jews, is to

combat, without waiting for the landing of the Allies. It's up to us to create a second front . . . leave the home and workshop, your life is in danger." See *En Avant*, no. 3 (February 1943): np.

166. See Lucien Rebatet, "La fait juive," *Je Suis Partout* (April 14, 1944), and "Fidelité," *Je Suis Partout* (July 28, 1944), 1. "I admire Hitler," he wrote.

167. See Serge Moreaux, "La musique," *La Gerbe* (February 3, 1944): 1.

168. See Camille Fegy, "De Gaulle a vendu son âme au diable!" *La Gerbe* (April 13, 1944): 1

169. Boris Vian, "Referendum en forme de ballade," cited in Noël Arnaud, *Les vies paralleles de Boris Vian* (Paris: Christian Bourgois, 1970), 101.

170. "Zazou n'est plus," *L'Assaut* (August 28, 1944): 2.

171. Marcel Landowski, "La vie musical: jeunesse du jazz," *Le Franc-Tireur* (October 7, 1944): 1.

172. See *Libération*, November 4, 1944.

173. Amouroux, vol. 9, *Les règlements de comptes* (Paris: Robert Laffont, 1991), 248.

174. See *Libération*, June 12, 1945.

175. Amouroux, vol. 10, *La page n'est pas encore tournée* (Paris: Robert Laffont, 1993), 133.

Chapter 7: *Assimilation, Absence, and the Liberation of French Discourse on Jazz*

1. See Richard Kuisel, *Seducing the French: The Dilemma of Americanization* (Berkeley: University of California Press, 1993), 36–44.

2. At the head of this cultural expansionism, of course, was Hollywood cinema, and American diplomats made an open market for American movies in France a condition for postwar aid, which amounted to around $1 billion annually between 1945 and 1954. See Irwin M. Wall, *The United States and the Making of Postwar France, 1945–1954* (Cambridge: Cambridge University Press, 1991), 2.

3. On Hodeir's activity after the war, see Ludovic Tournès, *New Orleans sur Seine: histoire du jazz en France* (Paris: Fayard, 1999), 265.

4. André Hodeir, *Le jazz, cet inconnu* (Paris: Collection Harmoniques, 1945), 13. The book's title alluded to Alexis Carrel's book *L'homme, cet inconnu*, which argued that society should be led by an elite group of intellectuals who would guide its development and growth from above, including enforcing eugenic selection to weed out inferior stock.

5. Ibid., 13.

6. Ibid.

7. Ibid., 49.

8. Ibid.

9. Ibid., 39.

10. Ibid.

11. Ibid.

12. Hugues Panassié, "Verité sur la musique de jazz," *Images Musicales*, no. 4 (November 2, 1945): 10.

13. Jean-Paul Sartre, "Paris sous l'occupation," *Situations, III* (Paris: Gallimard, 1949), 52.

14. Ibid., 61.

15. Ibid.

16. See "Hugues Panassié, Robert Goffin à Paris," *Jazz Hot,* no. 5 (March 1946): 2.

17. Hugues Panassié, "Appel à la tolérance," *Jazz Hot,* no. 9 (September–October 1946): 7.

18. Hugues Panassié, *Douze années de jazz, 1927–1938* (Paris: Corrêa, 1946), 1.

19. Hugues Panassié, *La véritable musique de jazz* (Paris: Robert Laffont, 1946), 1.

20. Ibid., 2.

21. Boris Vian, "Le Jazz en France," *Combat* (October 23, 1947). Citation from Boris Vian, *Autres écrits sur le jazz* (Paris: Christian Bourgois, 1981), 225.

22. Ibid.

23. Ibid.

24. *Hachebuisson* could be translated as "Bushwhacker."

25. Charles Delaunay, "De Charles Delaunay," *Jazz Hot,* no. 27 (November 1947): 27.

26. Ibid.

27. See Jean Wiéner, "L'orchestre Glenn Miller à L'Opéra," no. 5 (March 2, 1945); and "Le jazz et l'enseignement de la musique," *Arts,* no. 12 (April 20, 1945).

28. Marc Pincherle, "Où va le jazz?" *Arts* (October 31, 1947): 3.

29. Boris Vian, "Pas de chance, Monsieur Panassié," *Jazz Hot,* no. 19 (January 1948): 13.

30. Boris Vian, "Pour vous qu'est-ce que le jazz?" *Combat* (January 29, 1948): in *Autres écrits,* 236.

31. Ibid.

32. Ibid., 237.

33. See Colin Nettelbeck, *Dancing with de Beauvoir: Jazz and the French* (Carlton, Victoria: Melbourne University Press, 2004).

34. Boris Vian, "Louis Armstrong à Pleyel a triomphé 'comme prévu,'" *Combat* (March 3, 1948): in *Autres écrits,* 252.

35. Ibid.

36. See also G. B. Bernard, "Du style New Orleans au Be-Bop!" *Arts* (May 21, 1948): 7.

37. Michel Dorigné, *La guerre du jazz* (Paris, 1948), 124.

38. Ibid., 117.

39. Probably the most thorough and scathing critique of Panassié came in the first number of the second series of *La Revue du Jazz* in 1952. In it, Delaunay argued that Panassié was like a "modern Don Quixote." Lucien Malson wrote an article titled

"Panassié megalomaniac," which decried Panassié's dogmatic paternalism as a product of "mechanisms of resentment." Jacques B. Hess, who would become a leading critic in the late 1950s, wrote that Panassié's static position was characteristic of someone who looked at jazz as "folklore instead of art." His incapacity to accept new forms was understood as a sign of him being an "old man." Finally, André Hodeir revealed the stylistic and structural underpinnings of Panassié's authoritarianism and his pretension of being the only one to "understand the blacks": "In this way, Panassié pretends to have the absolute right of owning the expressions of jazz jargon. That is to push megalomania a bit too far." Hodeir thought that most of this dogmatism came from the desire to conceal a fundamental musical illiteracy. The authors all showed how, at base, Panassié's concerns were primarily commercial ones related to his role as a promoter: he wrote favorably only on those who made money for him.

40. See Hugues Panassié, "Les faux prophètes du jazz," *La Casserole*, no. 4 (August–November 1949): 1.

41. See Hugues Panassié, "Explication du Zazou," *Hébdo-Latin*, no. 20 (April 1949): 1.

42. See André Hodeir, "Miles Davis l'insaisissable," *Jazz Hot*, no. 32 (April 1949): 6. See also Hodeir, "Charlie Parker," *Jazz Hot* (no. spécial, 1948): 9. "And whatever admiration I have for Gillespie . . . Parker seems to me to have something more than him—that something is genius."

43. On Hodeir's work in the 1950s, see Jean-Louis Pautrot, "Le jazz français en grande forme: le contribution d'André Hodeir," *Nottingham French Studies* 43, no. 1 (Spring 2004): 19–29.

44. This trajectory would be most apparent in Hodeir's 1954 work *Hommes et problèmes du jazz* (Paris: Flammarion, 1954). Hodeir stated that he wanted his book to become the "discourse on method of jazz" (p. 19), in order to give readers a method for judging for themselves the value of jazz. Hodeir said that it was Malson who first formulated the conception of swing in Husserlian terms in his article "Où il le fallait, quand il le fallait," in the December 1949 issue of *Jazz Hot*. The translations and the page numbers are from André Hodeir, *Jazz: Its Evolution and Essence*, trans. David Noakes (New York: Grove Press, 1954).

45. See Frank Ténot, "À chacun sa vérité," *Jazz Hot*, no. 37 (October 1949): 16–18.

46. See Georges Daniel, "Le jazz: musique de jeunesse," *Jazz Hot*, no. 26 (October 1948): 18; "Public et évolution," *Jazz Hot*, no. 37 (October 1949): 16; and Georges Daniel and André Hodeir, "L'ABC du jazz: essais d'initiation," *Jazz Hot*, no. 26 (October 1948); no. 27 (November 1948); and no. 28 (December 1948).

47. Lucien Malson, "Musique et couleur de peau," *Jazz Hot*, no. 29 (January 1949): 7.

48. Ibid.

49. Michel Dorigné, "Editorial," *La Gazette du Jazz*, no. 1 (June 1949): 1.

50. See "Indiscretions," *La Gazette du Jazz*, no. 2 (July–August 1949): 2. The defense of Latin jazz was in response to Panassié's conference "Aux Societé Savantes" on the

"nefarious" influence of South American rhythms on jazz. See the follow-up on this "scandal" by J. F. Gievreuz, "Notes sur l'afrocubanisme," *La Gazette du Jazz,* no. 4 (November 1949): 2.

51. Michel Dorigné, "Editorial," *La Gazette du Jazz,* no. 4 (November 1949): 1. "We exiled Pétain, for we heard him say that he had done a great deal for the country. But we condemned him to death nonetheless. That Panassié be thus a bit wise, he should leave us alone once and for all."

52. Xavier Clarke, "Propositions: l'affaire Luter," *La Gazette du Jazz,* no. 2 (July–August 1949): 2. See also Michel Dorigné, "Editorial," *La Gazette du Jazz,* no. 9 (April–May, 1950): 1. Dorigné described how Panassié's denunciation of French jazz resulted in the decrease of record sales.

53. See "Editorial," *La Gazette du Jazz,* no. 7 (February 1950): 1.

54. Boris Vian, "Improvisation," in *Autres écrits,* 700.

55. Vian first translated *cats* this way in a conversation between Armstrong and Mezzrow in *Down Beat.* See "Revue des Presses," *Jazz Hot* (May 1948), in *Chroniques de Jazz,* 122.

56. See Boris Vian, "Lundi 9: compte rendu objectif et circonstancié de la soirée du Festival international de Jazz à Pleyel, le lundi 9 mai, en 1949 de l'ère chrétienne, au 29 de l'ère bisonique," *Jazz News,* no. 6 (June 1949), in *Autres écrits,* 382. The "ère bisonique" alluded to one of Vian's signature anagrams, Bison Ravi.

57. Boris Vian, "Le critique de jazz," *Jazz News,* no. 3 (March 1949), in *Autres écrits,* 378.

58. Ibid.

59. Ibid., 379.

60. Ibid.

61. Ibid.

62. Ibid.

63. Ibid.

64. See "Le jazz en France," *Combat* (October 23, 1947).

65. *Chroniques,* 158.

66. Ibid., 172.

67. Ibid., 161.

68. Ibid., 171.

69. Ibid., 181.

70. Boris Vian, "Bulles du Pape," *Jazz Hot* (no. spécial, 1950): in *Autres écrits,* 82.

71. Boris Vian, "Les grosses figures," *Jazz News,* no. 8 (November 1949): in *Autres écrits,* 386.

72. Vian's trial on charges of obscenity for the Vernon Sullivan novels *J'irais cracher sur vos tombes* and *Les morts ont tous la même peau* began on April 19, 1950. He was championed by Queneau, who responded that the "obscenity" of the novels was a mark of their authenticity. "I believe that the sexual aspect of the *nègre* question is absolutely preeminent. It's the most important, that which torments Americans the

most." In the end, Vian was charged a fine of 100,000 francs. The publicity of the trial, of course, made the sales of the Vernon Sullivan books soar. See *Boggio*, 287–92. For a full account of the trials, see also Arnaud Noël, *Dossier de "l'affair" J'irai cracher sur vos tombes* (Paris: Christian Bourgois, 1974).

73. From the March 1951 "revue de presse," in *Chroniques de jazz*, 161. The article in *Vie Catholique Illustrée* was in the no. 292 (February 11, 1951): issue. Armstrong had been received by Pope Pious XII in 1949. See *La Revue du Jazz*, no. 9 (December 1949): 308. Perhaps Panassié also drew this bit of cynical commercial wisdom from Satchmo himself, who declared in 1949: "Maybe the young people don't appreciate what we have done. Good! We will play for the old people. After all, they have all the money." Quotation from *Chroniques*, 131.

74. From the July–August 1950 "revue de presse" in *Chroniques de Jazz*, 95. The first phrase was written as "Peu de chose à se mettre sous l'Adam," which replaced "la dent" with "l'Adam," which sounds the same and thus riffs on the idea of "old as Adam" over the standard idiomatic expression.

75. Cecile Roux, "French Singer Charles Trenet Dies," Associated Press (February 19, 2001).

Index

MATTHEW F. JORDAN is an assistant professor of film, video, and media studies at Pennsylvania State University.

The University of Illinois Press
is a founding member of the
Association of American University Presses.

Composed in 10.5/13 Adobe Minion Pro
with Frutiger LT Std display
by Barbara Evans
at the University of Illinois Press
Manufactured by Thomson-Shore, Inc.

University of Illinois Press
1325 South Oak Street
Champaign, IL 61820-6903
www.press.uillinois.edu